INTRODUCTION TO
THE SCIENCES OF THE QUR'AN

VOLUME I

INTRODUCTION TO THE SCIENCES OF THE QUR'AN

Mohammad Hādī Ma'rifat

Translated by
Salim Rossier
Mansoor Limba

Abridged and introduced by
Mohammad Saeed Bahmanpour

Volume I

SAMT

ISBN: 978-1-910178-01-0 (hbk)
ISBN: 978-1-910178-00-3 (pbk)

SAMT Publications
www.samt.ac.ir

CONTENTS

INTRODUCTION

I

'Ulūm al-Qur'an, or Qur'anic sciences, is a discipline which deals with those aspects of the Qur'an which are not usually discussed in exegeses (*tafsīr*) of the Qur'an. In this discipline, unlike *tafsīr*, the contents of the verses are not discussed, rather general information about the Qur'an and different groups of verses are provided and analysed.

The scholars of *'Ulūm al-Qur'an* differ in the number of topics discussed in this discipline. Badr al-Dīn al-Zarkashī (d. 794/1392) has listed forty-seven related topics,[1] while Jalāl al-Dīn al-Suyūṭī (d. 911/1505) has increased this to eighty.[2] The range of titles includes historical discussions on topics such as the nature, duration, chronology and causes of revelation; compilation, the preservation and unification of the Qur'an; consonantal and vocal texts; and different modes of recitation and their origins. They also include theological and conceptual topics such as the immutability of the Qur'an, or the impossibility of its alteration; the inimitability of the text; and types of verses in terms of ambiguity or clarity, abrogation or continuity, and universality or contextuality.

As is manifest, there is no logical or didactic order between most of the above-mentioned topics. Thus the word 'sciences' is in the plural in order to denote the independence of most of these topics from each other. What brings all these together is the fact that they all revolve round the one unifying theme of the Qur'an.

---

[1] Badr al-Dīn Muhammad Zarkashī, *al-Burhān fī 'Ulūm al-Qur'an* (Beirut: Dār Iḥyā' al-Kutub al-'Arabiyyah, 1957), vol. 1, 9-12.

[2] 'Abd al-Raḥmān al-Suyūtī, *al-Itqān fī 'Ulūm al-Qur'an* (Beirut: Dār al-Fikr, 1996), vol. 1, 27-30.

However, certain classifications have been suggested for organising these sciences in a logical order. One suggestion is that these topics can be divided into three main categories: literal, conceptual and historical. The first category includes topics which deal with literal aspects of the Qur'an, and these include the science of pronunciation (*tajwīd*), recitation (*qirā'ah*), calligraphy (*rasm al-khaṭṭ*), and the number of chapters, verses, words and letters of the Qur'an. The second category includes topics such as exegeses (*tanzīl*) and figurative interpretation (*ta'wīl*), esoteric (*bāṭin*) and exoteric (*ẓāhir*) meanings, abrogation (*naskh*), univocal (*muḥkam*) and equivocal (*mutashābih*), and abstract (*mujmal*) and lucid (*mubayyan*) verses. The third category deals with historical issues such as the history and order of revelation, the history of its writing, collection and compilation, the phases of its preparation and so forth.

An analysis of Islamic traditions and historical records shows that some of the topics included in the sciences of the Qur'an date back to the time of the companions of the Prophet. These records show that not only were some of these topics discussed at that time, but they were also regarded as indispensible for anyone dealing with the Qur'an as a legal, theological or political source. In his *Path of Eloquence* (*Nahj al-Balāghah*), Sharīf al-Raḍī (d. 401/1010) reports from Imam Ali (d. 40/660) that *univocal* and *equivocal* verses of the Qur'an should be clearly distinguished, as well as *abrogating* and *abrogated* verses,[3] in a tone critical of those who disregarded this knowledge. The concepts of equivocality and abrogation are among the most discussed topics in the sciences of the Qur'an. Moreover, Imam Ali used to assert that he had learnt the knowledge of such verses from none other than the Prophet himself: 'No single verse of the Qur'an was revealed to the Prophet without him having me recite it. He dictated it to me and I wrote it in my own hand. He taught me its figurative interpretation (*ta'wīl*) and outer explanation (*tafsīr*), its abrogating and abrogated verses, as well as its univocal and equivocal verses.'[4] He also said: 'By God, there is no single verse in the Book of God of which I do

[3] Al-Sharīf Muhammad ibn al-Husayn al-Raḍī, *Nahj al-Balāghah* (Qum: Dār al-Dhakhā'ir, 1412 q.), sermon 1, 25.
(Note: In all footnotes q. refers to the Islamic lunar (*qamarī*) calendar and s. refers to the Islamic solar (*shamsī*) calendar)

[4] Abū Ja'far Muhammad ibn Ali ibn al-Ḥusayn ibn Bābawayh al-Ṣadūq, *Kamāl al-dīn wa Tamām al-Ni'mah* (Qum: Mu'assasat al-Nashr al-Islāmi, 1405 q.), 285.

not know whether it was revealed during the night or the day, or if it was revealed on a mountain or a plain,' and 'no verse was revealed that I know not where it was revealed, about what it was revealed, and with whom it was revealed.'[5] All these were topics which were later discussed in books of *'Ulūm al-Qur'an*.

Based on the above reports, it is but logical to find books and epistles written on different topics of these sciences from the early years of Islamic scholarship. However, such epistles, which started to appear early in Muslim history towards the end of the first/seventh century, beginning with *Kitāb al-Qirā'āt* (The Book of Recitations) of Yahyā ibn Ya'mur (d. 89/708), did not deal with all these sciences in one place. Ibn al-Nadīm (d. 385/995) lists 250 such books and epistles in his catalogue up to the year 377/987.[6] The more comprehensive books, with the newly coined title of *'Ulūm al-Qur'an,* started to appear at the beginning of 4th/10th century, notably with such works as *al-Ḥāwī fī 'Ulūm al-Qur'an* of Muhammad ibn Khalaf ibn Marzbān (d. 309/921) and *al-Mukhtazan fī 'Ulūm al-Qur'an* of Abu al-Hasan al-Ash'arī (d. 324/936). This era culminated in the monumental work of al-Suyūṭī (d. 911/1505), *al-Itqān fī 'Ulūm al-Qur'an,* in the 9th/15th century.

II

Since the early days, Shī'a scholars, showed great dedication to the sciences of the Qur'an, more than any other Islamic subjects. The Shī'a contribution to *'Ulūm al-Qur'an* is usually overlooked, therefore it would be appropriate to mention very briefly some of the work in this field.

Obviously, the initial concern of all Muslim scholars who were experts in the field of the Qur'an was the proper method of recitation and the orthography of the Scripture. Hence, we find books on *qirā'āt* and discussions on variant nuances of recitation to be among the foremost topics appearing in *'Ulūm al-Qur'an*. Great personalities with Shī'ī inclinations were among the first scholars to focus on the different aspects of *qirā'āt* such as grammar, recitation and orthography. These scholars were later followed by others who drew greatly on their expertise.

---

[5] Muhammad Ibn Sa'd, *al-Ṭabaqāt al-Kubrā* (Leiden, 1325 q.), vol. 2, 292.

[6] Muhammad ibn Isḥāq Ibn al-Nadīm, *al-Fihrist* (Cairo: Istiqāmah, n.d.), 37-41.

Despite the availability of other scripts such as Nabataean and Syriac, the early companions chose to transliterate the Qur'an in the Kūfic script. However, as is well known, the Kūfic script lacked dots or diacritics to indicate certain phonetic sounds and to distinguish graphically identical words. The onerous task of creating new signs for this script was first done by Abū al-Aswad al-Du'alī (d. 69/688), who introduced this development in the Kūfic script merely for the correct recitation of the Qur'an.

A close disciple of Imam Ali, al-Du'alī fought for him at the Battle of Ṣiffīn and was appointed by him as governor of Basra after 'Abdullāh ibn 'Abbās, a post held by Abū al-Aswad until his death. According to Shaykh Ṭūsī (d. 460/1068), al-Du'alī was a student of the first four Shī'a Imams.[7] Ibn Qutaybah (d. 276/889) reports that he was the first person to systematise Arabic grammar, a matter of utmost importance for the correct recitation of the Qur'an.[8] Al-Du'alī authored a text on grammar called *al-Ta'līqah* primarily composed of Imam Ali's instructions on grammar and his own annotations.[9] In order to assist the Muslims in reciting the Qur'an in a grammatically correct fashion, al-Du'alī improvised diacritical dots to distinguish different phonetic values.[10]

Abu al-Aswad al-Du'alī trained famous scholars including his Shī'a student, Yaḥyā ibn Ya'mur,[11] and others such as Naṣr ibn 'Āṣim and 'Abd al-Raḥmān ibn Hurmuz, all of whom became famous grammarians in their own rights and improved on his work. Additionally, two prominent reciters of the Qur'an (*qurrā'*), Abān ibn Taghlib (d. 141/758) and Ḥamrān ibn A'yan (d. 130/747), who were also disciples of the fifth and sixth Imams, are considered to have been his students.

Abu al-Aswad originally invented the system of dots to indicate vowel sounds (*i'rāb*) rather than consonantal sounds (*i'jām*). Dots were later

---

[7] Ayatollah Sayyid Abū al-Qāsim Al-Khoī, *Mu'jamu Rijāl al-Hadith* (Qum: Markaz Nashr al-Thaqāfah al-Islāmiyyah, 1413 q.), vol. 10, 187.

[8] Abdullāh ibn Muslim Ibn Qutaybah, *al-Ma'ārif* (Beirut: Dār Iḥyā' al-Turāth al-Arabi, 1390 q.), 434.

[9] Ibn al-'Asākir, *Tārīkh Madīnat Dimishq* (Beirut: Dār al-Fikr, 1415 q.), vol. 7, 55; Shihāb al-Dīn Ibn Ḥajar al-'Asqalānī, *Lisān al-Mīzān* (Beirut: Mu'assasat al-A'lamī, 1405 q.) vol. 1, 83.

[10] Shihāb al-Dīn Ibn Ḥajar al-'Asqalānī, *al-Iṣābah fī Ma'rifat al-Ṣaḥābah* (Beirut: Dār al-Kutub al-'Ilmīyyah, 1415 q.), vol. 3, 455; Sayyid Muḥsin al-Amīn al-'Āmilī, *A'yān al-Shī'ah*, 5th ed. (Beirut: Dār al-Ta'āruf li al-Maṭbū'āt, 1998), vol. 1, 130.

[11] Ibn Khallikān has regarded him as a Shī'a; see al-Amīn, *A'yān al-Shī'ah*, vol. 1, 163.

specified for *i'jām* and dashes for *i'rāb* by another Shi'a grammarian and lexicographer, Khalīl ibn Aḥmad al-Farāhīdī (d. 173/789), a philologist from what is today Oman who migrated to Basra at an early age. According to al-Suyūṭī, Khalīl invented the *hamzah*, the *tashdīd*, *rawm* and *ishmām*.[12] He is best known for introducing the current system of marking the Arabic consonantal sounds (*ḥarakāt*) in his *Kitāb al-Nuqāṭ wa al-Shakl*; for the invention of Arabic prosody (*al-'arūḍ*); and for *Kitāb al-'Ayn*, considered to be the first Arabic dictionary, which he arranged phonetically rather than alphabetically, following the pattern of pronunciation of the Arabic alphabet from the deepest letter from the throat, (*'ayn*), to the last letter pronounced by the lips, (*mīm*). The renowned Arabic grammarian Sībawayh (d. 180/796) was one of his students.

Grammar flourished in Kūfa through Shī'a students of al-Khalīl, such as Ali ibn Ḥamza al-Kisā'ī (d. 189/805), who was known as 'the leader of the Kufans in grammar' (*imām al-kūfiyyīn fī al-naḥw*), and Abū Ja'far Muhammad ibn al-Ḥasan al-Ru'āsi, a disciple of the fifth and sixth Imams and who, according to Ibn al-Nadīm, was the first Kufan to write about grammar,[13] and also authored a work on Qur'anic recitations known as *Kitāb al-Qirā'ah,*[14] which addressed an urgent need among Muslims in the first and second centuries to ascertain the correct recitation (*qirā'ah*) of the Qur'an, a topic of expertise for Shī'a scholars in Kūfa.

Of the seven famous masters of Qur'anic recitation (*al-qurrā' al-sab'ah*), four are thought to have been Shī'as. The first is 'Āṣim ibn Abi al-Najūd Bahdalah al-Kūfī (d. 128/745), who learned his recitation from the *tābi'ī* Shī'a master of recitation, Abū Abd al-Raḥmān al-Sulamī, who in turn learned it from Imam Ali. 'Āsim's *qirā'ah*, through Ḥafṣ ibn Sulaymān (d. 180/796), is now the commonest *qirā'ah*, according to which almost all Qur'ans are printed throughout the world. The second is Abū 'Amr ibn al-'Alā' al-Baṣrī (d. 154/771), who took his recitation from Sa'īd ibn Jubayr (d. 94/712), who was one of the closest disciples of Imam Zayn al-'Abidīn (d. 95/713). The third is Ḥamzah ibn Ḥabīb al-Zayyāt al-Kūfī (d. 156/773), who took his *qirā'ah* from Imam Ja'far al-Ṣādiq (d. 148/765)

---

[12] Al-Suyūṭī, *al-Itqān*, vol. 2, 454.

[13] Al-Amīn, *A'yān al-Shī'ah*, vol. 1, 163.

[14] Āghā Buzurg Tehrānī, *al-Dharī'ah ilā Taṣānīf al-Shī'ah* (Tehran: Islāmiyyah, 1398 q.) vol. 17, 53.

and learned from prominent Shī'a Qur'anic scholars such as Ḥamrān ibn A'yan and Ṣulaymān ibn Mihrān al-A'mash. He authored many books on different aspects of the Qur'an, including *Kitāb al-Qirā'ah* (*The Book of Recitation*), *Kitāb Asbā' al-Qur'an* (*Classification of the Qur'an in Seven Parts*), *Kitāb Ḥudūd Āy al-Qur'ān* (*The Number of the Verses of the Qur'an*), *Kitāb Mutashābih al-Qur'an* (*Equivocal verses of the Qur'an*) and *Kitāb fi Maqṭū' al-Qur'ān wa Mawṣūlih* (*Jointed and Disjointed Verses of the Qur'an*).[15] And the fourth is Abu al-Ḥasan Ali ibn Ḥamzah al-Kisā'ī al-Kūfī (d. 189/805), who took his recitation from Abān ibn Taghlib, and from Ḥamzah through Imam Ja'far al-Ṣādiq. According to Sayyid Muḥsin al-Amīn, Abān ibn Taghlib was the first person to author a book on *qirā'āt*.[16] The remaining three famous reciters were Ibn Kathīr (d. 120/738), Nāfi' (d. circa 170/786) and 'Abdullāh ibn 'Āmir (d. 118/736), from Mecca, Medina and Damascus respectively.

Shī'a scholars were also forerunners of *tafsīr* or Qur'anic exegesis. Kufan study of *tafsīr* can be traced back to Maytham ibn Yaḥyā al-Tammār, who was killed in 60/679 by 'Ubaydullāh ibn Zīyād. Records indicate that a complete book of *tafsīr* was written in Kūfa by Sa'īd ibn Jubayr (killed in 94/712 by al-Ḥajjāj) which, according to Ibn al-Nadīm, was the first book of *tafsīr* ever written in Islam. On mentioning his book, al-Suyūṭī reports from Qatādah that Ibn Jubayr was the most knowledgeable in *tafsīr* of the second generation of companions (*tābi'ūn*).[17] Mention is also made of a *tafsīr* authored by the controversial Shī'a scholar Jābir ibn Yazīd al-Ju'fī (d. 128/745).[18] There is a better known *tafsīr* by a more famous exegete, al-Suddī al-Kabīr (d. 127/744), a *mawlā* from Kūfa whose *tafsīr* is described by al-Suyūṭī as the best of all commentaries (*amthal al-tafāsīr*). He was a companion of the fourth, fifth and sixth Shī'a Imams.[19] According to Ibn 'Adī[20] (d. 365/975), the most sizable *tafsīr* was written by Muhammad ibn al-Sā'ib al-Kalbī (d. 146/763), another renowned Shī'a scholar of Kufa.

---

[15] Al-Sayyid Hassan al-Ṣadr, *Ta'sīs al-Shī'ah li 'Ulūm al-Qur'an* (Baghdad: Sharikat al-Ṭab' wa al-Nashr al-'Irāqiyyah, 1370 q.), 346-347.

[16] Al-Amīn, *A'yān al-Shī'ah*, vol. 1, 131.

[17] Ibid. 125.

[18] Abū al-'Abbās Aḥmad ibn Ali al-Najāshī, *Rijāl: Fihris Asmā' Muṣannifī al-Shī'ah* (Beirut: Dār al-Aḍwā', 1408 q.), 128.

[19] Al-Khoī, *Mu'jam Rijāl al-Hadith*, vol. 4, 63.

[20] Al-Amīn, *A'yān al-Shī'ah*, vol. 1, 125.

Since Ibn 'Adī died in 365/975, it could be assumed that no *tafsīr* was written as large or as famous as al-Kalbī's before the second half of the fourth century, including Ṭabarī's.

This early scholarly output shows the importance early Shī'a scholarship attached to the sciences of the Qur'an. Merely to list the names of known Shī'a Qur'anic scholars during this period would require numerous pages.

III

Early Muslim scholars had concerns about the translation of the Qur'an into other languages. The nature of the concern was of two types, and the first was that the Qur'an was the word of God revealed in Arabic, and so how could man change this revelation by translating it into another language? The second concern was about the beauty, tone and delicate nuances of meaning which would be lost in translation.

The Jewish philosopher, Moses ibn Ezra (d. 530/1135), is quoted as saying that once in his youth a Muslim scholar in Granada had asked him to translate the Ten Commandments into Arabic. In response, he asked the scholar to read for him the first chapter of the Qur'an in Latin, a language that the latter spoke fluently. The reading turned out to be awkward and unfamiliar, and the scholar realised the significance and did not insist on his request.[21]

This example shows how difficult it is to translate any religious or inspirational text into another language. However, none of these concerns prevented Muslims from translating the Qur'an from the very early days. During the lifetime of the Prophet those parts of chapter 19 of the Qur'an which relate the story of Mary were translated into Amharic for the Emperor Negus of Abyssinia. A group of Iranian Muslims had asked Salmān al-Fārisī, the Persian companion of the Prophet, to translate the Qur'an for them into Farsi, which he did with the Prophet's sanction.[22] Whether Salmān translated the whole Qur'an or only the first chapter, *fātihat al-kitāb,* is yet to be investigated.

---

[21] Kāmrān Fānī, *Bayt al-Ḥikmah wa Dār al-Tarjamah* (Tehran: Markaz-i Nashr-i Dāneshgāhī, 1365 s.), 113.

[22] Shāhfūr ibn Ṭāhir Isfarāyīnī, *Tāj al-Tarājim fī Tafsīr al-Qur'an li al-A'ājim* (Tehran: Intishārāt-i 'Ilmī Farhangī, 1375 s.), vol. 8, 8.

It was actually this translation which caused a controversy amongst some of the great jurists. Abū Hanīfa (d. 150/767) was of the opinion that, based on this approval, it was permissible to replace the Arabic text by the translation even in formal prayers, while other jurists were of the view that the translation, if at all permissible, was only for conveying the meanings and concepts, and could never replace the original Arabic in any ritual context.[23]

Historically the Iranians were the first nation to translate the whole Qur'an into their own language. This took place some time towards the end of the third/ninth and beginning of the fourth/tenth centuries. It was previously thought that the translation of Ṭabari's *Tafsīr* in 345/956, which naturally included the translation of all the verses, was the first Persian translation of the Qur'an, but the discovery of *Qur'an Quds*, which is dated about a century before that, means that this assumption is now under question.[24] However, the translation of Ṭabari's *Tafsīr* has a more established history. It was undertaken by order of the Sāmānid King, Mansūr ibn Nūḥ (d. 365/975), after he obtained a *fatwā* from the scholars of Khorāsān and Transoxiana regarding the permissibility of translating the Qur'an.

As for other languages, the oldest extant Turkish translation of the Qur'an dates back to 734/1333, while the first Urdu translation was completed much later in 1190/1775. It is interesting to know that a Malay translation was completed in the 11th/17th century before the Urdu version, by Sheikh Abdur Ra'ūf al-Fansūri of Aceh, in *Tafsīr Tarjumān al-Mustafīḍ*. This translation was in classical Malay, which later evolved into Indonesian and the modern Malaysian languages.

IV

The study of the Qur'an in the West has been marked historically by polemics and prejudice. This process began with the first translation of the Qur'an into a European language in the twelfth century by the English scholar Robertus Ketenensis (Robert of Ketton), and was completed in

[23] For an elaborate discussion of this subject see, Fakhr al-Dīn Rāzī, *Mafātīḥ al-Ghayb (al-Tafsīr al-Kabīr)* (Beirut: Dār Ihyā' al-Turāth al-Arabi, 1420 q.), vol. 1, 209-213.

[24] Bahā' al-Dīn Khorramshāhī, *Qur'an Shinākht* (Tehran: Nāhīd, 1387 s.), 113-114.

537/1143. He did not entitle his translation 'the Qur'an,' but *Lex Mahumet Pseudoprophete* (The Law of Muhammad the False Prophet). The translation was in Mediaeval Latin and was commissioned by Peter the Venerable (d. 1157), the great abbot of the monastery of Cluny in France.

Although the purpose of this translation was both to study and to refute Islam, it barely resembled the original, due to arbitrary omissions and additions and a preference for improbable and distasteful meanings over likely and appropriate ones. It was stored in the vaults of the church until it was published four centuries later, in 1543, by authorisation of Martin Luther in three editions, all of which were prefaced by Luther himself. This was the only Qur'an translation available to Europeans for more than five centuries, from which Italian, German, Dutch, French and Russian renditions were produced. The Italian translation was derived directly from Ketenensis, and was used to develop the German translation, which was used in turn for the Dutch.[25] It is not hard to imagine how poor and erroneous such translations would be by the time the second and third-hand renditions were produced.

The second Latin translation of the Qur'an was produced in 1698 by Father Ludovico Marracci (d. 1700), and was dedicated to the Holy Roman Emperor Leopold I. The book had an introduction containing *A Refutation of the Qur'an*, and its main purpose, as stated by the author himself, was to discredit Islam by inserting elaborate quotations from Muslim authorities themselves. Many European translations were based on Marracci's work, including the French translation of Savory (1751), which stated on the title page of one of its editions that it was published in Mecca in 1165 AH to give it a better sense of authenticity.[26]

Drawing on this work in attitude, and especially in its 'Preliminary Discourse,' George Sale (d. 1736) later compiled the first English translation of the Qur'an, which professed to have been derived directly from Arabic. Released in 1734, it was 'to expose the imposture' and to have 'the glory of its overthrow.'[27]

---

[25] Afnān Fatānī, 'Translation and the Qur'an,' in Oliver Leaman, *The Qur'an: an encyclopedia* (UK: Routledge, 2006), 667.

[26] Ibid.

[27] George Sale, *The Koran* (London: Frederick Warne and Co., 1801), v.

Sale's translation remained in circulation in successive editions. Compared to previous translations it was an impartial rendition, despite the fact that it makes a tedious reading, nothing at all like the original Arabic. It was after reading this translation that Thomas Carlyle (d. 1881) found the Qur'an as tedious a piece of reading as he did ever undertake, which was 'wearisome,' 'confused' and 'crude,' and advised that 'nothing but a sense of duty could carry any European through the Koran.'[28] Edward Gibbon (d. 1794) found it to be an 'endless incoherent rhapsody of fable' which did not excite any sentiment or any idea.[29]

This negative attitude towards the Qur'an did not improve later when polemicists were replaced by Orientalists. Parvez Manzoor, a critic of Orientalism, believes that the Orientalist method for studying the Muslim scripture may be called anything but the 'natural mode of apprehension of the rationalist man.'[30]

This generation includes personalities such as Reverend J. M. Rodwell (d. 1900), who published his English translation in 1861. He claimed that his translation attempted to imitate the 'imperfect style' of the original Arabic. His observation on the literary merit of the Qur'an proves nothing but his insufficient knowledge of Arabic literature, a deficiency which could be found in most members of this brand of translators. Rodwell believed that the Qur'an was the 'most unreadable and incongruous patchwork' of literature, which contained 'fragments of disjointed truth – that is based upon Christianity and Judaism partially understood.'[31] Another member of this group was E. H. Palmer, a Cambridge scholar who published his translation in 1880, and believed that the style of the Qur'an was 'rude and rugged,' and for that reason it had to be translated into colloquial language.[32]

The above statements about the literature of the Qur'an should be left to Arab littérateurs to judge in addition to chapter ten of this book

---

[28] James Kritzeck, *Anthology of Islamic Literature* (New York: Penguin Group, 1975), 22.

[29] Arthur J. Arberry, *The Koran Interpreted* (London: George Allen & Unwin, 1981), vol. 1, 11.

[30] Parvez Manzoor, 'Method against Truth: Orientalism and Qur'anic Studies,' in *The Qur'an – Style and Contents*, vol. 24 (ed.) Andrew Rippin (Hampshire: Ashgate Publishing, 1999), 382.

[31] J.M. Rodwell, *The Koran* (London: J.M. Dent & Sons Ltd. 1909), 2, 13 and 14.

[32] Fatānī, 'Translation and the Qur'an', 668.

where Ayatollah Ma'rifat elaborates on the inimitability of the Qur'an from a literary perspective.

The most notable of this group, however, is the German scholar Theodor Nöldeke (d. 1930), who, with the publication of his award-winning book *Die Geschichte des Qorans* (History of the Qur'an), advanced the first systematic work on the study of the Qur'an in the West based on a historical-critical approach. Unlike Sale, who saw beauty in the language of the Qur'an, Nöldeke views the Qur'an as a text in which 'little care is taken to express all the transitions of thought,' in which indispensable clauses are frequently omitted, and extended narratives are 'vehement and abrupt,' that uses a 'great deal of superfluous verbiage,' and whose syntax even 'betrays great awkwardness.'[33] Such statements are clearly contrary to the unanimous views of all Arabic littérateurs who have considered the Qur'an the most elegant and eloquent example of Arabic literature. It only implies a lack of literary comprehension in a non-Arab who tries to digest a Shakespearean-like text of Arabic literature.

Nöldeke's works, despite their academic value and their insightful analyses of the etymology and grammar of the Qur'an, betray a prejudice driven by religious motivations in an effort to defend Christianity and Judaism against Islam.[34] He is prejudiced against the Prophet of Islam and does not shy away from expressing this in language which is occasionally insulting.

Nöldeke is also critical of the content of the Qur'an, and considers it to be a bad copy of the Bible. This, in his view, is mainly because the Prophet did not read the scriptures, but his knowledge of them was 'by oral communications from the Jews who knew a little and Christians who knew next to nothing' about the scriptures. This knowledge was probably 'picked up in a conversation with any Jew or Christian,' and that is why the deviations from the biblical narratives in the Qur'an are conspicuous.

The eloquence of the text of the Qur'an was better appreciated by the Scottish scholar Richard Bell (d. 1952), who considered the Prophet to

---

[33] Theodor Nöldeke, *The Qur'an: An Introductory Essay*, (ed.) N. A. Newman (Hatfield: Interdisciplinary Biblical Research Institute, 1992), 5 and 12.
[34] Ibid. 29-31.

be a poet, 'but not of the ordinary Arab type,' for his themes were hardly touched upon by other poets.[35]

Following in the footsteps of Weil and Nöldeke, Bell's translation in 1937 suggested a rearrangement of the Qur'anic chapters. However, it took the sifting operation as far as reordering the whole text by separating it up into small fragments in order to 'unravel the composition of the separate suras' and 'remove the confusions' from the Qur'an.[36] To this end he undertook a verse by verse examination of the Qur'an, and tried to recast the entire text in a new mould.

Bell's method was based on the assumption that the Qur'anic literature suffered from abrupt changes of rhyme, the intrusion of extraneous subjects into passages otherwise homogeneous, breaks in grammatical structure, sudden changes of the dramatic situation, and other literary-based assertions.[37] Based on this conjecture, he theorised that the parts of the Qur'an he deemed disjointed were due to 'discarded material' being confused with the original text at the time of its collection and compilation. He explains that the Qur'an was revised in Medina by the Prophet, and while this revision was being done the scribes noted down the revised version on the back of the sheets on which the original verses were written. Later, editors inserted the old verses back in the text. It is to these 'scraps' that got into the Qur'an by mistake, Bell says in his preface, 'rather than to textual defects, or to confusion in Muhammad's own thought and style that the dreary welter of the Qur'an' is due.[38]

The reader can find adequate arguments in the second chapter of this book regarding the above which render most such perceived shortcomings to be due to the lack of proper knowledge of 'Shakespearian' Arabic.

In dealing with the Qur'an, Bell allowed himself the liberty of assuming that any perceived unevenness in the style would justify rearrangement of the verses according to his own ideas of stylistic fitness; something that no scholar after him would take up. In essence, Bell is not a translator, but

[35] Mohammad Khalīfa, *The Sublime Qur'an and Orientalism* (Karachi: International Islamic Publishers, 1989), 20.

[36] Richard Bell, *The Qur'an: Translated, with a critical re-arrangement of the Surahs* (Edinburgh: T. and T. Clark, 1937), vi.

[37] W. Montgomery Watt and Richard Bell, *Introduction to the Qur'an* (Edinburgh: Edinburgh University Press, 1970), 93.

[38] Bell, *The Qur'an: Translated*, vi.

an author. He not only rearranges the order of the chapters, but actually restructures the order of the verses according to what he believes to be the thematically correct order of the text. On the lexical level, some very common and familiar words in Arabic are mistranslated so as to make the text appear ludicrous. Moreover, in many instances he allows himself to comment on the content of the text he translates in an ostensibly biased way. For example, next to his rendering of the oath at the beginning of *sura* 89, he writes: 'An absurd oath.'[39]

I cannot imagine that anyone would allow himself the liberty of treating any text as Bell did in treating the Qur'an. His theory of unconnected pieces was so extreme that it was criticised by his student William Montgomery Watt (d. 2006). In his revised version of Bell's *Introduction to the Qur'an*, Watt argues that Bell was inconsistent in the application of his theory, and thus little was to be gained by his distinctive hypothesis.[40] However, no scholar has ethically criticised Bell for his adventurous attitude towards an established sacred text. As Fatānī reminds us: 'The fact that Bell took a coherent Arabic text, readily understood by any native speaker of the language, and cut and pasted it into something incoherent and disjointed clearly raises ethical questions that have yet to be addressed.' [41]

Generally speaking, the persistent problem with most Western translations of the Qur'an has been that they were undertaken by Christian missionaries and Orientalists who had hardly any rigorous knowledge of the Arabic language.[42] This problem has been addressed since the 1930s by Muslim translations of the Qur'an in different European languages.

V

The idea that the Qur'an was a distorted version of the Bible or heavily copied from it is not restricted to Nöldeke. It has been a common view among the Orientalists and later academics, and usually labelled as an historical-critical perspective. We can find this view in writings as early as the first half of the 19th century in the works of Abraham Geiger (d. 1874),

[39] Fatānī, 'Translation and the Qur'an', 659.

[40] Watt, *Introduction to the Qur'an*, 106.

[41] Fatānī, 'Translation and the Qur'an', 659.

[42] Ibid. 658.

the German rabbi and scholar who founded Reform Judaism,[43] and whose book could be regarded as a pioneering work in the historical approach. Although this allegation is as old as the Qur'an itself, and certain verses of the Qur'an speak of disbelievers charging the Prophet with rewriting the old fables of the past as dictated to him by another person (25:5), or being taught to him by a foreigner (16:103), the Orientalists believe that by the critical-historical method they have shed new light on this old allegation.

The nineteenth century is marked by a number of biographies of the Prophet Muhammad by Western Orientalists, notably Gustav Weil (1843), William Muir (1861) and Aloys Sprenger (1861-65). Inevitably these biographical works contained some introductory material related to the study of the Qur'an and its biblical provenance.

The German Orientalist Gustav Weil (d. 1889) believed that Muhammad learnt Jewish stories and concepts from existing Jewish tribes, and incorporated them into Islamic teachings with the help of figures like Waraqah ibn Nawfil, Abdullah ibn Salām, Salmān Fārisī and Baḥīrā, a monk Muhammad met on his way to Boṣrā and who was, according to Weil, a baptised Jew.[44] His references, however, are mainly to legends from biblical sources incorporated into Islamic traditions, commonly called *isrā'īliyyāt*, rather than the Qur'an.

Aloys Sprenger (d. 1893) rejects Muhammad's claim of revealed knowledge about the previous Books, and maintains that he learnt of them from Jewish and Christian sources. He even goes one step further to name his probable teachers in this regard. He believed Muhammad never named his teachers in order to pretend miraculous knowledge, and the fact that all his teachers died in the early days of his career allowed him to cover up for it.

One of the people he names as a secretive teacher of Muhammad is the 'eccentric' *Zayd* from the Addy tribe, who followed the true religion of Abraham. In *The Life of Mohammad, from Original Sources*, published in 1851, he postulates that it was Zayd who 'first instilled purer notions

[43] Abraham Geiger, *Judaism and Islam*, tr. F. M. Young, 1896, (http://answeringislam.org/Books/Geiger/Judaism/index.htm), xxx.
[44] Gustav Weil, *The Bible, the Koran, and the Talmud; or Biblical Legends of the Mussulmans* (New York: Harper & Brothers, 1855), viii-xi.

respecting God into his mind, and induced him to read biblical history.'[45] Then there was Waraqah, who, according to Sprenger, before his death had helped the Prophet to write the Qur'an. Addās, a monk of Nineveh who lived in Mecca and taught Muhammad biblical stories, is another figure, along with Rabbis of the Ḥijāz who taught him their legends.[46]

Learning about biblical history is one thing, but reading it was even more improbable for Muhammad, as he was known to be illiterate and, in any case, no Bible was translated into Arabic at the time. To overcome the first problem, Sprenger rejects the official Islamic view that the Prophet was illiterate, and believes that he pretended to appear illiterate 'in order to raise the elegance of the composition of the Qur'an into a miracle.'[47] To overcome the second issue he conjectures that there should have been Arabic translations of the Bible available at the time.[48]

To prop up his opinion he further argues that some of the closest companions of the Prophet, such as his stepson Zayd ibn Thābit and the Abyssinian ex-slave Bilāl, were former Christians who could have taught the Prophet about the biblical scriptures.[49]

Obviously, none of these claims could be supported by historical data; most of them are based on insignificant stories scattered around the sources which have been blown out proportion by Orientalist scholars. The story of Waraqah is given a good critical examination in the present book.

William Tisdall (d. 1928) is another figure of this ilk. A British historian and philologist who served as the Secretary of the Church of England's Missionary Society in Isfahan, he cites a number of events in the Qur'an that he believes had been copied from the Old Testament.[50] However, since there are certain clear discrepancies between the accounts in the Qur'an and those in the Bible, on these occasions Tisdall, like Nöldeke, concludes that Muhammad's knowledge of the Bible was imperfect and partial.

---

[45] Aloys Sprenger, *The Life of Mohammad, from Original Sources* (Oxford: Presbyterian Mission Press, 1851), 95.

[46] Ibid. 96-99.

[47] Ibid. 102.

[48] Ibid. 100 ft.

[49] Ibid. 161-162.

[50] William St Clair Tisdall, *The Sources of Islam*, tr. Sir William Muir (USA: CSPI, LLC, 1902), 9.

But if Muhammad was inspired by the Bible, where did these differences come from? Tisdall answers this question by resorting to the existence of unorthodox Christian sects in Medina and greater Arabia at the time of the Prophet. Muhammad's knowledge of the Bible came from the followers of these sects who did not have a proper knowledge of the Bible and taught Muhammad from their unorthodox sources.[51]

Apart from unorthodox Christian teachings, Tisdall further argues that Mohammad was influenced by other cultures that existed in the region, for example, Zoroastrianism and Hinduism. Muhammad's companions such as Salmān Fārisī informed Muhammad about Persian tales, and Muhammad subsequently introduced them into the Qur'an. Nevertheless, he fails to specify which Persian tales were included in the Qur'an.[52]

Hartwig Hirschfeld (d. 1934) widens the sources of such influences to other lettered communities. In his book, *New Researches into the Composition and Exegesis of the Qur'an*, published in 1902, he argues for a strong biblical influence on Muhammad which did not only come from Jews and Christians of Mecca and Medina, but also from the region of the Dead Sea which Muhammad passed through when he was leading a trading caravan to Syria.[53] However, he admits that these fleeting encounters did not consist of systematic study or regular instruction, and rejects Sprenger's view regarding the role of Baḥīrā as the secret tutor of Muhammad and the author of the *Ṣuḥuf*.

Throughout his work, Hirschfeld points to the similarities between Qur'anic concepts, such as 'human soul,' 'resurrection,' 'miracle' and so forth,[54] and biblical concepts.

It should be pointed out here that Muslims never deny the similarities between the concepts and the stories of the Qur'an and those of the Bible. On the contrary, the Qur'an insists on such a similarity.[55] The difference between Muslim scholars and the Orientalists is the paradigm in which they accommodate this fact. The Muslim paradigm is that the similarities are, and should be, there because both books come from the same source;

---

[51] Ibid. 30.

[52] Ibid. 50-61.

[53] Hartwig Hirschfeld, *New Researches into the Composition and Exegesis of the Qoran* (London: Royal Asiatic Society, 1902), 28.

[54] Ibid. 41-44.

[55] For example, see the Qur'an 5:48, 35:31, 41:43, 46:12, among many other verses.

they are both revealed books to chosen people. The Qur'an states that it approves of what is in previous books and is a yardstick for its accuracy: *We have sent you down the Book with the Truth, to confirm what was already there from the previous Book, and to safeguard it* (5:48). The Orientalists, on the other hand, by assuming that the Prophet of Islam was an imposter, have tried to find an alternative explanation for this similarity, and it could only be that he had taken it or learnt it from the Jews and Christians of his time. This latter paradigm, however, is lacking in historical fact, and to accept it one must draw on a creative imagination rather than solid data.

Such a creative imagination abounds in Alfred Guillaume's (d. 1966) article, 'The Influence of Judaism on Islam' (1927). According to him, Islam made use of Judaic sources through 'an intermediate legatee,' which was Christianity. He bases his argument on the existence of the Jewish diaspora throughout the Arabian peninsula at the time of the Prophet. These Jews had been present in the peninsula from the time of Solomon for commercial reasons, and by the seventh century they were well established in the various cities, including Khaibar, Medina and Ṭā'if.[56]

He rightly mentions the referential style of some Qur'anic stories, in the sense that certain stories in the Qur'an are unintelligible without referring them back to the Old Testament.[57] This observation is not out of place, since the Qur'an is to act as a safeguard for those stories, and is not in position of retelling them in full. For example, in chapter 38, Surah *Ṣād*, the accounts of David and Solomon appear as corrections and annotations to the biblical accounts, in order to acquit these two personalities of the faults attributed to them in the Bible. Thus, his conclusion that Muhammad was an unsuccessful 'interpreter of Judaism'[58] could only be acceptable according to the Orientalist paradigm, and not according to the Muslim paradigm.

The speculative venture of Orientalist paradigm reached its climax with Arthur Jeffery (d. 1959) in *The Foreign Vocabulary of the Qur'an*, published in 1938. By examining 318 non-Arabic words in the Qur'an and tracing them back to their original roots, Jeffery concludes that the Qur'an was

---

[56] Alfred Guillaume, 'The Influence of Judaism on Islam,' in *The Legacy of Israel*, (ed.) Edwyn R. Bevan and Charles Singer (Oxford: Clarendon Press, 1927), 129-133.

[57] Ibid. 39.

[58] Ibid. 147.

influenced by both Jewish and Christian sources, since followers of both religions were strongly visible in the Arabian Peninsula during the time of Muhammad, and, according to him, Muhammad was greatly impressed by the higher civilisation surrounding Arabia, 'particularly by the religion of the great Empire of Rome.' His conception of his mission was therefore to provide the Arabs with the benefits of such a civilisation. 'It was therefore natural that the Qur'an should contain a large number of religious and cultural terms borrowed from these surrounding communities.'[59]

It is difficult to imagine how a scholar like Jeffery is able to postulate such a grand theory merely by finding 318 non-Arabic words, most of which were used by Arabs of the time, among 77437 words of the Qur'an.

More strangely, Sir Hamilton Gibbs (d. 1971) believed that Syriac Christianity influenced the formation of the Qur'an, for although concepts such as *tawḥīd* (monotheism) were already known to the Arabs through the *ḥanīf*s, the significant concept of the Day of Judgment was clearly influenced by the works of the fathers and monks of Syriac Christianity. His evidence for this is the ignorance of the Arabs of such concepts as clearly reflected in the Qur'an.[60]

However, probably no one of the Orientalist paradigm has ever made as bold and as unwarranted a claim as Christoph Luxenberg, a pseudonym of the author of *The Syro-Aramaic Reading of the Koran*. Luxenberg claims in this book that he attempts to place the text of the Qur'an in its historical context, and to analyse it from a new philological perspective, with the aim of arriving at a more convincing understanding of the text.[61] His main thesis is that the 'Ur-Qur'an' was not written in Arabic, but in Syriac, yet later scholars either 'forgot or attempted to disguise' this fact. He further postulates that until the reign of 'Abd al-Malik the official language of the Islamic territories was Syriac, which he replaced with Arabic. Rejecting the Muslim heritage regarding the history of the Qur'an, he denies that there was any oral tradition of Qur'an transmission, and that the Muslims

---

[59] Arthur Jeffery, *The Foreign Vocabulary of the Qur'an* (Baroda, India: Oriental Institute, 1938), 30.

[60] Sir Hamilton Alexander Rosskeen Gibb, *Mohammedanism: An Historical Survey* (New York: Oxford University Press, 1962), 37-39.

[61] Luxenberg, Christoph, *The Syro-Aramaic Reading of the Koran: a Contribution to the Decoding of the Language of the Koran* (New York: Prometheus, 2007), 22.

were left with a text which they knew neither how to read, nor in what language it was written.[62]

Luxenberg uses all types of methods to restore the Qur'anic expressions to their original Aramaic and Syriac roots, and believes that by doing so many expressions of the Qur'an that previously did not make sense would become clear.[63]

I leave the judgment of such sweeping theories to the reader. However, one may question the ethical standards and academic etiquette that would allow a researcher to postulate such theories, which insult the intelligence and the very existence of scholars throughout the history of a great civilisation with 'findings' which indicate that they were so confused and stupid that they did not know what language their forefathers were speaking.

VI

Since Wansbrough, *'Ulūm al-Qur'an* in the Western academic sphere has been more than ever under Goldziher's spell, in the sense that his fabrication theory was extended to the Qur'an and the Qur'anic sciences. Influenced by this theory, Wansbrough and his students regarded *'Ulūm al-Qur'an* as a tool that was invented to give the Qur'an historical value, and to justify the religious edicts of different legal schools. Here the Orientalist's prideful narrow-mindedness reached its apogee, by assuming that all Muslim scholars without exception were either a collection of liars and fabricators, or stupid simpletons incapable of critical thought.

For Wansbrough, all literature regarding *asbāb al-nuzūl* was a fabrication by jurists to incorporate the scripture into the existing legal system. By means of this corpus of fake traditions, Muslim scholars could establish historical order to the text of the Qur'an; it was subjected to the same requirements as legal *ḥadith*s and was produced in much the same way.[64]

---

[62] Ibid. 78.

[63] Ibid. 327.

[64] Herbert Berg, 'The Skepticism and Literary Analysis of J. Wansbrough, A. Rippin, Et Al.,' in *The Koran: Translation and Exegesis*, (ed.) Colin Turner (London: Routledge, 2004), 273.

In *The Collection of the Qur'an*, John Burton comes to a completely different conclusion about the compilation of the Qur'an, and believes that it was collected at the time of the Prophet, yet his methodology suffers from the same prejudicial views.

Burton bases his argument on the conjectures of J. Schacht, who, following Goldziher, came to believe that Islamic legal traditions were all forgeries of the Islamic legal systems. There was such fierce rivalry between these legal schools that they were ready to defend their positions at any cost, which meant that each created a corpus of supporting *hadith*s, while disregarding the clear rulings of the scripture.[65] Burton extends this hypothesis to all traditions related to the Qur'an.

The process of fabrication needed a number of tools to give the forged traditions validity and credibility. Above all, they needed to devise a system by which they could establish the credibility of their own corpus of *hadith*s, and undermine those of rival schools. This gave rise to the introduction of the discipline of *hadith* criticism, and the creation of an *isnād* (chain of transmission) for every single tradition forged by any school of law. Traditions were classified according to the historical reliability of each individual who made up the chain of narration of the *hadith*.[66]

According to Burton, the jurists tried to solve the contradiction between the opinions of their legal schools and verses in the Qur'an by devising *asbāb al-nuzūl* ('occasions of revelation'). *Asbāb al-nuzūl* was a body of *hadith* literature which was created to give a 'context' to various Qur'anic verses, in order to bring them in line with the views of the legal schools.[67]

However, *asbāb al-nuzūl* alone was not enough to 'manipulate' the Qur'an. The Qur'an was a powerful source for the provision of legal rulings, and as such posed a serious obstacle for the legal schools to assert their arbitrary rulings. Hence, according to Burton, the method of *al nāsikh wa al mansūkh* ('abrogation and the abrogated') was improvised as a handy tool for the legal schools to offset the effect of certain verses that went against their legal judgments, as well as finding legitimacy for them in the Qur'an.[68]

---

[65] John Burton, *The Collection of the Qur'an* (Cambridge: Cambridge University Press, 1977), 10.

[66] Burton, *The Collection of the Qur'an*, 14-15.

[67] Ibid. 15.

[68] Ibid. 17.

The concept of abrogation worked well for dealing with most of the problematic verses of the Qur'an; however, an additional method was needed to deal with more 'inflexible' verses. Thus, the technique of variant readings of the Qur'an was devised. Through this technique, the legal schools could easily twist the Arabic grammar of the text to give the desired meaning and bear out their point of view.[69]

Burton tries to show how variant readings of the Qur'anic verses led to different legal rulings, and concludes that the assumption that *fiqh* was derived from the Qur'an is false, but that instead, the variant readings of the Qur'an were derived from *fiqh.* [70]

Most of the above issues, especially the issue of variant readings, are discussed extensively in the present book where the highly speculative nature of all such statements is made clear. Nonetheless, one has to admire such imaginative creativity in the academic circles. A fact that these Orientalists forget to consider is that the scholars about whom they are theorising were not machines, but ordinary human beings who have the right to be given credit for their scholastic knowledge and a degree of conscience and professional integrity; something it seems that many in the West have yet to learn about other people.

VII

As I mentioned above, both Muslim and Western scholarship equally accept certain facts about the Qur'an, yet they are often explained and accommodated by them in different ways. The example examined was about the similarities that exist between stories and concepts in both the Qur'an and the Bible. The dispute between Muslim scholars and Orientalists in this regard is not whether such similarities exist, but the paradigm in which they are accommodated. The Muslim paradigm is that the similarities are and should be there, because the Islamic faith is a continuation of the Jewish and the Christian faiths, and that the Qur'an and the Bible are both revealed from the same source. The overlapping of themes and motifs, and even linguistic expressions, in the Qur'an and other scriptures exhibit the identity of the transcendent Source of

[69] Ibid. 31-32.

[70] Ibid. 34

these Books, rather than 'borrowings' and 'appropriations.' The Qur'an has come 'to confirm what was already there from the previous Books, and to safeguard it' (5:48).

The Orientalist paradigm, on the other hand, is based on the belief that Muhammad was an imposter who tried to create a new religion for his people by copying and imitating the earlier scriptures, which he did rather poorly and inadequately. It should be clear that both of these paradigms are faith-based, and neither can claim to be more objective than the other, although, at least as a Muslim, I believe that the evidence adduced for the latter paradigm is lacking in strength and logic.

It would be futile to try to make a compromise between these two paradigms, since they diametrically oppose one another. However, this does not mean that the subscribers to either paradigm cannot benefit from the research and the studies of the other group. Despite the resentment and repugnance that the Orientalist view has created among Muslims in general, and Muslim scholars in particular, I still think that by taking a couple of steps back from each other, these two branches of scholarship can reinforce one other in their researches, and push forward our understanding of the content and history of the Islamic faith.

For its part, Western scholars should abandon their condescending and patronising attitude. They have to let go of the idea that they are the only ones free from prejudice by being unattached to the Islamic faith, and should realise that their rejection of Islam and its Prophet may be an equally misleading prejudice. They have to refrain from postulating rushed and unfounded theories based on gross and unwarranted conjectures, such as the 'Hagarian' theory of Cook and Crone or the Syriac literature theory of Luxenburg.

Western students of Islam work on the assumption of there being a total cultural void in pre-Islamic Arabia, and a complete lack of knowledge, discretion, acumen and integrity in the post-Islamic era. They work under the assumption that the traditional Muslim view is always influenced by theological and dogmatic considerations, and must of necessity be discarded. Such a pathological Islamophobic trait would leave no room for symbiotic interaction. Western scholarship should stop ignoring the huge contribution of Muslim scholarship over the centuries, and distrusting everything that is consensual and conformist in the Muslim tradition. In studying past Muslim scholarship, Orientalists could try to be more realistic, and could portray an appropriate etiquette by refraining from phantasmagorical theories which presume all Muslim scholars to be liars, fabricators and ignorant opportunists; something that could never happen in the real world.

Muslim scholars, on their part, could appreciate the critical studies of the history and content of Islam by scholars who are not attached to it; who can see things from a different angle, and consequently add insight and depth to different aspects of this huge body of knowledge through critical analysis. They should not insist on their traditional opinions if evidence is adduced against it. They could also appreciate that modern scholarship has a much broader knowledge of comparative philology and more sophisticated methods of linguistic analysis, which puts it in a better position to shed light on some 'obscure' words and terminology, provide more plausible explanations, give more solid etymologies and trace more foreign words than was possible for the traditional Muslim scholars.

And finally, they have to accept other people's rights to study Islam within the framework of their own paradigms, for Islam is a vast meta-historical event which has changed the topography of human history, and as such, people of all persuasions have a right to study and analyse it.

VIII

It is for all the aforementioned reasons that the present book makes an indispensible contribution to the field of Qur'anic studies. It is an example of a good academic endeavour which tries to address many critical issues about the Qur'an and its history in an unprejudiced manner. Although, as one should expect, it is set within the Islamic paradigm, its critical approach and cross-dimensional and denominational analyses makes it stand out as an example of a work which can form a bridge between two perspectictives.

The text is an abridged translation of Ayatollah Mohammad Hādī Ma'rifat's magnum opus, *al-Tamhīd fī 'Ulūm al-Qur'an* (Introduction to the Sciences of the Qur'an). The original work is in Arabic and is published in ten volumes. Although the book does not address the Orientalist theories directly, the richness of its investigation and the wealth of information it contains make most of their doubts and speculations irrelevant, for it shows the inadequacy of the information upon which the Orientalists have conjectured.

Ayatollah Ma'rifat (d. 2007) was one of the most prominent contemporary experts in *'Ulūm al-Qur'an*. He was born in Karbala to a family of the clerical tradition. His forefathers were all religious scholars going back to the famous Sheikh Ali ibn Abd al-'Ālī al-Maysī of Jabal 'Āmil (d. 938/1531). Al-Maysī was the author of *al-Risālat al-Maysiyyah*, and migrated to Isfahān at the invitation of the Safavid king along with his teacher al-Muhaqqiq al-Karakī; hence the Isfahāni origin of Ayatollah Ma'rifat.

More information about his personal life, his education and his other works can be found in his autobiography which follows this introduction. What I have to emphasise here are the innovative ideas he has contributed towards elevating our knowledge of the Qur'an to a higher level. His research and analysis clarify many previously vague aspects of *'Ulūm al-Qur'an*, and address many difficult questions in different areas of this discipline. In addition to the rich historical and conceptual information, the reader will find in the chapters of this book original theories and well considered suggestions for solving certain problematic matters related to this science.

An example of such a theory is his contribution regarding the orality of the Qur'an, which can be applied to the criticisms we discussed earlier regarding the abrupt transitions and disconnected nature of some sections of the Qur'an. Although he does not directly refer to Richard Bell or Theodor Nöldeke, and probably had never read their work, his theory is a clear response and the direct antithesis of their claims, and most certainly unravels Bell's theory on this issue.

Ayatollah Ma'rifat stipulates in this relation that the phraseology of the Qur'an is that of the spoken word, rather than that of a written book. One of the distinguishing features of the primarily written word is the coherence of the contents from beginning to end; something usually lacking in speech. Although a speaker should make sense in what is said, speech is not constrained by a strict verbal or conceptual order. In fact, unlike the written text, abrupt transitions are sometimes desirable. A speaker may jump from one subject to another on account of something which occurs to him while speaking. According to Ayatollah Ma'rifat, this is something we encounter in the Qur'an on many occasions.

This style involves switching from the third person to the second person or from the second person to the third person. It may also involve the use of different pronouns and demonstrative pronouns without matching the nouns to which they refer, or switching from explicit to implicit and other such features. These sudden shifts from one state to another are permissible and sometimes desirable in the style of spoken as opposed to written word. It is also permissible to use parenthetical remarks in the spoken word but not in the written word. Such instances, according to Ayatollah Ma'rifat, have occurred in the Qur'an in different forms as follows.

Sudden Switching: One of the unique features of oral communication is that it is permissible to switch suddenly from one subject to another or from one situation to another relying upon contextual indicators provided by the setting. He mentions *Surah al-Qiyāmah* as an example; this surah begins by talking about Man and his state with regard to the coming of the Hour. Then all of a sudden, the discourse turns to address the Prophet by saying: *Move not thy tongue with it to hasten it; Ours it is to gather it, and to recite it. So, when We recite it, follow thou its recitation. Then Ours it is to explain it* (75:16-19). After this interjection the discourse goes back to confront Mankind with an adjunct: *No indeed; but you love the hasty world, and leave the Hereafter* (75:20-21). Drawing on a tradition from Imam Riḍā, Ayatollah Ma'rifat explains that this sudden shift may have been due to the fact that upon revelation of these verses the Messenger hurried to recite them fearing they would get lost. So he was immediately told not to; and then the discourse on the subject continues.

Grammatical Shift for Rhetorical Purposes (*Iltifāt*): According to Ayatollah Ma'rifat such meandering in discourse is not appropriate in the written word while it is regarded as beauty of style in the spoken word. He cites many examples from different verses including *Fātiḥat al-Kitāb* where one begins by praising God in the third person, and then the discourse turns to petitioning Him in the second person, which is a beautiful grammatical shift in the spoken discourse.

Paying attention to rhyme: One of the distinguishing features of rhyming prose is being able to notice the rhyme if it is heard out loud as opposed to being written down. There is a lot of rhyming prose in the Qur'an – at the expense of articulated speech – which cannot be properly rendered in a mere book.

Among many examples is the verse: *Bal al-insānu 'alā nafsihī basīrah wa law alqā ma'ādhīrah* (75:14-15); the words only rhyme if there is a pause after both *basīrah* and *ma'ādhīrah* when it is uttered and recited with a *yā'*, *rā'* and *hā'* at the end of them; something which cannot be achieved in the written word. Another example is

Wa al-fajri wa layālin 'ashr wa al-shaf'i wa al-watr wa al-layli idhā yasr (89:1-4);

where the *yā'* at the end of *yasrī* has been omitted to preserve the rhyme when it is said aloud. This is how it was recited to the Prophet and how he recited it to the people, and it is always mandatory to copy it in this way. The written form therefore follows that of recitation, since the recitation of the Qur'an is what came first.

Melodies and tunes: An important feature of the Qur'an is its innovative vocal arrangement to melodies and tunes which has a captivating effect on the feelings of its audience. This can only be achieved by reciting it out loud as steered by the tune of the performance, not whispering it under the cover of secrecy. This is a matter overlooked by those who suppose that the formation of the Qur'an was composed in writing as opposed to epic oral performance.

Ayatollah Ma'rifat provides more evidence for his view which you can find in the related chapter in this book. This is not the only innovative view one can find in contributions of Ayatollah Ma'rifat. Unfortunately, some volumes of this huge work do not submit to translation as they discuss the eloquence and semantic aspects of the Qur'anic literature which only make sense in Arabic.

Notwithstanding, I am sure that the students of *'Ulūm al-Qur'an* will find many interesting and thought provoking ideas in this translation which makes this book an indispensible asset for the students of the sciences of the Qur'an.

IX

I cannot thank enough the people who made the creation of this English abridged edition of *al-Tamhīd fī Ulūm al-Qur'an* possible. First of all, I have to thank the SAMT Institute whose generous help, support and financial contribution was behind this project from day one to the end. I cannot name all the individuals at SAMT who worked hard for this project as it would make a long list, but special mention should be made of Dr Ahmad Ahmadī, Dr Abolghāsemī, Shaykh Muhammad Rezā Nūrullāhiyān and Dr Saeedī.

Special thanks and gratitude are due to Dr. Khalīl Tousī for his dedicated and diligent management of the project and for his enthusiasm, without which this project would neither have started nor come to fruition. I should say a big thank you to the translators of this highly technical text, Mr Salim Rossier of Cambridge and Dr Mansoor Limba of Manila, whose brilliant English rendition made the task seem easy. Also my thanks and appreciations are due to Mr Seyfeddin Kara and Ms Aliya Gokal for helping with the research.

Last but not least, I have to thank the English editor, Trevor Banyard, who added much beauty and smoothness to the text, and all those who helped out in proof reading, design, lay-out and printing.

All these helping hands and facilitating means did, of course, come together under the auspicious care of God, Whom we cannot thank enough.

Mohammad Saeed Bahmanpour

FOREWORD

An Overview of My Life

My name is Muhammad Hādī Ma'rifat, and I was born to a family of men of religion in the Holy City of Karbalā in the year 1349 AH. My father was Sheikh Ali ibn al-Mīrzā Muhammad Ali, one of the grandsons of Sheikh 'Abd al-'Ālī al-Maysī al-Iṣfahānī, a well-known preacher in Karbalā at that time. My father migrated with his parents from Iṣfahān to Karbalā in the year 1329 AH, when he was fifteen years old. He then died there in the year 1378 AH, when he was nearly 63 years of age, and was buried in the courtyard of the shrine of 'Abu al-Faḍl al-'Abbās. He was a brilliant scholar and preacher, and blessed with the respect of the people of Karbalā. All of my ancestors going back three centuries were from a noble chain of religious scholars.

As for my mother, she was Al-Sayyidah Zahrā', daughter of Al-Sayyid Hāshim al-Tājir (the trader) al-Rashtī, who settled in Karbalā, where he died in the year 1404 AH and was buried there.

Academic Career

When I reached the age of five, my father sent me to a private school set up by Sheikh Bāqir. I then studied the preliminaries (*al-muqaddimāt*) at the hand of Ustādh Hājj Sheikh Ali Akbar al-Nā'īnī and subsequently my father. After that I studied literature and logic with the teachers at the *ḥawzah* in Karbalā. I learned a number of astronomical and mathematical sciences. My teachers at this time were the following: my father, Al-Sayyid Sa'īd al-Tunikābūnī (a specialist Arabic literature teacher), Ayatullāh al-Sayyid Muhammad al-Shīrāzī, Sheikh Muhammad Husayn al-Māzandarānī and Sayyid Murtaḍā al-Qazwīnī.

The next phase in my studies consisted of jurisprudence and an introduction to philosophy. My teachers were my father, Sheikh Muhammad al-Kalbāsī, Sheikh Muhammad Husayn al-Māzandarānī, Sheikh Muhammad al-Khaṭīb (a *marja'* and great scholar at the *ḥawzah*), Sayyid Muhammad Mīr Qazwīnī (one of the most famous scholars in the *ḥawzah* and a student of the late Ākhund Khurāsānī), Sheikh Muhammad Mahdī al-Kābulī (with whom I studied some of *Qawānīn al-Usūl*), and Sheikh Yūsuf al-Biyārijmandī al-Khurāsānī (one of the late Nā'īnī's most famous students, and who was knowledgeable in the principles of jurisprudence), with whom I studied *al-Fuṣūl*, *al-Rasā'il*, *al-Makāsib*, a complete course in the principles of jurisprudence, and a large part of jurisprudence at *baḥth khārij* level. Since he was a student of the great literary expert al-Nīsābūrī,, I also studied *al-Muṭawwal* with him. This course lasted until the year 1379 AH.

Starting to Give Something Back

In addition to these studies, I also took up teaching and research in the literary and technical fields in the *ḥawzah 'ilmiyyah*s, as well as holding weekly religious circles for young people, activities which were warmly received and from which many students graduated. I also took the initiative of setting up and publishing a monthly magazine entitled *Ajwibat al-Masā'il al-Dīnīyyah* (Answers to Religious Questions) accompanied by and with the help of a number of *ḥawzah* luminaries, such as al-Sayyid Muhammad al-Shīrāzī, al-Sayyid 'Abd al-Riḍā al-Shahristānī, al-Sayyid Muhammad Ali al-Baḥrānī, al-Sheikh Muhammad Bāqir al-Maḥmūdī and others. We worked on it in all earnestness, and this led to its having a wide readership, especially in universities, and in particular a number of universities outside Iraq. The magazine had a long lifespan and contained articles on religion of a technical nature. Some of the articles were of such importance that they were later reprinted as a book or treatise, such as *Ḥuqūq al-Mar'ah fi al-Islām* (Women's Rights in Islam), *Tarjamat al-Qur'an: al-Imkāniyyah, Al-Naqd, al-Ḍarūrah* (Translation of the Qur'an: Whether It Is Possible, Criticism, and the Need for It), *Firqatā al-Sheikhiyyah* (The Two Sects of the Sheikhiyyah), *Ahamiyyat al-Ṣalāt wa Ta'thiruhā 'alā al-Ḥayāt al-Fardiyyah wa al-Ijtimā'iyyah* (The Importance of Prayer and its Impact on Individual and Social Life), and so forth. Some of these were translated into Persian.

In the Wake of the *Hawzah 'Ilmiyyah*

After my father's death in 1380 AH, I moved to the holy city of Najaf, accompanied by my family, with the purpose of completing my studies. The main goal was to participate in the study circles of the luminaries of scholarship and jurisprudence. I gained as much as possible from senior teachers and jurisprudents such as al-Sayyid Muḥsin al-Ḥakīm, al-Sayyid Abu al-Qāsim al-Khoī, al-Mīrzā Bāqir al-Zanjānī, al-Sheikh Husayn al-Ḥillī, al-Sayyid Ali al-Fānī al-Iṣfahānī and latterly the late Imam Khomeini, may God hallow all their souls.

Al-Sayyid al-Ḥakīm was exceptionally proficient and precise in setting out the opinions of the jurisprudents, and this meant that there was something special about his classes. He cared incessantly for the opinions of the early jurisprudents, as much as he did for the words of the Infallible Ones.

Al-Sayyid al-Khoī was brilliant at clarification and in his ability to reason, combining eloquence and depth with simplicity of expression. He was unrivalled in his ability to explain the principles of jurisprudence and related matters, replete with subtle technicalities, in record time.

Al-Sayyid al-Zanjānī specialised in presenting and clarifying different viewpoints, and had an agreeable way of explaining the profundities of an issue.

Al-Sheikh al-Ḥillī was characterised by his immense skill in presenting various opinions on every issue, studying their proofs and criticising them. He also has an unparalleled innovative legacy in the study of jurisprudence; the number of his pupils was limited, but they were among the best and most outstanding at the *Ḥawzah 'Ilmiyyah*. The late Sheikh had a unique style of teaching, and would not necessarily state his own opinion explicitly. Rather, it could be discerned by reading between the lines of his presentations of the opinions of others. Whenever he was asked to outrightly state his opinion, he would answer, 'It is not in your interest.' This was because pupils incline towards their teachers and may incline towards their opinion without realising it, when in fact this can be misleading and limit the thinking process. That was the way of the professor, and he was able to educate strong students who enjoyed freedom of thought.

As for al-Sayyid al-Fānī, he was a farsighted and knowledgeable researcher who exerted most of his efforts on giving select students an academic grounding. In addition to daily study circles, al-Sayyid Riḍwānī (a current member of the Constitutional Council in Iran), al-Sayyid Ghadīrī (currently responsible for answering jurisprudential questions in the leader al-Khāmeneī's office) and I would come to him on Thursdays and Fridays, from early morning until midday, to hold discussion sessions on various subjects through which we acquired great technical abilities.

Imam Khomeini was set apart by his special skill at presenting the opinions of great scholars and his extensive criticism and analysis of them. He believed that it was only the sayings of the Infallible Ones which were sacred, and he raised his students on that; the words of senior scholars were respected, but not considered sacred, and due deference towards them is based on criticism and analysis, not slavish acceptance. He would deal with the subject matter entirely appropriately, and not be disgruntled by questions or his students' refutations. Thus, he was able to kindle thought and prepare students with a critical eye; may God grant him the best reward.

At this stage, I studied a little philosophy, especially transcendental philosophy with the erudite scholar al-Riḍwānī. In addition to my studies at the academic centres, I also did some teaching; I spent the mornings studying and the afternoons teaching.

Nor did I neglect research or writing academic articles. We had weekly sessions with a number of the *ḥawzah*'s well-known luminaries, such as al-Sayyid Jamāl al-Dīn Khoī (Ayatollah Khoī's son), al-Sayyid Muhammad al-Nūrī, al-Sayyid 'Abd al-'Azīz al-Ṭabāṭabā'ī, al-Sheikh Muhammad Riḍā Ja'farī Ishkevārī, Dr Muhammad Ṣādiqī (the author of the exegesis) and Professor 'Amīd Zanjānī, in order to research various subjects, each according to his own specialisation and interest, wherein I chose the field of Qur'anic sciences. In addition, I published articles in magazines such as *Ajwibat al-Masā'il al-Dīniyyah* (Answers to Religious Questions), which was still being published at that time, and wrote on various matters including *Tanāsukh al-Arwāḥ* (Reincarnation), refuting this theory which was popular at the time. This book had a wide readership among university students in Baghdad, and was translated into Persian in Iran. I also had a treatise published under the title *Tamhīd al-Qawā'id* (Introduction to the Principles) on performing duties left undone (*qaḍā' al-fawā'it*), and which constituted a transcript of Ayatollah al-Khoī's lessons. This was the beginning of my work in discursive jurisprudence (*al-fiqh al-istidlālī*), where I shed light on jurisprudential matters in a new way.

The Pivotal Position of the Qur'an and its Exegesis

The impetus behind dealing with issues pertaining to the Qur'an – in addition to jurisprudence and the principles and practice of jurisprudence – was my clash with a bitter truth in the course of my reading and research in preparation for teaching the subject of exegesis. This involved the lack of a living study on Qur'anic matters in the Shi'a academic library at that time. I developed this impression whilst consulting the specialist Qur'anic library to write an article on the translation of the Qur'an. I came across many books on the subject, some of them in two volumes, and similarly several treatises and articles written by contemporary scholars in Egypt, whereas in the *ḥawzah* of Najaf I found no more than a catalogue entry for a single page by Ayatollah al-Sheikh Muhammad Husayn Kāshif al-Ghiṭā'. This weighed heavily upon me, and prompted me to set out the words of scholars past and present on Qur'anic issues. The result of that tireless work was *al-Tamhīd (The Introduction), in seven volumes, and al-Tafsīr wa al-Mufassirūn* (Exegesis and Exegetes), in two volumes. The latter was more or less a critical analysis of Muhammad Husayn al-Dhahabī, and a rectification of what had eluded him, when he had unfairly claimed not to know the status of the Shi'a in the field of Qur'anic studies.

From Najaf to Qum

In the year 1392 AH, the Ba'athist regime in Iraq issued an edict to expel Iranians, so I travelled with my family to the *Ḥawzah 'Ilmiyyah* in Qum, taking important books with me, in particular my handwritten manuscripts. The rest of my books were later sent on.

No sooner had I arrived in Qum, I began applying the methodology which I had followed in the *ḥawzah*s in Karbalā and Najaf. However, I only attended one class: that of the late Mīrzā Hāshim Āmulī. I devoted the rest of my time to teaching and academic research. With regards to teaching, I began teaching *al-Rasā'il*, *al-Makāsib* and *al-Kifāyah*, and then jurisprudence (*fiqh*) and its principles (*uṣūl*) at *dars al-khārij* level. In addition, I taught at Madrasah Ḥaqqānī al-'Āliyah (the Ḥaqqānī School of Advanced Studies), at the invitation of its director, Martyr Quddūsī, teaching matters pertaining to the Qur'an, especially the Qur'anic sciences (*'Ulūm al-Qur'an*). Worthy individuals who are now luminaries in that field would attend that class.

In addition to exegesis and Qur'anic sciences, I was asked to teach jurisprudence, based on *al-Makāsib* by al-Sheikh al-Anṣārī, and the principles thereof, based on his *al-Rasā'il.* As well as teaching, I settled down to some serious research and subjected the critical studies which I had completed in Najaf to a serious and comprehensive review. They were to become improved and honed into *al-Tamhīd*, each part coming to light one after another.

In the year 1399 AH, at the beginning of the Islamic Revolution, the third volume was ready for print. Then Mu'assasat al-Nashr al-Islāmī, attached to Jāmi'at al-Mudarrisīn, reprinted them in six volumes. Realising that after the Revolution had settled down the subjects set out in this book were deemed by the *ḥawzah* to be fundamental study material, I began teaching them at the *ḥawzah* centre. After these classes many people graduated, various academic fields such as exegesis and the Qur'anic sciences were modernised, some started writing and teaching in this field, and its influence spread to the point where we now have fourteen colleges specialising in Qur'anic sciences alongside the specialist academic *ḥawzahs* all over the country.

Pickings and Fruits

In this context, I wrote other books as circumstances dictated, including *Ṣiyānat al-Qur'an min al-Taḥrīf*[71] (The Qur'an's Being Immune to Tampering) in defence of the sacredness of the Holy Qur'an and as a response to a Pakistani writer Iḥsān Ilāhī Ẓāhir, who had written a book critical of the Shi'a, accusing them of believing that the Qur'an has been tampered with.

Striving on my part to refute this accusation and to defend the sacred essence of the Qur'an, I made a firm resolution to write this book, completing it in six months (Ramaḍān 1407 AH – 30 Ṣafar 1408 AH). It received a great deal of attention, was reprinted several times and was translated

[71] Muhammad Hādī Ma'rifat, *al-Tamhīd fī 'Ulūm al-Qur'an* (Qum: Jāmi'ah Mudarrisīn, 1396 q.), vol.8.

into Persian twice, once abridged and once unabridged. The same thing happened with *al-Tafsīr wa al-Mufassirūn* (Exegesis and Exegetes) in two volumes, which I also translated into Persian.

Regarding *al-Ma'ārif al-Qur'aniyyah*,[72] I wrote several magazine articles and a sum of five volumes ready for print.

The last work I have taken up, commencing at the beginning of 1421 AH, and which is of great importance, constitutes the collection and arrangement of both sects' exegetical traditions (*riwāyāt*). The work is proceeding quickly with the help of two panels of ten people from the *ḥawzah*s and graduates of the Qur'anic school. The exegetical traditions are there in the books in a raw format, untouched by the hand of personal judgement or critical examination, the way the traditions pertaining to laws and jurisprudence (*al-aḥkām al-fiqhiyyah*) have been dealt with, whereby the sound and valuable ones have been mixed up with the unsound ones of no value.

Besides the Qur'anic work, I have been involved in activity in the field of jurisprudence since the time I was in the Holy City of Najaf; I have written several books and treatises in this field, such as *Tamhīd al-Qawā'id* (Introduction to the Principles), *Ḥadīth La Tu'ād* (The Tradition Regarding Non-Repetition of Prayers), *Wilāyat al-Faqīh: Ab'āduhā wa Ḥudūduhā* (The Authority of the Jurist: Its Dimensions and Limits), *Mālikiyyat al-'Arḍ* (Land Ownership) and *Masā'il fi al-Qaḍā'* (Issues Pertaining to Judgment), all in Arabic.

As for the huge opus on jurisprudence which I was and still am dedicated to, it involves the derivation of modern jurisprudential opinions on the basis of the development of *ijtihād*[73] in the last few centuries. It is the result of jurisprudential classes at *khārij* level and arranged in the order of the jurisprudential chapters of *Jawāhir al-Kalām*, from the beginning

---

[72] This is a reference to a collection of studies on topics such as the matter of monotheism (*tawhid*), Divine Attributes, the present life and the Hereafter, the matter of volition and religious responsibility, predestination, free will, good and evil, divine laws, reward and punishment, and other matters which appear in the text of the Qur'an and which are studied by scholars and exegetes (see below). [Trans.]

[73] The derivation of laws based on textual evidence in the text where it is apparent, and the determination of an appropriate course of conduct based on legal presumptions where no textual basis can be found. [Trans.]

of *Kitāb al-Ṭahārah* (The Book on Ritual Purity) to the end of *Kitāb al-Diyāt* (Damages for Death or Personal Injury and Criminal Compensation for Offences Against the Person), and is entitled *al-Sharḥ wa al-Ta'līq li Jawāhir al-Kalām* (Explanation of and Commentary on *Jawāhir al-Kalām*). This work is nearly complete with the Almighty's help.

Today, in the year 1421 AH, I still practise – praise to Almighty God – with verve and vigour, inasmuch as I teach jurisprudence and its principles at *khārij* level and Qur'anic sciences in a modern style, and conduct research in the fields of jurisprudence and exegesis in accordance with the firm principles accepted by critical researchers.

It is God Who grants success.

Qum – Muhammad Hādī Ma'rifat
25/12/1421 AH

CHAPTER I

ON THE QUR'AN AND THE QUR'ANIC SCIENCES

THE QUR'AN AND ITS NAMES

The Qur'an is a proper noun and the name of the Scripture revealed to the Prophet of Islam.

The Scripture is mentioned by this name along with the definite article[74] more than fifty times within the text:

> *And this Qur'an (hādhā al-Qur'ān)[75] has been revealed to me that I may warn you thereby, and whomsoever it may reach (6:19);*

and without the definite article in fifteen places:

> *And a Qur'an We have divided, for thee to recite it to mankind at intervals, and We have sent it down successively (17:106).*

The name 'Qur'an' is used to refer to the text in its entirety as well as just part of it:

> *In whatever business thou mayest be, and whatever Qur'an thou may be reciting from it- and whatever deed ye may be doing - We are Witnesses thereof when ye are deeply engrossed therein...(10:61).*

This is because here an adjectival meaning – its being recited – is intended. Thus the universal applicability generated by the lack of qualification is correct.

The word has a deep Arabic root. At its root is the verbal noun (*maṣdar*) of *qara'a* (he recited), *yaqra'u* (he recites), *qirā'ah* (recitation), and *Qur'ān* (recital), derived from the same form as *ghufrān* (forgiveness), *rujḥān* (preferability) and *kufrān* (ungratefulness). It is used as a verbal noun in the following Words of God:

> *...and the recital (Qur'ān) of dawn; surely the recital of dawn is witnessed (17:78);*

---

[74] The definite article indicating a reference back to a previously used adjectival meaning; Ibn Mālik said that it is used with some proper nouns to refer back to something previously mentioned.

[75] The definite article in *hādhā al-Qur'an* is omitted in translation, i.e. 'this Qur'an.' [Trans.]

and:

> *It is for Us to gather it and to recite it (qur'ānahu): but when We have recited it, follow thou its recital (qur'ānahu) (75:17-18).*

Derived meanings with many possible conjugations and declensions – especially tri-radical – are indications that a word is a native part of the language.

According to Ibn Fāris:

> The *qāf, rā'* and the weak letter are a valid root which means 'collecting' and 'gathering.' The word *qariyah* (village) comes from that. It is so called because people gather there. If it is given a *hamzah* it equally means the same thing. They say that this also applies to the Qur'an. It is as if it were so called on account of its comprising rules, stories and other things.[76]

Al-Rāghib says:

> The root meaning of Qur'an is a *masdar* along the lines of *kufrān* and *rujḥān*. The Almighty said: *It is for Us to gather it (jam'ahu) and to recite it (qur'anahu): but when We have recited it (qara'nāhu), follow thou its recitation (qur'anahu)* (75:17-18). The name is exclusively used for the Scripture revealed to Prophet Muhammad and has become like a proper noun for it. According to some, out of all God's Scriptures, this Scripture was called the *Qur'an* on account of its combining the benefits of all His Scriptures and indeed of all fields of knowledge as mentioned in the verse:
>
> > *...and [it is] a detailed description of everything (12:111).*
>
> and:
>
> > *...as an explanation of everything (16:89).*
>
> Thus the conjecture of those who thought the word to be foreign and taken from a Syriac root, *Quryānah*, meaning 'the recitation of religious texts' is pointless, because there is nothing remarkable about Eastern languages, especially Semitic ones, having shared roots, as everybody knows.

---

[76] Abu al-Ḥusayn Aḥmad ibn Fāris, *Mu'jamu Maqāyīs al-Lughah* (Qum: Maktab al-I'lām al-Islamī, 1404 q.), vol.5, 78-79.

Furqān

Al-Furqān (the Criterion) is another name for the Qur'an on account of its being speech which distinguishes between truth and falsehood. The Almighty said:

> *Blessed be He who has sent down the the Criterion (furqān) upon His servant, that he may be a warner to all beings (25:1).*

This attribute is obvious in a verse such as:

> *...the month of Ramadan, wherein the Qur'an was sent down to be a guidance to the people, and as clear signs of the Guidance and the Criterion (furqān) (2:185).*

Imam Ja'far ibn Muhammad al-Ṣādiq has said, 'The Qur'an is the whole Book and the *Furqān* is the clear part which has to be acted upon.'[77]

This attribute was also used to describe Moses' Scripture:

> *And when We gave to Moses the Book and the Criterion (furqān), that haply you should be guided* (2:35).

"The Criterion" here is joined by a clarificatory conjunction to "the Book". Clearer than that are the Words of the Almighty:

> *We gave Moses and Aaron the Criterion and a Radiance, and a Remembrance for the God-fearing* (21:48).

In this respect the *Furqān* is not a name which is exclusive to the Qur'an. It was only used for it on account of its having that attribute.

Other Names

These two names – the Qur'an and the *Furqān* are the most well-known names of the Wise Remembrance. Two other names come after these in terms of how well they are known: *al-Kitāb* (The Book), which is a general noun, and *al-Dhikr* (The Remembrance) on account of its being a reminder (*mudhakkir*) and a general adjective.

---

[77] Aḥmad ibn Ali ibn Abī Ṭālib Ṭabrisī , *Majma' al-Bayān* (Tehran: Islāmiyyah, 1382 q.), vol.2, 276.

The author of *al-Burhān* and others got carried away with names by regarding all adjectives used in the Qur'an to describe the Book as names for it, such as:

> *...it is surely a noble (karīm) Qur'an* (56:77);
>
> *And this is a blessed (mubārak) Remembrance that We have sent down* (21:50).

They thought that *Karīm* was one name and *Mubārak* another, and so on up to fifty-five names according to the author of *al-Burhān*'s reckoning! One commentator went all the way up to ninety or so names,[78] which is clearly an affected expression of unnecessary prolix.

'Ulūm al-Qur'an (the Qur'anic Sciences)

'Ulūm al-Qur'an is the name of a variety of studies that seek a technical understanding of various matters mentioned in the Holy Qur'an, each in accordance with its own principles and criteria. These disciplines often differ significantly from one another in the principles and evidence they employ, as do their conclusions. They share neither fundamentals nor subsidiary matters. That is why each topic is a separate science in terms of its evidence, subject matter and the questions it raises, and they should be categorised as different sciences.

The study of divergent readings is an example. This includes the origin of various readings, how they vary, their being limited to seven, their being reported by so many sources as to be indubitable (*mutawātir*) and their evidential value. Matters such as this all revolve around discussions of a single topic – in this case recitation – and each forms a science in itself with no link between it and discussions on what abrogates and what is abrogated in the Qur'an. The same is true of what is clear and what is equivocal in the Qur'an, the collecting together and compilation of the Qur'an, its inimitability, its being protected from alteration and so forth. Every issue is a separate subject and has its own material. What brings them all together is that they are studies on various matters pertaining to the Qur'an. They form several rather than a single science on account

---

[78] Zarkashī, *al-Burhān fī 'Ulūm al-Qur'an*, 273-376.

of their different subject matter, and they are therefore not placed under one umbrella.

This is in contrast to another technical term which has recently come into circulation, namely *Ma'ārif al-Qur'an*, which refers to a collection of studies on subjects such as monotheism (*tawḥīd*), the Divine Attributes, the present life and the Hereafter, the matter of volition and religious responsibility, predestination, free will, good and evil, the Divine Law, reward and punishment, and other matters which appear in the text of the Qur'an and are studied by discerning scholars and senior exegetes. If such topics are thematically studied either all together or separately – by singling out related verses and studying them systematically – then this type of discussion and Qur'anic elaboration is regarded as thematic exegesis (*tafsīr mawḍū'ī*) and is an important exegetical discipline. We have referred to the importance of such studies in our work on methodologies of exegesis, *al-Tafsīr wa al-Mufassirūn* (Exegesis and Exegetes) (parts 9 and 10 of *al-Tamhīd*).

In *'Ulūm al-Qur'an* the subjects under discussion are Revelation and the sending down of the Qur'an, the duration and order of the Revelation, the circumstances surrounding it, the collection and recording of the Qur'an, the scribes who recorded it, the standardisation of the manuscripts, the origin and emergence of different readings (*qirā'āt*) of the Qur'an, the Qur'an's authority and immunity from distortion (*taḥrīf*), the issue of abrogation (*naskh*) in the Qur'an, equivocal verses (*mutashābihāt*) in the Qur'an, the Qur'an's inimitability (*i'jāz*) and so on. And since each of these issues has its own framework and is considered distinct from the others, this science is placed in the plural form, *'ulūm*, which literally means 'sciences.'

As for the reason for the importance of Qur'anic sciences – the study of various matters pertaining to the Qur'an – it suffices to know that one can only arrive at the true meaning of the Qur'an through these studies, and that they are the principles and stepping stones facilitating that desired objective.

If we look at the themes of this science issue by issue we find that each of them has a fundamental role in enabling one to derive benefit from the Qur'an. For example, studies of the value of evidence of the apparent meanings[79] of the Qur'an are what pave the way for the jurisprudent to deduce laws from the appropriate verses. The same applies to knowing the difference between verses that abrogate others and those which are abrogated, and between those which are capable of more than one interpretation and those which are clear. In the same way, the study of the evidential value of divergent readings and whether they are reported by enough sources as to be indubitable plays an important role in getting to know the text of the Qur'an. The same is true of studies refuting the allegation that the Qur'an has been altered, on the matter of its inimitability and other topics. They all have an indispensable part to play in familiarising oneself with the text.

The history of Qur'anic Sciences

From the beginning, the Prophet's most senior companions and eminent successors (*tābi'īn*) made great efforts studying various aspects of the Holy Qur'an. They concerned themselves with which parts abrogated others (*nāsikh*) and those which were abrogated (*mansūkh*), which parts were clear (*muḥkam*) and which were capable of sustaining more than one interpretation (*mutashābih*), literal (*tanzīl*) and allegorical interpretation (*ta'wīl*) of it, its general (*'āmm*) and particular parts (*khāṣṣ*), its unqualified (*muṭlaq*) and qualified parts (*muqayyad*), rhythmic recitation (*tartīl*) and beautiful recitation (*tajwīd*), and other disparate issues. Similarly, the scope of Qur'anic studies has flowed and expanded throughout the centuries, as hadith collections and exegetical texts with various functions have abounded.

Here I try to give an overview of the most important books written on the subject in a chronological order.

The First Century

Writings on the subject date back to the end of the first century of the Islamic calendar. The first to write about recitation was Yaḥyā ibn Ya'mur (d. 89 AH), one of Abū al-Aswad al-Du'alī's pupils. His book *al-Qirā'ah* (Recitation) was written in the village of Wāsiṭ. According to

[79] If a statement is capable of two or more interpretations, the principle of the 'evidential value of the apparent meaning' (*ḥujīyyat al-ẓuhūr*) establishes that the more apparent meaning (*ẓāhir*) that comes to mind before the others should have priority [Editor].

Fu'ād Sazgīn in *Tārikh al-Turāth al-'Arabī* (The History of Arab Culture), it comprises the differences noticed in the known Qur'anic codices.

The Second Century

In the second century, al-Ḥasan ibn Abī al-Ḥasan Yasār al-Baṣrī (d. 110 AH) wrote his book *'Adad Āy al-Qur'an* (The Number of Verses in the Qur'an).

'Abdullāh ibn 'Āmir al-Yaḥṣabī (d. 118 AH) wrote *Ikhtilāfu Maṣāḥif al-Shām wa al-Ḥijāz wa al-'Irāq* (The Difference Between Qur'anic Codices in Syria, the Hijaz and Iraq) and *al-Maqṭū' wa al-Mawṣūl* (The Disjointed and the Jointed) on pausing (*waqf*) or joining together (*waṣl*) the ends of phrases or verses.

Abū Muhammad Ismā'īl ibn 'Abd al-Raḥmān al-Suddī al-Kabīr (d. 128 AH) has a book *al-Nāsikh wa al-Mansūkh* (That Which Abrogates Other Parts and That Which is Abrogated).

Shaybah ibn Naṣṣāḥ al-Madanī (d. 130 AH) wrote *Kitāb al-Wuqūf* (The Book on Pausings).

Abān ibn Taghlib (d. 141 AH), a companion of Imam Ali ibn al-Husayn al-Sajjād, was the first to write on *al-Qirā'āt* (Divergent Recitations) after Ibn Ya'mur. He also wrote a book called *Ma'ānī al-Qur'an* (The Meanings of the Qur'an).

Muhammad ibn al-Sā'ib al-Kalbī (d. 146 AH) was the first to write on *Aḥkām al-Qur'an* (Laws Contained in the Qur'an).

Muqātil ibn Sulaymān the exegete (d. 150 AH) wrote a book called *al-Āyāt al-Mutashābihāt* (The Equivocal Verses).

Abū 'Amr ibn al-'Alā' Zabbān ibn 'Ammār al-Tamīmī (d. 154 AH) wrote *al-Waqf wa al-Ibtidā'* (Pausing and Starting) and *al-Qirā'āt* (Divergent Recitations).

Ḥamzah ibn Ḥabīb (d. 156 AH), one of the seven reciters and a companion of Imam Ja'far ibn Muhammad al-Sādiq, wrote *al-Qirā'ah* (Recitation).

Mūsa ibn Hārūn, one of Abān ibn Taghlib's pupils (d. circa 170 AH) wrote *al-Wujūh wa al-Naẓā'ir* (Different and Similar Meanings).

Ali ibn Ḥamzah al-Kisā'ī (d. 179 AH) wrote *al-Qirā'āt* (Divergent Recitations), *al-Hā'āt* – on the use of the pronoun *hā'* in the Qur'an – and other books.

Yaḥya ibn Ziyād al-Farrā' (d. 207 AH) wrote *Ma'ānī al-Qur'an* (Meanings of the Qur'an), which has been printed in three volumes, and *Ikhtilāf Ahl al-Kūfah wa al-Baṣrah wa al-Shām fī al-Muṣḥaf* (The Difference between the Kufan, Basran and Syrian Qur'anic Codices), *al-Jam' wa al-Tathniyah fī al-Qur'an* (The Plural and Dual in the Qur'an) and other books.

Muhammad ibn 'Umar al-Wāqidī (d. 207 AH), the erudite writer and famous historian, wrote *al-Raghīb* on Qur'anic sciences and misinterpretations.

Abū 'Ubaydah Mu'ammar ibn al-Muthannā (d. 209 AH) wrote *Majāz al-Qur'an* (Metaphors in the Qur'an), which has been printed in two parts, and *Ma'ānī al-Qur'an* (The Meanings of the Qur'an).

The Third Century

In the third century, Abū 'Ubayd al-Qāsim ibn Salām (d. 224 AH) wrote *Faḍā'il al-Qur'an* (The Merits of the Qur'an), *al-Maqṣūr wa al-Mamdūd* (That Which Is Not Drawn Out and That Which Is) on types of recitation, *Gharīb al-Qur'an* (Rare Words in the Qur'an), *al-Nāsikh wa al-Mansūkh* and other texts.

Al-Ḥasan ibn Ali ibn Faḍḍāl (d. 224 AH), one of al-Ridā's companions, wrote *al-Nāsikh wa al-Mansūkh.*

Ali ibn al-Madīnī (d. 234 AH) wrote on reasons for Revelation.

Al-Ḥārith ibn Asad al-Muḥāsibī (d. 236 AH) wrote *al-'Aql wa Fahm al-Qur'an* (The Intellect and Understanding the Qur'an).

Abu al-Faḍl Ja'far ibn Ḥarb (d. 236 AH) wrote *Mutashābih al-Qur'an* (Passages of the Qur'an Capable of Sustaining More than One Interpretation).

Aḥmad ibn Muhammad ibn 'Īsā al-Ash'arī (d. circa 250 AH), the sheikh and head of the people of Qum, wrote *al-Nāsikh wa al-Mansūkh.*

Abū 'Uthmān 'Amr ibn Baḥr al-Jāḥiẓ (d. 255 AH) wrote *Naẓm al-Qur'an* (The Coherence of the Qur'an).[80]

Abū Ḥātim Sahl ibn Muhammad al-Sijistānī al-Baṣrī (d. 255 AH) wrote *al-Qirā'āt* and *Ikhtilāf Maṣāḥif al-Amṣār* (The Difference between the Qur'anic Codices of the Metropolises).

Abū 'Abdillāh Aḥmad ibn Muhammad ibn Sayyār (d. 268 AH), the scribe for Āl Ṭāhir and a companion of the Imams al-Hādī and al-'Askarī, wrote *Thawāb al-Qur'an* (The Reward of the Qur'an) and *al-Qirā'āt*, which was also called *al-Tanzīl wa al-Taḥrīf* (Revelation and Falsification).

---

[80] Poets and composers of rhyming prose liken their work to arranging pearls on a string. This aspect of the Qur'an is examined in this and similar works. [Trans.]

Abū Muhammad 'Abdullāh ibn Muslim ibn Qutaybah (d. 276 AH) wrote *Ta'wīl Mushkil al-Qur'an* (The Interpretation of What is Ambiguous in the Qur'an), *Tafsīr Gharīb al-Qur'an* (Exegesis of Rare Words in the Qur'an), *Gharīb al-Qur'an* (Rare Words in the Qur'an) and *al-Qirā'āt*.

Abu al-'Abbās Muhammad ibn Yazīd al-Mubarrad the grammarian (d. 286 AH) wrote *I'rāb al-Qur'an* (Desinential Inflection in the Qur'an).

Abū 'Abdillāh Muhammad ibn Ayyūb ibn Ḍurays (d. 294 AH) wrote *Fīmā Nazala bi Makkah wa Mā Nazala bi al-Madīna* (On That Which Was Revealed in Mecca and That Which Was Revealed in Medina) and *Faḍā'il al-Qur'an* (Merits of the Qur'an).

Abu al-Qāsim Sa'd ibn 'Abdillāh al-Ash'arī al-Qummī (d. 299 AH) wrote a comprehensive treatise on categories of verses in the Qur'an, which 'Allāmah Majlisī came across and cited in chunks in his magnum opus, the encyclopedia called *Biḥār al-Anwār*.[81]

Abū 'Amr Muhammad ibn 'Umar ibn Sa'īd al-Bāhilī (d. 300 AH) wrote *I'jāz al-Qur'an* (Inimitability of the Qur'an), the first book by this title to appear, and which examines the inimitable quality of the Qur'an.

The Fourth Century

The fourth century was marked by the flourishing of the Islamic sciences and a variety of arts, especially on the subject of the various facets of the Qur'an.

One of those to write on Qur'anic sciences at the beginning of this century was Muhammad ibn Yazīd al-Wāsiṭī (d. 306 AH), one of the finest theologians and the author of *al-Imāmah* (The Imamate). Ibn al-Nadīm says he had a book on *I'jāz al-Qur'an fi Naẓmihi wa Ta'līfih* (The Inimitability of the Qur'an With Regard to Its Coherence and Composition). It is said that he was the first to elaborate further on the inimitability of the Qur'an. Sheikh 'Abd al-Qāhir al-Jurjānī wrote two brilliant commentaries on it.

Muhammad ibn Khalaf ibn Ḥayyān (d. 306 AH) wrote *'Adad Āy al-Qur'an* (The Number of Verses in the Qur'an).

Muhammad ibn Khalaf ibn Marzbān (d. 309 AH) wrote *al-Ḥāwī fī 'Ulūm al-Qur'an* (The All-in-One on Qur'anic Sciences) in 27 parts.

---

[81] 'Allāmah Muhammad Bāqir Majlisī, *Biḥār al-Anwār* (Beirut: Mu'assasat al-Wafā' 1403 q.), vol. 93, 97.

Abū Muhammad al-Ḥasan ibn Mūsā al-Nawbakhtī (d. circa 310 AH) wrote *al-Tanzīh wa Dhikr Mutashābihāt al-Qur'an* (The Refutation of Anthropomorphism and Discussion of the Passages of the Qur'an Capable of Sustaining More Than One Meaning).

Abu 'Ali al-Ḥasan ibn 'Ali al-Ṭūsī (d. 312 AH) wrote *Naẓm al-Qur'an.*

Abū Bakr ibn Abī Dāwūd 'Abdullāh ibn Sulaymān al-Sijistānī (d. 316 AH) wrote *al-Maṣāḥif, al-Nāsikh wa al-Mansūkh* and a treatise on divergent recitations.

Abū 'Abdillāh Muhammad ibn Aḥmad ibn Ḥazm al-Andalusī (d. 320 AH) wrote *al-Nāsikh wa al-Mansūkh.*

The authority on literature and linguist 'Allāmah Abū Bakr Muhammad ibn al-Ḥasan al-Azdī, known as Ibn Durayd (d. 321 AH), wrote a book on rare words in the Qur'an called *Gharīb al-Qur'an.*

Abū Zayd Aḥmad ibn Sahl al-Balkhī (d. 322 AH) wrote *Mā Ughliqa Min Gharīb al-Qur'an* (The Most Complicated Rare Words in the Qur'an), *al-Ḥurūf al-Muqaṭṭa'ah fi Awā'il al-Suwar* (The Disjointed Letters at the Beginning of Chapters), *al-Baḥth 'an Kayfiyyat al-Ta'wīlāt* (Study on How to Carry Out the Various Kinds of Exegesis) and other books.

Abū Bakr Aḥmad ibn Mūsā al-'Aṭshī, known as Ibn Mujāhid (d. 324 AH), wrote his famous book *al-Sab'ah* (The Seven) on the seven different recitations. It was he who limited them to seven.

Abū Bakr Aḥmad ibn Ali ibn Ikhshīd (d. 326 AH) wrote *Naẓm al-Qur'an.*

Thiqat al-Islam, Muhammad ibn Ya'qūb al-Kulaynī (d. 329 AH), wrote *Faḍā'il al-Qur'an*, which he included in the sublime *al-Uṣūl min al-Kāfī.*

Abū Bakr Muhammad ibn al-'Azīz al-Sijistānī (d. 330 AH) is famous for his book on *Gharīb al-Qur'an* which he called *Nuzhat al-Qulūb* (Delight of the Hearts), arranged in alphabetical order and completed in fifteen years.

Abū Ja'far Aḥmad ibn Muhammad al-Naḥḥās (d. 338 AH) wrote *I'rāb al-Qur'an, al-Nāsikh wa al-Mansūkh* and *Ma'āni al-Qur'an.*

Abū 'Abdillāh Muhammad ibn Ibrāhīm known as Ibn Abī Zaynab al-Kātib al-Nu'mānī (d. around 350 AH) wrote about categories of verses of the Qur'an which 'Allāmah Majlisī cited in *Biḥār al-Anwār.*[82] He was a close friend of al-Kulaynī and scribed *al-Kāfī* for him.

Abū Muhammad al-Qaṣṣāb Muhammad ibn Ali al-Karkhī (d. circa 360 AH) wrote *Nukāt al-Qur'an* (Subtleties of the Qur'an).

---

[82] See Majlisī, *Biḥār al-Anwār*, vol. 93, 3.

Abū Bakr Aḥmad ibn Ali al-Rāzī al-Jassās (d. 370 AH) wrote about laws contained in the Qur'an (*Aḥkām al-Qur'an*). It is a comprehensive and overflowing book printed in three large volumes, and is the most complete and most useful book on the subject.

Abū 'Ali al-Fārisī (d. 377 AH), one of the luminaries of the *Imāmiyyah,* is one of those who signalled the heyday of the fourth century in terms of merit, nobility and literary achievement. He wrote *al-Ḥujjah fī al-Qirā'āt* (The Proof on Divergent Recitations), which is the best, most complete and most accurate book on the subject.

Abū al-Ḥasan Ali ibn 'Īsā al-Rummānī (d. 384 AH) wrote *al-Nukāt fī I'jāz al-Qur'an* (Subtleties on the Inimitability of the Qur'an) and a short treatise pervaded with a deep theological flavour on polemical Mu'tazilism.

Abū al-Ḥasan 'Abbād al-Ṭāliqānī (d. 385 AH), the father of al-Ṣāḥib ibn Abbad, wrote a book on laws contained in the Qur'an (*Aḥkām al-Qur'an*).

Abū Muhammad 'Abdullāh ibn 'Abd al-Rahmān al-Qayrawāni (d. 386 AH), one of the north African luminaries of jurisprudence, wrote a book on the inimitability of the Qur'an.

Muhammad ibn 'Ali al-Adfawi (d. 388 AH) wrote *al-Istighnā'* (Sufficiency) in a hundred parts on Qur'anic sciences. The author of *al-Tāli' al-Sa'īd* (Fortuitous Star) had seen twenty of them.

One of Zayd ibn al-Khaṭṭāb's grandsons, Abū Sulaymān Hamad ibn Muhammad ibn Ibrāhīm al-Khaṭṭābī al-Bustī (meaning from Bust in the lands of Kabul) (d. 388 AH), wrote a short treatise on *Bayān I'jāz al-Qur'an* (Explanation of the Inimitability of the Qur'an) in which he treated the subject expertly, demonstrating its incomparability, explaining it in terms of coherence and that its arrangement and the selection of words are completely appropriate to their context. It may be the most complete study to ever appear which explores this aspect of the inimitability of the Qur'an.

Abu al-Fatḥ 'Uthmān ibn Jinnī (d. 392 AH) wrote *Al-Muḥtasab*, shedding light on the reasons for deviant recitations.

Al-Qāḍī (the Judge) Abū Bakr Muhammad ibn al-Tayyib al-Bāqillānī (d. 403 AH) wrote *I'jāz al-Qur'an* (The Inimitability of the Qur'an) and *Nukat al-Intisār* (Points of Triumph) on divergent recitations, and the gathering together and compilation of the Qur'an.

Abu al-Hasan Muhammad ibn al-Hasan al-Sharīf al-Raḍī (d. 404 AH) wrote *Talkhīs al-Bayān fī Majāzāt al-Qur'an* (Abridged Explanation of

Metaphors in the Qur'an) and *Haqā'iq al-Ta'wīl fī Mutashābih al-Tanzīl* (Truths about Interpretation of Revelation Capable of Sustaining More Than One Interpretation), of which only the fifth part has been found. Mu'assassat Muntadā al-Nashr (The Publication Forum Foundation) in the Holy City of Najaf happened across it, checked it and prepared it for publication in the year 1355 AH. Thereafter, it was printed in Najaf and Beirut.

The Fifth Century

In the fifth century, the Judge Abū Zar'a 'Abd al-Rahmān ibn Muhammad (d. circa 410 AH) wrote *Ḥujjat al-Qirā'āt* (The Proofs of Divergent Recitations), following the example of *al-Ḥujjah fī al-Qirā'āt* by Abu Ali al-Fārisī and copying its style and methodology. It was printed at Benghazi University in Tunis and thereafter several editions were printed in Beirut.

Abu al-Qāsim Hibatullah ibn Salamah (d. 410 AH) wrote *al-Nāsikh wa al-Mansūkh*.

Abū 'Abdillah Muhammad ibn Muhammad ibn al-Nu'mān (d. 413 AH), who was known as al-Sheikh al-Mufīd (The Enlightening Sheikh), wrote a book on *I'jāz al-Qur'an* and *al-Bayān* (The Explanation), on the various kinds of Qur'anic sciences.

Abu al-Hasan 'Imād al-Dīn al-Qāḍī 'Abd al-Jabbār (d. 410 AH), the Mu'tazilite theologian, wrote *Mutashābih al-Qur'an* in two parts and *Tanzīh al-Qur'an 'an al-Maṭā'in* (Declaring the Qur'an to Be Unharmed by Attacks).

Abu al-Qāsim al-Husayn ibn Ali (d. 418 AH), the Imami Moroccan vizier, the grandson of Ibn Abī Zaynab and of Persian origin, wrote *Khaṣā'iṣ al-Qur'an* (Unique Features of the Qur'an).

Muhammad ibn 'Abdullah al-Iskāfī (d. 421 AH), known as al-'Allāmah al-Musaddad (the Guided and Most Learned One), wrote *Durrat al-Tanzīl wa Ghurrat al-Ta'wīl* (The Pearl of Revelation and the Best Interpretation) on the allegorical passages in the Qur'an. It also contains wise sayings and proverbs from Qur'anic verses.

Abū al-Hasan Ali ibn Ibrāhīm ibn Sa'id al-Hūfī (d. 430 AH) wrote *al-Burhān fī 'Ulūm al-Qur'an* (The Rational Demonstration on Qur'anic Sciences), a study and exegesis of the Qur'an.

Abū al-Ma'ālī al-Sharīf al-Murtaḍā 'Alam al-Hudā Ali ibn al-Husayn al-Mūsawī (d. 436 AH) wrote *al-Durar wa al-Ghurar* (The Pearls and the Finest) and *al-Mūḍiḥ min Jihat I'jāz al-Qur'an* (The Expounder of the Aspect of the Inimitability of the Qur'an), in which he discussed the inimitability of the Qur'an from the viewpoint of the Obstruction Theory (*Ṣarfah*).[83]

Abū Muhammad Makkī ibn Abī Tālib (d. 437 AH) wrote *al-Kashf 'an Wujūh al-Qirā'āt al-Sab'* (Light on the Reasons for the Seven Ways of Reciting) in two large parts, a brilliant work wherein he discusses comprehensively the reasons for the divergent recitations and the proofs for them.

Abū 'Amr al-Dānī (d. 444 AH) wrote *al-Taysīr* on the seven divergent recitations, *al-Muḥkam* (The Strong) on dots in the text, and *al-Muqni'* (The Fulfilling Book) on the orthography of the Qur'anic codices of the various metropolises. They are highly respected books on this subject.

Abū Muhammad Ali ibn Aḥmad ibn Sa'īd (d. 456 AH), known as Ibn Hazm al-Ẓāhirī (The Literalist) al-Andalūsī, wrote a treatise on well-known recitations which were circulating widely enough in the metropolises for one to be sure of their validity.

In the introduction to his exegesis *al-Tibyān* (The Exposition), Abū Ja'far Muhammad ibn al-Hasan al-Ṭūsī (d. 460 AH) has splendid discussions on various matters pertaining to the Qur'an in which he refutes the beliefs in the allegations of alteration in the Qur'an, and shows that their attribution to the Shi'a Imamiyya – who are far from holding such beliefs – to be false. He also discusses other matters by providing well-established rational arguments.

Al-Khaṭīb (The Preacher) al-Nīshābūrī al-Hasan ibn al-Husayn al-Khuzā'ī (d. circa 460 AH) authored *I'jāz al-Qur'an.*

Abū al-Hasan Ali ibn Aḥmad al-Wāḥidī (d. 468 AH) wrote *Asbāb al-Nuzūl* (The Causes of Revelation), *Faḍā'il al-Qur'an*, *Nafy al-Taḥrīf 'an al-Qur'an* (Refuting the Allegation that the Qur'an Has Been Altered) and other treatises in which he discussed matters pertaining to the Qur'an.

Abū Bakr 'Abd al-Qāhir al-Jurjānī (d. 471 AH) authored *Asrār al-Balāghah* (Secrets of Eloquence), *Dalā'il al-I'jāz* (Proofs of Inimitability) and thirdly *al-Shāfiyah* (The Curative), in which he plays devil's advocate by challenging the Qur'an and demonstrating the inability of the Arab poets to match it.

[83] The theory of *Ṣarfah* holds that although imitating the Qur'an is potentially possible for ordinary man based on human capacities and talents, however, God in one way or another obstructs them from doing so [Editor].

Abū 'Abdillah Muhammad ibn Shurayḥ al-Ru'aynī (d. 476 AH), one of the luminaries from Seville, abridged *al-Ḥujjah* by Abu Ali al-Fārisī and wrote a book on divergent recitations entitled *al-Kāfī* (The Sufficient).

Abū Ma'shar 'Abd al-Karīm ibn 'Abd al-Samad al-Ṭabarī (d. 478 AH) wrote *al-Talkhīs* (The Summary) on eight divergent readings – the established seven plus Ya'qūb's. He also has books entitled *al-Waqf wa al-Ibtidā'*, *Hijā' al-Masāhif* (Alphabetical Index of Codices), *al-'Adad* (Numbers) and others.

Abu al-Qāsim al-Husayn ibn Muhammad al-Rāghib al-Iṣfahānī (d. 502 AH) wrote *al-Mufradāt fī Gharīb al-Qur'an* (The Vocabulary of Rare Words in the Qur'an). This work is astonishing in its excellence. He also wrote *al-Muqaddimah* (The Introduction), in which he discusses various matters pertaining to the Qur'an, especially studies linked to exegesis, its conditions and its etiquette. It is an excellent and sublime book. It is like an introduction to his exegesis *al-Jāmi'* (The Encyclopedia).

Abu al-Qāsim Maḥmūd ibn Ḥamzah al-Kirmānī (d. 505 AH) wrote *Asrār al-Tikrār fī al-Qur'an* (The Secrets behind Repetitions in the Qur'an), *'Ajā'ib al-Qur'an* (Wonders of the Qur'an) and *Lubāb al-Ta'wīl* (The Quintessence of Interpretation).

Abū Hāmid al-Ghazālī (d. 505 AH) wrote *Jawāhir al-Qur'an* (The Jewels of the Qur'an), in which he discusses the link between the Qur'an, the humanities and the secrets of nature, as well as the section in *Ihyā' 'Ulūm al-Dīn* (The Revival of the Religious Sciences) he dedicated to a discussion of matters pertaining to the Qur'an.[84]

As for my own work, from the time I first learned how to read I have been busy studying matters concerning the Holy Qur'an and reading books about its various facets. I derived from that such immense enjoyment that I waded into its depths. Indeed, it is a pressing need which every Muslim has to familiarise himself with if he aspires to be a strong support for this pure religion. I started studying the appropriate subject matter carefully and diligently, making notes on what I had read, either censuring views which I doubted or admiring what I thought to be original ideas.

---

[84] The author continues listing works of later centuries up to the present time, which we decided to omit in this abridgement. He emphasises that these are but a sample of the most important works on the subject. What follows here is the story of his own venture into the field of Qura'nic studies and the motives behind his extensive research on the topic [Editor].

Now, years later, a huge number of those large notebooks have accumulated and I have started putting them in order. They are even good enough to constitute a book with chapters and sections on various Qur'anic studies. I have called it *al-Tamhīd* (The Introduction) because I have made these studies an introduction to my exegesis *al-Wasīṭ* (The Intermediate). I ask the Almighty to grant me the success to complete it, and that I may have served my generation of Muslims with new views on the Holy Qur'an which might not be found elsewhere, or which may be in large volumes that are difficult for them to digest or beyond the general public's understanding.

What strengthened my resolve to complete this humble work was that, even though they had once been rich, I detected an absence in the Shi'a libraries of our times of books that deal exhaustively with Qur'anic studies, apart from a few documents dealing with certain aspects of the Qur'an. Many other aspects remained in obscurity, and should the researcher wish to apprise himself of the Shi'a opinion in the light of the school of Ahl al-Bayt he would be unable to find them.

Thus, I began studying works and views, criticising them objectively, scrutinising them against confirmed historical sources and traditions that either had been reported so widely as to generate certainty of their authenticity, or were surrounded by indubitable contextual evidence.

The extent of the deviation which took hold of many leading critics and researchers due to their rushed judgment, or their fanatical devotion to a *madhhab* or a particular way of investigating opinions and works, will be revealed through the discussions coming up. I did not conclude a matter until I was sure of its correctness and certain of its purity of origin to the best of my efforts.

Neither during the time I lived in the Holy City of Najaf (1379-1391 AH), nor after I migrated to the Holy City of Qum (at the end of 1391), did I neglect delivering university lectures to students of the higher religious institutes, and giving them the opportunity to debate amongst themselves. This was with the purpose of complete circumspection regarding whatever new views I had breathed fresh life into, and leaving it up to consensus to decide on matters which I had resolved to settle once and for all.

CHAPTER II

REVELATION *(WAḤY)* AND THE QUR'AN

The Phenomenon of Revelation

The linguistic meaning of *waḥy*

Waḥy means to pass information on quickly and secretly, whether by way of a signal, whisper or secret note. Anything passed swiftly to someone in order to make him understand is *waḥy*.

The Almighty said of Zakarīyyā:

> *So he emerged before his people from the Temple, and signalled (awḥā) to them that they should glorify God morning and evening* (19:11).

So he came forth to his people and made some kind of sign to them.

According to al-Rāghib:

> The root meaning of *waḥy* is a quick signal. On account of its incorporating the meaning of speed one says, *amrun waḥyun*, meaning a quick instruction. That can be orally by way of signal or insinuation, or it could be by way of a disjointed sound, signalling with one of one's limbs or in writing.[85]

Ibn Fāris explains:

> *W-ḥ-y* is a root which means to pass on knowledge in secret or in some other way to someone else. *Waḥy* can be a signal. *Waḥy* can be a book or message. Everything you pass to someone else to let him know is *waḥy*, no matter how it is done.[86]

It may be that the wider meaning accorded by Ibn Fāris to the concept of *waḥy* was part of the original meaning for which it was coined. However, it became used for that which is secret.

Abū Isḥāq says:

---

[85] Abu al-Qāsim al-Ḥusayn ibn Muhammad, known as al-Rāghib al-Iṣfahānī, *al-Mufradāt fī Gharīb al-Qur'an* (Cairo: Maṭba'at Muṣṭafā al-Bābī al-Ḥalabī, 1381 q.), 515.

[86] Ibn Fāris, *Mu'jam Maqāyīs al-Lughah*, 6:93.

The root meaning of *waḥy* throughout the language is to let someone know secretly. That is why inspiration (*ilhām*) is known as *waḥy*.

Ibn Birrī writes:

> *Waḥā ilayhi* and *awḥā* mean that he spoke to him in words which he hid from everyone else. Also, *waḥā* and *awḥā* mean 'he signalled.'

It may be that the meaning of secrecy is on account of the speed in it. A quick signal is normally inherently hidden from anyone else apart from the person who is being signalled to. One says *mawtun waḥyun,,* meaning a quick death. *Al-waḥā al-waḥā* comes from it, meaning: 'Hurry! Hurry!' One says that when one is in a hurry.

And al-Zamakhsharī comments:

> *Awḥā ilayhi* and *awmā* mean the same thing (he signalled to him). One says *waḥaytu ilayhi* or *awḥaytu* if one said to him what one had hidden from everyone else. *Tawaḥḥā* means hurry.

Waḥy in the Qur'an

The Qur'an uses *waḥy* in four senses:

1. The same dictionary meaning: a secret signal. It appears in the verse mentioned above in *Surah Maryam* (19:11).

2. A deep-seated natural instinct; it is natural disposition of things; the sense of communicating by words is metaphorically borrowed to refer to communication through a thing's essence. This is because of the secrecy common to the way in which the information is passed and received in both cases. Because *waḥy* is telling someone secretly, it is appropriate to borrow it to refer metaphorically to all hidden, natural feelings, including what appears in the following verse:

> *And thy Lord inspired (awḥā) the bee, saying: 'Choose thou habitations in the hills and in the trees and in that which they thatch. Then eat of all fruits, and follow the ways of thy Lord, made smooth (for thee)'* (16:68-69).

The bee follows its instinct and allows itself to be guided by the depth of its natural disposition, subject to the instinct of organised toil which has been placed in it. Hence it does not stray from that path.

Another example is the Almighty's Words:

> *...and inspired (awḥā) in each heaven its mandate* (41:12),

meaning 'He destined.'

3. Spiritual inspiration; a feeling or sensation inside, the source of which sometimes seems a mystery. One might think it is from God, but it may be from some other source.

This meaning is known to spiritualists as telepathy (mental communication at a distance). It is a momentary secret inspiration the source of which is unknown. They say that it is an idea which passes from one person's mind to another's, even though the distance between the two of them may be great. Alternatively, it is thought to be spiritual instruction from high or low spirits. It is also said that it is an idea from the All-Merciful which the angels inspire. They blow it into the heart of a person whom God wants to guide. Conversely, it may be satanic whispering which demonic *jinns* recite to lead a person astray.

An example of inspiration by the All-Merciful is the following:

> *And We inspired (awḥaynā) the mother of Moses, saying: 'Suckle him and, when thou fearest for him, then cast him into the river and fear not nor grieve. Lo! We shall bring him back unto thee and shall make him (one) of Our messengers'* (28:7).

According to al-Azharī:

> *Waḥy* here means instruction delivered by God to her heart. What comes next indicates – but God knows best – that it is inspiration from God to inform her, to reassure her, 'for We shall return him to thee...' It is said that *waḥy* means inspiration here. It is possible that God sent instruction to her heart that he would be returned to her and that he would be a Messenger. However, informing her is a clearer meaning for *waḥy* in this place.[87]

Sheikh Mufīd understood *waḥy* here to mean secretly communicating, as his book *Awā'il al-Maqālāt* says. However, in his book *Taṣḥīḥ al-I'tiqād* he construes it as a dream (*manām*), or words which Moses' mother heard in a dream. He says, by way of an explanation of *waḥy*:

[87] Muhammad ibn Mukarram Ibn Manẓūr, *Lisān al-'Arab* (Beirut: Dār Ṣādir, 1968), vol. 15, 380.

> The original meaning of *waḥy* is talking secretly. It may be used for anything intended to make the other person understand whilst keeping it secret from everyone else.[88]

As for using *waḥy* to refer to Satan's whisperings and his enticement to evil thoughts and corruption, it appears in the Almighty's Words:

> *Thus have We appointed unto every prophet an adversary - devils of men and jinn who inspire (yūḥī) in one another plausible discourse through guile* (6:112).

God also says:

> *Indeed the devils do inspire (layūḥūna) their minions to dispute with you...* (6:121);

which is explained by His Words:

> *...the sneaking whisperer, who whispereth in the hearts of mankind, of the jinn and of mankind* (114:4-6).

The Almighty's Words also use *waḥy* to refer to commands which God inspires in the angels for them to perform immediately:

> *When thy Lord inspired (yūḥī) the angels, (saying): I am with you. So make those who believe stand firm* (8:12).

The use of *waḥy* to refer to a message God passes to one of His prophets, with or without an angel as intermediary, is a fourth meaning used in the Qur'an, and is the subject of the discussion in the following section.

The Revelation of a Message (*al-Waḥy al-Risālī*)

'Revelation of a message' is a fourth meaning used in the Qur'an in more than seventy places, by referring to the Qur'an as *waḥy* passed down to the Prophet:

> *We relate unto thee (Muhammad) the best of narratives, in that We have revealed (awḥaynā) to thee this Qur'an* (12:3).

---

88 Sheikh Muhammad ibn Muhammad ibn Nu'mān al-Mufīd, *Awā'il al-Maqālāt fī al-Madhāhib wa al-Mukhtārāt* (Qum: Dāvarī, 1370 q.), 39, and al-Mufīd, *Taṣḥīḥu I'tiqādāt al-Imāmiyyah* (Qum: International Congress on the Thousandth Anniversary of the Birth of Sheikh Mufīd, 1413 q.), 56.

And thus We have revealed (awḥaynā) to thee an Arabic Qur'an, that thou mayest warn the Mother of Cities and all around her (42:7).

Recite that which has been revealed to thee (ūḥiya ilayka) of the Book (29:45).

The phenomenon of *waḥy* as God's Message is the primary characteristic distinguishing the prophets from pretenders and inspired reformers endowed with genius. Among the messengers, Muhammad was not unprecedented in having this prophetic characteristic, and he was not the first to address the people in the name of heavenly revelation (*waḥy*). Hence, there is no surprise in his being selected for such a mission. Throughout mankind's weary journey, there have been accompanying reformers who have called out to invite people to God in the name of revelation (*waḥy*) and the propagation of God's Message.

Is it a wonder for mankind that We have revealed (awḥaynā) to a man among them, saying: 'Warn mankind and bring unto those who believe the good tidings that they have a sure footing with their Lord'? The unbelievers say, 'Lo! this is a mere sorcerer' (10:2).

To rebut this strange rejection, the Qur'an says:

We have revealed (awḥaynā) to thee as We revealed to Noah and the prophets after him, and We revealed (awḥaynā) to Abraham, Ishmael and Isaac and Jacob and the tribes, and Jesus and Job and Jonah and Aaron and Solomon, and as We imparted unto David the Psalms; and messengers We have mentioned unto thee before and messengers We have not mentioned unto thee; and God spake directly unto Moses (4:163-164).

Revelation of a message (*al-waḥy al-risālī*) does not extend far beyond the dictionary meaning, given that it is a secret communication. It is a hidden link between God and His Messenger. It manifests in three forms, as this verse tells us:

And it was not [vouchsafed] to any mortal that God should speak to him unless (it be) by revelation (waḥyan) or from behind a veil, or [that] He sendeth a messenger to reveal (fa yūḥī) what He will by His leave. Lo! He is Exalted, Wise (42:51).

The first form is a casting into the heart and a blowing into the soul. The second is speaking from behind a veil by creating a voice in the air that reaches the Prophet's ears.[89] Since the form of the Speaker is unseen, the likeness of speaking from behind a veil is given. The third form is the sending to the Prophet of an angel, who may be either visible or invisible to him, although the Message is audible.

Thus the difference between revelation to a Messenger and all other kinds of secret communication is the aspect of its supernatural origin, transcending matter. It is secret communication from the world above.

Observation:

Since a revelation is a spiritual phenomenon, the place to where it descends to a prophet is his heart (his inner person, his soul), regardless of whether it is a revelation directly from God or through an intermediary such as Gabriel. The Almighty said:

> *For he it is who has revealed it to your heart* (2:97).
>
> *Which the True Spirit has brought down upon thy heart, that thou mayest be (one) of the warners* (26:193-194).

The heart is the essence of something and its true reality. Sayyid Ṭabāṭabā'ī writes in this regard:

> This is an allusion to the manner in which he received the Qur'an, and to the fact that that which received it from the Spirit was his noble soul without the involvement of external senses which are tools to perceive specific things in the outside world. He would see the form of the angel and hear the voice of revelation, but not with this physical sense of hearing or sight. Otherwise, it would have been something common to him and to other people, and he would not have heard or seen to the exclusion of everyone else. So the pangs of revelation took hold of him while he was among the people and he would receive revelation without anyone present knowing about it.[90]

---

[89] But not with the physical ear. The Almighty said: *For he (Gabriel) it is who hath revealed it to thy heart* (2:97).

[90] Al-Sayyid Muhammad Ḥusayn Ṭabāṭabā'ī, *al-Mīzān fī Tafsīr al-Qur'an (Tehran: Dār al-Kutub al-Islāmiyyah, 1392 q.)*, vol. 15, 346: 'the mill of revelation'; the severity of its

Details on the ways in which the Message was revealed, and what the Prophet would be exposed to, will be discussed later.

Explanation of the Revelation of the Message

The revelation of the Message is a type of direct spiritual link between the heavenly host and the Messenger's inner personality. This is because of exceptional traits within him which qualify him for this unique supernatural link. Hence, the spiritual revelations, in which he clearly sees the high heavens without confusion and without vagueness, are made possible for him. Such a revelation is different from being inspired with vague knowledge, as its source is as clear as the noonday sun, in contrast to inspiration, the source of which is a mystery to the person who is inspired.

Similarly, it is different from drawing inspiration from within oneself, insofar as the latter is reflecting personal thoughts which have accumulated and which sometimes become clear, perhaps without one's realising it. Revelation to a Messenger is drawn from outside the self, from the Heavenly Host, from the presence of the Lord of All Worlds. It is known to the Prophet with certainty, without hesitation or doubt, that what has been revealed to him is a revelation from heaven. Hence, he is not fearful or anxious, as we shall discuss in more detail.

Ways in Which a Message Is Revealed

> *It is not fitting for a man that God should speak to him except by revelation or from behind a veil, or by the sending of a messenger to reveal, with God's permission, what God wills: for He is Most High, Most Wise* (42:51).

Three ways for the revelation of a message are alluded to in the above verse. Here *by revelation* indicates that it is like an inspiration and a flashing within the Prophet's soul, casting within him what seems to be a brilliant page written on his soul. This type of revelation may also occur in a vision or dream.

Or from behind a veil is when God speaks to him in plain speech; he hears the sound without seeing a form, in the way God spoke to Moses by creating a voice in the air, shrilling in his ears, or coming at him from everywhere, and likewise in the way He spoke to the Prophet on the Night

---

discomfort and pain.

of the Ascension (*al-mi'rāj*). Speaking from behind a veil is a metonym likening God to someone speaking while hidden away. Alternatively, what is meant by the veil is figurative, on account of the enormous gulf separating the perfection of the Necessary Being from the imperfection of the contingent beings.

Or by the sending of a messenger, that is, one of the angels, *to reveal, by God's permission, what God wills,* by either casting it upon his hearing or reverberating in his heart.

> *And thus* (i.e., in either of these three ways – inspiration, speech or by sending an angel)[91] *have We revealed to thee a Spirit of Our command; thou knowest not (before) what was the Book and what was faith; but We have made it (the Qur'an) a Light, wherewith We guide such of Our servants as We will; and verily thou dost guide (men) to the straight way* (42:52)

These methods of revelation are meant generally. As for the Prophet Muhammad, revelation would sometimes come to him in dreams – this was mostly at the beginning of his prophethood – and at other times as direct revelation from God without an angel as intermediary, and thirdly, with Gabriel as an intermediary. However, the Qur'anic revelation was exclusively via the latter two – either directly or with an angelic intermediary. Some details follow.

1- Dreams which came true

The Revelation started with dreams which came true. The Prophet would not have any dream which did not come true like the break of dawn – a metonym for a shining radiance which would reveal itself to his soul as a prelude to the outpouring of the Holy Spirit. At such a time he preferred being alone, and he would spend time in solitude in the Cave at Ḥirā', seeking religious purification (*yataḥannath*)[92] for several nights before returning to his wife. He would thus prepare himself, then go back to Khadījah, who

[91] Majlisī, *Biḥār al-Anwār*, vol. 18, 246.

[92] *Taḥannuth* or *taḥannuf* means inclining towards purity, which is the servant's worship as a means of purification. Ibn Hishām says, 'The Arabs say *al-taḥannuth* or *al-taḥannuf.* They use a *fā'* instead of a *thāh* as in *jadath* and *jadaf*, meaning 'grave.'' He also says, 'Abū 'Ubaydah told me that the Arabs say *fumma* instead of *thumma* (for 'then').' See

would once more give him provisions to return again to Ḥirā', where on one such occasion the Truth took him by surprise and the angel came to him and said: *Recite.*

Ali ibn Ibrāhīm al-Qummī reports:

> When the Prophet turned thirty-seven, he would in his sleep see as if someone was coming towards him, calling him, 'Messenger of God.' He was like that for a while throughout which time he hid it, when all of a sudden one day, while he was herding one of Abū Ṭālib's flocks, in the crevices between the mountains he saw a person say to him, 'Messenger of God!' He asked him, 'Who are you?' He replied, 'I am Gabriel. God sent me to you to appoint you as a Messenger.'[93]'

Imām al-Bāqir is reported to have said:

> A prophet, he it is who sees a vision like Abraham's in his sleep and like the effects of prophethood that the Messenger of God [the Prophet Muhammad] would see before revelation until Gabriel brought him the Message from God.[94]

What he means by 'before revelation' is before the revelation of the message which he was commanded to propagate, because this explanation is an interpretation of the concept of a 'prophet' before he becomes a 'messenger.' It is a person who has received a revelation without being commanded to propagate it. He is spiritually linked to the Heavenly Host and the heavens are revealed to him, as happened to our Prophet shortly before his prophetic mission.

Ṣadr al-Dīn al-Shīrāzī writes in this regard:

> This means that his holy self had the attribute of prophethood and the Message came to him from God covertly and secretly before he had the attribute of being a Messenger, that is, Gabriel's visibly descending on him with audible speech. In other words,

---

Muhammad ibn Isḥāq, corrected by Abū Muḥammad 'Abd al-Malik ibn Hishām, *al-Sīrat al-Nabawiyyah* (Cairo: Muhammad Ali Ṣubayḥ & Sons, 1963), vol. 1, 251.

[93] Majlisī, *Biḥār al-Anwār*, vol. 18, 184, hadith 184; vol. 14, 194, hadith 30.

[94] Abū Ja'far Muhammad ibn Ya'qūb ibn Isḥāq al-Kulaynī al-Rāzī, *al-Kāfī* (Tehran: Dār al-Kutub al-Islamiyyah, 1363 s.), vol 1, 176; Majlisī, *Biḥār al-Anwār*, vol. 18, 266.

> Gabriel only came to him in visible form once he had all the means of accomplished prophets like Abraham – dreams which came true, consecutive notifications, true knowledge of things and revelations of hidden things. In a nutshell, the Prophet's inside and soul attained perfection before the attribute hidden in him crossed into the open, thus characterising his outside with the attribute of his inside, in harmony with it. The former is the end of the journey from creature to the Truth, and the latter is the end of the journey from the Truth via the Truth to the creature.[95]

It is agreed that, at times, dreams which came true were the means by which he was sent revelation, and sometimes knowledge would be passed to him in dreams, as the Commander of the Faithful said, 'Prophets' dreams are revelation.'[96] However, none of that was the Qur'an. The Qur'anic revelation never happened to him in a dream, even though it is true that some of his dreams were causes for Qur'anic revelations, as we are told in the verse:

> *Truly did God fulfil the vision for His messenger: Ye shall enter the Sacred Mosque, if God wills ...* (48:27).

For the Prophet had seen this during the year of Ḥudaybiyyah (sixth year AH), and it came true during the year of the Conquest (Year eight AH).

Also there is the verse:

> *We granted the vision which We showed thee, but as a trial for men – as also the cursed tree (mentioned) in the Qur'an* (17:60).

Ibn Abī Ḥātim, Ibn Mardawayh, al-Bayhaqī and Ibn 'Asākir cite Sa'īd ibn al-Musayyab as saying that:

> The Messenger of God saw the Umayyads on the pulpits. That saddened him and so God revealed to him: It is just worldly gain which they have been given. And this is the meaning of *We granted the vision...*[97]

---

[95] Ṣadr al-Dīn Shīrāzī, *Sharḥ Uṣūl al-Kāfī*, lithograph (Tehran: Maktabah Maḥmūdī, 1391 q.), vol. 3, 454.

[96] Abū Ja'far Muhammad ibn al-Ḥasan Ṭūsī, *al-Amālī* (Qum: Dār al-Thaqāfah, 1414 q.), 315; Majlisī, *Biḥār al-Anwār*, vol. 11, 64.

[97] Jalāl al-Dīn 'Abd al-Raḥmān ibn Abī Bakr al-Suyūṭī, *al-Durr al-Manthūr* (Beirut: Dār al-Fikr, 1993), vol. 4, 191; Abū Ja'far Muhammad ibn Jarīr al-Ṭabarī, *Jāmi' al-Bayān fī Tafsīr al-Qur'an* (Beirut: Dār al-Ma'rifah, 1972), vol. 15, 77.

Nevertheless, some have stated that *Sūrah al-Kawthar* was revealed to the Messenger of God in a dream, on account of Anas ibn Mālik's narration:

> While the Messenger of God was among us, he dozed off. He then raised his head, smiling, and we asked, 'What made you laugh, Messenger of God?' He said, 'A chapter was just (*ānifan*) revealed to me.' So he recited: *In the Name of God, the Merciful, the Compassionate: Surely We have given thee abundance...*(108:1)[98]

Al-Rāfi'ī says about this:

> They understood from that that the chapter was revealed during that nap. However, what is more likely is that *al-Kawthar*, which had been revealed to him prior to that, came to his mind during that slumber and so he recited it to them and explained it to them.

He further says:

> It could also be construed as the state which would possess him when revelation came down upon him. It is referred to as the paroxysm of revelation. It is a lethargy similar to sleepiness which would affect him from the weight of the revelation.

Jalāl al-Dīn opines:

> What al-Rāfi'ī says is extremely sound. The second explantion is more correct than the first, because the term *ānifan* negates the possibility of its having been revealed prior to that [since *ānif* means shortly before this time]. In fact it was revealed in that state. The lethargy was not the lethargy of sleep. On the contrary, it was the state which possessed him when revelation occurred.[99]

However, it should be noted that *Sūrah al-Kawthar* is Meccan without any doubt. This is the majority opinion among exegetes to such an overwhelming extent that it nearly reaches indubitability (*tawātur*).[100] It was revealed in Mecca when the pagans found fault

---

[98] Al-Ṣuyūṭī, *al-Durr al-Manthūr*, vol. 6, 401.

[99] Al-Suyūṭī, *al-Itqān*, Vol. 1, 65-66.

[100] Reported through so many different chains of transmission as to generate certainty of its authenticity. [Trans.]

in him for being *abtar* – not having any children – or for being cut off from his people – ostracised.

> Thus, when his son 'Abdullāh died, the Quraysh went to each other to give each other the 'good' news. They said: 'This juvenile one was cut off (*butira*) tonight.'[101]

And Ibn 'Abbās reports:

> The Messenger of God entered through the Ṣafā Gate and went out through the Marwah Gate. Al-'Ās ibn Wā'il al-Sahmī met him and went back to the Quraysh. The Quraysh said to him, 'Whom did you just meet, Abū 'Amr?' He said, 'That *abtar*,' by which he meant the Prophet, and so God, Sublime is His Majesty, revealed *Sūrah al-Kawthar* to console His Prophet's pure soul.[102]

Further, Anas had not reached twenty years of age at the time of the Prophet's death. Thus, when he came to Medina, he was a child who was no older than nine. It is said he was eight years old. How can we be sure of a hadith from him which contradicts the unanimous agreement that the opposite was the case, i.e., that it was revealed in Mecca, the story behind which is reported by a number of sources which exceeds the level of *tawātur*?

This is a matter which gives credence to Imām Rāfi'ī's first choice. Alternatively, we disregard Anas' tradition altogether.

It is true that Muslim and Bayhaqī cite this narration from another source which does not contain '...was revealed to me.' It says that the Prophet dozed off, then he raised his head and recited *Sūrah al-Kawthar.*

Bayhaqī says:

> This wording is more appropriate, because it does not contradict what the exegetes and panegyrists say – that the chapter entitled *al-Kawthar* was revealed in Mecca.[103]

---

[101] See Jalāl al-Dīn 'Abd al-Raḥmān ibn Abī Bakr al-Suyūṭī, *Lubāb al-Nuqūl fī Asbāb al-Nuzūl* (in the margin of *Tafsīr al-Jalālayn*, Cairo: Dār Iḥyā' al-Kutub al-'Arabiyyah, n.d.), vol. 2, 142; al-Suyūṭī, *al-Durr al-Manthūr*, vol. 6, 401.

[102] 'Izz al-Dīn Abu al-Ḥasan Ali ibn Abī al-Karam Ibn al-Athīr, *Usd al-Ghābah fī Ma'rifat al-Ṣaḥābah* (Tehran: Ismā'īliyān, n.d.), vol. 1, 127.

[103] *Al-Suyūṭī, al-Durr al-Manthūr*, vol. 6, 401.

2- Gabriel's Descent

It was the angel Gabriel who brought the revelation down to the Prophet and recited it. Sometimes the Prophet would see him either in his original form – this happened twice – or resembling the form of a man called Diḥyah ibn Khalīfah. At other times he would not see him, and the angel would just bring the revelation down upon the Prophet's heart: *With it [the Revelation] came down the Spirit of Faith and Truth [Gabriel] - to thy heart and mind* (26:193-194).

In respect of Gabriel, an elaboration could be found in *Sūrah al-Najm: Your companion [the Prophet] is neither astray nor being misled, nor does he say (aught) of (his own) desire. It is naught but a revelation sent down to him: he was taught by one mighty in power* (53:2-5), meaning Gabriel, an emanation of the force of the Almighty's Power. *For he appeared (in stately form)* (53:6), remaining firm in his original form – this was the first time at the outset of the Revelation; *While he was in the higher (part of the) horizon* (53:7), thereby blotting out everything between the east and the west. *Then he approached and descended* (53:8), coming closer to the Prophet... *at a distance of but two bow-lengths or (even) nearer* (53:9); and thus through the intermediary of Gabriel, *So did (God) reveal to His servant [Muhammad] what He revealed* (53:10). *The (Prophet's) (mind and) heart in no way falsified that which he saw* (53:11), meaning that his heart discerned the truth of what his eyes saw. *Will you then dispute with him concerning what he saw? For indeed he saw him at another descent* – at another time on a lower level than the first – *near the Lote Tree of the utmost boundary: near it is the Garden of Refuge. Behold, the Lote Tree was shrouded (in mystery unspeakable). (His) sight swerved not, nor did it go wrong* (53:12-17). Therefore, what he saw was true reality, neither illusion nor imagination.

And in other verses:

> *Verily the Qur'an is a word (conveyed by) a noble messenger [Gabriel], endued with Power, with rank before the Lord of the Throne secure, with authority there, (and) faithful to his trust. And your companion [Muhammad] is not one possessed; and without a doubt he saw him [Gabriel] in the clear horizon* – another allusion to the first occasion (81:19-23).

Ibn Mas'ūd said that the Messenger of God saw Gabriel in his true image only twice: once when he asked him if he could see him in his true form, and he showed him his true form, thus blocking the horizon, and the second time was when Gabriel took him up on the Night of the Ascension, to which the verse *while he was in the higher horizon* alludes.[104]

The truth is that the first of these two occasions was at the beginning of the Revelation at Ḥirā'. Gabriel appeared to him in the form in which God had fashioned him, filling the sky's horizon from the east to the west. The Prophet was extremely afraid of him, and so Gabriel came down to him in human form and hugged him to his chest. Thereafter, he would only come down to him in a beautiful human form.

The second time was when the Prophet asked him to do so, according to traditions. Gabriel had continued coming to him in human form, and so the Messenger of God asked him to show himself to him for a second time in the form in which God had fashioned him. So he showed him his form and blocked the horizon. Therefore, *while he was in the higher horizon,* refers to the first time while *another time* refers to the second time.[105]

The Messenger of God said, 'Sometimes the angel appears to me in the form of a man and speaks to me, and I hear what he says.'[106]

Imām al-Ṣādiq comments:

> Gabriel would come to the Prophet and not enter until he had asked permission. When he came in, he would sit before him the way a slave sits.[107]

Moreover, whenever Gabriel appeared to the Messenger of God, he would appear in a form resembling Diḥyah ibn Khalīfah al-Kalbī, as Ibn Shihāb says:

> The Messenger of God would compare Diḥyah al-Kalbī with Gabriel whenever he appeared to him in human form.[108]

---

[104] Al-Suyūṭī, *al-Durr al-Manthūr*, vol. 6, 123.

[105] Ṭabrisī, *Majma' al-Bayān*, vol. 9, 173, vol. 9, 175; vol. 10, 446; Muhammad al-Muḥsin ibn Murtaḍā ibn Maḥmūd al-Fayḍ al-Kāshānī, *al-Ṣāfī fī Tafsīr al-Qur'an* (Tehran: Maktabat al-Ṣadr, 1416 q.), vol. 2, 618.

[106] Abū Abdillāh Muhammad ibn Ismā'īl Bukhārī, *Ṣaḥīḥ al-Bukhārī* (Cairo: Maṭābi' al-Sha'b, 1378 q.), vol. 1, 3.

[107] Al-Ṣadūq, *Kamāl al-Dīn*, 85,

[108] Abū 'Umar Yūsuf ibn Aḥmad Ibn 'Abd al-Barr, *al-Isti'āb fī Ma'rifat al-Aṣḥāb bi Hāmish al-Iṣābah* (Cairo: al-Sa'ādah, 1328 q.), vol. 1, 474.

That is because Diḥyah was the most handsome man in Medina. Whenever he came to town, the girls would come out to look at him.[109]

The Messenger of God said, 'Gabriel would come to me in the form of Diḥyah al-Kalbī' and, 'Dihyah was a handsome man.' However, It is likely that the latter phrase is from Anas, the narrator of the hadith.[110] This form that resembled Diḥyah caused the companions to imagine that he really was Diḥyah. Hence, the Messenger of God would tell them not to come and see him if they saw Diḥyah with him. He said, 'If you see Diḥyah al-Kalbī with me, no one should come and see me.'[111]

Gabriel would also appear in Diḥyah's form to the companions in battles like the one against Banī Qurayẓah, in the fifth year after the Hijra. The companions saw him on a white mule.[112]

Ali also saw him a number of times in the Prophet's presence, speaking to him while the Prophet was asleep.[113]

Yet the angel also frequently brought down revelation to him without his seeing him, either by reciting to his ears with the Prophet listening attentively, or by inspiration in his heart that stayed there indelibly. The Almighty said:

> *Verily this is a Revelation from the Lord of the Worlds: with it came down the Spirit of Faith and Truth, to thy heart and mind, that thou mayest be one of the warners, in a clear, Arabic tongue* (26:192-195).

When the angel first started bringing him the Revelation, the Prophet feared he would forget the words. Hence, he would move his tongue and lips to try to remember it. Thus, he would immediately repeat every letter Gabriel recited to him, but the Almighty told him not to, promising him that it would be preserved and guarded by Him:

> *Move not thy tongue (with it) to make haste therewith. Indeed, upon Us is the collection (in thy heart) and to (make possible) its recitation.*

---

[109] Ibn Ḥajar, *al-Isābah*, vol. 1, 473.

[110] Ibn Ḥajar, *al-Iṣābah*, vol. 1, 473; Ibn al-Athīr, *Usd al-Ghābah fī Ma'rifat al-Ṣaḥābah*, vol. 2, 130.

[111] Majlisī, *Biḥār al-Anwār*, vol. 37, 326 citing Ibn al-Athīr.

[112] Ibn Hishām, *al-Sīrat al-Nabawiyyah*, vol. 3, 245.

[113] Majlisī, *Biḥār al-Anwār*, vol. 20, 210; vol. 22, 331-332; Ṭabrisī, *Majma' al-Bayān*, vol. 8, 351.

So when We have recited it, follow thou its recital. Then upon Us is its clarification (75:16-19).

Sometimes the Prophet would recite the Qur'an to his companions as soon as Gabriel had recited it to him, and before the Revelation had ended or the verses were finished, keen to have a verbatim record made of it. The Almighty told him not to do this also, saying:

Be not in haste with the Qur'an before its revelation to thee is complete, but say, 'O my Lord, increase me in knowledge ...' (20:114).

And so the Almighty reassured him it would be remembered and preserved in its entirety. Thereafter when Gabriel came to him, the Messenger of God would listen to him, and when he had gone, he would recite it as he had made him recite.[114] This is also mentioned in:

By degrees shall We teach thee to recite (the Message), so thou shalt not forget (87:6).

Alluding to this kind of revelation – which is like an itch in the heart – he said:

'The Holy Spirit blew into my *raw'*.'[115]

Raw' is the blackness of the heart, and represents the hidden interior which in turn alludes to his noble soul.

3- Direct Revelation

According to the companions' description of the Prophet's condition at the time when a revelation came down, it may be that most of it was direct and not through the intermediary of an angel. His soul would experience severe pressure that required a great exertion to withstand, and a feeling of faintness would take hold of him. He would lower his head, his face would become cold and he would sweat. Terrible fear would assail those present. They would also lower their heads on account of the frightening scene. The Almighty said:

Verily, soon shall We shall cast upon thee a weighty word (73:5).

According to Imām al-Ṣādiq:

[114] Ibn Sa'd, *al-Ṭabaqāt al-Kubrā*, vol. 1, 198-199.
[115] Al-Suyūṭī, *al-Itqān*, vol. 1, 127.

> That was when revelation came without an angel between him and God. A lethargy (*sabtah*)[116] would take hold of him, and that particular state fell on him as it did on account of the weight of revelation upon him, whereas when Gabriel brought him revelation, he would say, 'This is Gabriel,' or say, 'Gabriel said to me...'[117]

Sheikh Abū Ja'far al-Ṣadūq writes in this regard:

> The Prophet would be among his companions and he would faint and sweat. When he came to, he would say, 'God said such and such,' or 'He commanded you to do such and such and told you not to do such and such.'

He continues:

> Most of our opponents have claimed that that was when Gabriel came down to him, and so Imām al-Ṣādiq was asked about the fainting which would come over the Prophet. Was it when Gabriel came down? He said, 'No. When Gabriel came to the Prophet, he would not enter without asking his permission. When he entered, he would sit before him the way a slave sits. It only happened when God spoke to him directly, without an interpreter or intermediary.'[118]

In what follows are descriptions in the words of the companions of what would happen, referring to the state they witnessed taking hold of the Messenger of God at the time when revelation came to him:

The Commander of the Faithful said:

> *Sūrah al-Mā'idah* (The Table) was revealed to the Prophet while he was on his grey mule. The revelation weighed so heavy upon him that it stopped and stretched out its stomach until I saw its navel nearly touch the ground. The Messenger of God fainted until he put his hand on Shaybah ibn Wahb al-Jamaḥī's forelock.[119]

---

[116] It means a lethargy which looks like sleepiness.

[117] Abū Ja'far Aḥmad ibn Muhammad ibn Khālid al-Barqī, *al-Maḥāsin* (Qum: al-Majma' al-'Ālamī li Ahl al-Bayt, 1413 q.) vol. 1, 69; Majlisī, *Biḥār al-Anwār* vol. 18, 271.

[118] Al-Ṣadūq, *Kamāl al-Dīn*, 85-86; Majlisī, *Biḥār al-Anwār*, vol. 18, 260.

[119] Abū Naẓr Muhammad ibn Mas'ūd ibn 'Ayyāsh al-Sulamī al-Samarqandī, *Tafsīr al-'Ayyāshī* (Tehran: al-Maktabat al-'Ilmīyyah al-Islāmiyyah, n.d.), vol. 1, 288; a *dhu'ābah* is a lock of hair at the front of the head.

'Ubādah ibn al-Ṣāmit said:

> When revelation came down upon the Prophet, it would burden him and his face would glower.[120]

And in another report:

> He would lower his head and his companions would lower their heads. Then, when it had quit him he would raise his head.[121]

'Ikrimah said:

> When revelation came down to him, the Prophet would be felled (*wuqidha*) by it for an hour, looking like a drunk person.[122]

Ibn Arwā al-Dūsī said:

> I saw revelation come down upon the Prophet when he was on his mount. It brayed and spread its front legs until I thought that its front legs would break. It may have knelt down or stood up, its front legs rigid until the weight of revelation was quit of him. [Sweat] poured from him like pearls.[123]

'Ā'ishah recalls:

> I saw revelation come down to him on a bitterly cold day. It was quit of him and his forehead poured with sweat.[124]

She also said:

> Revelation would come to the Messenger of God while he was on his mount and he would strike the front part of its neck.[125]

Ibn 'Abbās explains:

---

[120] Ibn Sa'd, *al-Ṭabaqāt al-Kubrā*, vol. 1, 131; *kuriba* in the passive means his soul would be taken and his state would change; *tarabbada* means the colour of his face changed to a dusty hue.

[121] Muhammad Farīd Wajdī, *Dā'irat Ma'ārif al-Qarn al-'Ishrīn, 4th ed.* (Dā'irat Ma'ārif al-Qarn al-'Ishrīn Printing Press, 1386 q.), vol. 10, 712.

[122] Ibn Sa'd, *al-Ṭabaqāt al-Kubrā*, vol. 1, 197; *wuqidha* in the passive means that he fainted. A *mawqūdh* is someone overcome by sleepiness; hence he became like a drunk person.

[123] Ibn Sa'd, *al-Ṭabaqāt al-Kubrā* vol. 1, 131.

[124] *Ṣaḥīḥ al-Bukhārī*, vol. 1, 3.

[125] Ṭabrisī , *Majma' al-Bayān*, vol. 10, 378; Majlisī, *Biḥār al-Anwār*, vol. 18, 263.

> When revelation came to the Prophet he would have to deal with hardship, severe pain and weight from that and his head would ache.[126]

Ibn Shahr Āshūb writes:

> It is narrated that when revelation came to him, he would lower his head and his companions would lower their heads. Because of that one speaks of the paroxysm of revelation.[127]

Ibn Qayyim narrates:

> One time revelation came to him and his thigh was on Zayd ibn Thābit's thigh. It weighed so heavy on him that it nearly crushed it.[128]

The author of *al-Muntaqā* narrates that:

> An accepted (*maqbūl*) hadith says that revelation came to him while he was on his camel, and so it knelt down and laid the front part of its neck on the ground, unable to move. 'Uthmān [ibn Maẓ'ūn] used to act as a scribe for the Prophet, and so his thigh was on 'Uthmān's thigh. The revelation made him pass out. His thigh weighed so heavily on 'Uthmān's thigh that he said, 'I was afraid it would crush it.'[129]

Finally, the Prophet described in astonishing terms how revelation came to him:

> 'Abdullāh ibn 'Umar asked him, 'Do you feel the revelation?' So he said, 'I hear clanking. Then I go quiet at that. There is not a single time when revelation came to me that I did not think that my soul would be taken.'[130]

---

[126] Majlisī, *Biḥār al-Anwār* vol. 18, 261.

[127] Muhammad ibn Ali Ibn Shahr Āshūb, Māzandarānī, *Manāqib Āl Abī Ṭālib* (Najaf: al-Maṭba'at al-Ḥaydariyyah, 1956), vol. 1, 41.

[128] Muḥammad Ibn-Abī-Bakr : Ibn Qayyim al-Jawziyyah, *Zād al-Ma'ād fī Hady Khayr al-'Ibād* (Beirut: Mu'assasat al-Risālah, 1998), vol. 1, 18.

[129] Majlisī, *Biḥār al-Anwār,* vol. 18, 263-264, 268, 269. This 'Uthmān is 'Uthmān ibn Maẓ'ūn, as explicitly stated in a narration on the authority of Imām al-Bāqir in Abu al-Qāsim Ali ibn Mūsā ibn Ja'far ibn Muhammad ibn Ṭāwūs, *Sa'd al-Su'ūd* (Qum: Manshūrāt al-Raḍī 1363 q.), 122.

[130] Al-Suyūṭī, al-Itqān, vol. 1, 128, citing Aḥmad ibn Ḥanbal, *Musnad Aḥmad* (Beirut: Dār Ṣādir), vol. 2, 222.

> Al-Ḥārith ibn Hishām asked him, 'Messenger of God, how does revelation come to you?' So he said, 'Sometimes it comes to me like the clanking (*ṣalṣalah*) of a bell. It is the most difficult kind for me. When it leaves me I remember what it said.[131] Sometimes the angel comes to me in the form of a man and speaks to me, and I remember what he says.[132] It is the easiest for me.'[133]

Following on from this tradition – which is almost *mutawātir* – we have to draw the reader's attention to some important points.

Firstly, the clanking of a bell in this tradition indicates a repetitive, ringing sound, and would signal a direct revelation. He would listen attentively with his entire being until he had received it in its entirety. It would have a severe impact on his soul. This expression – 'the clanking of a bell' – informs us of the severity of the impact, because the repetitiveness of incessant noise has an effect on one's hearing, and penetrates into the depths. So it is as if it was repeatedly and forcefully grabbing the core of the heart. Hence he said, 'I thought that my soul would be taken.'

Recognising that this clanking was likely to be a prelude to revelation coming to him, he could prepare himself for the powerful spiritual link. Hence he said, 'Then I go quiet at that,' meaning, 'I listen attentively at the indication that revelation is coming down.'

True, revelation itself made an extremely loud noise which the inhabitants of the highest heavens could not withstand.

Abū Ja'far Muhammad ibn Ali al-Bāqir said by way of exegesis of the Almighty's Words:

> *So far that when terror is lifted from their hearts, they will say, 'What is it that your Lord commanded?' They will say, 'That which is true and just; and He is the Most High, Most Great'* (34:23).

> The people of heaven had not heard revelation in the period between Christ and Muhammad's prophetic mission. When God despatched Muhammad on his mission, the people of heaven

[131] These words are among the things explained *infra*.

[132] *Ṣaḥīḥ al-Bukhārī*, vol. 1, 3; Ibn Sa'd, *al-Ṭabaqāt al-Kubrā*, vol. 1, 132; Majlisī, *Biḥār al-Anwār*, vol. 18, 260-261; *ṣalṣala* is the sound of iron beating on iron.

[133] This addition appears in Abū 'Awān's narration in his *Ṣaḥīḥ* ; see al-Suyūṭī, *al-Itqān*, vol, 129; Ibn Ḥajar al-'Asqalānī, Shihāb al-Dīn, *Fatḥ al-Bārī fī Sharḥ al-Bukhārī* (Beirut: Dār al-Ma'rifah, 1400 q.), vol. 1, 20.

> heard the sound of the revelation of the Qur'an like the sound of iron falling upon rock and they were all dumbfounded. When God finished the revelation, Gabriel descended. As he passed by the inhabitants of each heaven, he would remove the fear from their hearts – meaning he would clear that covering from them – and they would start saying to each other, 'What said your Lord?' They would say, 'The Truth; and He is the Most High, Most Great.'[134]

Ibn Mas'ūd's narration says:

> When God spoke through revelation, the people of heaven heard a clanking like the clanking of a chain on *ṣafwān* (a smooth stone), and so they were afraid.[135]

Ibn 'Abbās said:

> When revelation came, its sound was like iron falling on smooth stone. The people of heaven would be dumbfounded, 'until the terror was lifted from their hearts, and they would say 'What said your Lord?' The Messengers would say, 'The truth...''[136]

It is narrated that the Messenger of God said:

> When God wanted to reveal a commandment, he would speak through revelation. When He spoke, severe trembling from fear of Almighty God would take hold of heaven, and the people of heaven would be dumfounded and throw themselves down prostrate.[137]

Therefore, if the people of heaven could not withstand the terrifying sound, we can hardly be surprised at the fainting which would take hold of the Messenger of God when revelation came to him.

Secondly, this kind of powerful revelation which fell upon his noble soul was exclusive to direct revelation as mentioned above, just as the tradition itself informs us, because the first category it lists is the clanking of a bell, so it was the sound of revelation coming to him directly – hence, he said, 'It was the most difficult for me' – and the second category it

[134] Abu al-Ḥasan Ali ibn Ibrāhīm al-Qummī, *Tafsīr al-Qummī* (Najaf: Maṭba'at al-Najaf, 1387 q.), vol. 2, 202.

[135] Al-Suyūṭī, *al-Itqān*, vol. 1, 126.

[136] Al-Suyūṭī, *al-Durr al-Manthūr*, vol. 5, 235.

[137] Al-Suyūṭī, *al-Durr al-Manthūr*, vol. 5, 236.

lists is when the angel spoke to him and he would understand what was revealed to him that very moment, because he was in his normal state.

Jalāl al-Dīn claims that one of the two kinds referred to by the tradition was when the angel bringing down the revelation was hidden from sight, and the other was when he appeared in a form,[138] but this contradicts what the tradition itself says, as our Sheikh Ṣadūq points out[139] and as Imām al-Ṣādiq's hadith[140] says.

Thirdly, the powerful spiritual pull of the first kind may have given the impression that some of the revelation may have escaped him when he would visibly lose consciousness. However, he dispelled this impression by finding everything that had been revealed to him there in his mind when he recovered. It was just as if it had been written in a book, with none of it eluding him. This is what he means by, 'When it leaves me I remember what it said.'

The reason for that is that revelation in its direct form would seep into the depths of his being, God having caused it to penetrate his heart:

> *By degrees shall We teach thee to declare [recite] (the Message),so that thou shalt not forget* (87:6).

Thus the meaning of the hadith narrated by Ibn Abī Salāmah on the authority of his uncle becomes clear.

> It reached him that the Messenger of God would say: 'Revelation would come to me in two ways. Gabriel would come to me and recite it to me the way a man recites to another man[141]. That is what slips away from me. Alternatively, it comes to me in something[142] like the sound of a bell until it blends with my heart. That is what does not slip away from me.[143]

---

[138] Al-Suyūṭī, *al-Itqān*, vol. 1, 128-129.

[139] Al-Ṣadūq, *Kamāl al-Dīn*, 85; Majlisī, *Biḥār al-Anwār*, vol. 18, 260.

[140] Al-Barqī, *al-Maḥāsin: Kitāb al-'Ilal*, vol. 1, 69; Majlisī, *Biḥār al-Anwār*, vol. 18, 271.

[141] i.e. the way a man recites his words to his companion. This is the second kind, as mentioned above.

[142] i.e. the revelation came to him without an angel as intermediary. It is the first kind as mentioned above.

[143] Ibn Sa'd, *al-Ṭabaqāt al-Kubrā*, vol. 1, 131.

His words: 'That is what slips away from me,' mean 'what would *almost* slip away from me' because it was hearing the revelation directly from the angel, for as soon as a person hears something from someone else, he forgets it if he does not memorise it. This kind of revelation is what was at risk of being forgotten and was feared to slip away – as is the case with hearing only, if it is not recorded by writing it down straight away – not that it would *actually* slip away from him. As for direct revelation, because it would blend with his heart by penetrating to its depths, he would have no fear that it would slip away from him.

This is what was about this hadith that caused some researchers to fall into error[144] and others to reject it. However the meaning as we have stated is correct and in accordance with all the other traditions.

The Wording of the Qur'an is the Product of Revelation

The Holy Book – in addition to traditions reported by so many sources as to be indubitable – explicitly states that both the exact wording and meaning of the Qur'an came down in its entirety from God's presence, and that the composition and arrangement of all its sentences and expressions is the precise phrasing of the revelation and the product of heaven. No one else whatsoever had a hand in it, neither Gabriel the entrusted one, nor the Prophet. Various verses of the Qur'an explicitly state that it is the Word of God.[145] Words cannot be attributed to anyone unless they are his own work in terms of arrangement, composition, phraseology and meaning.

The same is true of the explicit statement that it is what God recited to the Prophet.[146] It does not qualify as recitation unless it is a recitation word

---

[144] Ibn Ḥajar, *Fatḥ al-Bārī*, vol. 118.

[145] *They wish to change God's decree ...* (48:15); and *If one amongst the idolaters seeks of thee protection, grant it to him, so that he may hear the Word of God* (9:6). The Messenger of God said: 'Almighty God said: He who explains my Words in accordance with his own opinion does not believe in Me' (al-Sheikh al-Ṣadūq Abū Ja'far Muhammad ibn Ali ibn al-Ḥusayn ibn Mūsā ibn Bābawayh al-Qummī: *al-Amālī*, (Najaf, n.d.), 6. Imam Ali, the Commander of the Faithful, said of the Qur'an: 'It is the Word of God and interpretation of it is not like human speech (Ṣaduq, Abū Ja'far Muhammad ibn Ali ibn al-Ḥusayn ibn Bābawayh, *al-Tawḥīd*, Beirut: Dār al-Ma'rifah, 1346 q. 264.)

[146] *It is for Us to gather it and to recite it: but when We have recited it, follow thou its recitation* (75:17-18).

for word. Simply conveying the meaning is not good enough, because that is not recitation of the Qur'an. It is no more than conveying the meaning.

Similar to that is the word used to signify that it is an instructed recitation (*iqrā'*) received by the Prophet.[147] The same is true of its saying that he 'received' the Qur'an.[148] Receipt (*talaqqī*) of the Qur'an means word for word in a given order, and not just the meaning of it, for the Qur'an is that which is recited and not that which is understood and perceived.

In the same vein, there are the verses specifying that the Prophet used to recite and not 'speak' the Qur'an.[149] This is in addition to the fact that the Qur'an is the eternal miracle of Islam, for mankind in its entirety is unable to produce the likes of it, even if they all work together. This sweeping statement also applies to the Prophet himself. It is beyond the Prophet's capability as a man to compose words the way the Qur'an is composed. How can it be thought that it is his creation, given that he would be unable to come up with the likes of it even with the help of all mankind?

Imām Badr al-Dīn al-Zarkashī reports someone quoting al-Samarqandī[150] as citing three views on what was revealed to the Prophet:

> 1) The dominant opinion is that what was revealed to the Prophet was both the words and the meanings as the Qur'an explicitly states.
>
> 2) That Gabriel just brought the meanings and the Prophet would word them in the phrasing of the language of the Arabs. Those who ascribe to this rely on the apparent meaning of the verses such as *Which the True Spirit hath brought down upon thy heart'* (26:193-194) and *For he (Gabriel) it is who hath revealed it to thy heart by God's leave* (2:97), claiming that what the heart can retain is just the

[147] *By degrees shall We teach thee to recite (sanuqri'uka) (the Message), so thou shalt not forget* (87:6).

[148] *The Qur'an is bestowed upon thee from the presence of One Who is Wise and All-Knowing* (27:6).

[149] *A Qur'an which We have divided, in order that thou mayest recite it unto mankind at intervals* (17:106).

When thou recitest the Qur'an We place between thee and those who believe not in the Hereafter a hidden barrier (17:45).

And when thou recitest the Qur'an, seek refuge in God from Satan the outcast (16:98).

[150] Abū Bakr Muhammad ibn al-Yamān al-Samarqandī (d. 268). He was a Ḥanafī jurisprudent and theologian.

meanings and not specific words, which have to be picked up by one's hearing.

3) That Gabriel, having received it, would discharge the recitation in packages of words in Arabic to the Prophet. Thus, the inhabitants of Heaven would listen to Gabriel's Qur'an and start reciting it in Arabic. However, there is no evidence for this opinion apart from purported traditions on the sending down of the complete Qur'an to *al-Bayt al-Ma'mūr* or to *Bayt al-'Izzah* in the lowest or the Fourth Heaven. It would then have been sent down gradually to the Messenger of God over twenty years.[151]

Al-Juwaynī has this to say on the matter:

> There are two kinds of revelation. One is where God would tell Gabriel to say to the Prophet, 'Do such-and-such a thing,' or 'God commands such-and-such a thing.' Gabriel would receive the meaning and cast it into the Prophet's heart. The second is where He would say to him, 'Recite such-and-such a thing to the Messenger of God.' This he would deliver in the wording he received without any change, just as kings would write down messages and send them in the hands of messengers for them to deliver without any paraphrasing or change.

After citing the above from al-Juwaynī, Jalāl al-Dīn al-Suyūṭī opines that:

> The Qur'an is like the second kind. Gabriel would receive it word for word and recite it to the Prophet as he had received it, without making any change either to its wording or to its meaning. It was not permissible for him merely to convey the meaning. The secret behind that is that what is intended by the Qur'an is to adhere explicitly (*ta'abbud*) to its exact wording in addition to acting explicitly in accordance with its meaning. Because this is evidence of its inimitability, no one – neither Gabriel nor anyone else – can come up with a word to take the place of another. Behind every letter of it there are meanings too numerous to reckon. No one can come up with a substitute which would cover them.[152]

---

[151] See Zarkashī, *al-Burhān*, vol. 1, 229-230; also cited by al-Suyūṭī in *al-Itqān*, vol. 1, 126.

[152] Al-Suyūṭī, *al-Itqān*, vol. 1, 127-128.

Al-Zarqānī also says that:

> Some people sank low, claiming that Gabriel would bring the Prophet the meanings of the Qur'an and the Messenger would express them in the language of the Arabs. Others claimed that the wording was Gabriel's, and that God would only reveal the meaning to him. Both opinions are false and sinful, and clash with the explicit words of the Scripture, Sunnah and consensus. They are not worth the ink they were written with. My belief is that it was interpolated into the Muslims' books. Otherwise, how could the Qur'an be a miracle if the wording was either Muhammad's or Gabriel's? Further, how could it be validly attributed to God if the wording is not God's?[153]

As for the verses relied upon by those who propose such an interpretation, they are more indicative of the opposite! That is because what is meant by the heart is the Messenger's hidden personality which was qualified to receive revelation from God's presence, and not the circulatory organ hidden in the chest. Our senses are not equipped to receive such metaphysical things, and they only work within a limited framework.

A parallel to this limitation in material matters is wireless wave broadcasts received by purpose-built machines. They receive the exact same words, and even pictures, forms and colours, from a distant place which cannot be received by a normal external sensor. The same is true of souls which deserve to perceive matters which ordinary senses are unable to perceive, and which do not reach the level of refinement suited to the Heavenly Host!

Furthermore, the verse from *Sūrah al-Shu'arā'* (The Poets), *'brought down by the Trusted Spirit upon thy heart'* is followed by the phrase *'in a clear, Arabic language'* (26:193-195), which specifies that what is revealed from God's presence and at the hand of Gabriel, the Trusted Spirit, is this Qur'an, verbatim, in its clear Arabic wording! So the verse is more indicative of the opposite of what it was claimed to prove.

---

[153] Al-Sheikh Muhammad 'Abd al-'Aẓīm al-Zarqānī, *Manāhil al-'Irfān fī 'Ulūm al-Qur'an* (Cairo: Maṭba'ah Muṣṭafā al-Bābī al-Ḥalabī, 1362 q.), vol. 1, 49.

At any rate, some have attributed this opinion to Mu'ammar ibn 'Abbād al-Sulamī (d. 215 AH), one of the leaders of the Mu'tazilites,[154] on the basis of syllogism by equations (*qiyās al-musāwāt*), for he makes no explicit statement to that effect. It is just concomitant with his position on the Almighty's speech, according to their claim. This is because he says that speech as such is an accident (*'araḍ*), and an accident, according to the Mu'tazilites, is movement which subsists within the body (*jism*). It is, therefore, impossible for it to subsist in the Almighty, because He cannot be a locus (*maḥall*) for accidents. Thus God's Words are no more than what issues from the locus – be it a tree or a human being. Speech which issues from the tree is its action, and speech which issues from humans is their action, even if it is by God's will.[155]

What that means, according to them, is that God's Words which issue from the locus are tantamount to the capacity to receive – created by God in the tree or the human being. Thus the locus recites the speech through which God's will manifests. The speech issuing from the locus is its own action, even though it may be attributed to God, since it only issues forth in accordance with God's Will.

They further rely on what al-Rāwandī attributes to Mu'ammar:

> He claimed that the Qur'an is not God's action or one of His Attributes within Himself as the common people believe. Rather, it is one of Nature's acts.

However, Abū al-Ḥasan al-Khayyāṭ al-Mu'tazilī categorically rejects this attribution, saying:

> Know – may God guide you to goodness – that Mu'ammar used to claim that it was God who spoke the Qur'an, that the Qur'an

---

[154] Abu al-Mu'tamir ibn 'Amr. It is also said that he was Ibn 'Abbād al-Baṣrī. There were debates and disputes between him and the government. Al-Dhahabī, *Siyar A'lām al-Nubalā* (Beirut: Mu'assasat al-Risālah, 1993), vol. 10, 546 no. 176.

[155] Abu al-Hasan Ali ibn Ismā'īl Ash'arī, *Maqālāt al-Islāmiyyīn wa Ikhtilāf al-Muṣallīn* (Beirut: Dār Ṣādir, 1980.), vol. 1, 268. He states: 'The fifth group is the followers of Mu'ammar. They claim that recitation (*al-Qur'an*) is an accident (*'arḍ*) and that it is impossible for God to have truly done it, because they believe it to be impossible for accidents to be actions performed by God. They claim that recitation (*al-Qur'an*) is an action performed by the locus from which it is heard. If it is heard from a tree then it is the tree's action. From whence it is heard is the locus in which it inheres.'

> is God's speech, His words and His revelation and His sending down. No one but He said it or spoke it. He also believed that the Qur'an was temporally created (*muḥdath*), brought into being after it did not exist.[156]

However, in spite of that we find that one foreign orientalist[157] followed by one Muslim writer[158] – who did so without checking – held the view that Mu'ammar said that the Qur'an is not God's Words and that God, Exalted is He, gave His Prophet the licence to formulate words into which the Will of God poured, which he would receive through revelation into his soul.

It is an erroneous conclusion based as it is on pure analogy and not on his explicit words. Further, God's Words, *and unto Moses God spoke directly (taklīman)* (4:164), confirm that God Himself uttered these aforementioned words and that it really was speech, and not figurative expression (*majāz*) or metaphorical borrowing (*isti'ārah*). Otherwise this emphasis through the *maf'ūl muṭlaq*[159] would not be possible. What Mu'ammar said can be construed as meaning that speech which is heard from any thing was only made by God to be heard from that thing, not that it is the product of that thing. And so, if it is heard from the wind it is the wind's action, i.e., it issues from the wind even though God caused it to do so. It is then the same case with the tree. As for what issues from a human being like the Prophet, it is through the inspiration of God to him, produced by God and not the Prophet himself.

The Qur'an Phrased as Spoken Word rather than as Book

One of the distinguishing features of books is the coherence of the contents from beginning to end. There is not a single article in a newspaper, treatise in a book or publication which is not interconnected and arranged coherently, each part joined to another like links in a chain.

---

[156] See Abu al-Ḥusayn 'Abd al-Raḥīm ibn Muhammad ibn al-Khayyāṭ al-Mu'tazilī, *al-Intiṣār 'alā Ibn al-Rāwandī al-Mulḥid*, (Cairo: Maktabat al-Thaqāfah al-Dīniyyah, n.d.), 104.

[157] Harry Austryn Wolfson in *The Philosophy of the Kalām* (Harvard University Press, 1979, translated by Aḥmad Ārām), 298, 302.

[158] Maqṣūd Farāsatkhāh, *Zabān-e Qur'an* (Tehran: Intishārāt-i 'Ilmī-Farhangī, 1376 s.), 305.

[159] A literal translation of Qur'an 4:164 might be '*and unto Moses God spoke a speaking.*' The words 'a speaking' are rendered by a single word in Arabic – *taklīman* – which is an adverb or *maf'ūl muṭlaq*. It is considered to be emphatic, and is often translated as 'utterly' or 'thoroughly,' e.g. 'destroyed them utterly' as opposed to 'destroyed them a destroying,' and 'cleanse you thoroughly' as opposed to 'cleanse you a cleansing.'

Such coherence is frequently lost in speech, since the speaker is not so constrained by word order, either verbally or in terms of meaning. He may jump from one subject to another on account of something which occurs to him as appropriate while speaking, even if there is not such a strong link between the subject matter. This is something we encounter often in the Qur'an. The tendency to switch from the third person to the second person and vice versa, the use of pronouns and demonstrative pronouns that do not match the nouns to which they refer, switching from explicit to implicit meanings, as well as other characteristics, all indicate that it is composed in the style of the spoken word rather than written prose. Otherwise, the abrupt changes from one form to another would simply be poor grammar! When speaking it is also permissible to use types of parenthetical remarks which would not work well in writing. There follow some examples that demonstrate unique features of the spoken word which we find in the Qur'an.

1- Sudden Switching

A unique feature of oral communication is switching suddenly from one subject to another by relying on contextual indicators provided by the setting. There may not be any apparent link between the two, which would be considered to be a flaw in the discourse's coherence if it were a book and not the spoken word.

Take for example *Sūrah al-Qiyāmah* (The Resurrection), which begins by talking about Mankind, his state with regard to the coming of the Hour, up until it comes to the Almighty's Words:

> *O, but man is a telling witness against himself, although he tenders his excuses* (75:14-15).

Then suddenly the discourse turns to address the Prophet:

> *Stir not thy tongue herewith to hasten it. Lo! upon Us (resteth) the putting together thereof and the reading thereof. And when We recite it, follow thou its recitation; then upon Us (resteth) the explanation thereof* (75:16-19).

It abruptly goes back to confront Mankind with an adjunct:

> *Nay, but you love the fleeting world and neglect the Hereafter* (75:20-21).

Then it turns to talk about man's condition on the Day of Resurrection:

> *Upon that day will faces be resplendent, looking toward their Lord* (75:22-23).

And so on right up to verse 30. After that it talks about the arrogant person who did not believe or pray, but instead denied and turned away, gleefully going back to his household. Thus we find the thread twists and turns. One moment there is condemnation, the next rebuke, and then fearful warnings up until the end of the chapter.

So this kind of advance and withdrawal occurs for no other reason than its being in the thread of the spoken word. The switch is made six times in this chapter, and is without a doubt one of the innovative features which makes the Qur'an unique.

Commentating on the words *Stir not thy tongue herewith ...* (75:16), Imām Rāzī says by way of defending this type of radical and sudden grammatical shift for rhetorical purposes (*iltifāt*):

> It is possible that it so happened that, when these verses were revealed, the Messenger hurried his recitation of them fearing they would get lost. So of course he was immediately told not to. This is like when a teacher is giving his pupil a lesson, the pupil starts turning to the right and the left, the teacher brings his attention to it immediately, saying, during the lesson, 'Do not turn to the right or to the left,' and then goes back to the lesson. If that entire lecture is recorded along with the interruption – such as if it is put onto tape – someone with no knowledge of the situation would not understand the reason, whereas someone who knows would realise that it is in order.[160]

2- Grammatical Shift for Rhetorical Purpose (*Iltifāt*)

Within *Sūrah Yā Sīn* one finds a clear example of the rhetoric beauty known as *iltifāt*:

> *Lo! those who merit Paradise this day are happily employed, they and their wives, in pleasant shade, on thrones reclining; theirs the fruit (of their good deeds) and theirs (all) that they ask; the word from a Merciful*

[160] See Rāzī, *al-Tafsīr al-Kabīr*, vol. 30, 222-223. Here, as elsewhere, the author combines paraphrasing with his own commentary. [Trans.]

> *Lord (for them) is: Peace! But avaunt ye, O ye guilty, this day! Did I not charge you, O ye sons of Adam, that ye worship not the devil – Lo! he is your open foe! – but that ye worship Me? That was the right path. Yet he has led astray of you a great multitude. Had ye then no sense? This is hell which ye were promised (if ye followed him). Burn therein this day for that ye disbelieved. This day We seal up their mouths, and their hands speak out to Us and their feet bear witness as to what they used to earn* (36:55-56).

One may notice here that initially the discourse relates to the inhabitants of Heaven, in the third person. Then it turns to sending them a greeting, addressing them in the second person. The second person address suddenly turns to the sinners in *But avaunt ye* ('begone,' 'away with you'). Then, however, it goes back to the third person with the words *This day We seal up their mouths.*

This kind of meandering in a written discourse is usually inappropriate, but is regarded as beauty of style in the spoken word.

Another example can be seen in *Sūrah al-Fatḥ* (The Victory):

> *God was well pleased with the believers when they swore allegiance unto thee beneath the tree, and He knew what was in their hearts, and He sent down peace of reassurance on them, and hath rewarded them with a near victory, and much booty that they will capture. God is ever Mighty, Wise. God promiseth you much booty that ye will capture ...* (48:18-20).

This starts with God addressing the Prophet in the second person, talking about the believers in the third person, and then turns to address the believers themselves in the second person.

This style is very elegant for the spoken word, but unsuitable for prose.

In *Sūrah al-Fatihah* or *al-Ḥamd* (The Praise) one begins by praising God in the third person, then the discourse turns to petitioning the Almighty in the second person. This is wonderful grammatical shift.

3- Attention to Rhyme

One of the distinguishing features of rhyming prose emerges when hearing it as opposed to reading it. There is a much rhyming prose in the Qur'an – at the expense of articulated speech – which cannot be adequately rendered in a written text.

For example:

> Bal al-insānu 'alā nafsihi baṣīra[tun] wa law alqā ma'ādhirah[ū]
>
> *O, but man is a telling witness against himself, although he tender his excuses* (75:14-15).

The words only rhyme if there is a pause after both *baṣīra* and *ma'ādhirah* when they are pronounced with a *yā'*, *rā'* and *hā'* at the end, which cannot be achieved in the written word.

The same is true in the following:

> *Wa [i]ltaffati [a]l-sāqu bi al-sāq[i] ilā Rabbika yawma'idhini [a]l-masāq[u]*
>
> *And (the) leg is wound about (the) leg; unto thy Lord that day will be the procession* (75:28-29).

The prose only rhymes when it is recited with a pause after *bi [a] l-sāq* and *al-masāq.*

> *Fa ammā man ūtiya kitābahu bi yamīnihī fa yaqūlu hā'umu [i]qra'ū kitābiyah. Innī ẓanantu annī mulāqin ḥisābīyah fa huwa fī 'īshatin rāḍīya[tin] fī jannatin 'ālīya[tin] quṭūfuhā dāniya[tun]*
>
> *Then, as for him who is given his record in his right hand, he shall say: Here, take and read my book! Surely I knew that I should have to meet my reckoning. Then he will be in a blissful state in a lofty Garden whereof the clusters are in easy reach* (69:19-23).

This only rhymes in articulated speech when there is a pause after every *tā' marbūṭah.*

> *Wa ammā man khaffat mawāzīnuhū fa ummuhū hāwīya[tun] wa mā hiyah nārun ḥāmiya[tun]*
>
> *But as for him whose scales are light, his refuge will be an abyss. And what will convey unto thee what that is?* (101:8-10).

This only rhymes if there is a pause after the *tā' marbūṭah* in both *hāwiya* and *ḥāmiya*, making them consistent with the pausal *hā'* in *māhiyah*. This is exclusive to recitation as opposed to the written word.

This is how it was recited to the Prophet and how he recited it to the people. It is mandatory to follow this way forever more. Even the written form here follows the style of recitation, because recitation of the Qur'an is what came first.

4- Melodies and Refrains

An important feature of the Qur'an, which suits its being recited as the spoken word rather than read as written lines, is its innovative vocal arrangement in melodies and refrains, which is what initially had the effect of captivating the Arabs' feelings before they could proceed further. The Prophet had instructed that the Qur'an be read in these melodies in Arabic as the first step. This can only be done by reciting it aloud, guided by the tunefulness of the performance, as opposed to saying it quietly to oneself.

This is in addition to the fact that the tune followed in its phrases is either threatening, frightening, informative of glad tidings or warnings, wistful, sorrowful or something similar. It is only giving voice to it using one of those melodies that makes it effective.

This is a matter overlooked by those who suppose that the composition of the Qur'an was in writing rather than epic oral performance.

Indeed, there is an old adage that says, 'The Qur'an is preserved through its recitation not through its writing.'

5- Reliance on Sources Beyond the Confines of the Text

If communication is in the form of a book, its meaning has to come across in the actual wording, either before, after or during the expression (adjunct contextual indicators). Reliance on evidence unconnected to the text[161] is not permissible – but is allowed if the communication is in the form of the spoken word. The Qur'an is of the latter type. To understand its meanings one must normally rely on knowledge of the reasons for revelation (*asbāb al-nuzūl*).

It is not permissible for someone who composes a text to rely on specific events which are generally unknown to others and expect them to understand it, because the readership is general and not restricted to just those who know about the events. As for the Qur'an, it relies on many matters of context separated from its text – known as the reasons for

[161] It is worth pointing out that if rational evidence – like rational deduction – can be clearly inferred from the text, then it is deemed to be adjunct contextual evidence and not evidence disconnected from the text.

revelation – to convey its meanings. In order to recognise the contextual meanings within the Qur'an, there is no recourse other than to have prior knowledge of them, because the text becomes impossible to understand if one does not know the rationale behind the various sections.

Take as an example the following:

> *Lo! (the mountains) of Ṣafā and Marwah are among the indications of God. It is therefore no sin for him who is on pilgrimage to the House (of God) or visiteth it, to go around them. And he who doeth good of his own accord, (for him) God is Responsive, Aware* (2:158).

Whoever does not know the reason why this verse was revealed would think - on the basis of the literal meaning of *it is therefore no sin for him* – that going back and forth between Ṣafā and Marwah is not mandatory. However, if one knows that it was revealed regarding those believers who were too reluctant to go back and forth between Ṣafā and Marwah – after the idols were returned to them – out of fear that it would amount to veneration of them in the way the pagans venerated them, one realises that the verse was revealed to rebut this misconception. It is, therefore, not a mere licence to perform it without fear of doing something wrong, but rather the licence to perform it as a mandatory act without fear of proscription. However, this cannot be understood from the verse until one knows the reason why it was revealed, for there is no indication of it in the explicit wording.

There are many verses like this, which would be most unsuitable for writing a book intended as a general manifesto and a universal call.

This is the most important evidence that the wording of the Qur'an is that of the spoken word as opposed to that of the written word.

The Prophets and Revelation

At this juncture there are two very important matters pertaining to the Message of the Prophets and the truthfulness of their call to God which need to be dealt with in a scientific and acceptable way. *Ahl al-Sunnah* have all spoken of it in uncustomary ways which are perhaps not easy for instinctive reason to digest. As for our scholars – the *Imamiyya* – they have spoken of it rationally on the basis of logical reasoning supported by evidence transmitted on the authority of the Imams from the People of the Household.

Firstly, how did the Prophet know that he had been given a mission? Why did he not think that perhaps the one who had come to him was a devil? Why was he sure it was Gabriel?

Secondly, is it possible:

i) for the Prophet to make a mistake with regard to what is revealed to him;

ii) for false things which he had imagined to fool him to present themselves to him in the form of revelation, or,

iii) for the deceiver (*Iblīs*) to recite to him what he thinks is revelation from God?

With regard to the first matter, the majority hold that the Prophet was at first terrified, fearing that he had been touched by madness. He sought refuge in the embraces of his loyal wife, who in turn sought the help of her uncle Waraqah ibn Nawfil to reassure him and confirm that he was a Prophet, thus calming him and setting his mind at rest.

As for the second matter, it has been said that it was possible for the deceiver to interfere with revelation from heaven, and to recite to the Prophet what he thought was revelation – as in the cranes hadith – were it not for Gabriel's putting things right and foiling the Devil's plot.

In relation to both matters, the Imams of the Household have taken the position that neither case applies, since the Prophet is too precious to God for Him to let this happen, and not to illuminate him with clear evidence of his prophethood at that difficult time. Similarly, He would not allow the Devil to take hold of the Prophet's feelings:

So wait patiently for thy Lord's decree, for surely thou art in Our sight; and proclaim the praise of thy Lord when thou risest up (52:48).

Furthermore, in order to maintain the dignity of the Messenger of God, it is worth discussing each of these issues comprehensively.

Propethood Linked to Shining Proofs

It is God's duty – in the sense of a duty dictated by His Grace and Compassion for His Servants – to link His appointment of a Prophet with shining proofs which leave no room for doubt to creep into his soul, just as He showed Abraham the Kingdom of Heaven and Earth so that he would be certain,[162] and as with Moses:

---

[162] Paraphrased from 6:75.

... he was called by name: O Moses, I am thy Lord... (20:11-12);

Lo! it is I, God, the Mighty, Wise (27:9);

O Moses! fear not! Indeed, the emissaries fear not in My presence (27:10).

This is what the Rule of Grace (*qā'idat al-luṭf*) dictates, and which theologians (*'ulamā' al-kalām*) have discussed.

Zurārah ibn A'yan says on this topic:

> I asked Abū 'Abdillāh how the Messenger of God was not afraid that what came to him from God was not something the Devil insinuated. So he said: 'If God makes a servant a Messenger he sends assuredness [*al-Sakīna*] and mental balance [*al-Waqār*] down upon him. So what came to him from God was like what he saw with his own eyes.[163]

This means the plain truth which was unobscured. He clearly sees the truth, and there is no doubt or disturbance in his mind. The Imam made that plain in another tradition, when he was asked how the Messengers knew that they were Messengers? He said:

> The veil was lifted from them.[164]

'Allāmah Ṭabrisī explains:

> God only ever reveals to His Messenger with bright proofs and clear signs to prove that what has been revealed to him is from God Almighty alone, so he does not need anything else apart from them. He is not terrified and he is not dismayed.[165]

Al-Qāḍī 'Ayād al-Yaḥṣabī writes:

> It is not right [i.e. in the Almighty's Wisdom – an allusion to the Rule of Grace (*Qā'idat al-Luṭf*)] for the Devil to appear to him in the form of an angel and to confuse matters for him, not at the outset of the Message or thereafter. The Prophet's confidence in that is evidence of its being a miracle. Indeed, the Prophet does not doubt that what comes to him from God is the angel and His

---

[163] *Tafsīr al-'Ayyāshī*, vol. 2, 201; Majlisī, *Biḥār al-Anwār*, vol. 18, 262.

[164] Majlisī, *Biḥār al-Anwār*, vol. 11, 56.

[165] Ṭabrisī , *Majma' al-Bayān*, vol. 10, 384.

> true messenger, either through instinctive knowledge God has created in him or through clear proof which God shows him, so that your Lord's Words can be perfect in truth and justice, with no man capable of changing God's Words.[166]

So when the Prophet is despatched as a Prophet, he has to have knowledge of certainty (*'ilm yaqīn*), or indeed the heart of certainty (*'ayn al-yaqīn*), about his task without doubting or being agitated. His mind is convinced and reassured through Almighty God's care, protection and Grace, assisting him and supporting him, especially at the outset of the mission. So the Clear Truth (*al-Nāmūs al-Akbar*) comes to him as though he sees it with his eyes and witnesses it in his heart. It is a defining and critical point at which a prophet should not waver or be afraid:

> *... the emissaries fear not in My presence* (27:10).

Furthermore, God only chose the Prophet for his mission once He had perfected his mind and taught him those secrets of the heavens and the earth of which he was worthy, so that he could perform his task as ambassador and propagator of God's Message among all beings, just as He had done with His bosom friend (*al-Khalīl*) Abraham. Imām Ali, the Commander of the Faithful, said:

> From the time he was weaned, God linked His greatest angel to him to lead him night and day to the world's best and finest of manners.[167]

Imām 'Askarī said that God found the Prophet's heart to be:

> ... the best and most attentive of hearts, and so He chose him as a prophet.[168]

Similarly, he said:

[166] Abu al-Faḍl 'Ayāḍ ibn Mūsā al-Yaḥṣabī, *al-Shifā bi Ta'rīf Ḥuqūq al-Muṣṭafā* (Beirut: Dār al-Kitāb al-'Arabī, 1984), vol. 2, 112.

[167] Al-Raḍī, *Nahj al-Balāghah, : al-Khuṭbah al-Qāṣi'ah* (*The Sermon of Disparagement*) (no. 192), 300.

[168] Majlisī, *Biḥār al-Anwār*, vol. 18, 205-206.

> God did not send a single prophet or messenger until his intellect had been perfected, and thus his mind was better than all the minds of his nation.[169]

'Allāmah Majlisī explains:

> From the time that God perfected his intellect, he remained supported by the Holy Spirit. He would speak to him, and he would hear His voice and have dreams which came true until God sent him on his mission as a messenger and prophet.[170]

The proofs that he had received God's Grace and special attention from the very beginning are many. His people knew him to be a genius and inherently worthy. They recognised his honesty and astuteness, and found him to be a blend of rectitude and soundness of judgment, until he became dear to all the people and they nicknamed him 'the trustworthy, truthful one' (*al-Ṣādiq al-Amīn*), whose judgment and behaviour they could trust.

According to Ali ibn Ibrāhīm's tradition,[171] the signs of prophecy appeared in him three years before he was given his mission, when he was thirty-seven. He would have dreams which came true and spend time on his own in the Cave at Ḥirā' pondering the Essence of God and the secrets of the Heavens and Creation, until the truth suddenly came upon him at the age of forty. His soul was prepared and he knew the signs of what was to happen – something which had been on the brink of happening for some time.

Such a person is not terrified and is not dismayed. He does not think he is insane or vulnerable to evil, or seek refuge in a woman with no experience of the secrets of prophecy or a man[172] whose knowledge was based on corrupted and extinct books – works which had not been proven at that time to have touched on truths regarding the dominion (*mulk*) and heaven (*malakūt*) and not to have been transformed from their original form.

[169] Kulaynī, *al-Kāfī*, vol. 1, 12-13.
[170] Majlisī, *Biḥār al-Anwār*, vol. 18, 277.
[171] Majlisī, *Biḥār al-Anwār*, vol. 18, 184 and 194.
[172] Namely, Waraqah ibn Nawfil, Khadījah's paternal cousin.

Thus, the Prophet's position with regard to the revelation of the Truth to him at the outset of his mission was that of someone who is aware of the true state of the matter, knowing the essence of the Truth being revealed to him, and extremely confident and self-composed. We may rest assured that he did not hesitate or doubt, and was neither agitated, terrified nor dismayed. We shall tell the story of the outset of this mission according to the traditions of the People of the Household, which explain aspects of the Prophet's position at the time, and which are majestic, deferential, reverent and sublime.

The Story of Waraqah ibn Nawfil

What was mentioned above is the story of the Despatch according to the traditions of the People of the Household, and who know best what went on in their own domestic situation. There follows another account regarding the Prophet Muhammad's despatch according to what other traditions say:

Bukhārī, Muslim, Ibn Hishām, Ṭabarī and the like narrate:

> While the Prophet was spending time alone in the Cave at Ḥirā', all of a sudden he heard someone calling him. Terror took hold of him and he raised his head. Why, it was a terrifying form which was calling him. The terror grew in him and the horror of his position stopped him dead. He began turning his face away from what he saw and lo, he saw it on all horizons of the sky drawing near and moving away. The form would not go away no matter which way he turned. He occupied himself with that for a time, oblivious to himself. He almost threw himself from the top of the mountain on account of the severity of the horror of the terrifying scene which had overcome him. Meanwhile, Khadījah had sent someone to look for the Prophet in the cave, but he could not find him. This continued until the form went away. He went back, his heart agitated, full of fear and dread until he walked in on Khadījah, shivering from fear as if he had a fever. He looked at his wife the way one seeking refuge and help looks, saying, 'Khadījah, what is wrong with me?' He told her what he had seen and informed her of his fears that his eyes were deceiving him. He said, 'I felt sorry for myself. The only thing I think can be wrong with me is

that I have been touched by a jinn.[173] The cursed one [meaning his own self] is a soothsayer or a madman!'

His faithful wife looked at him with a sympathetic glance and said, 'Not so, cousin. Rejoice and be strong. God will never disgrace you. By Him in whose hand Khadījah's soul rests, I wish you to be this nation's Prophet. You will maintain good relations with kin, speak the truth, entertain your guests generously and assist in the face of calamity. You have never committed a lewd act.' In this way she calmed him with her sharpened words.

Then she carried out a successful experiment. She said, 'Cousin, can you tell me about this friend of yours who comes to you?' 'Yes,' he replied. She continued, 'When he comes, tell me.' So the angel came as he would come to him and the Messenger of God then said, 'Khadījah, this is he who has come to me.' She replied, 'Get up cousin and sit on my left thigh.' So the Messenger of God got up and sat on [her thigh]. She asked, 'Can you see him?' He replied, 'Yes.' She said, 'Turn around and sit on my right thigh.' So the Messenger of God turned around and sat on her right thigh. She asked, 'Can you see him?' He replied, 'Yes.' 'So turn around and sit on my lap.' He then turned around and sat on her lap. She then bared her head and cast off her headscarf with the Messenger of God sitting on her lap. She asked, 'Can you see him, cousin?' He replied, 'No,' and so she said, 'Cousin, rejoice and be strong. By God, it is an angel and not a devil.'

Then to corroborate what she had deduced from her experiment, she set off to her cousin Waraqah ibn Nawfil. He had become a Christian and read the Scriptures. She told him the story of her cousin Muhammad, and so Waraqah said, 'Holy! Holy! If you were to believe me, Khadījah, the Archangel Gabriel who used to come to Moses has come. So tell him to be strong and that he is this nation's Prophet. I wish I could stay alive for his days, to protect him and help him.' Khadījah went back to the Messenger of God

[173] Ibn al-Athīr's interpretation of *'uriḍa lī.*

> and told him what he had said. At that, his mind was put at rest, his fear subsided and he was convinced that he was a Prophet.[174]

There is no doubt that the story of the Prophet's being terrified by that shocking image is a myth weaved by feeble minds ignorant of the sacredness (*maqām*) of God's noble Prophets , and hence of their elevated importance.

First of all, it is surprising that scholars, who are people of analytical reasoning, prefer the intellect of a person who had nothing to do with the secrets of prophecy over the intellect of a perfect man, who had reached a pinnacle entitling him to carry God's Message, then for her to carry out a critical experiment unknown to the Messenger of the Lord of All the Worlds, for him to be reassured by what she said, or by what was said by a man whose prestige rested on his knowledge of books which had undoubtedly been corrupted. We do not know what it was that the Messenger of God found in what she said that was the source of his reassurance, which he did not find in the Truth revealed to him from the presence of God, the Mighty and Wise.

Did not the true dreams which preceded his despatch on his mission, the angel's greeting him with 'Peace be upon you, Messenger of God' at the time of the despatch, the trees, stones and everything he passed on his way home to Khadījah's house greeting him, and his inherent knowledge which had deepened during the time spent alone at Hirā' convince him of the matter, such that he had to seek the reassurance of a woman, or a man who had become a Christian? This is nothing but a terrible detraction from the sacred standing of God's Messenger, if not an atrocious sacrilege.

Also, there is discrepancy in the rendition of the account which does not fit together, evidence *ab initio* that it does not stand up. According to one narration, Khadījah set off alone to Waraqah and told him what had happened. In another:

---

[174] See Ibn Hishām, *al-Sīrat al-Nabawiyyah*, vol. 1, 252-255; *Ṣaḥīḥ al-Bukhārī*, vol. 1, 3-4; *Ṣaḥīḥ Muslim*, vol. 1, 97-99; Abū Ja'far Muhammad ibn Jarīr Ṭabarī, *Tārīkh al-Rusul wa al-Mulūk (Tārīkh al-Ṭabarī),* (Cairo: al-Istiqāmah, 1358q.), vol. 2, 298-303; Ṭabarī, *Jāmi' al-Bayān*, vol. 30, 161; Muhammad Ḥasanayn Haykal, *Ḥayāt Muhammad* (Cairo: Maṭba'at Dār al-Kutub al-Miṣriyyah, 1354 q.), 95-96.

> ... she set off with me to Waraqah and said, 'Hear from your nephew.' He asked me and I told him. He said, 'This is the Archangel Gabriel who was sent down to Moses.

There is another narration according to which Waraqah ibn Nawfil met him while he was circumambulating the House and said, 'Nephew, tell me what you have seen and heard.' Thereafter the Messenger of God told him and so Waraqah said to him, 'I swear by Him in Whose Hand rests my soul that you are this nation's Prophet. If I live to see that, God knows what help I will give Him. Another says, on the authority of Ibn 'Abbās, that Waraqah ibn Nawfil said, 'I said, "Muhammad, tell me about this one who comes to you," meaning Gabriel. He said, "He comes to me from Heaven, his wings are pearl and the bottoms of his feet are green."'[175] This is not in Khadījah's accounts regarding Waraqah or according to what the aforementioned authentic books (*ṣiḥāḥ*) say. Yet another says that Abū Bakr went to see Khadījah and she said, 'Set off with Muhammad to Waraqah,' and they set off together and told him the story.[176]

If the account is true, why did Waraqah not believe in him at that time, if he knew that he was a Prophet who had been sent?

According to the correct hadith, he died an unbeliever, not believing in the Prophet. Sibṭ ibn al-Jawzī says:

He was the last person to die during the period [the first years of the prophetic mission] and he was buried in al-Ḥujūn.

And adds:

> He was not a Muslim.

The same is narrated on the authority of Ibn 'Abbās:

> He died as a Christian.[177]

The matter of the Prophet's dream – where Waraqah was dressed in white – is also fabricated, and its chain of narration is broken. Otherwise, Waraqah would have been recorded among those who believed in the Prophet. Ibn 'Asākir says:

---

[175] Ibn al-Athīr, *Usd al-Ghābah*, vol. 5, 88; the narration is weak on account of Rawḥ ibn Musāfir. Waraqah died before Ibn 'Abbās was born.

[176] Al-Suyūṭī, *al-Itqān*, vol. 1, 71.

[177] See Ali ibn Burhān al-Dīn al-Ḥalabī al-Shāfi'ī, *al-Sīrat al-Ḥalabiyyah* (Beirut: Dār al-Fikr, n.d.), vol. 1, 250.

I do not know anyone who has said that he became a Muslim.[178]

This is in spite of the fact that Waraqah lived beyond the commencement of the prophetic mission – the author of *al-Imtā'* says that Waraqah ibn Nawfil died after the fourth year. Burhān al-Dīn al-Ḥalabī writes:

What *Sīrat ibn Isḥāq* says agrees with it, as does *Kitāb al-Khamīs*.[179]

It is narrated that he passed by Bilāl while he was being tortured.[180] Ibn Ḥajar says that this proves that he lived beyond the beginning of the Prophet's call, his invitation to Bilāl and the latter's becoming a Muslim.

So why did he remain an unbeliever and not become a Muslim the way other people did? Why did he not help him the way other people helped him? He broke the promise mentioned in the myth.

Revelation Cannot Be Confused with Anything Else

This is the second matter referred to above. The Prophet cannot make a mistake over what is revealed to him. The matter can never be confused with anything else. When revelation was sent to the Prophet, the veil would be lifted from his eyes and he would see reality through his spiritual aspect, cut off from the vicissitudes of matter. At such a time, he would perceive manifestations and radiant illumination covering him from the heavenly realm, so that he could devote himself completely to meeting God's Spirit and receiving His Words. He would see the Essence of the Truth revealed to him with understanding and piercing vision, like someone who sees the sun in broad daylight. There is no possibility of error in his vision or confusion over what he understands.

Thus, revelation was not an idea which sprang from inside his mind, making it prone to error by inferring conclusions or the possibility of confusion in its application.[181] On the contrary, it is the clear perception of a present reality that rules out the possibility of error.

---

[178] Ibn Ḥajar, *al-Iṣābah*, vol. 3, 633.

[179] Ibn Hishām, *al-Sīrat al-Nabawiyyah*, vol. 1, 250.

[180] Ibn Ḥajar, *al-Iṣābah*, vol. 3, 634.

[181] Error is only possible in two fields: either in the field of thought or seeing things in the real world, for example, because rational deduction has conditions and rules, which, if are ignored by the thinker, cause him to fall into error. The same applies to seeing things in the real world – if seen from afar, there may be error in terms of the application of deep-seated principles and information within oneself to the particulars

This illustrates a practical, philosophical method[182] which leads us to acknowledge the impossibility of revelation being erroneous. Hence God's law (*sharī'ah*) as revealed to His messengers is clear from the beginning of any possibility of error.

There is another rational method which demonstrates the infallibility of the prophets regarding what they communicate from God. Theologians discuss this in detail, and it can be summed up by saying that the prophet who communicates from God must, in accordance with the Law of Grace (*qā'idat al-luṭf*), be blessed with complete soundness of sensory perception and intellect, as well as in his opinions, speculation, moral behaviour, and even disposition and form. In a nutshell, God has to choose as a messenger someone with perfect formal qualities and ethics, so that people do not turn away from him, and instead have confidence in what he communicates from God. Otherwise, it would defeat the purpose of devising a code of law (*tashrī'*).

Therefore the Prophet is protected (*ma'sūm*) from error and forgetfulness, especially with regard to communicating the laws of the sharī'ah. This is the consensus of Muslims and other rational people who obey the Message of the Prophets. Otherwise, adhering to religious laws would be a folly which good sense would been inclined to reject.[183]

Also, it is impossible for Iblīs to come in disguise and interfere with what is revealed to the Prophet, by making evil insinuations in the form of revelation and tricking the Prophet into claiming that it is from God, because the Devil cannot take possession of the minds of God's messengers and honoured servants:

---

observed. The error lies in this personal application and not in the actual thing seen, because seeing means imprinting an image from outside – an unchangeable reality – on the mind through the medium of the eye. This is a natural phenomenon which happens under given conditions. Admittedly, it is one's self which makes a decision on what is observed: 'That it is such-and-such,' But the error can only occur in the interpretation, and not in the actual perception. Therefore, insofar as revelation has nothing to do with either, that is, thinking or seeing from afar, and is the perception a present reality, there is no room for error.

182 See Tabātabā'ī, *Wahy Ya Shu'ūr-e Marmūz* (Qum: Dār al-Fikr. n.d.), 104.

183 See *Mabāhith al-'Iṣmah*, which is the third matter in the fourth *Maqṣad* (objective) of *Mabāhith al-Nubuwwah al-'Āmmah* (The Discussions on General Prophethood) in Jamāl al-Dīn al-Hasan ibn Yūsuf ibn 'Ali ibn al-Muṭahhar al-'Allāmah al-Hillī, *Kashf al-Murād fī Sharh Tajrīd al-I'tiqād* (Qum: Mu'assasatal-Nashr al-Islāmī, 1417 q.), 195.

> *Lo! My (faithful) bondmen – over them thou hast no power ...* (17:65);

for it would contradict the Almighty's Words:

> *And if he had invented false sayings concerning Us, We assuredly had taken him by the right hand ...* (69:44-45);

and:

> *Nor doth he (Muhammad) speak of (his own) desire. It is naught but an inspiration that is inspired, which one of mighty powers (Gabriel) hath taught him* (53:3-5);

the Devil having already said:

> *But I had no authority over you, save that I called unto you, and you responded to me* (14:22).

Therefore the supposition contradicts the Rule of Grace (*qā'idat al-luṭf*) referred to above and is inconsistent with the Almighty's Wisdom in sending prophets as explained earlier on.

It is true that Sunni hadith scholars believe that it is possible for the Devil to take possession of the Messenger's mind, as their tradition on the story of the cranes says, but this is something we believe to be impossible and, accordingly, a fabrication interpolated by those who want to detract from the Messenger's status and capture feeble minds. It is a story ripe for the picking by the enemies of Islam. Here is the text of the myth followed by a critique of it:

The Myth of the Cranes

Ibn Jarīr al-Ṭabarī narrates via a chain of narration which he claims to be authentic, on the authority of Muhammad ibn Ka'b, Muhammad ibn Qays, Sa'īd ibn Jubayr, Ibn Abbās and others, that the Prophet was among a group of pagans from Quraysh in the open area around the Ka'bah or in one of its outhouses. It afflicted his soul if some of the Qur'an brought about fierce quarrelling between him and his people, because he was upset at being distanced from them and wished for harmony, at no matter what cost. When the chapter entitled *The Star* (*Sūrah al-Najm*) was revealed to him, he began reciting it until he reached:

> *Have ye thought upon Al-Lāt and Al-'Uzzā and Manāt, the third, the other?* (53:19-20);

and then the Devil recited to him: 'Those high cranes – their intercession is desired.'[184]

He thought it was revelation and recited it to the crowd of Quraysh. Then he carried on and recited the remainder of the chapter. When he completed it, he prostrated, the Muslims prostrated and the pagans also prostrated out of deference for the agreement Muhammad had shown them in honouring their gods and desiring their intercession. This news spread until it reached the migrants in Ethiopia, and they began returning to their homes in Mecca, joyful over this sudden accord, just as the Prophet, too, was joyful at the realisation of his old dream of uniting his people.

It is said that a white devil is what appeared to the Prophet in Gabriel's form and recited the words to him.

It is also said that the Prophet was praying by Abraham's footprints (*Maqām*) when drowsiness took hold of him, and the words rolled across his tongue without his realising it.

Alternatively, it is said that the Prophet spoke the words of his own accord, out of desire for Quraysh's hearts to be in accord, and later regretted it, for it was a lie about God.

Then, when night came, Gabriel came and said to him, 'Read me the chapter.' So the Prophet began reciting it until he reached the point in question. Then Gabriel said, 'Indeed! From where did you get these words?' So the Messenger of God felt remorse and said, 'I attributed them falsely to God and said that God had said what He did not say.' Then he felt severe sorrow and had a great fear of God.

It is said that the Prophet said to Gabriel, 'Someone who came to me in your form brought it to me and cast it upon my tongue.' So Gabriel said, 'God forbid that I should have recited this to you.' That troubled the Messenger of God and the following was revealed:

> *And they indeed strove hard to beguile thee from that wherewith We have inspired thee, that thou shouldst invent other than it against Us; and then would they have accepted thee as a friend. And if We had not*

[184] Cranes (*gharānīq*); here, *gharnūq* (sing.) means a soft, white youth. Its root meaning is the name of a waterbird (*mālik al-ḥazīn*), and it likens the pagan gods to white birds hovering in the sky, symbolising their nearness to God.

> *made thee wholly firm, thou mightest almost have inclined unto them a little. Then had We made thee taste a double (punishment) of living and a double (punishment) of dying, then hadst thou found no helper against Us* (17:73-75).

The Messenger's sorrow over this surprising incident was profound, and he remained grief-stricken and worried until the following was revealed:

> *Never sent We a messenger or a prophet before thee but when he recited (the message) Satan proposed (opposition) in respect of that which he recited thereof, but God abolisheth that which Satan proposeth. Then God establisheth His revelations. God is the Knower, Wise* (22:52).[185]

This was a consolation for his sorrowful heart, and his worry went away and his soul was happy.[186]

Criticism of the Hadith's Chain of Narration

Orientalists and those attacking the pure Islamic faith have become fond of this fabricated myth of the cranes, which is falsely attributed to the Prophet, and have broadcast it and stirred up false suppositions,[187] whereas it is a lie forged by the talents of storytellers and attributed by them to some of the successors (*tābiʻīn*) and companions up to Ibn 'Abbās. The proof that it is a lie and falsely attributed is clear from its content.

Firstly, the chain of narration does not go back without a break to any of the companions. It is merely attributed to a number of successors and others who were not present at the time of the Prophet. Accordingly, the hadith has an unspecified source (*mursal*) and therefore lacks an unbroken chain of narration.

As for its being attributed to Ibn 'Abbās, this can hardly be the case, since Ibn 'Abbās was born in the third year before the Migration, and could not possibly have witnessed the incident. It could only possibly have been narrated to him.

Thus in all its forms, the tradition does not have an unbroken chain of narration going back to any witness to the incident, assuming it actually

---

[185] This is discussed at the end of the section.

[186] Ṭabarī, *Jāmiʻ al-Bayān*, vol. 17, 131-134; al-Suyūṭī, *al-Durr al-Manthūr*, vol. 4, 194 and 366-368; *Fath al-Bārī*, vol. 8, 333.

[187] See *The History of the Islamic Peoples* by Karl Brockelmann, 34.

happened. The rules governing the chains of narrations do not allow such a *mursal* hadith to be relied upon as evidence.

Secondly, Ahmad ibn al-Husayn al-Bayhaqī, the Shafi'ī Imam known widely for his precise scrutiny says:

> This hadith is not proven in terms of narration. Its narrators are all disparaged.[188]

And al-Qāḍī 'Ayāḍ has said:

> None of the authors of authentic collections have cited this hadith, nor has it been narrated by any reliable source via a sound, unbroken chain of narration. Only historians enamoured of every strange thing and who piece together from pages every sound and sickly thing are enamoured of it.

Thirdly, the consensus of the critical judges among the scholars of Islam, both historically and latterly, is that the hadith is fabricated. They have decided it is an obvious lie, without paying attention to whether its chain of narration is unbroken or broken, sound or 'sickly,' because above all it contradicts the explicit text of the Qur'an, according to which:

> *Falsehood cannot come at it from before it or from behind it. (It is) a revelation from the Wise, the Owner of Praise* (41:42).

Imam Rāzī says:

> This is the account of all literalist exegetes. As for critical judges, they deem it to be false and fabricated. It has been argued against using many rational and textual arguments.[189]

Sayyid Ṭabāṭabā'ī says that the indisputable proofs of the infallibility of the Prophet refute the wording of the hadith even if its chain of narration is presumed to be authentic. It is essential to clear the Prophet's holiness of falsehoods like these which detract from the esteem in which the prophets are held.[190]

---

[188] Rāzī, *al-Tafsīr al-Kabīr*, vol. 23, 50.
[189] Ibid.
[190] Ṭabāṭabā'ī, *al-Mīzān*, vol. 14, 435.

Scribes of the Revelation

Ali, peace be on him, was the first to act as scribe for the Prophet in Mecca, and continued until the end of his lifetime.

One of his unique characteristics was that he did not let any revelation elude him and would write it all down in a book. The Prophet would even keep that which was revealed in his absence for him until he came back, and dictate it to him.

Another unique characteristic was that he would not restrict himself to writing down the text of the revelation, but would accompany it with whatever interpretation it needed and write that down as well.

Sulaym ibn Qays al-Hilāli al-'Āmirī (who died around 90 AH and was one of the most eminent companions) narrates:

> I sat with Ali in Kufa in the mosque, and the people were around him. He said, 'Ask me before you lose me. Ask me about the Book of God, for I swear by God, not a single verse of the Book of God was revealed without God's Messenger making me recite it and teaching me the interpretation of it.' So Ibn al-Kawwā'[191] said, 'What about that which was revealed while you were away?' So he said, 'Yes. He would keep what I had missed and when I came to him, he would say to me, "Ali, God has revealed such-and-such and such-and-such while you were away." Then he would recite it to me. "The interpretation of it is such-and-such," and he would teach it to me.'[192]

The first to act as a scribe in Medina was Ubayy ibn Ka'b al-Anṣārī. He was one of the few who could write well at that time. He was the first to end letters with 'and So-and-So wrote.' The Prophet personally presented him with the Qur'an in its entirety, and he was among those

---

[191] His name was 'Abdullāh of Banī Yashkur. He was one of the Khārijite chiefs when they rebelled against Ali at the Battle of Ṣiffīn. He and a group then returned to the fold after being advised by Ibn 'Abbās. He would stay close to Ali asking him difficult questions, not with the intention of trying to understand but rather with the intention of trying to cause annoyance. Nevertheless, the Imām would give him wise answers a large number of which, filled with various fields of knowledge and humanities, have been preserved for us.

[192] Sulaym ibn Qays al-Hilālī, *Kitāb Sulaym ibn Qays* (Qum: Dār al-Kutub al-Islāmiyyah, n.d.), 213-214.

who attended the last presentation. Later, he took on the supervision of the scribes during 'Uthmān's time, and was the authority they turned to whenever they disagreed with each other.[193]

Zayd ibn Thābit used to live near the Prophet and was a fortitudinous youth who wrote well. If Ubayy was away, the Prophet would send for Zayd to act as a scribe for him until he became one of the official scribes. Mostly he would attend to writing his letters and orders. The Prophet instructed him to learn Hebrew in Jewish schools of the time, called *māsilah*, to help him write his letters in Hebrew.

The main official scribes were Ali, Ubayy and Zayd, while others were secondary. Ibn al-Athīr writes:

> 'Abdullāh ibn al-Arqam al-Zuhrī was a regular letter writer. As for covenants and treaties, Ali would write them. A number of Companions were deemed to be his scribes including the three caliphs, Zubayr ibn al-'Awām, Khālid and Abān sons of Sa'īd ibn al-'Āṣ, Ḥanẓalah al-Usaydī, 'Alā' ibn al-Haḍramī, Khālid ibn al-Walīd, 'Abdullāh ibn Rawāḥah, Muhammad ibn Maslamah, 'Abdullāh ibn Ubayy ibn Sullūl, Mughīrah ibn Shu'bah, 'Amr ibn al-'Āṣ, Mu'āwiyah ibn Abī Sufyān, Jahm or Juhaym ibn al-Ṣalt, Mu'ayqab ibn Abī Fāṭimah and Sharḥabīl ibn Ḥasanah.

He adds:

> The first from Quraysh to write for him was 'Abdullāh ibn Sa'd ibn Abī Sarḥ. He migrated with him to Medina, then he apostatised and fled to Mecca, denouncing the Messenger of God, making fun of the matter of revelation. He would say to the Quraysh: 'I would turn Muhammad any way I wanted. He would dictate to me: 'Mighty, Wise,' and I would say, 'Or All-Knowing, Wise?' He would say, 'Yes, it's all correct.' On the day of the Conquest, the Prophet wanted to spill his blood. However, 'Uthmān – who was his milk brother through sharing the same wet nurse – interceded on his behalf, persisted and continued to do so until the Prophet

[193] See Ibn Sa'd, *al-Ṭabaqāt al-Kubrā*, vol. 3, part 2, 59; Ibn Ḥajar, *al-Iṣābah*, vol. 1, 19; Ibn 'Abd al-Barr, *al-Istī'āb*, vol. 1, 50-51; Abdullāh ibn Abī Dāwūd al-Sijistānī, *al-Maṣāḥif* (Cairo, 1355 q.), 30

> forgave him after a long silence, wanting someone to take the initiative and kill him. He died under Mu'āwiyah's sponsorship in the year thirty-seven.[194]

Ibn Abī al-Ḥadīd says:

> What biographers say is that Ali, Zayd ibn Thābit and Zayd ibn Arqam used to write down the revelation. Ḥanẓalah ibn al-Rabī' al-Taymī and Mu'āwiyah ibn Abī Sufyān used to write to kings and tribal chiefs for him, write down his daily requirements, and write down what charity monies came in and what shares were given to whom.[195]

It appears that those we mentioned were the number known for their knowledge of writing and the Messenger of God's using them for his needs in this respect.

Al-Balādhurī cites al-Wāqidī as saying:

> Islam appeared among the Quraysh when seventeen men knew how to write: Ali ibn Abī Ṭālib, 'Umar ibn al-Khaṭṭāb, 'Uthmān ibn 'Affān, Abū 'Ubaydah ibn al-Jarrāḥ, Talḥah ibn 'Ubaydillāh, Yazīd ibn Abī Sufyān, Abū Ḥudhayfah ibn 'Utbah ibn Rabī'ah, Ḥāṭib ibn 'Amr brother of Suhayl ibn 'Amr al-'Āmirī, Abū Salamah ibn 'Abd al-Asad al-Makhzūmī, Abān ibn Sa'īd ibn al-'Āṣ ibn Umayyah, Khālid ibn Sa'īd and his brother 'Abdullāh ibn Sa'd ibn Abī al-Sarḥ al-'Āmirī, Ḥuwayṭib ibn 'Abd al-'Uzzā al-'Āmirī, Abū Sufyān ibn Ḥarb ibn Umayyah, Mu'āwiyah ibn Abī Sufyān, Juhaym ibn al-Ṣalt ibn Makhramah ibn al-Muṭṭalib ibn 'Abd Manāf and al-'Alā' ibn al-Ḥaḍramī.
>
> Among the women who knew how to write when Islam appeared were: Umm Kulthūm bint 'Uqbah, Karīmah bint al-Miqdād and al-Shifā' bint 'Abdillāh al-'Adawiyyah. The Messenger of God asked the latter to teach Ḥafṣah bint 'Umar how to write the way she

[194] Ibn al-Athīr, *Usd al-Ghābah*, vol. 1, 50 at the end of the entry for Ubayy ibn Ka'b and vol. 3, 173 under the entry for 'Abdallāh himself.

[195] Ibn Abī al-Ḥadīd, *Sharḥ Nahj al-Balāghah* (Beirut: Dār Iḥyā al-Kutub al-'Arabiyyah, 1959), vol. 1, 338.

> had taught her *raqnat al-namlah.*[196] Umm Salamah knew how to read the Codex (*al-Muṣḥaf*) but did not know how to write. The same is true of 'Ā'ishah bint Abī Bakr.

He further reports from al-Wāqidī:

> Ḥanẓalah ibn al-Rabī' ibn Rabāḥ al-Usaydī from Banū Tamīm happened to write in front of the Messenger of God once and he was named Ḥanẓalah the scribe.

And also:

> Few among the Aws and Khazraj knew how to write Arabic. Some of the Jews knew how to write Arabic and the children in Medina had learnt from them since olden times. So when Islam came along there were among the Aws and Khazraj a number who knew how to write: Sa'd ibn 'Ubādah ibn Dulaym, al-Mundhir ibn 'Amr, Ubayy ibn Ka'ab and Zayd ibn Thābit – he could write Arabic and Hebrew[197] – Rāfi' ibn Mālik, Usayd ibn Ḥuḍayr, Ma'an ibn 'Udayy al-Balawī, Bashīr ibn Sa'd, Sa'd ibn al-Rabī', Aws ibn Khūllī and 'Abdullāh ibn Abī al-Munāfiq.[198]

---

[196] *Al-Raqnah* means making oneself up with henna and saffron. *Raqnat al-namlah* may have been a way in which women made themselves up.

[197] Al-Wāqidi states via his chain of narration going back to Khārijah ibn Zayd that his father Zayd ibn Thābit said: The Messenger of God told me to learn Jewish writing. He said to me, 'I do not trust any Jew to do my writing for me. It only took me a little while to learn it. Then, I would write to the Jews for him. If they wrote to him I would read their letter.

[198] Al-Balādhurī, *Futūḥ al-Buldān*, 456-460.

CHAPTER III

THE DESCENT OF THE QUR'AN

There is an important matter linked to the revelation of the Qur'an and how it ties in with the beginning of the Message. This is because the commencement of the Prophetic Mission, which was in the month of Rajab, coincided with the revelation of some of the Qur'an (five verses from the beginning of *The Blood Clot* (*Surah al-'Alaq*), whereas the Qur'an explicitly states that it was revealed on the Night of Destiny during the month of Ramaḍān. How can this be reconciled? The same applies to determining the period over which the Qur'an was gradually revealed and the chapters which were revealed before the Migration, technically making them Meccan, and which were revealed after that, making them Medinan. Are there any verses which are exceptions regarding the chapters in which they are placed? The best answer is that there are no exceptions. If a chapter is Meccan, then all its verses are Meccan. The same principle applies to the Medinan chapters, because there is no reliable evidence of any exceptions, as we will explain in the detailed discussion of these elements which follows.

The Start of the Revelation - the Prophetic Mission

According to the eminent and reliable Sheikh Ali ibn Ibrāhīm al-Qummī, when the Prophet turned thirty-seven, he would see someone coming towards him in his dreams saying, 'Messenger of God!' He kept that to himself for some time. One day he was tending one of Abū Ṭālib's herds along the clefts in the mountains, when he saw someone who said to him, 'Messenger of God!' He asked, 'Who are you?' and the other replied, 'I am Gabriel; God sent me to you to make you a messenger.' He began teaching him ablution from minor impurity, and prayer. That was when he was forty. So one day Ali came in while he was praying. He asked, 'Abu al-Qāsim, what is this?' He replied, 'It is the prayer which God has told me to perform.' So he began praying with him. Khadījah joined them as a third. Ali would pray on the Messenger of God's right hand side and

Khadījah would be behind him. Thereafter, Abū Ṭālib told his son Ja'far to pray on the Messenger of God's left hand side. Zayd ibn Ḥārithah, the slave freed by the Messenger of God,[199] had become a Muslim when the Messenger of God became a Prophet and he would also pray with them. Through this group the seed of Islam was planted.[200]

The Imam's exegesis[201] says that:

> The Messenger of God would go out to Ḥirā' every morning and look at the signs of God's Mercy, pondering on the Kingdom of Heaven and the Earth and worshipping God as He should be worshipped until he was about to turn forty. God found his noble heart to be the best, most sublime, most obedient and humblest of hearts. He granted permission for the Gates of Heaven to open. He granted the angels permission to descend and for Muhammad to observe. Mercy came down upon him from the leg of the Throne. He looked at the trustworthy one, Gabriel, crowned with light. He came down to him, grabbed his upper arm, shook it and said, 'Muhammad, recite!' He asked, 'What shall I recite?' He replied:

---

[199] It is said that the Messenger of God bought him for Khadījah. When he married her she gave him to him as a gift. The Messenger of God freed him. Alternatively, it is said that Khadījah asked her nephew Ḥakīm ibn Ḥuzām ibn Khuwaylid to give him to her as a gift when he came to Mecca with slaves, among whom was Zayd, who was still a boy who had not yet reached adolescence. He said to her, 'Aunt, choose whichever of these slaveboys you like.' She chose Zayd, then gave him to the Messenger of God as a gift. The Messenger of God freed him and adopted him.

[200] Majlisī, *Biḥār al-Anwār*, vol. 18, 184 and 194.

[201] *Tafsīr al-Imām*, 157. This exegesis is attributed to the eleventh Imām, al-Ḥasan ibn Ali al-'Askarī. Some careful critics have refuted this attribution because of the shocking things it contains. However, if what is meant is that it is the Imām's work written by him personally and his own composition, then it is categorically unacceptable. However, if the imputation is with regard to the narrator's having attended the Imām's class and asked him things pertaining to the exegesis of verses of the Qur'an, then having returned home and written down what he remembered, possibly adding or omitting things in accordance with his personal knowledge, then it is something which cannot be denied. This is what we believe. Thus, we rely on much of what is included in this exegesis that is in accordance with other authentic sources. See also Majlisī, *Biḥār al-Anwār*, vol. 18, 205-206.

> *Recite: In the Name of thy Lord Who createth, createth man from a blood clot. Recite: And thy Lord is the Most Bounteous, Who teacheth by the pen, teacheth man that which he knew not* (96:1-5).
>
> Then he revealed to him what he revealed. Gabriel ascended to his Lord and Muhammad came down from the mountain. He had fainted from God's greatness and the sublimity of His splendour which gave him a severe fever. The fear of Quraysh's calling him a liar and attributing it to insanity weighed on him, his being the most rational of God's creatures and the noblest of his created beings. The thing he hated most was the devil and the things mad people do, so God wanted to encourage his heart and sooth his breast, so every time he passed by a stone or tree it would call out to him, 'Peace be upon you, Messenger of God.'

In his commentary on Nahj al-Balāghah, Ibn Abī al-Ḥadīd says:

> One of Abū Ja'far Muhammad ibn Ali al-Bāqir's companions asked him about God's Words, Mighty and Sublime is He:
>
> > *... save unto every messenger whom He hath chosen, and then He maketh a guard to go before him and a guard behind him ... (72:27).*
>
> He replied, 'Almighty God appoints angels for His prophets to count their deeds and to report to Him on their propagation of the message. He appointed a great angel for Muhammad from the time he was weaned to guide him towards good deeds and the best manners and keep him away from evil deeds and bad manners. It was he who would call out to him, 'Peace be upon you, Muhammad, Messenger of God,' when he was a young man and had not yet reached the state of being a messenger. He would think it was coming from a stone or the earth and look closely but not see anything.'[202]

See the Sermon of Disparagement for some of the Commander of the Faithful's words on this matter, some of which is cited above. It is Sermon no. 238 in *Sharḥ Nahj al-Balāghah* by Ibn Abī al-Ḥadīd.

According to *Tārīkh al-Ṭabarī*:

---

[202] Ibn Abī al-Ḥadīd, *Sharḥ Nahj al-Balāghah*, vol. 13, 207.

> Before Gabriel appeared to the Messenger of God with God's Message to him, he would receive and be marked out with the signs of someone whom God wants to honour and single out for His favour. An example of that was the aforementioned tradition about the two angels who came to him, cleft open his belly,[203] and extracted the rancour and impurity from it while he was with his wetnurse Ḥalīmah. Another example was his never passing a tree or stone when walking along a road without their greeting him.

Similarly:

> When he went out on errands he would go out so far that he could not see any houses. He would reach the clefts [between mountains] and the bottoms of valleys and not pass by a single stone or tree without its saying, 'Peace be upon you, Messenger of God.' He would turn to the right, left and right around but not see anyone.[204]

Based on al-Ya'qūbī's account:

> Gabriel would appear to him and speak to him or perhaps call to him from Heaven, from a tree or from a mountain. Then, he would say to him, 'Your Lord commands you to avoid the impurity of idols.' That was his first order. The Messenger of God would come to Khadījah, daughter of Khuwaylid, tell her what he had heard and talk about it. She would say to him, 'Keep it quiet, cousin. I swear by God that I hope God will do you good.[205]

The Messenger of God was forty when he was despatched on his prophetic mission. It was ten years into the reign of Khusraw Abarwīz ibn Hurmuz ibn Anushirwan.[206] According to al-Ya'qūbī:

---

[203] These words do not appear in any hadith transmitted from the People of the Household. They may signify intangible matters, and be for protecting him from shameful characteristics.

[204] *Tārīkh al-Ṭabarī*, vol. 2, 294-295.

[205] Aḥmad ibn Abī Ya'qūb ibn Ja'far ibn Wahb ibn Wāḍiḥ, *Tārīkh al-Ya'qūbī* (Najaf: al-Maktabat al-Ḥaydariyyah, 1384 q.), vol. 2, 17.

[206] 'Izz al-Dīn ibn al-Athīr, *al-Kāmil fi al-Tārīkh* (Beirut: Dār Ṣādir, 1399 q.), vol. 2, 29-30.

> He was despatched on the prophetic mission in the month of Rabīʿ al-Awwal, or as stated in the alternative, Ramaḍān. According to the non-Arab calendar it was in February.

He continues:

> Gabriel came to him on Friday night and Saturday night. Then, he appeared to him with the Message on Monday.[207]

Ibn Saʿd states:

> The angel came down to the Messenger of God in Ḥirā' on Monday the seventeenth of the month of Ramaḍān.[208]

According to Abū Jaʿfar al-Ṭabarī:

> This, that is, the revelation of the Message to him on a Monday, is something over which no people of knowledge disagree. They only disagree over which Monday it was. Some of them say that the Qur'an was revealed to God's Messenger on the eighteenth of Ramaḍān. Others say the twenty-fourth. Others say the seventeenth of the month of Ramaḍān. They rely on the Almighty's Words, *and that which We revealed unto Our slave on the Day of Separation, the day when the two armies met* (8:41), as evidence of that. It refers to God's Messenger's confrontation with the pagans at Badr, which was on the morning of the seventeenth of Ramaḍān.[209]

However, there is no indication in the verse that his despatch coincided with that date, first of all, because what is meant is the proofs of truth and signs of victory sent down to him, not the entire Qur'an or the commencement of its revelation. Secondly, we shall refer to the fact that the commencement of the revelation of the Qur'an, as heavenly scripture, came after the day he was despatched with the message, for he was despatched as a messenger to the people on 27 Rajab, and the Qur'an was revealed to him in the month of Ramaḍān on the Night of Destiny. It is possible that it was after a period of three years, as stated below. Thirdly, 'the Day of Separation' means the day on which truth was separated from and defeated falsehood, making it wane. It was a critical

---

[207] Ibn Wāḍiḥ, *Tārīkh al-Yaʿqūbī*, vol. 2, 17-18.

[208] Ibn Saʿd, *al-Tabaqāt al-Kubrā*, vol. 1, 129.

[209] *Tārīkh al-Ṭabarī*, vol. 2, 293-294.

day in the life of the Muslims. The Devil despaired on that day of ever being worshipped or obeyed.[210]

According to al-Mas'ūdī:

> The first part of the Qur'an to be revealed to him was:
>
> *Recite: In the Name of thy Lord...*
>
> Gabriel came to him on Friday night, then on Saturday night and addressed him, and communicated the Message to him on Monday. That was in Ḥirā'. It was the first place in which the Qur'an was revealed. He uttered the first chapter to him up to the words:
>
> *taught man what he knew not,*
>
> and the rest was revealed after that.That was five years after the Ka'bah was built, at the beginning of the twentieth year into Khusraw Abarwīz's reign and at the beginning of the two hundredth year after the treaty at Rabadhah.[211]
>
> It was six hundred and nine years after the birth of Christ.[212]

In our opinion, the correct date for his despatch on the mission was the twenty-seventh day of the month of Rajab, according to the People of the Household's traditions. It is commendable to fast and perform rites exclusive to that day, which the Imami Shi'a adhere to every year in veneration of this hallowed day on which blessing descended upon all people of the earth from the Gates of Heaven. It is because the Prophet was sent as a mercy to all the worlds that is is such a blessed day.

According to Imām al-Ṣādiq:

> On the twenty-seventh day of Rajab, prophethood came down upon the Messenger of God.[213]

He says:

[210] See al-Sayyid 'Abdallāh Shubbar, *Tafsīru Shubbar* (Cairo: al-Sayyid Murtaḍā al-Raḍawī, 1966), 195.

[211] Ali ibn al-Husayn al-Mas'ūdi, *Murūj al-Dhahab* (Beirut: al-Sharikah al-'Ālamiyyah li al-Nashr, 1989), vol. 2, 282.

[212] Jurjī Zaydān, *Tārīkh al-Tamaddun al-Islamī*, (Cairo: Dār al-Ḥilāl, 1958), vol. 1, 43.

[213] Ibn al-Sheikh, *al-Amālī* (Najaf, n.d.) 28; see Majlisī, *Biḥār al-Anwār*, vol. 18, 189.

> Do not fail to fast on the twenty-seventh day of Rajab, for it is the day on which prophethood came down upon Muhammad.[214]

Imām Riḍā explains:

> God, Mighty and Sublime is He, sent Muhammad as a mercy to all the worlds on the twenty-seventh of Rajab. God will record sixty months' fasting for whoever fasts on that day.[215]

The People of the Household's traditions on this matter are numerous.[216] Similarly, Ahl al-Sunnah have traditions specifying the same day.

In his biography, Ḥāfiẓ Dimyāṭī cites Abū Hurayrah:

> Almighty God will record sixty months' fasting for whoever fasts on the twenty-seventh of Rajab. It is the day on which Gabriel brought the Message down to the Prophet and the first day on which Gabriel came down.[217]

Bayhaqī narrates on the authority of Salmān al-Fārisī in *Shu'ab al-Īmān*:

> There is a night and day in Rajab. Whoever fasts that day and stands that night in prayer will be as one who has fasted for a hundred years and stood in prayer for a hundred years. It is three days before the end of Rajab. On that day God despatched Muhammad on the mission.[218]

The author of al-Manāqib narrates on the authority of both Ibn 'Abbās and Anas ibn Mālik:

> God revealed to Muhammad on Monday the twenty-seventh of Rajab. He was forty years old.[219]

According to 'Allāmah Majlisī:

---

[214] Kulaynī, *al-Kāfī*, vol. 4, 149.

[215] Kulaynī, *al-Kāfī*, vol. 4, 149.

[216] See Muhammad ibn al-Ḥasan al-Ḥurr al-'Āmilī, *Wasā'il al-Shī'ah* (Beirut: Dār Iḥyā' al-Turāth al-'Arabī), vol. 7, 329.

[217] Ibn Hishām, *al-Sīrat al-Nabawiyyah*, vol. 1, 238.

[218] Ali ibn Ḥasān al-Muttaqī al-Hindī, *Muntakhab Kanz al-'Ummāl*, (printed in the margin of Musnad Aḥmad ibn Ḥanbal, Beirut: Dār Ṣādir, n.d.), vol. 3, 362.

[219] Ibn Shahr Āshūb, *Manāqib Āl Abī Ṭālib*, vol. 1, 173; Majlisī, *Biḥār al-Anwār*, vol. 18, 205.

> They have five divergent opinions on the day on which the Prophet was despatched:
>
> First: the seventeenth of the month of Ramaḍān;
>
> Second: the eighteenth of the month of Ramaḍān;
>
> Third: the twenty-fourth of the month of Ramaḍān;
>
> Fourth:the twentieth of Rabīʿ al-Awwal;
>
> Fifth: the twenty-seventh of Rajab.
>
> The Shiʿa are agreed on the last one.[220]

My comment is that there are two more opinions – the eighth of Rabīʿ al-Awwal and the third of Rabīʿ al-Awwal – referred to by Ibn Burhān al-Ḥalabī in his biography. He then states the opinion that it was the twelfth of Rabīʿ al-Awwal – the day of the Prophet's birthday – to conform with the opinion that he was despatched at the beginning of the fortieth year.[221]

We consider that the majority of those who say that he was despatched in the month of Ramaḍān may have confused the beginning of his prophethood with the commencement of the revelation of the Qur'an as a Book in which there is clarification of everything. This confusion seems to arise from the interpretation of everything that indicates that the Qur'an was revealed on the Night of Destiny in the month of Ramaḍān as evidence of the date of his despatch. We can demonstrate that there is no link between the two incidents. He was despatched on the 27th Rajab. However, the Qur'an began to be revealed to the Prophet in the month of Ramaḍān – on the Night of Destiny– three years after he had become a prophet. The duration of his prophethood was twenty three years. However, the revelation of the Qur'an was spread over twenty years. It commenced at the beginning of the fourth year after the despatch and ended with his death in the tenth year after the Migration.

---

220 Majlisī, *Biḥār al-Anwār*, vol. 18, 190.

221 Ibn Hishām, *al-Sīrat al-Nabawiyyah*, vol. 1, 238.

The Beginning of the Revelation of the Qur'an

There is no doubt that the Qur'an was revealed to the Messenger of God on the Night of Destiny in the blessed month of Ramaḍān according to the Almighty's Words:

> *The month of Ramaḍān in which was revealed the Qur'an* (2:185);
>
> *We have sent it down in a blessed night* (44:3)

and:

> *Lo! We revealed it on the Night of Destiny* (97:1).

According to us, the Night of Destiny is one of two of the last ten nights of the blessed month of Ramaḍān – either the 21st or the 23rd. It is more likely to be the latter on the basis of al-Juhanī's tradition.[222]

According to al-Ṣadūq:

> Our Sheikhs unanimously agree that it is the twenty-third night.[223]

Working out the date of the Night of Destiny is not the matter at hand. All that concerns us is the assessment of certain aspects of it, such as the revelation of the Qur'an on a single night – the Night of Destiny – within the month of Ramaḍān.

Firstly, it appears to contradict what we have stated above regarding the Shi'a consensus and a number of traditions circulated by others which say that the despatch was in Rajab. There is no doubt that the despatch coincided with the revelation of some verses – five verses from the beginning of *The Blood Clot* (*Sūrah al-'Alaq*) – so how can that be, considering the belief that the Qur'an was revealed in its entirety or partially at the beginning of its revelation in the month of Ramaḍān on the Night of Destiny?

Secondly, what is meant by the Qur'an being revealed on a single night – the Night of Destiny? Was the entire Qur'an revealed in one go on that night, even though we know that the Qur'an was revealed in instalments

---

222 See al-Ḥurr al-'Āmilī, *Wasā'il al-Shī'ah*, vol. 7, 262.

223 Abū Ja'far Muhammad ibn Ali ibn al-Ḥusayn ibn Bābawayh al-Qummī al-Ṣadūq, *al-Khiṣāl* (Qum: Jāmi'at al-Mudarrisīn, 1403 q.), 519.

over a period of twenty or twenty-three years, coinciding with various incidents and circumstances called the reasons for revelation (*asbāb al-nuzūl*)? How do these matters relate to each other?

And thirdly, what was the first verse or chapter of the Qur'an to be revealed? If it were *The Blood Clot* (*Sūrah al-'Alaq*), or verses from it, why is *The Praise* (*al-Ḥamd*) called *The Opening of the Book* (*Fātiḥat al-Kitāb*)? It cannot mean that it was written at the beginning of the codex, because this arrangement came after the death of the Prophet, or at the very least during a late stage in his life, in spite of the fact that it had from the time it was first revealed been known as *The Opening*. According to a tradition from the Prophet's tongue, there is no prayer without *The Opening*[224].

To answer these three questions in broad terms, we say that the beginning of the mission is different from the commencement of the Qur'an's revelation as Heavenly Scripture, because the Prophet was only commanded to tell everyone that he was a prophet three years after having become one, during which period he invited people in secret, until the following verse was revealed:

> *So proclaim that which thou art commanded, and withdraw from the idolaters* (15:94).

From that time onwards, the Qur'an began to be revealed serially as a Book sent down from Heaven. It was recorded over twenty years on palm leaves and pottery, written down by a small number of believers who knew how to write.

The revelation of the Qur'an commenced after the initial phase, on the Night of Destiny, in the month of Ramaḍān. In this respect, it is true to say that the Qur'an was revealed on the Night of Destiny, even though its revelation was spread over twenty years, because every important event has a particular duration, and history records its first appearance, as will be discussed in detail.

As for the earliest revelation, it was the first five verses of *The Blood Clot* (*Sūrah al-'Alaq*). The rest of it was revealed later on. However, the first complete chapter of the Qur'an to be revealed was *The Praise* (*Sūrah al-Ḥamd*), and hence it was called *The Opening* (*al-Fātiḥah*). This is a summary of these matters which are followed up in more detail below.

---

[224] Al-Muttaqī al-Hindī, *Muntakhab Kanz al-'Ummāl*, vol. 3, 180.

The period of three years

Let us suppose that the despatch was in Rajab, in line with the tradition of the People of the Household and a number of others. However, the Qur'an, as a Heavenly Book and eternal, divine constitution, was only revealed three years later; in the interim, the Prophet hid his mission from the people at large and invited individuals to God in secret. Hence, apart from verbal attacks, the pagans did not set about harassing him, because they did not see in his affair anything to fear for their religion.

Four people would pray with the Messenger of God at that time: Ali, Ja'far, Zayd and Khadījah. Every time a crowd of Quraysh passed by them they would mock them.

According to Ali ibn Ibrāhīm al-Qummī:

> After three years, God revealed to him: *So proclaim that which thou art commanded, and withdraw from the idolaters. Lo! We defend thee from the scoffers ...* (15:94-95). He says that that was three years after he was made a Prophet.[225]

Al-Ya'qūbī states:

> The Messenger of God remained in Mecca for three years, hiding his mandate.[226]

Muhammad ibn Isḥāq says:

> Three years after he was despatched, *So proclaim that which thou art commanded...* was revealed and he was instructed to make his call public and issue counsel for everyone.[227]

According to Imām al-Ṣādiq:

> The Messenger of God remained in Mecca for thirteen years after revelation came to him from Blessed and Almighty God, including three years out of view and afraid, not exposing his mandate

[225] *Tafsīr al-Qummī*, vol. 1. 378; Majlisī, *Biḥār al-Anwār*, vol. 18, 53 and 179.

[226] Ibn Wāḍiḥ, *Tārīkh al-Ya'qūbī*, vol. 2, 19.

[227] Ibn Hishām, *al-Sīrat al-Nabawiyyah*, 1:280; Ibn Shahr Āshūb, *Manāqib Āl Abī Ṭālib*, vol. 1, 43; Majlisī, *Biḥār al-Anwār*, vol. 18, 193-194.

> until God told him to proclaim what he had been commanded and make his call known.[228]

If we consider these traditions in conjunction with the traditions that say that the Qur'an was revealed to the Prophet over a period of twenty years, they tell us that the Qur'anic revelation comenced three years after the despatch, because there is no doubt that the revelation continued right up until the year of his death. This fits in with the opinion that the Qur'anic revelation commenced in the month of Ramaḍān on the Night of Destiny, as explicitly stated in the Holy Qur'an itself.

Imām al-Ṣādiq said:

> Then the Qur'an was revealed over twenty years.

This is according to Kulaynī's[229] and al-'Ayyāshī's[230] traditions, and al-Ṣadūq[231] and Majlisī[232] alluded to it; there are many texts which specify that the period during which the Qur'an was revealed was twenty years.[233]

The tradition on the authority of Sa'īd ibn al-Musayyab makes a similar allusion:

> Revelation came down to the Prophet when he was forty-three years old.[234]

This would be so, because there is no doubt that prophethood devolved upon him when he had completed forty years. If everyone else agrees on this, then how can it elude someone like Sa'īd?

Al-Wāḥidī narrates via a chain of narration going back to al-Sha'bī:

---

228 Abū Ja'far Muhammad ibn al-Ḥasan al-Ṭūsī, *al-Ghaybah* (Qum: Mu'assasat al-Ma'ārif al-Islamiyyah, 1411 q.), 333; al-Ṣadūq, *Kamāl al-Dīn*, vol. 2, 344; Majlisī, *Biḥār al-Anwār*, vol. 18, 177.

229 Kulaynī, *al-Kāfī*, vol. 2, 628-629.

230 *Tafsīr al-'Ayyāshī*, vol. 1, 80.

231 Abū Ja'far Muhammad ibn Ali ibn al-Ḥusayn ibn Mūsā ibn Bābawayh al-Qummī al-Ṣadūq, *al-I'tiqādāt fī Dīn al-Imāmiyyah* (lithograph, Tehran: Markaz Nashr Kitāb, 1370 s.), 101.

232 Majlisī, *Biḥār al-Anwār*, vol. 18, 250 and 253.

233 See al-Suyūṭī *al-Itqān*, vol. 1, 118 and *Tafsīru Shubbar*, 350.

234 Abū 'Abdillāh al-Ḥākim al-Naysābūrī, *al-Mustadrak 'alā al-Ṣaḥīḥayn* (Beirut: Dār al-Ma'rifah), vol. 2, 610.

> God divided up His Revelation and its beginning to end was a period of twenty years, or roughly twenty years.[235]

Even clearer is what Imām Aḥmad narrates via an unbroken chain back to 'Āmir al-Sha'bī:

> Prophethood came down upon the Messenger of God when he was forty years old, so Raphael was linked to his prophethood for three years. He would teach him, but the Qur'an was not revealed. After three years, Gabriel was linked to his prophethood and the Qur'an was revealed upon his tongue over twenty years, ten in Mecca and ten in Medina. He died when he was sixty-three years old. According to Ibn Kathīr, it is an authentic chain of narration back to al-Sha'bī.[236]

Even though this tradition contains things which we do not concede, which may be the result of al-Sha'bī's own interpretation (*ijtihād*), what is of use to us in this narration is the reference to the Qur'an's revelation taking twenty years, and that it commenced three years after the despatch. This is something upon which there is consensus.

Views and Interpretations

Scholars have various opinions and interpretations of what is meant by the revelation of the Qur'an on the Night of Destiny in the month of Ramaḍān. In view of the fact that we know that the Qur'an was revealed serially over twenty or twenty three years, and at particular times and in various circumstances, the following assertions have been made:

1) That the revelation began on the Night of Destiny in the month of Ramaḍān.

This is the view of Muhammad ibn Isḥāq[237] and al-Sha'bī[238]. According to Imām Rāzī:

---

[235] Abu al-Ḥasan Ali ibn Aḥmad al-Wāhidī, *Asbābu Nuzūl al-Āyāt* (Cairo: Mu'assasat al-Ḥalabī wa Shurakā'ihi li al-Nashr wa al-Tawzī', 1968), 3.

[236] Abu al-Fidā' Ismā'īl ibn Kathīr al-Dimashqī, *al-Bidāyah wa al-Nihāyah* (Beirut: Dār Ihyā' al-Turāth al-'Arabī, 1988), vol. 3, 4; al-Suyūṭī, *al-Itqān*, vol. 1, 128; Ibn Sa'd, *al-Ṭabaqāt al-Kubrā*, vol. 1, 127; Ibn Wāḍiḥ, *Tārīkh al-Ya'qūbī*, vol. 2, 18.

[237] Ṭabrisī, *Majma' al-Bayān*, vol. 2, 276.

[238] Al-Suyūṭī, *al-Itqān*, vol. 1, 119.

> That is because calendars are based on when nations and states begin, on account of their being the most important times, and because they are also precise, known times.[239]

Zamakhsharī also explains the verse this way:

> Its revelation to him began then.[240]

This is the opinion we adopt in view of the fact that if any important event is protracted over a period of time, history records its start date, just as with the time of the formation of a state, foundation or particular group, or some other particular event; for if one is asked about such things, the answer will invariably be the date when it began.

Also, there are God's Words, *wherein the Qur'an was sent down* (2:185), and other such verses, for if it were otherwise, they would be in the present tense or adjectival. These very words are evidence that some of the Qur'an was revealed after the Night of Destiny, unless of course they are interpreted without reference to evidence, as will be explained below, just as the the relevence of different verses accord with particular circumstances. This the greatest proof that they were revealed in different places, because it links every specific verse with a particular time and place. This is true of every verse that pertains to a particular incident at a particular time – the verse is revealed there and then, to address the situation. All this proves that the Qur'an was not all revealed at once. Otherwise, there would have been no reason for the pagans to say:

> *Why is the Qur'an not revealed to him all at once?* (25:32).

The Almighty responded as follows:

> *(It is revealed) thus that We may strengthen thy heart therewith; and We have arranged it in right order* (25:32)

This means that it was more supportive for the revelation to be in instalments and at appropriate times, so that the Prophet's heart would be reassured with the realisation of the presence of God's continuous care at all times and on every occasion.

---

[239] Rāzī, *al-Tafsīr al-Kabīr*, vol. 5, 85.

[240] Abu al-Qāsim Jārallāh Maḥmūd ibn 'Umar al-Zamakhsharī, *al-Kashshāf 'an Ḥaqā'iq al-Tanzīl wa 'Uyūn al-Aqāwīl* (Beirut: Dār al-Kitāb al-'Arabī, 1947), vol. 1, 227.

Ibn Shahr Āshūb also expresses this opinion in *Manāqib Āl Abī Ṭālib*, where he says:

> The month of Ramaḍān wherein the Qur'an was sent down means the revelation began.

In *Mutashābihāt al-Qu'rān* he contends that:

> The correct view is that 'Qur'an' here does not mean the whole of it. Instead it means the genus. Anything revealed fits the literal meaning.[241]

It appears from the end of his response to Abū Ja'far al-Ṣadūq *infra* that Sheikh Mufīd is also of this opinion:

> What may be meant by the tradition which says that the Qur'an was revealed *jumlatan* on the Night of Destiny is that a portion (*jumlatun*) of it was revealed on the Night of Destiny. Then, it was followed by revelations up until the Prophet's death. As for its being revealed in its entirety on the Night of Destiny, that is far from what the literal meaning of the Qur'an, indubitable traditions (*al-mutawātir min al-akhbār*) and the consensus of the scholars dictate, in spite of the difference in their opinions.[242]

2) What people needed that year from the Qur'an would be revealed to the Prophet every Night of Destiny. Then, as needed, Gabriel would bring down what Almighty God told him to. Thus, what is meant by 'Ramaḍān' is every Ramaḍān, not a specific Ramaḍān. It is an explanation which Imām Rāzī believed to be possible.[243]

This opinion is adopted by Ibn Jurayj[244] and al-Suddī, and also attributed by the latter to Ibn 'Abbās.[245] Al-Qurṭubī cites it on the authority of Muqātil ibn Ḥayyān, and al-Ḥalīmī and al-Mārūdi agree with it.[246]

---

[241] Ibn Shahr Āshūb, *Manāqib Āl Abī Ṭālib*, vol. 1, 173; Ibn Shahr Āshūb, *Mutashābih al-Qur'an wa Mukhtalafuh* (Qum: Bīdār, 1328 s.), vol. 1, 63.

[242] Mufīd, *Taṣḥīḥu I'tiqādāt al-Imāmiyyah*, 58.

[243] Rāzī, *al-Tafsīr al-Kabīr*, vol. 5, 85.

[244] Al-Suyūṭī, *al-Durr al-Manthūr*, vol. 1, 189.

[245] Ṭabrisī , *Majma' al-Bayān*, vol. 2, 276.

[246] Al-Suyūṭī, *al-Itqān*, vol. 1, 118.

However, this choice contradicts the literal meaning of the Almighty's Words *wherein...was sent down* (2:185) and *We sent it down* (97:1), which refer to a past event, otherwise it would have been more appropriate to say, 'We are sending it down (*nunazziluhu*).'

Another problem with this is what we think to be remote about the fifth opinion (see *infra*), which asks why the Qur'an would be revealed before it is needed. And this is indicative of its being revealed in relation to particular incidents, and not before.

3) *Shahru Ramaḍān alladhī unzila fīhi al-Qur'an* means 'The month of Ramaḍān, about which the Qur'an was revealed,' and is used in this context to mean that fasting was made mandatory, just as one says the Qur'an was revealed about So-and-So or about such-and-such an occasion. What is meant here by 'the Qur'an' is one or more verses of it.[247]

According to al-Ḍaḥḥāk, *Shahru Ramaḍān alladhī unzila fīhi al-Qur'an* (2:185) means the month of Ramaḍān regarding which the duty to fast was revealed in the Qur'an.[248] This is the opinion chosen by al-Husayn ibn al-Faḍl and Ibn al-Anbāri.[249]

However, this explanation is restricted to the verse in *The Cow* (*Sūrah al-Baqarah*). It does not apply to the verses in *The Smoke* (*Sūrah al-Dukhān*) and *The (Night of) Destiny* (*Sūrah al-Qadr*), as is obvious, not to mention that it is an interpretation (*ta'wīl*) of the wording for which there is no reason or evidential basis.

4) Most of the Qur'an was revealed in the month of Ramaḍān. Hence it is correct to attribute the whole of it to it. This is a second explanation considered to be possible by Sayyid Quṭb. He asserts:

> The month...wherein the Qur'an was sent down means either that its revelation began in the month of Ramaḍān or that most of it was revealed during months of Ramaḍān.[250]

However, there is no evidence that most of the verses of the Qur'an were revealed during months of Ramaḍān, or specifically on the Night of Destiny. It may be more realistic to dismiss this possibility altogether.

---

[247] Ṭabrisī, *Majma' al-Bayān*, vol. 1, 276; Zamakhsharī, *al-Kashshāf*, vol. 1, 227.

[248] Al-Suyūṭī, *al-Durr al-Manthūr*, vol. 1, 190.

[249] Rāzī, *al-Tafsīr al-Kabīr*, vol. 5, 85.

[250] Sayyid Quṭb, *Fī Ẓilāl al-Qur'an* (Cairo: Dār al-Shurūq, 1400 q.), vol. 2, 245.

5) The Qur'an was sent down complete on one night, namely the Night of Destiny, to the House of Might (*Bayt al-'Izzah*) or the Inhabited House (*al-Bayt al-Ma'mūr*). Then, it was sent down to the Messenger of God at different times in relation to particular events over a period of twenty or twenty- three years. A number of hadith scholars believe this in light of the literal meaning of various traditions.

Sheikh Ṣadūq states:

> The Qur'an was sent down complete in the month of Ramaḍān on the Night of Destiny to the Inhabited House in the Fourth Heaven. Then it was sent down from the Inhabited House over a period of twenty years. God gave the knowledge to the Prophet in one go. Then, He said to him: *And hasten not with the Qur'an ere its revelation hath been perfected unto thee...* (20:114).[251]

'Allāmah Majlisī says as a follow-up to this statement:

> Verses indicate that the Qur'an was sent down on the Night of Destiny. It is likely that it was sent down in its entirety. Textual evidence and oral narrations indicate that it was sent down over twenty[252] or twenty-three years.[253] Some traditions say that the Qur'an was sent down on the first night of the month of Ramaḍān. Some indicate that its revelation began with the despatch.[254] They can be reconciled by saying that on the Night of Destiny, the Qur'an came down complete from the Guarded Tablet (*al-lawḥ al-maḥfūẓ*) to the Fourth Heaven (the Inhabited House), to come gradually down from the fourth heaven to the earth.
>
> The whole of the Qur'an came down to the Prophet on the first night of the month of Ramaḍān for him to know, but not to recite to the people. Then, it began to be revealed verse by verse and

---

[251] Al-Ṣadūq, *al-I'tiqādāt fī Dīn al-Imāmiyyah*, 101.

[252] Kulaynī, *al-Kāfī*, vol. 2, 628-629.

[253] The length of his prophethood, assuming that the revelation began on the day he was despatched on the prophetic mission and ended with his passing.

[254] Narrations indicating that the first chapter to be revealed was *The Blood Clot*, revealed at the beginning of the despatch on 27 Rajab. See Majlisī, *Biḥār al-Anwār*, vol. 92, 39; vol. 18, 206.

> chapter by chapter at the despatch and at other times for him to recite to the people.[255]

Ṭabarānī and others cite on the authority of Ibn 'Abbās that the Qur'an was sent down complete on the Night of Destiny to the Lower Heaven and it was placed in the House of Might (*bayt al-'izzah*). Thereafter, it was sent down to the Prophet serially over twenty years.

According to Jalāl al-Dīn, this is the likeliest and most commonly held opinion. Many traditions, most of which are deemed to be authentic, are narrated to that effect on the authority of Hākim, Ṭabarānī, Bayhaqī, Nisā'ī and others.[256]

Ṭabarī narrates via his chain of narration on the authority of Wāthilah ibn al-Asqa' that the Prophet said:

> The scrolls of Abraham were sent down on the first night of the month of Ramaḍān, the Torah was sent down six days into Ramaḍān, the Gospel was sent down thirteen days in, and the Qur'an was sent down on the twenty-fourth of Ramaḍān.[257]

Ṭabarī also says that al-Suddī says on the authority of Ibn 'Abbās:

> 'The month of Ramaḍān' and 'the Blessed Night' mean the Night of Destiny, for the Night of Destiny is the Blessed Night. And it is in Ramaḍān. The Qur'an was sent down in one go to the Inhabited House. It is the position of the stars in the world's heaven where the Qur'an fell. Then it came down to Muhammad after that, with regard to commands and prohibitions and about wars, little by little.[258]

Doubt about this verse had crept into 'Aṭiyyah ibn al-Aswad's soul, because the Qur'an had come down in all the months of the year. So he asked Ibn 'Abbās about it and he gave him the above answer.[259]

So, too, narrates Jalāl al-Dīn via his chain of narration back to Jābir ibn 'Abdillāh al-Anṣāri:

---

[255] Majlisī, *Biḥār al-Anwār*, vol. 18, 253-254.

[256] Al-Suyūṭī, *al-Itqān*, vol. 1, 116-117.

[257] Ṭabarī, *Jāmi' al-Bayān*, vol. 2, 84.

[258] Ṭabarī, *Jāmi' al-Bayān*, vol. 2, 84-85.

[259] Al-Suyūṭī, *al-Durr al-Manthūr*, vol. 1, 189.

> God sent the scrolls of Abraham down on the first night of Ramaḍān, sent the Torah down to Moses six days into Ramaḍān, sent the Psalms down to David twelve days into Ramaḍān, sent the Gospel down to Jesus eighteen days into Ramaḍān, and sent the Furqān down to Muhammad twenty-four days into Ramaḍān.[260]

Via our chains of narration, 'Ayyāshī narrates that Ibrāhīm asked Imām al-Ṣādiq about the Almighty's Words:

> *The month of Ramaḍān in which was revealed the Qur'an...* (2:185)
>
> How was the Qur'an sent down in this way when the Qur'an was sent down over twenty years from beginning to end?

The Imām replied:

> The Qur'an came down complete in the month of Ramaḍān to the Inhabited House. Then it was sent down from the Inhabited House over twenty years.

He then continued:

> The Prophet said, 'The scrolls of Abraham came down on the first night of the month of Ramaḍān, the Torah was sent down six nights into the month of Ramaḍān, the Gospel thirteen nights into the month of Ramaḍān, the Psalms were sent down on the eighteenth of Ramaḍān, and the Qur'an was sent down on the twenty-fourth of Ramaḍān.[261]

The same hadith also appears in *al-Kāfī*, except that it says at the end:

> ...and the Qur'an was sent down on the twenty-third of the month of Ramaḍān.

The narration is on the authority of al-Ḥafṣ ibn Ghiyāth.[262]

Part of the hadith appears in *Tahdhīb al-Aḥkām*, narrated by Abū Baṣīr. At the end it says:

---

[260] Ibid.

[261] *Tafsīr al-'Ayyāshī*, vol. 1, 80.

[262] Kulaynī, *al-Kāfī*, vol. 2, 628-629.

> ...and the Furqān came down on the Night of Destiny.[263]

These are collected traditions which explain the Qur'an's being sent down in one go in one night, either to the Inhabited House in the Fourth Heaven according to Shi'a narrations, or to the House of Might in the Lower Heaven according to some Sunni narrations; from there, its verses came down separately, little by little to the Messenger of God in relation to particular circumstances.

Hadith literalists take these traditions at face value, and seek comfort for themselves by straightforward acceptance.

In contrast, critical scholars were not content to merely accept what seemed incomprehensible; there is, after all, no duty to slavishly accept anything which has nothing to do with the fundamentals of worship. Hence, they began criticising these hadiths in a scholarly fashion, asking themselves what palpable good there was in the Qur'an's coming down all at once to one of the High Heavens, then coming down gradually to the Messenger of God.

In answer to this question, Fakhr Rāzī says that it may be that it was to make it easy for Gabriel, or for the benefit of the Prophet who would be awaiting revelation from the nearest point.[264]

However, this response is very weak and has no foundation. Furthermore, it is conjecture about the unseen. We are surprised at such empty words issuing from someone so skilled in analysis.

Mawlā[265] Fayḍ Kāshānī says:

> It is as if this means its coming down to the Prophet's heart, as in the Almighty's Words, *Which the True Spirit brought down upon thy heart*...(26:193-194). Thereafter it came down in instalments spread over twenty years, from the bottom of his heart to the tip of his tongue, every time Gabriel brought him revelation and recited it to him in words.[266]

---

[263] Abū Ja'far Muhammad ibn al-Ḥasan al-Ṭūsī, *Tahdhīb al-Aḥkām fī Sharḥ al-Muqanni'ah li al-Sheikh al-Mufīd* (Tehran, Dār al-Kutub al-Islamiyyah, 1365 s.), vol. 4, 193-194.

[264] Rāzī, *al-Tafsīr al-Kabīr*, vol. 5, 85.

[265] Honorific title translatable as 'Master.' [Trans.]

[266] Fayḍ Kāshānī, *al-Ṣāfī fī Tafsīr al-Qur'an*, vol. 1, 42.

He interprets the Inhabited House as the Messenger's heart, and it is possible that al-Ṣadūq also means the same by saying that:

> He gave the knowledge to the Prophet in one fell swoop.

Sheikh Abū 'Abdillāh al-Zanjānī also favours the same interpretation of this tradition. He contends:

> We may say that the spirit of the Qur'an, namely the universal objective for which it is intended, manifested to his noble heart on that night: *Which the True Spirit brought down upon thy heart...* (26:193-194). Then it appeared on his actual tongue spread over twenty years: *And (it is) a Qur'an which We have divided, that thou mayst recite it unto mankind at intervals, and We have revealed it by (successive) revelation* (17:106).[267]

'Allāmah Ṭabāṭabā'ī takes this interpretation and explores it further, asserting:

> The Book has another reality beyond what we comprehend through ordinary understanding. It is a reality with a coherent unity which cannot be divided up or broken into parts, on account of its going back to a single meaning with no parts or sections. This division into sections seen in the Scripture only happened subsequent to the coherent unity. God said, *(This is) a Book whose verses are perfected (uḥkimat) and then expounded (fuṣṣilat), from One Wise, Informed ...* (11:1); *this is indeed a noble Qur'an in a Book kept hidden which none toucheth save the purified* (56:77-79); and, *Verily We have brought them a Scripture which We expound with knowledge, a guidance and a mercy for a people who believe* (7:52).
>
> So what is meant by the Qur'an's being sent down on the Night of Destiny is the Book's consolidated reality being sent down, all at once, to the Messenger's heart, just as the divided up Book was gradually sent down in parts, also to his heart, throughout the duration of his calling as a prophet.[268]

---

[267] See *Tārīkh al-Qur'an*, 10.

[268] Ṭabāṭabā'ī, *al-Mīzān*, vol. 2, 14-16. This is heavily paraphrased as is the author's custom when quoting. [Trans.]

What he says is all very well. However, it is no more than a particular reading which has no evidence. Above all, the matter is textual, and neither rational nor academic. Hence we might ask these luminaries what the basis is for interpreting the Inhabited House – which is in the Fourth Heaven according to Shi'a traditions, or the House of Might according to Sunni traditions – as the Prophet's heart. Why was this expression worded this way?

In the section on allegorical verses, we shall debate Sayyid 'Allāmah's view of there being more than one dimension to the Qur'an.

A useful enquiry

According to al-'Allāmah al-Sheikh Abū 'Abdillāh al-Mufīd:

> The basis of the position taken by Abū Ja'far under this heading is a *khabar wāḥid* i.e. it is not indubitable (*al-mutawātir al-maqtū' bihi*). It does not make knowledge or action necessary. Revelation of the Qur'an for reasons occurring, incident by incident, indicate the opposite of what this hadith says. For the Qur'an contains rulings on what happened, and states what occurred the way it occurred. That is only plausible if revelation occurred at the time of the reason for the said revelation.
>
> For example there are the Almighty's Words, *God has heard the saying of her that disputeth with thee concerning her husband, and complaineth unto God. And God heareth your dialogue ...* (58:1).
>
> This verse was revealed in relation to Khawlah bint Khuwaylid, who came to complain about her husband Aws ibn al-Ṣāmit, who had divorced her by way of *ẓihār* – a type of divorce which was valid during the days of ignorance.[269]
>
> Other examples are the Almighty's Words, *But when they spy some merchandise or pastime they break away to it and leave thee standing* (62:11); and, *Of the believers are men who are true to what they covenanted with God. Some of them have fulfilled their vow by death (in battle), and some of them still are waiting; and they have not altered in the least ...* (33:23).

[269] Ṭabrisī, *Majma' al-Bayān*, vol. 9, 246.

> Words in the past tense – 'they said' (*qālū*), 'they came' (*jā'ū*) and 'he came' (*jā'a*) – are common in the Qur'an. It also contains that which abrogates and that which has been abrogated. None of this is compatible with its having been revealed complete, at a time before any of that had happened.

He says further:

> If we follow up the stories in the Qur'an, we find that what we have referred to comes up frequently – there is not enough room in the treatise to deal with it all. How similar this hadith is to the position (*madhhab*) of the anthropomorphists who claim that God has always spoken the Qur'an, i.e., belief in the sempiternity of the Qur'an, telling of what will be using the past tense. Monotheists (*ahl al-tawḥīd*) have responded to them in the way we have stated.
>
> It is possible that the tradition which says that the Qur'an was sent down *jumalatan* on the Night of Destiny means that the essential meaning (*jumlah*) of it came down on the Night of Destiny, then it was followed by what came down periodically up to the death of the Prophet. The whole of it coming down in its entirety on the Night of Destiny is a departure from what is dictated by the literal meaning of the Qur'an, unquestionable traditions and the consensus of scholars, despite the different opinions of the latter.[270]

According to al-Murtaḍā 'Alam al-Hudā:

> If the position taken by Abū Ja'far ibn Bābawayh – certainty of its being revealed in one go – is based on traditions narrated by him, those traditions are hadiths narrated via one or only a very few chains (*āḥād*), and this is not grounds for certainty. Conversely, there are many other more widely circulated traditions which state that it was not revealed all at once, that some of it was revealed in Mecca and some in Medina. That is why some of the Qur'an is said to be Meccan and some Medinan. When events such as *ẓihār* divorce and other such things occurred, he would wait for what would be revealed to him from the Qur'an, saying, 'Nothing has been revealed to me on this matter.' Had the Qur'an been sent

[270] Mufīd, *Taṣḥīḥu I'tiqādāt al-Imāmiyyah*, 58.

> down all at once, that would not have happened, and the ruling on *ẓihār* and other matters over which he hesitated would have been known to him. One does not resile from such evident, widely circulated matters solely on the basis of isolated narrations.
>
> As for the Qur'an itself, it states, *And those who disbelieve say: Why is the Qur'an not revealed unto him all at once?* (25:32). If it had been sent down all at once, the response to them would have been that it was sent down as you suggested, and not, *(It is revealed) thus that We may strengthen thy heart therewith; and We have arranged it in right order (wa rattalnāhu tartīlā)* (25:32).

All the exegetes have interpreted that by saying that it means: 'We sent it that way, i.e., in instalments, to give it a chance to be heard and to progress gradually, enabling it to be digested. *Tartīl* also means 'one thing appearing after another.' Construing it otherwise is incorrect, because the literal meaning contradicts it, and the people did not say, 'Why did we not know that the Qur'an was sent down all at once?' They said, 'Why has the Qur'an not been revealed all at once?' If it had been sent like that, the response would have been, 'It was as you asked,' and there would have been no argument for it being revealed in instalments as the end of the verse states.

As for the verse, *The month of Ramaḍān in which was revealed the Qur'an* (2:185), it indicates that the genus of the Qur'an – most of it or the beginning of it – came down in this month. It does not indicate that the whole of it came down then.

And as for the verse, *And hasten not with the Qur'an ere its revelation hath been perfected unto thee* (20:114), we do not understand how it can mean that it was sent down all at once. It should be explained how it could mean that. The verse is more indicative of the opposite, because the Almighty said, *Ere its revelation hath been perfected unto thee*, which indicates that more was to come before it was completed.

A long time ago I was asked to write an interpretation of this verse and wrote a comprehensive treatise on it. I cited two explanations given by the exegetes and added a third explanation which was mine alone. One of the two exegeses was that when the angel brought some of the Qur'an, the Prophet would recite before the angel had finished, keen to remember and master it. So he was told to wait until the recitation was finished, because parts of it depended on others.

The second one was that he was told not to pass on any of the Qur'an before it had been revealed to him, along with its meaning and interpretation.

My own explanation was that he was told not to demand what had not yet been revealed to him of the Qur'an, because whatever he needed would inevitably be revealed to him without his asking, because God does not withhold what he needs. What he does not need is not sent down in any event, and so there is no need to ask. Thus the verse has nothing to do with the matter at hand.[271]

The Difference between *Inzāl* and *Tanzīl*

Another point relied upon by those who say that the Qur'an was sent down twice – first complete and then gradually – is the difference between the words, *inzāl* and *tanzīl*, which are used in this context. They say that whenever *inzāl al-Qur'an* is used, what is meant is its entire revelation. Examples of this phraseology are in God's words:

> *The month of Ramaḍān in which the Qur'an was revealed* (unzila) (2:185);

> *Lo! We revealed it* (anzalnāhu) *on a blessed night* (44:3);

and:

> *Lo! We revealed it* (anzalnāhu) *on the Night of Destiny*(97:1).

As for the word *tanzīl*, it means coming down gradually:

> *And (it is) a Qur'an that We have divided, that thou mayest recite it unto mankind at intervals, and We have revealed it* (wa nazzalnāhu) *by (successive) revelation.* (17:106).

Al-Zamakhsharī asks rhetorically why it is that God says *nazzala* in respect of the Book, and *anzala* regarding the Torah and the Gospel, in the following:

---

[271] *Jawāb al-Masā'il al-Ṭarābulusīyyāt* (Answer to the Three Questions from Tripoli), in the first group of treatises in al-Sharīf al-Murtaḍā, *Rasā'il al-Sharīf al-Murtaḍā* (Qum: Dār al-Qur'an al-Karīm, 1405 q.), 403-405.

> *He hath revealed* (nazzala) *unto thee the Scripture with truth, confirming that which was before it, even as He revealed* (wa anzala) *the Torah and the Gospel* (3:3).

And he answers himself by saying that the Qur'an came down in instalments whereas the other two Scriptures came down all at once.[272]

According to al-Rāghib:

> The difference between *inzāl* and *tanzīl* describing the Qur'an and the angels is that *tanzīl* is exclusively used to indicate that it is sent down one instalment after another whereas *inzāl* is general.

His comment on the first three verses is:

> The only reason for using the word *inzāl* instead of *tanzīl* is because of what is narrated – that the Qur'an came down all at once to the lower heaven and then came down instalment by instalment. In the Almighty's Words, *The wandering Arabs are more hard in disbelief and hypocrisy, and more likely to be ignorant of the limits which God hath revealed* (anzala) *unto His Messenger* (9:97).
>
> The word *inzāl* is used to refer to either. Also in the verse, *If We had caused* (law anzalnā) *this Qur'an to descend upon a mountain...* (59:21), God did not say *law nazzalnā*, thus drawing attention to the fact that if it had been revealed to the mountain once what was conferred upon the Prophet in several parts, then *...thou wouldst have seen it humbled...*(59:21).[273]

Our Sayyid 'Allāmah Ṭabāṭabā'ī followed them in that and confirmed it, insisting that *inzāl* was only used on account of the non-composite (*basīṭ*) reality of the Qur'an coming down all at once on the Night of Destiny in the month of Ramaḍān. As for its *tanzīl*, it means its distinct parts coming down gradually throughout the Prophet's lifetime.[274]

However, the truth appears to be something else, for the unbelievers asked:

> *Why is the Qur'an not revealed* (nuzzila) *unto him all at once?* (25:32).

---

[272] Zamakhsharī, *al-Kashshāf*, vol. 1, 336.

[273] Al-Rāghib, *al-Mufradāt*, 489.

[274] Ṭabāṭabā'ī, *al-Mīzān*, vol. 2, 14.

So the Qur'an coming down all at once is referred to as *tanzīl*. There is also:

> ...*We would have sent down* (nazzalnā) *for them from heaven an angel as messenger* (17:95).

But an angel is an individual entity, and does not come down gradually in parts.

And even though the sign comes down alone, the same is true in the following:

> *They say: Why hath no portent been sent down* (nuzzila) *upon him from his Lord?* (6:37).

The same applies to God's Words:

> *And those who believe say: O, if only a chapter were revealed* (nuzzilat)*!* (47:20),

meaning all at once,

And:

> *Had We sent down* (nazzalnā) *unto thee (actual) writing upon parchment, so that they could feel it with their hands...*(6:7),

which here means all at once.

And in the Almighty's Words:

> *It is He who sent down* (anzala) *upon thee the Book, wherein are verses clear that are the Essence of the Book, and others allegorical* (3:7),

the phraseology challenges the 'Allāmah's assertion that the word *inzāl* is exclusive to those things which are non-composite, because the Book sent down (*munzal*) has verses which are clear and others which are allegorical, therefore the Qur'an can be said to have distinct parts.

God has said:

> *Shall I seek other than God for judge, when He it is Who hath revealed* (anzala) *unto you this Scripture, fully explained? Those unto whom We gave the Scripture aforetime know that it is revealed* (nuzzila) *from thy Lord in truth.* (6:114).

That which came down fully explained is the Qur'an which came down in instalments.

Both words are used in relation to the Qur'an in a single verse:

> *...and We have revealed* (anzalnā) *unto thee the Remembrance that thou mayest explain to mankind that which hath been revealed* (nuzzila) *for them* (16:44).

Zamakhsharī makes two mistakes here. Firstly, he considers the Gospel to be a Scripture, when in fact it was nothing but good news which Jesus recited to the Apostles. He did not have a Scripture in the technical sense of the word,[275] for what is meant in the verse where Jesus says:

> *...He hath given me the Scripture...* (19:30),

is the code of religious law (*al-sharī'ah*), since it is a commonly used technical term. Also, where the Qur'an states:

> *... to instruct them in the Scripture and in wisdom...* (2:129),

this means to teach them the code of religious law (*sharī'ah*) as well as wisdom or insight into the religion.

Secondly, he regarded the Torah as coming down from Heaven in the form of a book, when in fact it was stone tablets which Moses took with him to write down what the Merciful dictated to him on Mount Sinai. Moses' Book, according to the Qur'an,[276] was written by his own hand. What came to Moses was what God dictated to him gradually throughout his stay on Mount Sinai.[277]

The First Revelation

Researchers disagree over various matters pertaining to the Qur'an, including concerns over which verses or chapters came down first. There are three opinions on the matter:

1) *The Blood Clot* (*Sūrah al-'Alaq*), because the prophetic mission began with the revelation of three or five verses from the beginning of *The Blood*

---

[275] See Ma'rifat, *al-Tamhīd fī 'Ulūm al-Qur'an*, vol 8, 'What happened to the Gospel which came down to Christ' (not included in this abridgment); 'Abd al-Wahhāb al-Najjār, *Qiṣaṣ al-Anbiyā'* (Beirut: Mu'assasat al-Ḥalabī, 1386 q.), 399.

[276] *Yet before that, the Book of Moses was an example and a mercy* (46:12).

[277] See Exodus 34:27.

Clot. That was when the truth came to the Prophet by surprise while he was in the Cave at Ḥirā' and the angel told him, 'Recite.' He then protested, 'I cannot recite.' Thereafter, he covered him completely and told him:

> *Recite: In the Name of thy Lord who createth, createth Man from a clot. Recite: And thy Lord is the Most Bounteous,*[278] *Who teacheth by the pen, teacheth Man that which he knew not* (96:1-5).[279]

Tafsīr al-Imām (The Imam's Exegesis) states that Gabriel:

> ...came down to him, grabbed his upper arm, shook it and said, 'Muhammad, recite!' He said, 'What shall I recite?' He said, 'Muhammad, *Recite: In the Name of thy Lord who createth, createth Man from a clot. Recite: And thy Lord is the Most Bounteous, Who teacheth by the pen, teacheth Man that which he knew not*' (96:1-5).[280]

It is narrated on the authority of Imām al-Ṣādiq that:

> The first thing to be revealed to the Messenger of God was, *In the Name of God, the Merciful, the Compassionate; Recite: In the Name of thy Lord*; and the last thing to be revealed to him was *When comes the help of God.*[281]

2) *The Shrouded* (*Sūrah al-Muddaththir*), on account of what is narrated by Umm Salamah:

> I asked Jābir ibn 'Abdillāh al-Anṣārī, 'Which part of the Qur'an was revealed first?' He replied, '*O thou shrouded in thy mantle*.' I suggested, 'Or *Recite: In the Name of thy Lord?*' He replied, 'I will tell you what the Messenger of God told me: 'I confined myself at Ḥirā' and then, when I finished my confinement, I went down and headed for the bottom of the valley. Then I looked towards the sky, and there he was,' meaning Gabriel. 'Trepidation took

---

[278] *Saḥīḥ al-Bukhārī*, vol. 1, 3.

[279] See *Ṣaḥīḥ Muslim*, vol. 1, 97.

[280] Imam al-Ḥasan 'Askarī ('Alayhi al-Salām), *Tafsīr* [attributed to] *al-Imām* (Qum, 1409 q.), 157; Majlisī, *Biḥār al-Anwār*, vol. 18, 206; al-Sayyid Hāshim al-Baḥrānī, *Tafsīr al-Burhān* (Tehran: Āftāb Printing Press, 1374 q.), vol. 4, 478 .

[281] Kulaynī, *al-Kāfī*, vol. 2, 628-629; Abū Ja'far Muhammad ibn Ali ibn al-Ḥusayn ibn Bābawayh al-Qummī, *'Uyūn Akhbār al-Riḍā* (Beirut: Mu'assasat al-A'lamī li al-Maṭbū'āt, 1984), vol. 1, 9; Majlisī, *Biḥār al-Anwār*, vol. 92, 39; Baḥrānī, *Tafsīr al-Burhān*, vol. 1, 29.

> hold of me and I went to Khadījah. I told her to shroud me in my mantle and she did so. Then, God revealed to me: *O thou shrouded in thy mantle, arise and warn!*"[282]

On the other hand Jābir may have worked out for himself that it was the first chapter, because there is no other indication in the Prophet's words. The preferred opinion is that Jābir said this after a period during which revelation had come to a halt, therefore he thought it was the commencement of the revelation.[283] Here is the hadith on the period during which the revelation had come to a halt, also in accordance with Jābir's narration:

> I heard the messenger of God speak of the time of revelation. He said, 'While I was walking, I heard someone call out from heaven, so I raised my head and there was the angel who had come to me at Ḥirā', sitting on a chair between heaven and earth. I was terrified of him, so I went back. I said, 'Wrap me up, wrap me up, shroud me in my mantle,' and so Blessed and Almighty God revealed: *O thou shrouded in thy mantle, arise and warn! Thy Lord magnify, thy raiment purify, defilement shun* (74:1-5),'meaning the idols. He said: 'Then revelation resumed.'[284]

In Bukhārī's words:

> revelation increased and resumed.[285]

3) *The Opening* (*Sūrah al-Fātiḥah*). According to Zamakhsharī:

> Most exegetes say that *The Opening* (*al-Fātiḥah*) was the first thing to be revealed.[286]

'Allāmah Ṭabrisī narrates on the authority of his teacher Aḥmad al-Zāhid's book *al-Īḍāḥ* via its chain of narration back to Sa'īd ibn al-Musayyab, that Ali ibn Abī Ṭālib said:

---

[282] *Ṣaḥīḥ Muslim*, vol. 1, 99.

[283] Zarkashī, *al-Burhān*, vol. 1, 206.

[284] *Ṣaḥīḥ Muslim*, vol. 1, 98; *Ṣaḥīḥ al-Bukhārī*, vol. 1, 4.

[285] *Ṣaḥīḥ Muslim*, vol. 1, 98; *Ṣaḥīḥ al-Bukhārī*, vol. 1, 4.

[286] Zamakhsharī, *al-Kashshāf*, vol. 4, 775; Ibn Ḥajar challenges it superficially, but there is no room to include it after the explanation below on how to reconcile the three opinions. See Ibn Ḥajar, *Fatḥ al-Bārī*, vol. 8, 548.

> I asked the Prophet about the reward in the Qur'an and so he told me about reward, chapter by chapter, in the order it came down from heaven. The first thing that came down to him in Mecca was *The Opening of the Book* (*Fātiḥat al-Kitāb*), then *Recite in the Name of thy Lord*, then *Nūn, The Pen...*[287]

Al-Wāḥidī narrates in *Asbāb al-Nuzūl*, via his chain of narration back to Abū Maysarah 'Amr ibn Sharḥabīl, that when the Messenger of God was off on his own, he would hear a call and be terrified by it. The last time, the angel called to him, 'Muhammad.' He replied, 'I am at your service.' He continued, '*In the Name of God the Merciful, the Compassionate: Praise be to God, the Lord of the Worlds*' until he reached, '*Nor of those who go astray.*'[288]

My comment is that there is no doubt that the Prophet prayed from the time he was despatched, and that Ali, Ja'far, Zayd ibn Ḥārithah and Khadījah would pray with him,[289] and that there is no prayer for someone who has not recited *The Opening of the Book.*[290] The tradition says that Gabriel began by teaching him ablution and prayer,[291] so *The Opening* had to have been linked with the despatch.

According to Jalāl al-Dīn al-Suyūṭī:

> It is not recorded that there was ever any prayer without *the Opening of the Book* in Islam.[292]

Furthermore, we do not see any fundamental contradiction between the three opinions in view of the fact that the three or five verses from the beginning of *The Blood Clot* only came down to give glad tidings of the Messenger's prophethood. This is the consensus of all. Secondly, after a while, verses also came to him from the beginning of *The Shrouded*, as Jābir's hadith says. As for *The Opening*, it was the first complete chapter to be revealed. As for other verses which were revealed before it, they came down for other purposes, although they were recorded later on within the verses and chapters of the Qur'an.

---

[287] Ṭabrisī, *Majma' al-Bayān*, vol. 10, 405.

[288] Al-Wāhidī, *Asbābu Nuzūl al-Āyāt*, 11.

[289] *Tafsīr al-Qummī*, vol. 1, 378.

[290] Naysābūrī, *al-Mustadrak 'alā al-Ṣaḥīḥayn*, vol. 1, 238-239; *Ṣaḥīḥ Muslim*, vol. 2, 9.

[291] Ibn Hishām, *al-Sīrat al-Nabawiyyah*, vol. 1, 260-261; Majlisī, *Biḥār al-Anwār*, vol. 18, 184; vol. 14, 194.

[292] Al-Suyūṭī, *al-Itqān*, vol. 1, 30.

Thus it is correct to refer to *The Praise* as *The Opening*, meaning the first complete chapter revealed in this specific capacity. The extreme importance given to it at the beginning of the prophetic mission, and its unique aspect of being mandatory in all prayers, made it equivalent, in terms of merit, to the whole of the Qur'an:

> *We have given thee seven of the oft-repeated (verses) and the great Qur'an* (15:87).

God conferred this special revelation as a grace to His Messenger equivalent to the rest of the Qur'an.

True, if you count chapters by their beginnings, *Praise* comes fifth according to Jābir ibn Zayd's tradition[293] – *infra.*

The Last to be Revealed

Our traditions say that the last to be revealed was *The Help* (*Sūrah al-Naṣr*). It is narrated that when it came down and the Prophet read it to his companions, they were happy and rejoiced, except for 'Abbās ibn 'Abd al-Muṭṭalib, who wept. The Prophet asked, 'What is making you cry, Uncle?' 'Abbās replied, 'I think that you have announced your death to yourself, O Messenger of God,' and he said, 'It is as you say,' and so he only lived for two more years after that.[294]

According to Imām al-Ṣādiq:

> The last chapter to come down was *When comes the help of God, and victory...*[295]

Muslim cites Ibn 'Abbās as saying:

> The last chapter to come down was *When comes the help of God, and victory...*[296]

It is narrated that the last chapter to be revealed was *The Repudiation* (*Sūrah al-Barā'ah*). It came down in the ninth year, after the year of the Conquest on the return from the Battle of Tabūk. Verses from the beginning

---

293 Al-Suyūṭī, *al-Itqān*, vol. 1, 72.

294 Ṭabrisī, *Majma' al-Bayān*, vol. 10, 554.

295 Baḥrānī, *Tafsīr al-Burhān*, vol. 1, 29.

296 Al-Suyūṭī, *al-Itqān*, vol. 1, 79.

of it were revealed, and the Prophet sent them with Ali to recite them to an assembly of pagans.[297]

Alternatively, it is narrated that the last verse to be revealed was *And guard yourself against a day in which ye will be brought back to God. Then every soul will be paid in full that which it hath earned, and they will not be wronged* (2:281), which Gabriel brought down and told the Prophet to put after verse 280 of *The Cow*. The Messenger of God only lived another twenty-one days – some say seven days – after that.[298]

According to Ibn Wāḍiḥ al-Ya'qūbī:

> It is said that the last to be revealed to him was, *This day I have perfected your religion for you and completed My favour unto you, and have chosen for you as religion al-Islam* (5:3).

His comment on the above is that:

> It is the authentic, confirmed and explicit narration. Its revelation was on the day of the Commander of the Faithful Ali ibn Abī Ṭālib's appointment at Ghadīr Khumm.[299]

My comment is that there is no doubt that *The Help* (*Sūrah al-Naṣr*) was revealed before *The Repudiation*, because it was glad tidings of the Conquest. Alternatively, it was in Mecca, during the year of the Conquest.[300] *The Repudiation* was revealed a year after the Conquest. The way to reconcile these traditions is that the last complete chapter to be revealed was *The Help*, when the Prophet said, 'My soul has announced my death.'[301] The last chapter opening to be revealed was *The Repudiation*.

As for the verse, *And guard yourself against a day in which ye will be brought back to God* (2:281), if it is true that it was revealed at Minā on the day of the ritual slaughter during the farewell pilgrimage, as Māwardī's tradition says,[302] the last verse to be revealed was the verse of completion (*āyat al-ikmāl*) – as al-Ya'qūbī says – because it was revealed on the 18th of Dhū al-Ḥijjah during the return from the farewell pilgrimage. Otherwise, if it is correct that the

---

[297] Fayḍ Kāshānī, *al-Ṣāfī fī Tafsīr al-Qur'an*, vol. 1, 680.
[298] *Tafsīru Shubbar*, 83.
[299] Ibn Wāḍiḥ, *Tārīkh al-Ya'qūbī*, vol. 2, 35.
[300] Al-Suyūṭī, *Lubāb al-Nuqūl*, vol. 2, 145.
[301] Ṭabrisī , *Majma' al-Bayān*, vol. 2, 394.
[302] Zarkashī, *al-Burhān*, vol. 1, 187.

Prophet lived for another twenty-one, seven or nine days after the verse *And guard against...* was revealed, then it was the last verse to be revealed.

In our view, the most correct opinion is al-Ya'qūbi's, in view of the fact that it is the verse telling of the completion of the religion, and so a warning to the Prophet, upon the end of the revelation, to be delivered and carried out. It may be the former verse was the last of the verses pertaining to laws (*āyāt al-aḥkām*) and the latter was the very last verse of revelation.

There are other opinions which have no value, and are not based on the evidence of an explicit statement by one of the Infallibles.

Al-Qāḍī (Judge) Abū Bakr says in *al-Intiṣār*:

> There is nothing in any of these opinions which was raised with the Prophet. It is possible that whoever said them did so based on his own judgment and putting his assumption first. Knowledge of that is not one of the duties of the religion such that critics have to criticise, as they have done, for lack of precision. It is possible that each of them narrated, on the authority of someone else, what he had heard on the authority of the Messenger of God, and someone else heard him after that; and it is also possible that the verse which was the last one to be revealed, was recited by the Messenger along with other verses revealed with it. So, the order was given to write down what had been revealed with it, and for it to be recited to them after having written down and reciting the last verse to be revealed, leading the listener to think that it was the last in order to be revealed.[303]

Meccan or Medinan

There is a great benefit in knowing where the verses and chapters were revealed – whether Mecca or Medina – and their relevance to particular reasons for revelation. This helps the exegete and jurist work out the general meaning of the verse, determine aspects of abrogation, distinguish the general from the particular and the qualified from the unqualified and so on. Hence, scholars have made great efforts to tell apart the Meccan and Medinan revelations. They have reached a consensus on a large

[303] Zarkashī, *al-Burhān*, vol. 1, 210.

number of them and disagree on others. Similarly, they have said that there are Medinan verses within Meccan chapters and vice versa. This will be discussed with a fresh approach later on.

Different Ways of Telling Meccan from Medinan

The criteria for distinguishing Meccan from Medinan varies in line with different views on the matter. In what follows are three general perspectives.

The first is a determination based on the Migration and the Prophet's arrival in the Radiant city of Medina (*al-Medina al-Munawwarah*). Whatever was revealed before setting off for the Migration, including during the journey itself, is Meccan, whereas whatever was revealed after that is Medinan.

The criterion for this is that of time. Whatever was revealed before the time of the Migration, even if was not actually in Mecca, is Meccan. Whatever was revealed after the Migration, even if it was not actually in Medina, and even if it was revealed in Mecca the year of the Conquest or on the farewell pilgrimage, is Medinan, in light of its having been revealed after the Migration. According to this terminology, all the verses which were revealed in relation to wars and journeys are Medinan, since they were revealed after the Migration.

According to Yaḥyā ibn Salām:

> Whatever was revealed in Mecca or on the way to Medina before he got there is Meccan. Whatever was revealed after his arrival in Medina, on his travels or during battles, is Medinan.

Jalāl al-Dīn's comment is:

> This is a subtle distinction. From it can be understood that whatever was revealed on the journey of Migration is Meccan, according to the terminology.[304]

An example of this is God's Words:

> *He who hath given thee the Qur'an for a law will surely bring thee home again* (28:85).

---

[304] Al-Suyūṭī, *al-Itqān*, vol. 1, 23.

It is said that it was revealed at Juḥfah when the Prophet was in flight on the way to Medina.[305]

The second method of determination is that whatever was revealed in Mecca and its environs is Meccan, even if came after the Migration. Whatever was revealed in Medina and its environs is Medinan. Whatever was revealed outside both towns and far away from both is neither Meccan nor Medinan, according to God's Words:

> *Thus We send thee unto a nation, before whom other nations have passed away, that thou mayest recite unto them that which We have inspired in thee, while they are disbelievers in the Beneficent. Say: He is my Lord; there is no god save Him. In Him do I put my trust and unto Him is my recourse* (13:30).

It is said that this was revealed at Ḥudaybiyyah when the Prophet made a peace treaty with the pagans from Quraysh. The Messenger of God told Ali, 'Write in the Name of God, the Merciful, the Compassionate...,' and Suhayl ibn 'Amr and the rest of the pagans said, 'We do not know any Merciful apart from the man in charge of Yamāmah,' meaning Musaylamah al-Kadhdhāb (Musaylamah the Liar), and so the verse was revealed.[306] Similarly, the verse in The *Spoils of War* (8:1) revealed at Badr when the Muslims argued amongst themselves about how to divide the booty,[307] is neither Meccan nor Medinan according to this terminology.

The third determination is that whatever addresses the people of Mecca is Meccan and whatever addresses the people of Medina is Medinan. This is taken from Ibn Mas'ūd's words:

> Everything that says, 'O people...,' was revealed in Mecca, and everything which says, 'O ye who believe...,' was revealed in Medina.[308]

Zarkashī adds:

> ...because what took hold of the people of Mecca was infidelity, and what took hold of the people of Medina was faith.[309]

---

[305] Zarkashī, *al-Burhān*, vol. 1, 197.

[306] Ṭabrisī , *Majma' al-Bayān*, vol. 6, 293.

[307] See Ibn Hishām, *al-Sīrat al-Nabawiyyah*, vol. 2, 322.

[308] Naysābūrī, *al-Mustadrak 'alā al-Ṣaḥīḥayn*, vol. 3, 18.

[309] Zarkashī, *al-Burhān*, vol. 1, 187

This difference of opinion caused disagreement over whether many verses and chapters are Meccan or Medinan.[310] However, of all these definitions the first is predominant, and is the majority opinion of scholars.[311] Our arrangement of the chapters in the order in which they were revealed, as set out below, relies on this definition.

It is a fact that there are very few ways to ascertain the actual places of revelation – whether Mecca, Medina or elsewhere – because the earliest scholars did not pay attention to this important aspect, except what they stated by way of digression in their expositions, and it is thus of precious little benefit. Therefore, to find out it is necessary to refer to the evidence of contextual indicators within the wording of verses, such as deducing information from the tone of what is said and the situation in which the people are addressed, whether it was in battle or not, whether it is a promise, a threat, guidance or dispensing duties. Where that generates a decisive solution to any confusion arising from the wording of a verse such as the following:

> *It is therefore no sin for him who is on pilgrimage to the House (of God) or visiteth it, to go around them ...* (2:158),

the problem of whether it means unqualified permission rather than an obligation is solved by what the reason for the revelation is claimed to be.[312] This generates confidence in the authenticity of the tradition, regardless of the chain of narration. Hence, the above verse is Medinan.

According to al-Ja'barī, there are two ways to distinguish Meccan from Medinan:

> ...the method based on tradition (*simā'i*), and the method based on analogical reasoning (*qiyāsī*): *simā'i* is word that has reached us telling us that it was revealed in one of the two. *Qiyāsī* is as 'Alqamah ibn Mas'ūd said: every chapter containing, 'O, people...' as the only form of address, or '*kallā*', or at the beginning of which are letters

[310] As with the verse on trusts (4:58). Al-Naḥḥās claims that it is Meccan on account of Ibn Jurayj's tradition. See Ṭabrisī , *Majma' al-Bayān*, vol. 3, 63.

[311] Zarkashī, *al-Burhān*, vol. 1, 187 and al-Suyūṭī, *al-Itqān*, vol. 1, 23.

[312] The Muslims were embarrassed to walk and run between Ṣafā and Marwah, claiming that it was a custom of the days of ignorance to venerate the position of Isāf and Nā'ilah,, and so the verse was revealed to nullify this misconception. See Ṭabrisī , *Majma' al-Bayān*, vol. 1, 240.

> of the alphabet – with the exception of the *zahrāwayn* (*The Cow* and *The Family of Imran*) and *The Thunder* – or which contain the story of Adam and Iblīs, with the exception of the longest (*The Cow*), or which contains stories of the prophets and extinct nations, is Meccan. Every chapter containing a punishment or duty is Medinan. Every chapter containing, 'O ye who believe...' is Medinan.

The Order of Revelation

In this exposition we have relied on several traditions upon which there is a consensus and upon which the majority of scholars rely. The most important of them is Ibn 'Abbās' tradition narrated via chains of narration acknowledged by leading scholars on the subject.[313]

According to Imam Badr al-Zarkashī:

> The tradition of reliable narrators has settled on this arrangement.[314]

We have adopted this as the authoritative statement in this exposition, and filled in the gaps using traditions of Jābir ibn Zayd and others along with reliable historical texts.[315] It is true that there is some disagreement between them, either over which were Meccan or Medinan chapters or over the number of each. This amounts to a disagreement over whether more than thirty chapters are Meccan or Medinan.

In this exposition a preponderance was given to the beginnings of the chapters, so if some verses from the beginning of a chapter were revealed, then another chapter was revealed and the first one was completed afterwards, the first one comes before the second according to this terminology.

There follows a list of Meccan chapters, which are eighty-six in number, followed by the Medinan chapters, of which there are twenty-eight. Chapters over which there is disagreement are discussed in a later section.

[313] See Ṭabrisī, *Majma' al-Bayān*, vol. 10, 405-406 and al-Suyūṭī, *al-Itqān*, vol. 1, 26 and 72.

[314] Zarkashī, *al-Burhān*, vol. 1, 193-194.

[315] See Ibn al-Nadīm, *al-Fihrist*, 44 and Ibn Wāḍiḥ, *Tārīkh al-Ya'qūbī*, vol. 2, 26.

Meccan Chapters

ORDER OF REVELATION	CHAPTER	ORDER AS PER THE MUṢḤAF
1	The Blood Clot (*al-'Alaq*)	96
2	The Pen (*al-Qalam*)	68
3	The Enwrapped (*al-Muzzammil*)	73
4	The Shrouded (*al-Muddaththir*)	74
5	The Opening (*al-Fātiḥah*) [*The Opening* is omitted in Ibn 'Abbās' tradition. We have included it on the basis of Jābir ibn Zayd's narration – see al-Suyūṭī, *al-Itqān*, vol. 1, 25 – and the text of Ibn Wāḍiḥ, *Tārīkh Ya'qūbī*, vol. 2, 26.]	1
6	Palm Fibre (*al-Masad*)	111
7	The Rolling Up (*al-Takwīr*)	81
8	The Most High (*al-A'lā*)	87
9	The Night (*al-Layl*)	92
10	The Dawn (*al-Fajr*)	89
11	The Forenoon (*al-Ḍuḥā*)	93
12	The Expanding (*al-Sharḥ*)	94
13	The Declining Day (*al-'Aṣr*)	103
14	The Chargers (*al-'Ādiyāt*)	100
15	The Abundance (*al-Kawthar*)	108

ORDER OF REVELATION	CHAPTER	ORDER AS PER THE MUṢḤAF
16	Rivalry (*al-Takāthur*)	102
17	Charity (*al-Mā'ūn*)	107
18	The Unbelievers (*al-Kāfirūn*)	109
19	The Elephant (*al-Fīl*)	105
20	The Daybreak (*al-Falaq*)	113
21	Mankind (*al-Nās*)	114
22	The Unity (*al-Tawḥīd*)	112
23	The Star (*al-Najm*)	53
24	He Frowned (*'Abasa*)	80
25	The (Night of) Destiny (*al-Qadr*)	97
26	The Sun (*al-Shams*)	91
27	The Constellations (*al-Burūj*)	85
28	The Fig (*al-Tīn*)	95
29	Quraysh (*Quraysh*)	106
30	The Great Calamity (*al-Qāri'ah*)	101
31	The Resurrection (*al-Qīyāmah*)	75
32	The Traducer (*al-Humazah*)	104
33	Those Sent Forth (*al-Mursalāt*)	77
34	Qāf (*Qāf*)	50

ORDER OF REVELATION	CHAPTER	ORDER AS PER THE MUṢḤAF
35	The City (*al-Balad*)	90
36	The Night Star (*al-Ṭāriq*)	86
37	The Moon (*al-Qamar*)	54
38	Ṣād (*Ṣād*)	38
39	The Heights (*al-A'rāf*)	7
40	The Jinn (*al-Jinn*)	72
41	Yā Sīn (*Yā Sīn*)	36
42	The Criterion (*al-Furqān*)	25
43	The Originator (*Fāṭir*)	35
44	Mary (*Maryam*)	19
45	Ṭā Hā (*Ṭā Hā*)	20
46	The Inevitable (*al-Wāqi'ah*)	56
47	The Poets (*al-Shu'arā'*)	26
48	The Ant (*al-Naml*)	27
49	The Narrations (*al-Qaṣaṣ*)	28
50	The Night Journey (*al-Isrā'*)	17
51	Jonah (*Yūnus*)	10
52	Hūd (*Hūd*)	11
53	Joseph (*Yūsuf*)	12

ORDER OF REVELATION	CHAPTER	ORDER AS PER THE MUṢḤAF
54	al-Ḥijr (*al-Ḥijr*)	15
55	The Cattle (*al-An'ām*)	6
56	Those Arrayed in Ranks (*al-Ṣāffāt*)	37
57	Luqmān (*Luqmān*)	31
58	Sheba (*Saba'*)	34
59	The Troops (*al-Zumar*)	39
60	The Believer/The Forgiver (*al-Mu'mīn/Ghāfir*)	40
61	Explained in Detail *(Fuṣṣilat)*	41
62	The Counsel *(al-Shūrā)*	42
63	The Adornments (*al-Zukhruf*)	43
64	The Smoke (*al-Dukhān*)	44
65	The Crouching (*al-Jāthiyah*)	45
66	The Sand Dunes (*al-Aḥqāf*)	46
67	The Winds That Scatter (*al-Dhārīyāt*)	51
68	The Enveloper (*al-Ghāshiyah*)	88
69	The Cave (*al-Kahf*)	18
70	The Bee (*al-Naḥl*)	16
71	Noah (*Nūḥ*)	71
72	Abraham (*Ibrāhīm*)	14

ORDER OF REVELATION	CHAPTER	ORDER AS PER THE MUṢḤAF
73	The Prophets (*al-Anbīyā'*)	21
74	The Believers (*al-Mu'minūn*)	23
75	The Prostration (*al-Sajdah*)	32
76	The Mount (*al-Ṭūr*)	52
77	The Kingdom (*al-Mulk*)	67
78	The Indubitable (*al-Ḥāqqah*)	69
79	The Ways of Ascent (*al-Ma'ārij*)	70
80	The Good Tidings (*al-Naba'*)	78
81	Those Who Tear Out (*al-Nāzi'āt*)	79
82	The Rending (*al-Infiṭār*)	82
83	The Sundering (*al-Inshiqāq*)	84
84	The Romans (*al-Rūm*)	30
85	The Spider (*al-'Ankabūt*)	29
86	The Dealers in Fraud(*al-Muṭaffifīn*)	83

Medinan Chapters

ORDER OF REVELATION	CHAPTER	ORDER AS PER THE MUṢḤAF
87	The Cow (*al-Baqarah*)	2
88	The Spoils of War (*al-Anfāl*)	8
89	The Family of Imran (*Āl 'Imrān*)	3
90	The Confederates (*al-Aḥzāb*)	33
91	She Who is Tested (*al-Mumtaḥanah*)	60
92	The Women (*al-Nisā'*)	4
93	The Earthquake (*al-Zilzāl*)	99
94	Iron (*al-Ḥadīd*)	57
95	Muhammad (*Muhammad*)	47
96	The Thunder (*al-Ra'd*)	13
97	The Merciful (*al-Raḥmān*)	55
98	The Man (*al-Insān*)	76
99	Divorce (*al-Ṭalāq*)	65
100	The Clear Sign (*al-Bayyinah*)	98
101	The Mustering (*al-Ḥashr*)	59
102	The Help (*al-Naṣr*)	110
103	The Light (*al-Nūr*)	24

ORDER OF REVELATION	CHAPTER	ORDER AS PER THE MUṢḤAF
104	The Pilgrimage (*al-Ḥajj*)	22
105	The Hypocrites (*al-Munāfiqūn*)	63
106	The Dispute (*al-Mujādalah*)	58
107	The Chamber (*al-Ḥujurāt*)	49
108	The Prohibition (*al-Taḥrīm*)	66
109	The Congregation (*al-Jumu'ah*)	62
110	The Mutual Disillusion (*al-Taghābun*)	64
111	The Ranks (*al-Ṣaff*) [In *al-Burhān*, Zarkashī placed the chapter entitled *The Ranks* after *Prohibition* and before *The Congregation.*]	61
112	The Victory (*al-Fatḥ*)	48
113	The Table (*al-Mā'idah*) [In *al-Burhān*, Zarkashī put *The Repentance/ The Disavowal* before *The Table* and made the latter the last chapter.]	5
114	The Repentance (*al-Tawbah*)	9

Chapters over which there is disagreement

Based on the above, the Meccan chapters are eighty-six in number. The first is *The Blood Clot* (*al-'Alaq*) and the last is *The Dealers in Fraud* (*al-Muṭaffifīn*). The Medinan chapters are twenty-eight in number, the first of which is *The Cow* (*al-Baqarah*) and the last *The Repentance* (*al-Barā'ah*).

However, not everyone agrees on this order as set out in the two tables, in certain cases on more than thirty chapters. A brief exposition of the disagreement follows, along with a short outline of how we arrived at our conclusion on the matter. We shall postpone a detailed discussion of this to our *tafsīr* book, *al-Tafsīr al-Wasīṭ*.

1- The Opening (*al-Fātihah*)

According to Mujāhid it is Medinan.[316]

Al-Husayn ibn al-Faḍl says:

> This is a mistake on Mujāhid's part, because scholars disagree with what he says[317] on account of what Ali said:
>
> > *The Opening of the Book came down in Mecca from a treasure trove under the Throne.*[318]
>
> and because of the Almighty's Words:
>
> > *We have bestowed upon thee the seven oft-repeated (verses) and the mighty Qur'an (15:87).*
>
> *and because it is the first complete chapter to be revealed to the Messenger of God, taught to him by Gabriel,*[319] *and it was named the Opening of the Book.*[320] *Further, 'There is no prayer without the Opening of the Book.'*[321]

According to Jalāl al-Dīn:

> It is not recorded that there was ever any prayer without the Opening of the Book.[322]

---

[316] Ṭabrisī, *Majma' al-Bayān*, vol. 1, 17.
[317] Al-Suyūṭī, *al-Itqān*, vol. 1, 30.
[318] Al-Suyūṭī, *al-Itqān*, vol. 1, 30.
[319] Ḥalabī, *Al-Sīrah al-Nabawiyyah bi Hāmish al-Sīrah al-Ḥalabiyyah,* vol. 1, 161.
[320] As mentioned under 'The First to be Revealed.'
[321] *Ṣaḥīḥ Muslim,* vol. 2, 9; Naysābūrī, *al-Mustadrak,* vol. 1, 238 and 239.
[322] Al-Suyūṭī, *al-Itqān*, vol. 1, 31.

2- The Women (*al-Nisā'*)

Al-Naḥḥās claims that it is Meccan in view of the Almighty's Words:

> *God doth command you to render back your trusts to those to whom they are due ...* (4:58).

Ibn Jurayj says that it was revealed in Mecca in the year of the Conquest and relates to the key to the Holy House. The Prophet wanted to give it to 'Abbās ibn 'Abd al-Muṭṭalib, but God told him to give it to 'Uthmān ibn Ṭalḥah, because he had taken it from him.[323]

However, exegetes agree that it is Medinan in view of the weakness of the chain of narration of this hadith, and also based on the fact that the revelation of a verse or chapter in Mecca in the year of the Conquest does not make it Meccan. According to the terminology used by the majority, whatever was revealed after the Migration is Medinan, even if it was revealed in Mecca.

Finally, an entire chapter does not get classified according to a single verse within it, where the revelation of that verse does not concur with that of the chapter as such.

3- Jonah (*Yūnus*)

A 'rogue' tradition on the authority of Ibn 'Abbās says that it is Medinan.[324] This tradition has not been confirmed, irrespective of the fact that it contradicts the aforementioned explicit statement (*naṣṣ*) on the authority of Ibn 'Abbās himself on the order in which the chapters were revealed, and upon which there is practically a consensus.

4- The Thunder (*al-Ra'd*)

According to Muhammad ibn al-Sā'ib al-Kalbī, Muqātil and 'Aṭā', it is Meccan.[325] The same is true of a tradition on the authority of Mujāhid, based on the authority of Ibn 'Abbās.[326]

Sayyid Quṭb has the following view:

> This chapter's being Meccan is painfully clear, both with regard to the nature of its subject matter, the way in which it is recited

---

[323] Ṭabrisī, *Majma' al-Bayān*, vol. 3, 63.

[324] Al-Suyūṭī, *al-Itqān*, vol. 1, 31.

[325] Al-Suyūṭī, *al-Durr al-Manthūr*, vol. 4, 42; Ṭabrisī, *Majma' al-Bayān*, vol. 6, 273.

[326] Al-Suyūṭī, *al-Itqān*, vol. 1, 24.

> and its general atmosphere, the fragrance of which cannot be mistaken by anyone who lives under the shade of this Qur'an.[327]

However, the consensus of the traditions regarding the order is that it is Medinan, and was revealed after the chapter on fighting, according to 'Ikrimah and al-Husayn ibn Abī al-Ḥasan's tradition, as well as Khuṣayf's tradition on the authority of Mujāhid, which has authority from Ibn 'Abbās himself.[328] Al-Ḥasan and Qatādah agree.[329]

As for the context of the chapter, it includes various concepts from general directives for mankind to the verses of 'the challenge' (*al-taḥaddī*), something common to both Meccan and Medinan chapters, like many verses in *The Cow* and other Medinan chapters. The main evidence is the consensus of traditions on the sequential order, which will become clearer in the discussion on *The Merciful*.

5- The Pilgrimage (*al-Hajj*)

According to Abū Muhammad al-Makkī ibn Abī Ṭālib, it is Meccan.[330] On the authority of Mujāhid via his chain of narration, which, however, has some weakness in it,[331] he narrates:

> I asked Ibn 'Abbās about the revelation of the chapters until he reached *The Pilgrimage*. He said, 'It was revealed in Mecca except for three verses from it (19, 20 and 21) which were revealed in Medina.[332]

---

[327] Sayyid Quṭb, *Fī Ẓilāl al-Qur'an*, vol. 13, 63, ft.

[328] Al-Suyūṭī, *al-Itqān*, vol. 1, 27.

[329] Ṭabrisī, *Majma' al-Bayān*, vol. 6, 273; al-Suyūṭī, *al-Durr al-Manthūr*, vol. 4, 42.

[330] Abū Muhammad Makkī ibn Abī Ṭālib, *al-Kashf 'An Wujūh al-Qirā'āt al-Sab'* (Damascus: Majma' al-Lughah al-Arabiyyah, 1974), vol. 2, 116.

[331] Because of Abū 'Ubaydah Mu'ammar ibn al-Muthannā (d. 210), regarding whom it is said: 'He believed in the Khārijites' belief; despicable and sacrilegious, he paid little attention to the Qur'an. When he recited it, he would recite it based on opinion. He was one of the biggest linguists and literary experts. He was the first to write on *Gharīb al-Qur'an* (unusual vocabulary in the Qur'an). He wrote a book on the Arabs' shortcomings cited by Abū 'Ubayd al-Qāsim ibn Salām.' See Ibn al-Nadīm, *al-Fihrist*, 85, Shams al-Dīn Muhammad ibn Aḥmad al-Dhahabī, *Mīzān al-I'tidāl* (Egypt: Dār Iḥyā' al-Kutub al-'Arabiyyah, 1386 q.), vol. 4, 155 and Shihāb al-Dīn Ibn Ḥajar al-'Asqalānī, *Tahdhīb al-Tahdhīb* (Beirut: Dār al-Ṣādir, 1325 q.), vol. 10, 247.

[332] Al-Suyūṭī, *al-Itqān*, vol. 1, 24.

What Ṭabarī says regarding the hadith on the cranes,[333] along with its severe tone, is consistent with its having been revealed in Mecca.

My comment is that all of this does not overcome the consensus of the traditions on the order of the revelation of the chapters together with historical documents, not to mention the weakness of the chain of narration of Mujāhid's tradition.[334] As for the cranes hadith, it is a folk tale with no basis to it. As for the tone, it works most of the time, but not throughout, so it is not a suitable evidential basis for arriving at a ruling on the matter.

6- The Criterion (*al-Furqān*)

Al-Daḥḥāk claims that it is Medinan in view of the verses at the end of it, and it is indeed said that it is Medinan.[335] Yet this on its own is not suitable evidence for its being Medinan, given the consensus of the traditions on the order of the revelation of the chapters.

7- *Yā Sīn*

It has been said to be Medinan,[336] but the person who made this claim and the evidence upon which he relied are not known. The consensus is that it is Meccan.

8- *Ṣād*

It is also said to be Medinan,[337] but this is a rogue opinion contrary to the consensus.

9- *Muḥammad*

There is a weak claim that it is Meccan,[338] which is strange given that it is a chapter on fighting!

10- The Chambers (*al-Ḥujurāt*)

It has been said to be Meccan, but the consensus is that it is Medinan.[339]

---

[333] Ṭabarī, *Jāmi' al-Bayān*, vol. 17, 131-132.

[334] See al-Suyūṭī, *al-Itqān*, vol. 1, 27 and 72; Ibn al-Nadīm, *al-Fihrist*, 44 and al-Suyūṭī, *al-Durr al-Manthūr*, vol. 4, 342.

[335] Al-Suyūṭī, *al-Itqān*, vol. 1, 27.

[336] Ibid.

[337] Al-Suyūṭī, *al-Itqān*, vol. 1, 32.

[338] Ibid.

[339] Ibid.

11- The Merciful (*al-Raḥmān*)

According to the text of *al-Fihrist* and *al-Ya'qūbī* it is Meccan. The majority also take that position. Jalāl al-Dīn agress that this is correct, on account of what al-Tirmidhī and al-Hākim say on the authority of Jābir:

> When the Messenger of God recited *The Merciful* to his companions, after he had finished, he said, 'How come I see you silent? The jinn had a better response than you! I did not once recite: *Then which of the bounties of your Lord will ye deny?* (55:13) without their saying, 'And we do not deny any of Your bounties, O Lord, so praise be to Thee."

According to Jalāl al-Dīn:

> The story of the jinn happened in Mecca.[340]

He says:

> More explicit than that is what Aḥmad narrates in his *Musnad* on the authority of Asmā', daughter of Abū Bakr: 'I heard and the pagans heard the Messenger of God say while he was praying near the corner (*al-rukn*), before shouting what he was commanded: *O which of your Lord's bounties will ye deny?* (55:13).[341]

His comment is that:

> This proves that it was revealed before *al-Ḥijr*.

Sayyid Quṭb says:

> Characteristics of the Meccan Qur'an are clear in the arrangement of the chapter.[342]

My own comment is that there is no doubt that its reproachful tone resembles the tone of the majority of the Meccan chapters, and indeed the heaviest of them upon the soul's ears. However, this alone is not proof that it is Meccan, given that it is not a unique feature, and can also be found in Medinan chapters such as *The Earthquake*, *The Clear Sign*, *The Man*

---

[340] Al-Suyūṭī, *al-Itqān*, vol. 1, 33.
[341] Ibn Ḥanbal, *al-Musnad*, vol. 6, 349.
[342] Sayyid Quṭb, *Fī Ẓilāl al-Qur'an*, vol. 27, 670.

and others. Further, many Meccan chapters such as *Joseph*, *Jonah*, *Hūd*, *The Cattle*, *The Heights* and several others have a dulcit tone.

As for the hadith about the jinn, there is no evidence that it is Meccan, since there is no concomitance between this hadith and the hadith on the revelation in Mecca of *The Jinn*. It is possible that it happened in Medina.

As for tradition regarding Asmā', assuming it to be authentic, it indicates that it was revealed in the early days of the transmission – which no one claims – because she said, '...before shouting what he was commanded.' This is in addition to the weakness of the hadith as it appears in the *Musnad*, due to the inclusion of Luhay'ah, a judge of Egypt, in its chain of narration. He has been criticised, and therefore Ibn Mu'īn considers him to be weak. He says:

> His narration cannot be relied upon as evidence. Yaḥyā ibn Sa'īd did not think he amounted to anything.[343]

Finally, such weak reasons do not overcome the traditions on the order of the revelation of the chapters, upon which there is agreement.[344]

12- Iron (*al-Ḥadīd*)

A number have said that it is Meccan, relying on the hadith on 'Umar ibn al-Khaṭṭāb becoming a Muslim as evidence. He went to see his sister and found in her possession a scroll which had the chapter *Iron* on it. He read it until he reached *What cause have ye why ye should not believe in God?* (57:8) and found Islam was to his liking, so he went to the Prophet and became a Muslim at his hands.[345]

This hadith contradicts Ibn Isḥāq's hadith, in which *Ṭā Hā* was on the scroll, and he read it until he reached *...that every soul may receive its reward by the measure of its endeavour* (20:15). Alternatively, it is said that *Ṭā Hā* was on the scroll and that 'Umar read it until he reached *...then shall each soul know what it has put forward* (81:14) and his heart inclined to Islam.[346]

It also contradicts Shurayḥ ibn 'Ubayd's hadith, which claims that 'Umar said, 'I went out to raise objections with the Messenger of God before I became a Muslim, and found that he had beaten me to the Mosque, so

---

[343] See al-Dhahabī, *Mīzān al-I'tidāl*, vol. 2, 475 and Ibn Ḥajar, *Tahdhīb al-Tahdhīb*, vol. 5, 374.

[344] See Ṭabrisī, *Majma' al-Bayān*, vol. 10, 405 and al-Suyūṭī, *al-Itqān*, vol. 1, 27 and 72.

[345] Ibn al-Athīr, *Usd al-Ghābah*, vol. 4, 54.

[346] Ibn Hishām, *al-Sīrat al-Nabawiyyah*, vol. 1, 370.

I stood behind him; he began *The Indubitable* (*al-Ḥāqqah*) and I began to be amazed at the Qur'an's composition. When he finished it, Islam fell right into my heart.'[347]

These two hadiths both have broken chains of narration (*mursal*) cited by those who cannot be relied upon. According to Ibn Ḥajar:

> The hadith is via a chain of narration which contains Isḥāq ibn 'Abdillāh ibn Abī Farwah.[348]

He alluded thereby to a flaw in the chain of narration, because this Ibn Abī Farwah is criticised and his traditions are rejected.[349]

Some rely on Ibn Mas'ūd's hadith as evidence:

> There were only four years between our becoming Muslims and our being reproached by the Almighty's Words, *Has not the time arrived for the believers that their hearts in all humility should engage in the remembrance of God ... and that they should not become like those to whom was given revelation aforetime ... and their hearts grew hard? For many among them are rebellious transgressors* (57:16), and so the believers began reproaching each other.[350]

My comment is that his hadith is also contradicted by others which either explicitly state that it was revealed in reference to the hypocrites a year after the Migration,[351] or that it was after some of the believers had become wealthy and their hearts had become somewhat mean.[352]

13- The Ranks (*al-Ṣaff*)

According to Ibn Ḥazm it is Meccan.[353] However, a majority of the scholars and traditions on the order of the revelation of the chapters

---

[347] Ibn al-Athīr, *Usd al-Ghābah*, vol. 4, 53; Ibn Ḥajar, *al-Iṣābah*, vol. 2, 519.

[348] Ibn Ḥajar, *al-Iṣābah*, vol. 2, 519.

[349] See Ibn Ḥajar, *Tahdhīb al-Tahdhīb*, vol. 1, 240; Shams al-Dīn Muhammad ibn Aḥmad al-Dhahabī, *al-Mughnī fi al-Ḍu'afā'* (Aleppo: Dār al-Ma'ārif, 1391 q.), vol. 1, 71 and al-Dhahabī, *Mīzān al-I'tidāl*, vol. 1, 193.

[350] Ṭabrisī, *Majma' al-Bayān*, vol. 9, 237; al-Suyūṭī, *al-Itqān*, vol. 1, 33.

[351] Ṭabrisī, *Majma' al-Bayān*, vol. 9, 237.

[352] Al-Suyūṭī, *Lubāb al-Nuqūl fi Asbāb al-Nuzūl*, vol. 9, 94.

[353] Ali ibn Aḥmad ibn Sa'īd Ibn Ḥazm al-Andalusī, *al-Nāsikh wa al-Mansūkh fi al-Qur'an al-Karīm* (Beirut: Dār al-Kutub al-'Ilmiyyah, 1406 q.), vol. 2, 199.

contradict what he says. The correct opinion is that it is Medinan, since Ibn al-Gharas attributes that to the majority.[354]

14- The Congregation (*al-Jumu'ah*)

This is Medinan by consensus. There is an unknown scholar who claims otherwise. Jalāl al-Dīn says it is confirmed in authentic texts that it is Medinan in its entirety.[355]

15- The Mutual Loss and Gain (*al-Taghābun*)

According to 'Abdullāh ibn al-Zubayr, it was revealed in Mecca. He attributed that to Ibn 'Abbās,[356] except that the consensus of the traditions on the order of the revelation of the chapters is that it is Medinan in its entirety.

16- The Kingdom (*al-Mulk*)

There is a strange claim that it is Medinan,[357] but the correct view by consensus is that it is Meccan.

17- The Man (*al-Insān*)

According to 'Abdullāh ibn al-Zubayr, and a number of those who like denying the People of the Household's having any merit, it was revealed in Mecca.[358] The core of this strange claim[359] is Ibn al-Zubayr's enmity towards the People of the Household, which is well known.

Similarly, Sayyid Quṭb insists that it is Meccan in a similar context:

> The possibility that this chapter is Medinan is in our opinion very weak, and can almost be ignored.[360]

Ḥāfiẓ Ḥasakānī asserts:

---

[354] Al-Suyūṭī, *al-Itqān*, vol. 1, 33.
[355] Al-Suyūṭī, *al-Itqān*, vol. 1, 34.
[356] Ṭabrisī, *Majma' al-Bayān*, vol. 10, 296.
[357] Al-Suyūṭī, *al-Itqān*, vol. 1, 34.
[358] Al-Suyūṭī, *al-Durr al-Manthūr*, vol. 6, 297; *Tafsīru Shubbar*, 542.
[359] 'Ubaydullāh ibn Abdillāh Ḥākim Ḥasakānī, *Shawāhid al-Tanzīl* (Beirut: Mu'assasat al-A'lamī, 1393 q.), vol. 2, 299.
[360] Sayyid Quṭb, *Fī Ẓilāl al-Qur'an*, vol. 29, 391.

> Some of the Nawāṣib[361] have objected by saying that this chapter is Meccan according to the consensus of the exegetes. This story, if anything, is Medinan, so how can it have been the reason for the revelation of the chapter?

He says in response:

> How can he claim consensus when the majority agree that it is Medinan?

He then makes reference to the clear statements (*nuṣūṣ*) of the leading scholars on the order of the revelation of the chapters which make it clear that it was revealed in Medina after *The Merciful* and before *Divorce*, in line with what we have stated above.[362]

Ṭabrisī confirms the same in his exegesis, as do other cautious exegetes.

The main evidence is the consensus of the traditions on the order of the revelation of the chapters to which there is not a single exception.[363] Thus, the matter of context is weak, given that it is not a universal rule which always applies.

According to al-Sayyid Shubbar, the claim that it is Meccan is disproven by authentic textual evidence.[364]

18- The Dealers in Fraud *(al-Mutaffifīn)*

Al-Ya'qūbī states that it was the first chapter to be revealed in Medina.[365] It is said that it was revealed to the Prophet during the Migration to Medina.[366] According to Jalāl al-Dīn:

> When the Prophet arrived in Medina, the people there were most devious with regard to weights and measures, and so God revealed this chapter. Thereafter, they were fair in their weights and measures.[367]

---

361 The *Nawāṣib* (singular: *Nāṣibī*) are those who show open enmity to the Prophet's family through word or deed (translator).

362 Ḥasakānī, *Shawāhid al-Tanzīl*, vol. 2, 310 and 315.

363 See Ṭabrisī, *Majma' al-Bayān*, vol. 10, 405.

364 *Tafsīru Shubbar*, 542.

365 Ibn Wāḍiḥ, *Tārīkh al-Ya'qūbī*, vol. 2, 35.

366 Ibn Ḥazm, *al-Nāsikh wa al-Mansūkh*, vol. 2, 202.

367 Al-Suyūṭī, *al-Itqān*, vol. 1, 34.

My comment is that this contradicts the traditions on the order of the revelation of the chapters, on which there is consensus, which say that it was the last Meccan chapter. Similarly, the harsh tone of the chapter is incompatible with the Prophet of Mercy's arrival in Medina and first dealings with its people, who were, after all, giving themselves over to him, especially given the repetition of the word[s] 'No indeed' (*kallā*), which indicates stubbornness on the part of the audience and is inconsistent with the environment of healthy belief which the people of Medina displayed at that time. What al-Ja'barī says – that every chapter containing *kallā* is Meccan – was discussed above.[368]

19- The Most High (*al-A'lā*)

It is said that it is Medinan because of the Almighty's Words: *But those will prosper who purify themselves, and mention the name of their Guardian Lord, and (lift their hearts) in prayer* (87:14-15), an allusion to the Eid (*'Īd*) prayer and Zakāt al-Fiṭrah.[369]

My comment is that the verse is general, and the tradition – assuming it is authentic – came along to apply this general rule to one of its instances; it is not meant to inherently exclude anything else. Further, even if we were to concede that these two verses were revealed in Medina, this does not indicate that the entire chapter is Medinan.

What is correct is that the chapter is Meccan even if some of its verses are Medinan, not to mention its tone's testifying to its being Meccan.

20- The Dawn *(al-Fajr)*

This is Meccan by consensus. No one is known to say otherwise.[370]

21- The City *(al-Balad)*

This is Meccan by the consensus which avers it refers to the blessed city of Mecca. It would be very difficult to claim that it is Medinan.[371]

---

[368] *Supra* under the heading: 'Different Ways of Telling Meccan from Medinan.'

[369] Al-Suyūṭī, *al-Itqān*, vol. 1, 34. Zakāt al-Fiṭrah is the charity given on the day of the 'Īd before the 'Īd prayer. The 'Īd to which this refers comes immediately after the month of Ramadan on the first day of Shawwal. (translator).

[370] Al-Suyūṭī, *al-Itqān*, vol. 1, 35.

[371] Ibid.

22- The Night *(al-Layl)*

It is said that it is Medinan based on a tradition concerning the reason it was revealed. A date palm overhung the home of a poor man, and his children would eat its dates. The owner of the date palm - a rich man - would treat them harshly, and so the Prophet tried to bargain with him, offering a date palm in heaven, but he refused until an Anṣārī man bargained with him over forty date palms. He bought them from him and gave them to the Prophet as a gift. The Prophet then gave them to the poor man as a gift. It is said that thereafter was revealed: *But as for him who hoardeth and deemeth himself independent, and disbelieveth in goodness ...* (92:8-9). However, the chain of narration is broken, not uninterrupted. Furthermore, the verse does not completely fit the intended meaning of the story.

The correct opinion according to many of our traditions and those of many others is that the verse is universally applicable to anyone who is miserly with God's right, and does not fear His punishment.[372]

23- The (Night of) Destiny *(al-Qadr)*

According to Ibn Ḥazm and Abū Muhammad, it is Medinan,[373] on account of what al-Hākim narrates on the authority of al-Ḥasan ibn Ali:

> The Prophet saw the Umayyads jumping on his pulpit like monkeys and this upset him, so it was revealed to console his noble mind.[374]

Jalāl al-Dīn reports al-Mazzī as saying that it is a disavowed hadith,[375] but this is an ignominious prejudice, since al-Ḥākim narrates it via an authentic chain of narration and al-Ḥāfiẓ al-Dhahabī confirms it in *al-Talkhīṣ*. He adds another chain of narration and confirms that, too, to be reliable. He continues:

> I do not know where the hadith's unsoundness comes from.[376]

---

[372] See Ṭabrisī, *Majma' al-Bayān*, vol. 10, 502; Ṭabarī, *Jāmi' al-Bayān*, vol. 3, 142 and Fayḍ Kāshānī, *al-Ṣāfī fī Tafsīr al-Qur'an*, vol. 2, 825.

[373] Makkī ibn Abī Ṭālib, *al-Kashf*, vol. 2, 385 and Ibn Ḥazm, *al-Nāsikh wa al-Mansūkh*, vol. 2, 203.

[374] Naysābūrī, *al-Mustadrak 'alā al-Ṣaḥīḥayn*, vol. 3, 171.

[375] Al-Suyūṭī, *al-Itqān*, vol. 1, 36.

[376] Shams al-Dīn al-Dhahabī, *Talkhīṣ al-Mustadrak bi al-Hāmish* (Abridged Version of *al-Mustadrak* In the Margin of Nayshābūrī, *al-Mustadrak*), vol. 3, 170.

My comment is that the claim of its unsoundness came from an Umayyad grudge which infused hearts overcome by ignorant and tribalistic (*qawmiyyah*) leanings, thus making it difficult for them to bow to the truth even when it is at the level of indubitability (*tawātur*) and certainty.[377]

However, this alone does not prove the point, because it is possible that he was shown it in Mecca before his migration as glad tidings of the elevation of his position, as well as giving him a brief view of the usurpation which would be perpetrated by the most evil ones from his nation. So there is no conflict at all between this tradition and the traditions on the order of the revelation of the chapters.

To support this, we assert that the verse *We granted the vision which We showed thee, but as a trial for men – as also the cursed tree in the Qur'an* (17:60) alludes to the same vision mentioned above. The verse is from *The Night Journey* which by consensus is Meccan. No one claims that any of this chapter is an exception, even if they believe that verses in other chapters are exceptions, as will be discussed below.

Ibn Abī Hātim cites Ibn 'Umar as saying that the Prophet said:

> I saw the progeny of al-Ḥakam ibn Abī al-'Āṣ on the pulpits like monkeys and God revealed with regard to that: *We granted the vision which We showed thee, but as a trial for men – as also the cursed tree in the Qur'an* (17:60). The cursed tree means al-Ḥakam and his progeny.

He also cites Ya'lā ibn al-Murrah as saying on the authority of the Messenger of God:

> I was shown the Umayyads on the earth's pulpits. They will speak to you and you will find them to be evil-doers. The Messenger of God became saddened and so the verse was revealed.

Ibn Mardawayh also cites 'Ā'ishah as saying that it was revealed about Marwān ibn al-Ḥakam:

> I heard the Messenger of God say to your father and grandfather: 'Verily you are the cursed tree in the Qur'an.'

---

[377] See Ṭabarī, *Jāmi' al-Bayān*, vol. 15, 77 and vol. 30, 167; al-Suyūṭī, *al-Durr al-Manthūr*, vol. 4, 191 and vol. 6, 371 and al-Mas'ūdi, *Murūj al-Dhahab*, vol. 3, 250.

Ibn Abī Ḥātim, Ibn Mardawayh, al-Bayhaqī and Ibn 'Asākir cite Sa'īd ibn Musayyab as saying:

> The Messenger of God saw the Umayyads on the pulpits and that upset him. Thereafter God revealed to him that it was just wordly gain given to them and so he was glad (*qarrat 'aynuhu*). That is what the Almighty's Words: *We granted the vision which We showed thee, but as a trial for men - as also the cursed tree in the Qur'an* (17:60) are about. It means a trial for men.[378]

24- The Clear Sign (*al-Bayyinah*)

According to Makkī ibn Abī Ṭālib it is Meccan.[379]

However, the consensus of the traditions and explicit statements on the order of the revelation of the chapters is that it is Medinan. What is reported about the Prophet's calling Ubayy ibn Ka'b when it was revealed to him and reciting it to him[380] supports that – Ubayy was Anṣārī and became a Muslim at the hands of the Messenger of God in Medina.

25- The Earthquake (*al-Zalzalah*)

Al-Daḥḥāk and 'Aṭā' claim that it is Meccan. So, too, says Makkī ibn Abī Ṭālib and Sayyid Quṭb agrees with them, in view of its rousing tone.[381] However, it is the consensus of the traditions that it is Medinan.[382] Further, Ibn Abī Ḥātim cites Abū Sa'īd al-Khidri as saying:

> When *and whoso has done an atom's weight of good shall see it* (99:7) was revealed, I said, 'Messenger of God, I will see my deeds?' He replied, 'Yes.' I asked, 'The major, major ones?' He replied, 'Yes.' I said, 'The tiny, tiny ones?' He replied, 'Yes.' I said, 'Then my mother should be bereaved of me!'[383].

[378] Al-Suyūṭī, *al-Durr al-Manthūr*, vol. 4, 191.
[379] Makkī ibn Abī Ṭālib, *al-Kashf*, vol. 2, 385.
[380] Al-Suyūṭī, *al-Durr al-Manthūr*, vol. 6, 378.
[381] Ṭabrisī, *Majma' al-Bayān*, vol. 10, 524; Makkī ibn Abī Ṭālib, *al-Kashf*, vol. 2, 386; Sayyid Quṭb, *Fī Ẓilāl al-Qur'an*, vol. 30, 639.
[382] Ibn al-Nadīm, *al-Fihrist*, 44; Ṭabrisī, *Majma' al-Bayān*, vol. 10, 405; al-Suyūṭī, *al-Itqān*, vol. 1, 27; *al-Suyūṭī, al-Durr al-Manthūr*, vol. 6, 379.
[383] *Al-Suyūṭī, al-Durr al-Manthūr*, vol. 6, 381.

Abū Sa'īd al-Anṣārī (i.e., Abū Sa'īd al-Khidri) only attained puberty after the Battle of Uḥud.[384]

26- The Chargers (*al-'Ādiyāt*)

According to Qatādah, it is Medinan[385] on account of a tradition attributed to Ibn 'Abbās:

> It was revealed about horses which the Messenger of God despatched in a military detachment. They were late back and it troubled him, so God told him what had happened to them.[386]

However, there is obvious intrigue and incoherence in the tradition, and at the same time, it is contradicted by what is also narrated on the authority of Ibn 'Abbās by Ibn Jurayr, Ibn Abī Ḥātim, Ibn al-Anbārī, al-Ḥākim – who further says it is authentic – and Ibn Mardawayh:

> Ali reproached him for interpreting the chargers as horses becoming fervent in God's cause.

He explained to him:

> It is the flood (of people) from 'Arafāt to Muzdalifah.

Ibn 'Abbās comments:
So I gave up what I had been saying and went back to what Ali said.[387]

27- Rivalry *(al-Takāthur)*

Jalāl al-Dīn's chosen view is that it is Medinan and he relies on the following matters as evidence for this:

1) Ibn Buraydah's tradition that it was revealed about two Anṣārī tribes who were boasting to each other.
2) Qatādah said that it was revealed about the Jews.
3) It is reported from Ubayy ibn Ka'ab, the Anṣārī:

> We used to believe that [the Prophet's statement], 'If the son of Adam had two valleys of gold he would wish for a third' was a Qur'anic verse until *al-Takāthur* was revealed.

---

384 Al-Suyūṭī, *al-Itqān*, vol. 1, 36; Naysābūrī, *al-Mustadrak 'alā al-Ṣaḥīḥayn*, vol. 3, 563.
385 Ṭabrisī, *Majma' al-Bayān*, vol. 10, 527.
386 *Al-Suyūṭī, al-Durr al-Manthūr*, vol. 6, 383.
387 Al-Suyūṭī, *al-Durr al-Manthūr*, vol. 6, 383; Ṭabarī, *Jāmi' al-Bayān*, vol. 30, 177.

4) That it is reported from Ali:

> We used to doubt in the punishment of the grave until it was revealed.

Jalāl al-Dīn's comment is:

> Punishment of the grave was only mentioned in Medina, in accordance with the authentic narration on the story of the Jewish woman.[388]

However, all the evidence he relied on is invalid:

Firstly, this chapter has nothing to do with boasting to each other, and only addresses the aspect of rivalry.

Secondly, how could Ubayy ibn Ka'b, given that he was his chief scribe, remain in doubt about a Qur'anic verse until his doubt was dispelled by the revelation of a chapter that had no involvement in proving something else not to be of the Qur'an, and not ask the Messenger of God?

Thirdly, how can we allow ourselves to believe a tradition that attributes doubt about matters pertaining to the Hereafter to someone like Ali, the Commander of the Faithful and gateway of the Prophet's knowledge?

As for its being revealed exclusively about the Jews, it is restriction of the general intended meaning of the chapter, which deals with mankind's life being wasted on lowly pursuits.

The correct view, according to the consensus of traditions on the order of the revelation of the chapters, is that it was one of the first Meccan chapters. Jalāl al-Dīn himself explicitly states so in *al-Durr al-Manthūr*, narrating on the authority of Ibn 'Abbās.[389]

This is in addition to the stern tone we note in the chapter that suits the environment of Mecca, which was strongly dominated by materialistic tendencies. Use of the word[s]: 'No, indeed!' (*kallā*) exclusively to the people of Mecca – as mentioned above – emphasises this sternness.

28- Charity *(al-Mā'ūn)*

According to al-Ḍahhāk, it is Medinan.[390] However, the traditions on the order of revelation and explicit statements upon which there is consensus refute this statement. Added to that is the chapter's tone

[388] Al-Suyūṭī, *al-Itqān*, vol. 1, 37.

[389] Al-Suyūṭī, *al-Durr al-Manthūr*, vol. 6, 386.

[390] Ṭabrisī, *Majma' al-Bayān*, vol. 10, 546.

of stern rebuke of those who do not believe in the Day of Judgment, so it is more likely to be one of the earliest Meccan chapters. It was the seventeenth in order of revelation, after *Rivalry.* [391]

29- The Abundance *(al-Kawthar)*

According to 'Ikrimah and al-Ḍahhāk, it is Medinan.[392] Jalāl al-Dīn prefers this opinion, as does al-Nawawī in *Sharḥ Muslim*, on account of what Muslim narrates on the authority of Anas:

> While the Messenger of God was among us, he dozed off. He then raised his head and ... said, 'A chapter was just (*ānifan*) revealed to me.' So he recited it.

However, we have discussed this hadith[393] and shown that it does not mean that the Qur'an was revealed to him in that state, with reference to al-Rāfi'ī's interpretation of the hadith as its occurring to the Prophet in that state followed by his reciting it to them. Further, Muslim himself supports that – he narrates this hadith without the words '...was...revealed to me' via another chain of narration. He says:

> The Prophet dozed off, then he raised his head and recited it.[394]

Finally, the consensus of the exegetes is that it is Meccan, and was revealed to console the Messenger of God's mind when that accursed, childless man (*abtar*) showed hate for him.[395] This is in addition to the traditions on the order of revelation all saying that it was revealed in Mecca. Therefore, it is inappropriate for such an unreliable hadith to create doubt regarding the consensus.

30- The Unity *(al-Tawḥīd)*

Jalāl al-Dīn prefers the view that it is Medinan on account of traditions concerning its revelation. He asserts:

---

[391] Ibn al-Nadīm, *al-Fihrist*, 28; Ṭabrisī, *Majma' al-Bayān*, vol. 10, 405; al-Suyūṭī, *al-Itqān*, vol. 1, 27.

[392] Ṭabrisī, *Majma' al-Bayān*, vol. 10, 548.

[393] Under the heading 'Dreams which came true'.

[394] Al-Suyūṭī, *al-Durr al-Manthūr*, vol. 6, 401.

[395] Al-Suyūṭī, *Lubāb al-Nuqūl*, vol. 2, 142; al-Suyūṭī, *al-Durr al-Manthūr*, vol. 6, 404; Ṭabrisī, *Majma' al-Bayān*, vol. 10, 549.

> It was revealed about a group of Jews in Medina who asked the Messenger of God to describe his Lord to them. So Gabriel brought down *The Unity*.[396]

However, there are other traditions which refer to the pagans' question:

> They said: 'Relate your Lord to us, Muhammad,' and so it was revealed.[397]

This is in addition to the consensus of the traditions on the order of revelation.

Hence, some researchers have said that it was revealed twice!

My comment: That would not be surprising. However, the revelation of a chapter on two occasions means that the second time was a reminder to the Prophet of its relevance to the matter at hand. It is possible, based on this hypothesis, that the Jews asked the Prophet a question similar to one the pagans had already asked, and so the Prophet hesitated in reciting to them the same chapter that had answered the pagans' earlier question. That was in view of the difference in level between the Jews and the pagans. So Gabriel revealed the adequacy of the original response, given that Qur'anic chapters are neither particular to one people to the exclusion of others, nor to one level, because in spite of the difference in their levels, all people can benefit from all the verses of the Qur'an, even though the type of benefit may vary according to their cultural level.

Thus, the chapter is Meccan, even if it was revealed again in Medina.

31 & 32- The *Mu'awwidhatān*[398]

Al-Ya'qūbī considers them to be among the last of the Medinan,[399] and Jalāl al-Dīn says:

> The preferred view is that they are Medinan, because they were revealed with regard to the story of Lubayd ibn al-A'ṣam's sorcery.[400]

---

[396] Al-Suyūṭī, *Lubāb al-Nuqūl*, vol. 2, 147; al-Suyūṭī, *al-Itqān*, vol. 1, 37.

[397] Al-Suyūṭī, *al-Durr al-Manthūr*, vol. 6, 410.

[398] The name given to the last two chapters of the Qur'an, because after 'In the Name of God, the Merciful, the Compassionate,' they commence with the words: 'Say: I seek refuge... (*Qul A'ūdhu...*).' [Trans.]

[399] Ibn Wāḍiḥ, *Tārīkh al-Ya'qūbī*, vol. 2, 35.

[400] Al-Suyūṭī, *al-Itqān*, vol. 1, 37.

The story, as reported in the two 'authentic' books (*al-Ṣaḥīḥayn*),[401] is told by 'Ā'ishah:

> A man among the Jews of Banī Zurayq, called Lubayd ibn al-A'ṣam, bewitched the Messenger of God.

She continues:

> It reached the point that the Messenger of God was made to think that he was doing something which he was not. In other words he was bewitched, making him think he had been intimate with his wives when he had not.

Sufyān says:

> This is the most powerful sorcery there can be.[402]

She states:

> Then one day or one night the Messenger of God invoked God, and kept on invoking Him and invoking Him. Thereafter, he said to me: 'Do you realise that God has given me a ruling on what I asked Him for a ruling on? Two men[403] came to me, and one of them sat at my head and the other at my feet. The one who was at my head asked the one who was at my feet: 'What is ailing this man?'
>
> He replied: 'Magic has been cast on him.'
>
> He asked: 'Who cast it on him?'
>
> He replied: 'Lubayd ibn al-A'ṣam.'
>
> He asked: 'Using what?'
>
> He replied: 'On a comb, the hair on it, and the husk of a male palm spathe.'
>
> He asked: 'Where is it?'
>
> He replied: 'In Dharwān's well.'

---

401 *Ṣaḥīḥ al-Bukhārī*, vol. 4, 148; *Ṣaḥīḥ Muslim*, vol. 7, 14.

402 *Ṣaḥīḥ al-Bukhārī*, vol. 7, 77.

403 One tradition says: 'Gabriel and Michael...So the former asked the latter...' See Ibn Ḥajar, *Fatḥ al-Bārī*, vol. 10, 194.

She continues:

> So the Messenger of God went there with some of his companions, came back and said: 'Ā'ishah, I swear by God its water was the colour of an infusion of henna and its palms like devils' heads.'

She said:

> So I asked him: 'Did you try to take it out?'
>
> He replied: 'No. As for myself, God cured me, and I feared that that would stir up evil against the people.'
>
> Then he ordered that the well be filled up with earth.

In a different version of hadith, the first man asked, 'Where is it?' and the other replied, 'On the husk of a male spathe under a stone (*rā'ūfah*)[404] in Dharwān's well.' And 'A'ishah said:

> So the Prophet went to the well and got it out. He said: 'This was the well I was shown. Its water was like an infusion of henna and its palms like devils' heads.'
>
> She asked: 'So would you not?' meaning, 'Would you not expose it?'
>
> He replied: 'As for myself, God cured me, and I recoil from stirring evil against any of the people.'[405]

This story, as mentioned in the two authentic books, does not contain any reference to the revelation of the two chapters. Al-Suyūṭī noticed that, hence, he sought evidence for the matter from sources of which the chains of narration are not authentic. In *Dalā'il al-Nubuwwah* (Evidence of Prophethood), Bayhaqī cites 'Ā'ishah as follows:

> The Messenger of God had a Jewish slave boy called Lubayd ibn A'ṣam who served him. The Jew remained with him until he cast magic upon the Prophet. He was wasting away, not knowing what was causing his pain.

According to another version:

---

[404] A *ra'ūfah* is a solid rock or stone put at the mouth of a well and which cannot be removed. The person drawing water stands on it. Alternatively, it is put at the bottom for whoever cleans the well to sit on.

[405] *Ṣaḥīḥ al-Bukhārī*, vol. 7, 178.

He was turning over, not knowing what was causing his pain.[406]

While the Messenger of God was asleep one night, two angels came to him and sat down, one of them at his head and the other at his feet. The former said to the latter, 'What is causing his pain?' The latter replied, 'He's had magic cast upon him.'

The first asked, 'Who cast it upon him?'

The second replied, 'Lubayd ibn A'ṣam.'

The first then asked, 'What did he use to cast it upon him?'

And the second replied, 'A comb, the hair on it and the husk of a male palm spathe at Dhū Arwān. It is under the well's stone.'

When the Messenger of God woke up in the morning, he set off for the well, his companions with him, and a man went down and took the spathe out. Why, God's Messenger's comb and some of the hair of his head was in it, and lo and behold, there was a candlewax doll – a doll of the Messenger of God. And there were pins sticking out of it and a rope with eleven knots on it. So Gabriel brought him the *mu'awwidhatayn* and instructed:

O Muhammad, say, *I take refuge with the Lord of the Daybreak...*

A knot came undone.

...From the evil of what He has created...

Another knot came undone, and so on until he reached the end of it and all the knots had come undone. He started pulling the pins out and did not pull a single one out without feeling pain. Thereafter he found comfort. He was asked, 'Messenger of God, why don't you kill the Jew?' He replied, 'God cured me. God's punishment, which will come to him, is more severe.'

Another tradition says:

A Jew cast magic on the Prophet and he suffered, so Gabriel brought him the *mu'awwidhatayn*. He said: A Jewish man has cast magic on you. The charm is in So-and-so's well.

[406] Ibn Ḥajar, *Fatḥ al-Bārī*, vol. 10, 193.

> So he sent Ali, and he came to it. He told him to undo the knots and recite a verse. He began reciting and untying until the Prophet got up as though he had been released from hobbling.[407]

It is also said:

> Lubayd's daughters were witches, so they and their father used magic on the Messenger of God and knotted eleven knots against him. So God sent down the *mu'awwidhatayn* – eleven verses, one for each knot – and God cured the Messenger of God.[408]

However, even if we were to accept this story, there is no evidence in the narrations in the authentic books that the *mu'awwidhatayn* verses were revealed in relation to it. As for the rest of the sources, they cannot be relied on as evidence, let alone their forming the evidential basis for a ruling in relation to matters pertaining to the Qur'an, on which a Muslim should not speak without knowledge or without reliable evidence.

According to Jalāl al-Dīn:

> As for the entire basis of the story, it is evidenced by the two authentic books with the exception of the revelation of the two chapters.

He then comments:

> However, there is evidence from elsewhere.

By this he means what al-Bayhaqī cites, on the authority of al-Kalbī, on the authority of Abū Ṣāliḥ, on the authority of Ibn 'Abbās, which contains a reference to the story and the revelation of the two chapters.[409]

However, Jalāl al-Dīn himself, in al-Itqān, states that the weakest chain of narration back to Ibn 'Abbās is al-Kalbī, then Abū Ṣāliḥ, then Ibn 'Abbās.[410] He then refers to further evidence in what Abū Nu'aym cites in *Dalā'il al-Nubuwwah* via Abū Ja'far al-Rāzī on the authority of al-Rabī' ibn Anas, on the authority of Anas ibn Mālik.[411]

---

[407] Al-Suyūṭī, *al-Durr al-Manthūr*, vol. 6, 417.

[408] Muhammad ibn Aḥmad Ibn Juzzī al-Kalbī, *al-Tas-hīl li 'Ulūm al-Tanzīl*, (Beirut: Dār al-Kitāb al-Arabī, 1393 q.), vol. 4, 225.

[409] Al-Suyūṭī, *Lubāb al-Nuqūl*, vol. 2, 148.

[410] Al-Suyūṭī, *al-Itqān*, vol. 4, 209.

[411] Al-Suyūṭī, *Lubāb al-Nuqūl*, vol. 2, 148.

Further, Ibn Ḥibbān contends:

> Hadith specialists stay clear of al-Rabīʿ ibn Anas' hadith if Abū Jaʿfar al-Rāzī is narrating on his authority, because there is much disorder in his hadiths.[412]

So is it not surprising how a man so well-versed in the arts of hadith and exegesis could get himself embroiled in contradictory rulings and fall into disorder by adducing inappropriate evidence, and thereafter speak on matters of the Qur'an without reliable evidence?

As for the Shiʿa, the fundamentals of our beliefs negate the possibility of influence on the Prophet's heart – the safe repository of God's revelation and His knowledge. In other words, Lubayd was incapable of manipulating a mind like that of God's Messenger, the best of God's creation and the noblest of prophets.

The Qur'an says:

> *Lo! My faithful bondmen – over them thou hast no power, and Thy Lord sufficeth as (their) guardian* (17:65).

Therefore, even less would Lubayd be able to possess the heart of God's noblest servant, since his heart is the property of Almighty God, and pollution could never approach it.

Thus, if we entertained the possibility of the Prophet being influenced in such a way that he could be made to imagine he had done something which he had not, faith would be lost in what he says being revelation. It could just be the work of an unclean sorceror that would cause him to think that it is revelation.

According to ʿAllāmah Ṭabrisī :

> This is not possible, because it is to describe him as touched by magic, as if his mind had been befuddled. God refutes such a thing in His Words, *And the evil-doers say, 'Ye are but following a man bewitched.' See how they coin similitudes for thee, so that they are all astray...* (25:8-9).

However, it is possible that the Jew and his daughters, according to what is narrated, strove to do so but were unable, and God apprised His Prophet of the despicable act they had carried out, enabling him to

[412] Ibn Ḥajar, *Tahdhīb al-Tahdhīb*, vol. 3, 239.

remedy it. This is evidence of his truthfulness, for how could the illness have been a result of what they did? If they had been able to do that, they would have killed him and many of the believers, given the strength of their enmity towards them.[413]

'Allāmah Majlisī says:

> General opinion among the Shi'a is that magic does not have any effect on the Prophets and Imāms (God's blessings be upon them). Hence they have interpreted some of the traditions in this connection in a non-literal manner and rejected others, that is, those which cannot be interpreted.[414]

Al-Quṭb al-Rāwandī states:

> It is narrated that a Jewish woman made a charm against him and thought that her scheme would work – but magic is futile and impossible – except that God showed him to it and so he sent someone to take it out (of the well). It was as they described it with the same number of knots, some of which someone would not even have noticed if they had seen it.[415]

According to *Ṭibb al-A'immah*:

> Gabriel came to the Prophet and said to him, 'So-and-so the Jew has charmed you.' He described the charm and where it was, and so the Prophet sent Ali to the well. He looked for it but could not find it. He struggled to find it, eventually did so, and then took it back to the Prophet. Why, it was real. It had a piece of the lower ends of palm branches inside comprising a cord with eleven knots in it. Gabriel had sent down the *mu'awwidhatayn* and so the Prophet told Ali to recite them at the cord. Every time he recited, a knot came undone until he reached the end. Thus, God relieved the Prophet of what had charmed him, and cured him.[416]

Even though this tradition's chain of narration is not authentic, it does not say anything about any influence on the Messenger's mind. It is

---

[413] Ṭabrisī, *Majma' al-Bayān*, vol. 10, 568.

[414] Majlisī, *Biḥār al-Anwār*, vol. 18, 70.

[415] Majlisī, *Biḥār al-Anwār*, vol. 57, 11.

[416] Abdullah ibn Sābūr al-Zayy al-Naysābūrī, *Ṭibb al-A'immah* (Qum: Amīr, 1411 q.), 118.

true that another tradition does mention an effect on his body that made him feel severe pain. This is the meaning of 'God relieved the Prophet of what had charmed him, and cured him' in the narration in *Ṭibb al-A'immah*, i.e., He cured him of the pain he felt. This is something which is possible. However, the more correct opinion in our view is what al-Quṭb al-Rāwandī said, namely, that magic has no effect on him. They wanted to scheme against him but they ended up as the losers.

Verses Which Are Exceptions

The earliest scholars said that certain verses are exceptions – they were revealed in a different place to the chapters in which they appear, so a Meccan chapter may contain Medinan verses and vice versa. Jalāl al-Dīn al-Suyūṭī dealt with this thoroughly in *al-Itqān*. However, he relied on traditions which we consider to be weak, and then later scholars relied on his findings without checking,[417] when in fact the majority who attest to these exceptions have done so on the basis of conjecture or exercising

---

[417] Exceptions appear in large letters in the Amīrī codex printed in Cairo with the permission of the Sheikhs of al-Azhar and under the supervision of the Board for Monitoring Islamic Studies (*Lajnat Murāqabat al-Buḥūth al-Islāmiyyah*). However, this is simply the copying of texts the overwhelming majority of which have no basis. It is also how Sheikh Abū 'Abdillāh al-Zanjānī records them in his book, *Tārīkh al-Qur'an*. Add to that the contradictions which appear in such texts. For example, the Amīrī codex says that the chapter *Alif Lām Mīm Tanzīl* (*Sūrah Sajdah*) was revealed after *The Believer* (*al-Mu'min*) and that the *Ḥā MīmTanzīl* (*Sūrah Fuṣṣilat*) was revealed after *The Forgiver* (*al-Ghāfir*), even though *The Believer* and *The Forgiver* are, in fact, two names for the same chapter.

Abū 'Abdillāh sets out two tables in *Tārīkh al-Qur'an* with regard to the order of the chapters, and states in the first table that the chapter entitled *The Cattle* (*al-An'ām*) was revealed after *al-Ḥijr*, and in the second table, that it was revealed after *The Cave*. He also states in the first one that *The Heights* (*al-A'rāf*) was revealed after *Ṣād* and in the second one that it was revealed after *The Spoils of War*. He states that there are eighty-five Meccan chapters and twenty-eight Medinan chapters without noticing that that is one short of the total number of chapters in the Qur'an. I think in so doing he was just copying Imām Badr al-Dīn al-Zarkashī.

A codex printed in Iran during the time of the Qājārs contains two lists, the first showing the year each chapter was revealed, the second recording the order of revelation. The first list says that *Those Arrayed in Ranks* (*al-Ṣāffāt*) was revealed in the fifth year of the despatch (*bi'thah*) and that *The Cattle* (*al-An'ām*) was revealed in the thirteenth. Then, the second list says that *Those Arrayed in Ranks* was revealed after *The Cattle*. There are many such contradictions.

their own judgement, without relying on any text containing an authentic tradition as evidence. Ibn al-Ḥaṣṣār says:

> There are among the people those who have relied on deduction as opposed to orally transmitted evidence with regard to exceptions.[418]

In knocking on this door we shall cast aside everything they have said on the matter, because it is not based on any acceptable evidence. For there is no doubt that the verses were recorded one after the other in a natural order, in line with the revelation in every chapter, after 'In the Name of God, the Merciful, the Compassionate,' which appears at the beginning of them. As for a Meccan verse remaining unentered in any chapter until a chapter was revealed in Medina and then being inserted, or Medinan verses inserted in Meccan chapters, it is irregular and outside the known method of recording, and therefore needs to be proven with an explicit statement. Conjecture and theoretical deduction do not enter into the matter.

According to Ibn Ḥajar:

> As for part of a chapter being revealed in Mecca and the revelation of the main part of the chapter being delayed till Medina, I have only seen this rarely. They are in agreement that *The Spoils of War* (*al-Anfāl*) is Medinan. However, it is said that God's Words, *And when the unbelievers plot against thee* (8:30), were revealed in Mecca, then *The Spoils of War* was revealed in Medina. This is very strange.[419]

We shall come to the refutation of this claim.

There follow some examples of both interpretations, along with a summary of the correct view.

Exceptions Within Meccan Chapters

1- The Opening (*al-Fātihah*): Meccan

Abū Layth al-Samarqandī reports an opinion stating that half of it was revealed in Medina.

Jalāl al-Dīn's comment is:

[418] Al-Suyūṭī, *al-Itqān*, vol. 1, 38.

[419] Ibn Ḥajar, *Fatḥ al-Bārī*, vol. 9, 38.

> There is no evidence for this opinion.[420]

As stated above, it was one of the first chapters to be revealed in its entirety in Mecca, and the Muslims would recite it in prayer.

2- The Cattle (*al-An'ām*): Meccan

It was revealed in Mecca and a thousand angels followed in procession. They gave off a soft humming sound of glorification and praise, and filled the whole space between heaven and earth. It was a Thursday night and they descended in grandeur. The Messenger of God began saying, 'Exalted is God, the Great, Exalted is God, the Great,' and fell down prostrate. Then he called the scribes and they wrote it down that very night.

This hadith is widely circulated (*mustafīḍ*), narrated by both sects via channels which support each other.[421] Jalāl al-Dīn's comment is:

> These are pieces of evidence which add strength to each other.[422]

Hence there is no weight to Abū 'Amr ibn al-Ṣalāḥ's claim:

> The aforementioned tradition comes from Ubayy ibn Ka'b's hadith, and there is weakness in his chain of narration. We have not seen an authentic chain of narration for it. That which contradicts it has been narrated.[423]

My own comment is that the numerous channels back to a number of other companions in addition to Ubayy ibn Ka'b means it is reliable evidence. Furthermore, the tradition which contradicts it is weak and unconfirmed.

Ibn Haṣṣār states:

> Nine verses are said to be exceptions, but there is no authentic hadith to support this.[424]

---

[420] Al-Suyūṭī, *al-Itqān*, vol. 1, 30 and 38.

[421] *Tafsīr al-'Ayyāshī*, vol. 1, 353; Ṭabrisī, *Majma' al-Bayān*, vol. 4, 271; al-Suyūṭī, *al-Durr al-Manthūr*, vol. 3, 2.

[422] Al-Suyūṭī, *al-Itqān*, vol. 1, 108.

[423] Zarkashī, *al-Burhān*, vol. 1, 199.

[424] Al-Suyūṭī, *al-Itqān*, vol. 1, 38.

We shall discuss what are claimed to be authentic traditions regarding the exceptions.[425]

The Amīrī Codex and those who copied it say, with no corroboration, that nine verses are exceptions. We shall discuss each one of them in what follows:

1) the Almighty's Words:

> *Those unto whom We have given the Book recognise (this revelation) as they recognise their sons* (6:20).

2) the Almighty's Words:

> *Then will they have no contention save that they will say, 'By God, our Lord, we never were idolators'* (6:23).

There is no evidence at all for claiming that these two verses are exceptions. The reason may be that they refer to the People of the Book, though this is not entirely clear in the second one, since there is no evidence for that, given that the People of the Book are mentioned in several Meccan verses such as:

> *And argue not with the People of the Book unless it be in (a way) that is better...* (29:46).

No one has claimed that to be an exception.

The same is true of God's Words:

> *In like manner We have revealed unto thee the Book, and those unto whom We gave the Book aforetime will believe therein ...* (29:47).

There are several others which are similar.

3) the Almighty's Words:

> *And they measure not the power of God its true measure when they say, 'God hath naught revealed unto any mortal.' Say: 'Who revealed the Book which Moses brought, a light and guidance for mankind, which ye have put on parchments which ye show, but ye hide much (thereof), and (by which) ye were taught that which ye knew not yourselves nor (did) your fathers (know it).' Say: 'God.' Then leave them to their play of cavilling* (6:91).

---

[425] Exceptions are nos. 7, 8 and 9.

Ibn Kathīr and Abū 'Amr read it as:

> They put it on parchments, revealing them but hiding much...[426]

It is said that it was revealed in relation to a group of Jews who asked, 'Muhammad, has God sent a Book down to you?' He replied, 'Yes.' Their response was, 'We swear by God, that He has not sent any Book down from Heaven.

It is also said that it was revealed in relation to Mālik ibn al-Ṣayf, who was one of the rabbis among the Jews of Qurayẓah – hence revealed in Medina. He was fat, and so the Prophet said to him:

> I implore you by Him who sent the Torah down to Moses, did you not find in the Torah, 'Verily, God hates fat rabbis?' He became angry and said, 'God has not sent anything down to any man.'

It is further said that the one who opposed the Prophet with regard to these words was Fanḥāṣ ibn 'Āzurā' the Jew.

It is said also that it was revealed in relation to the pagans from Quraysh because they denied all prophethood.[427]

Abū Ja'far Ṭabarī says:

> The most likely to be correct is the last of these opinions, because there had been no mention of the Jews before that. Denial of revelation to mankind is not something the Jews ascribe to. On the contrary, what is known of their religion is a confirmation of Abraham and Moses' Scrolls and David's Psalms. The tradition saying that it was revealed in relation to the Jews is not an authentic tradition with an unbroken chain of narration, nor have exegetes reached a consensus on that. Further, the context of the chapter from start to finish pertains to the pagans, so it is appropriate that this verse should also be linked to what precedes it and not cut off therefrom. We can only claim that it is separate on the basis of indubitable proof, either traditional or rational.

---

426 Makkī ibn Abī Ṭālib, *al-Kashf*, vol. 1, 440.

427 Ṭabarī, *Jāmi' al-Bayān*, vol. 7, 177; Ṭabrisī, *Majma' al-Bayān*, vol. 4, 333.

> What made this person fall into the aforementioned misconception is his reading it as 'You put it...,' in the second person. However, the correct reading is in the third person.[428]

My comment is that while we agree with Abū Ja'far with regard to this finding, we add that the story they mention on the matter of the dispute between Mālik ibn al-Ṣayf and the Prophet is wholly incompatible with the Messenger of God's impeccable manners. The Prophet never hurt a person's feelings at all, and similarly, God's Book is far above addressing such petty matters which are of no value, or for a verse to be revealed in relation to them.

Thus, the words *...ye were taught...* addresses the pagans in the second person after the account of the People of the Book in the third person – as preferred by Abū Ja'far.

As for the generally accepted reading – in the second person for all – it does not necessarily mean it is addressed to the People of the Book alone, but rather to all mankind, on account of the actions of some of those to whom the Book was revealed, especially in view of the pagan Arabs' contact and mingling with the Jews in the peninsula. Hence, there is a lot of talk about the Children of Israel in many Meccan chapters, such as *The Heights* (*al-A'rāf*), 7:102, 7:160.

The Almighty's Words addressed to the people of Mecca testify to that:

> *Ask the followers of the Remembrance if you know not* (16:43).

The same statement is also found in *The Prophets* (*al-Anbīyā'*), which is also Meccan. As a matter of fact, the Arabs had strong links with and trust in the People of the Book. They knew them as people of knowledge and that they could be relied upon. They would often ask them about the history of peoples and prophets and rely on what they said, and therefore they liaised with the Jews round about them, with whom they mingled and whom they trusted.

4) the Almighty's Words:

> *Who is guilty of more wrong than he who forgeth a lie against God, or saith: 'I am inspired,' when he is not inspired in aught; and who saith: 'I will reveal the like of that which God hath revealed'?* (6:93).

[428] Ṭabarī, *Jāmi' al-Bayān*, vol. 7, 178. Similarly, Sayyid Quṭb agrees with him in *Fī Ẓilāl al-Qur'an*, vol. 7, 302-303.

Concerning this they say:

> The Almighty's Words, *Who is guilty of more wrong...*, were revealed in relation to 'Abdullāh ibn Sa'd ibn Abī Sarḥ, who was breastfed by the same woman as 'Uthmān. He had become a Muslim and acted as a scribe for the Messenger of God. When *We created man from a product of wet earth* (23:12) was revealed, the Prophet summoned him and dictated to him. When he reached the words, *and then produced it as another creation* (23:14), 'Abdullāh was amazed by the details of man's creation, and so he said, 'Blessed be God, the fairest of creators.' And so the Messenger of God said: 'That is how it was revealed to me.'
>
> At that point 'Abdullāh had doubt, and said, 'If Muhammad is telling the truth, revelation will come to me the way it has come to him. If he is lying, I will say as he has said,' and so he apostasised from Islam and rejoined the people of Mecca. They began to ask him, 'How did you write the Qur'an for the son of the father of a sheep?' He replied, 'I would write as I liked.' That is because the Messenger of God would dictate to him, 'All-Knowing, All-Wise,' and he would write, 'All-Forgiving, All-Merciful,' interpolating, deleting and making changes to the Book of God without the Prophet's realising. Hence he doubted his being a messenger, became an unbeliever and rejoined Quraysh. So the Prophet wanted to spill his blood. However, 'Uthmān gave him shelter on the Day of the Conquest and pestered the Messenger of God until he pardoned him.[429]

They also say in relation to God's Words, *he who... saith, 'To me it has been revealed,' when aught has been revealed to him*, that they were revealed in relation to Musaylamah and al-Aswad al-'Anasī. who both claimed to be prophets within the Messenger's lifetime.[430]

[429] See Ṭabrisī, *Majma' al-Bayān*, vol. 4, 335; al-Suyūṭī, *al-Durr al-Manthūr*, vol. 3, 30; Ṭabarī, *Jāmi' al-Bayān*, vol. 7, 181; Rāzī, *al-Tafsīr al-Kabīr*, vol. 13, 84; Sayyid Quṭb, *Fī Ẓilāl al-Qur'an*, vol. 7, 306; Zarkashī, *al-Burhān*, vol. 1, 200.

[430] See Ṭabrisī, *Majma' al-Bayān*, vol. 4, 335; al-Suyūṭī, *al-Durr al-Manthūr*, vol. 3, 30; Ṭabarī, *Jāmi' al-Bayān*, vol. 7, 181; Rāzī, *al-Tafsīr al-Kabīr*, vol. 13, 84; Sayyid Quṭb, *Fī Ẓilāl al-Qur'an*, vol. 7, 306; Zarkashī, *al-Burhān*, vol. 1, 200.

However, the hadith is entirely fabricated, because *The Believers* (*al-Mu'minūn*) is Meccan and nobody has said that any of its verses are an exception. So how can Ibn Abī Sarḥ have acted as a scribe in Medina and then retreated back to Mecca? Further, far be it from a man to forge lies against God, claiming to be inspired, when God has guaranteed the protection of His Noble Book, and for the Messenger not to be aware of interpolations by a liar, falsely attributing things to God with regards to what God has revealed? If this possibility is accepted, can any faith remain in the Qur'an being exempt from false interpolations?

It is true that there are three verses from three chapters which are said to have been revealed in relation to Ibn Abī Sarḥ, and this is one of them. The second is:

> *but whoso findeth ease in disbelief...*(16:106),[431]

and the third:

> *Those who believe, then disbelieve and then (again) believe, then disbelieve, and then increase in disbelief ...* (4:137).

This last one is most appropriate and worthy of being accepted as narrated on the authority of the two Imāms Muhammad ibn Ali al-Bāqir and Ja'far ibn Muhammad al-Ṣādiq.[432]

Therefore the correct opinion on the first verse is what Abū Ja'far Ṭabarī said:

> It is general, describing mankind's overall position towards the messages of the prophets. Among them are stubborn people who do not accept any message sent by God. Others are gullible and weak, and believe any claim to be a messenger, even if it is Satanic insinuation, without hesitation or proper thought. Hence, the verse admonished this latter category of lowly gullibility and the former one of iniquitous insolence towards the Lord of Glory,

---

431 See Ṭabarī, *Jāmi' al-Bayān*, vol. 7, 181.

432 *Tafsīr al-'Ayyāshī*, vol. 1, 281. As for what appears in the exegesis attributed to Ali ibn Ibrāhīm al-Qummī, vol. 1, 210 about the verse from *The Cattle* (6:93) being revealed in relation to Ibn Abī Sarḥ, there are shocking things within it which negate the possibility of its having issued from an Infallible, for it says that the Messenger of God endorsed the changing of the text and said, 'It is the same thing...'

leading to the false and hostile forging of lies against Him. So the verse has nothing to do with the matter of Ibn Abī Sarḥ specifically.

Furthermore, the words, *I will reveal the like of that which God hath revealed* (6:93), do not apply to Ibn Abī Sarḥ's position towards the Messenger of God. They might have applied if the verse had said, 'I will reveal the like of that which Muhammad hath revealed...'

Sayyid Quṭb contradicts himself in relation to the verse. In one place he considers it more likely that the chapter is Meccan, and in another he relies on the traditions on exceptions.[433]

5) the Almighty's Words:

> *Shall I seek other than God for judge, when He it is Who hath revealed unto you (this) Book, fully-explained? Those unto whom We gave the Scipture (aforetime) know that it is revealed from thy Lord in truth* (6:114).

There is nothing in this verse that makes one think that it is Medinan except for the reference to the People of the Book. It was stated above that this alone is not proof. The likes of it appear in several Meccan verses. The reason goes back to the trust the pagan Arabs had in the People of the Book neighbouring their towns. They saw them as people of knowledge and cognisance. Hence the Almighty said, *Ask the followers of the Remembrance if ye know not!* (16:43),[434] meaning the People of the Book, especially the Jews. This verse is Meccan by consensus, except what is attributed to Jābir ibn Zayd. However, al-Suyūṭī refutes it on two counts.[435]

6) the Almighty's Words:

> *He it is Who produceth gardens trellised and untrellised... Eat ye of the fruit thereof when it fruiteth, and pay the due thereof upon the harvest day...* (6:141).

It may be that whoever said it was Medinan interpreted 'the due' as *zakāt*, and *zakāt* was only decreed on defined amounts of agriculture and fruit in Medina.

However, this meaning is not specified in the verse because it has been explained as *ṣadaqah* (charity) generally without any qualification.

---

433 Sayyid Quṭb, *Fī Ẓilāl al-Qur'an*, vol. 7, 106 and 306.

434 Also 21:7, but without the ending.

435 Al-Suyūṭī, *al-Itqān*, vol. 1, 9.

This general sense was compulsory in Mecca, and there is reference to it in, *And in their wealth the beggar and the outcast had due share* (51:19), the nineteenth verse of *The Winds That Scatter* (*al-Dhārīyāt*), which is Meccan by consensus. References to provision for and charity appear in several Meccan verses.

Several traditions say that the 'share' in these verses means providing for orphans and the destitute, on the authority of Sa'īd ibn Jubayr and others. They were then later abrogated by the verse on *zakāt*.[436] This is also narrated on the authority of Imam Abū 'Abdillāh al-Ṣādiq, on the authority of his forefathers.[437]

7) the Almighty's Words:

> *Say: 'Come, I will recite unto you that which your Lord hath made a sacred duty for you...'* (6:151).

8) the Almighty's Words:

> *And approach not the wealth of the orphan save with that which is better...*(6:152).

9) the Almighty's Words:

> *This is My straight path, so follow it* (6:153).

According to al-Suyūṭī:

> The narration on the authority of Ibn 'Abbās that these three verses are exceptions is authentic.[438]

This tradition is what Abū Ja'far al-Naḥḥās cites in his book, *al-Nāsikh wa al-Mansūkh*, via Abū 'Ubaydah Mu'ammar ibn al-Muthannā on the authority of Yūnus, on the authority of Abū 'Amr, on the authority of Mujāhid, on the authority of Ibn 'Abbās.[439]

This Abū 'Ubaydah was a man with odd views; he believed what the Khārijites believed, was foulmouthed, sacrilegious and paid little attention to the Qur'an. If he recited it, he would recite it according to his own

---

[436] See al-Suyūṭī, *al-Durr al-Manthūr*, vol. 3, 49 and Ṭabarī, *Jāmi' al-Bayān*, vol. 8, 44.
[437] Ṭabrisī, *Majma' al-Bayān*, vol. 4, 375.
[438] Al-Suyūṭī, *al-Itqān*, vol. 1, 39.
[439] Al-Suyūṭī, *al-Itqān*, vol. 1, 24.

opinion.[440] Hence any narration of his on scripture or the *sunnah* is not relied upon, unless of course it is a narration on poetry and literature. We do not know on what basis Jalāl al-Dīn considered the chain of narration of this tradition to be authentic.

Furthermore, Abū Nu'aym and al-Bayhaqī both narrate in *Dalā'il al-Nubuwwah* that Ali ibn Abī Ṭālib said:

> When God commanded His Prophet to put himself out there in front of the tribes, he went out to Minā. I was with him and so was Abū Bakr who was an expert on genealogy. So he stood at their campsites at Minā, greeted them and they replied. He spoke with the people until they asked him, 'What are you calling to, brother of Quraysh?'
>
> So the Messenger of God recited, *Come, I will recite unto you that which your Lord hath made a sacred duty for you...*, reciting all three verses.
>
> God's Words amazed them and they said, 'We swear by God, these are not the words of the people of earth. If they were, we would know them.'[441]

So the verses were revealed at that time in Mecca,[442] in addition to the fact that the tone of the verses and their style of expression also testify to their being Meccan.

In summary, the whole of *The Cattle* is Meccan. There is not a single Medinan verse in it. None of what is said to be an exception has been corroborated, either by way of hadith or rational proof, as stated above.

3- The Heights *(al-A'rāf)*: Meccan

Ibn Ḍurays, al-Naḥḥās and Ibn Mardawayh cite Ibn 'Abbās as saying, via many chains of narration, that it was revealed in Mecca.[443]

Qatādah says:

> Except for one verse:

---

[440] Ibn al-Nadīm, *al-Fihrist*, 85; Ibn Ḥajar, *Tahdhīb al-Tahdhīb*, vol. 10, 247; al-Dhahabī, *Mīzān al-I'tidāl*, vol. 4, 155.

[441] Al-Suyūṭī, *al-Durr al-Manthūr*, vol. 3, 54.

[442] Ṭabarī, *Jāmi' al-Bayān*, vol. 8, 60.

[443] Al-Suyūṭī, *al-Durr al-Manthūr*, vol. 3, 67.

And ask them of the township that was by the sea... (7:163),

which according to him was revealed in Medina.[444]

Another source says up to the end of verse 171, i.e., the words:

And when We shook the mountain above them as if it were a canopy...

My comment is that Qatādah's contention is that it addresses the Jews, which fits in, according to his claim, with its being in Medina. However, there is no evidence that the pronouns refer to the Jews. It may refer to the pagans themselves on account of their familiarity with the story of the people who transgressed the Sabbath. The township of Eilat was beside the Red Sea, towards the limit of the Ḥijāz in the environs of Syria, and was a small but prosperous Jewish town[445] which the summer caravans of the Quraysh would pass. News from there would reach them, hence they were familiar with its Jewish inhabitants who had broken their Lord's commandment.

As for what the other source said, there is no evidence at all for it, and no recognised chain of narration. So the correct view is that these verses fit in with other such stories passed down to Quraysh for those of the Prophets' people with the sense to learn from them. Thus, the opinion that all of it is Meccan without exception is favoured.

4- Jonah *(Yūnus)*: Meccan

Some them say that four of the verses are exceptions:

1) the Almighty's Words:

And of them is he who believeth therein, and of them is he who believeth not therein, and Thy Lord is best aware of those who corrupt (10:40).

Some claim that it was revealed in relation to the Jews. However, the context refutes this.

2) the Almighty's Words:

And if thou art in doubt concerning that which We reveal unto thee, then question those who read the Scripture (that was) before thee (10:94).

3) the Almighty's Words:

[444] Makkī ibn Abī Ṭālib, *al-Kashf*, vol. 1, 460.

[445] Shihāb al-Dīn Yāqūt ibn 'Abdillāh al-Ḥamawī, *Mu'jam al-Buldān* (Beirut: Dār Ṣādir, 1376 q.), vol. 1, 292.

And be not thou of those who deny...(10:95).

4) the Almighty's Words:

Those for whom the Word of thy Lord hath effect... (10:96).

It is claimed that they, too, were revealed in relation to the Jews, but they have no evidence for it. Furthermore, it is a single, unbroken thread. It may be that the reference to the People of the Book is what provoked this claim, even though it is plain that these verses are no more explicit than His Words, *Ask the followers of the Remembrance...* (16:43), a Meccan verse by consensus.

It is also said that verse 40 and right up to the end of the chapter was revealed in Medina,[446] but there is no evidence at all for this opinion. In addition, the tone and vernacular of the verses also refute this.

In summary, whoever says that there are exceptions within this chapter has no reliable evidence on which to rely. Similarly, the context indicates that it is clearly Meccan. Hence, we prefer the view that it is Meccan in its entirety.

5- *Hūd*: Meccan

Three of its verses have been said to be exceptions:

1) the Almighty's Words:

A likely thing, that thou wouldst forsake aught of that which hath been revealed unto thee, and that thy breast should be straitened for it, because they say: 'Why hath not a treasure been sent down for him, or an angel come with him?' (11:12).

However, the context clearly testifies to its being Meccan. What also incontrovertibly makes it Meccan has been narrated regarding the reason for its revelation.[447]

2) the Almighty's Words:

Is he (to be counted equal with them) who relieth on a clear proof from his Lord, and a witness from Him reciteth it, and before it was the Book of Moses, an example and a mercy? Such believe therein, and whoso disbelieveth therein of the clans, the Fire is his appointed place... (11:17).

---

[446] Al-Suyūṭī, *al-Itqān*, vol. 1, 40.

[447] Ṭabrisī, *Majma' al-Bayān*, vol. 5, 146.

Those who say that it is Medinan rely on the words 'the Book of Moses' and 'of the clans' (*min al-aḥzāb*).

However, neither phrase proves this, given that Moses is referred to in several Meccan verses.

'The clans' is a reference to the Arab tribes who resisted the Messenger. They had banded together since the time the pagans first sensed that there was a danger of Islam penetrating the peninsula and spreading quickly.[448] There is no evidence that it refers to the Battle of the Clans (*Waq'at al-Aḥzāb*).

3) the Almighty's Words:

> *Establish worship at the two ends of the day and in some watches of the night. Lo! good deeds annul ill-deeds* (11:114).

Abū Ja'far narrates via his chain of narration that Abū Maysarah said:

> A woman came to me to buy dates, and so I said to her, 'There are better dates in my house.' So I let her into my house, felt a desire to kiss her and get everything from her that a man gets from his wife except sexual union, to the point that I touched her bottom. Then I went out and mentioned it to Abū Bakr and 'Umar.
>
> They said, 'Keep that to yourself and don't tell anyone.'
>
> I then mentioned it to the Prophet and he asked, 'Have you equipped a warrior?'
>
> I replied, 'No.'
>
> He asked, 'Have you looked after the family of a warrior?'
>
> I replied, 'No.'
>
> He said, 'Seek your Lord's forgiveness and pray four *rak'ahs*.'
>
> He then recited, *Establish worship at the two ends of the day and in some watches of the night. Lo! good deeds annul ill- deeds*, and said, 'It is for people generally.'

Another tradition says that Gabriel brought it down at that very moment.[449]

---

[448] Abū Ja'far Muhammad ibn al-Ḥasan al-Ṭūsī, *al-Tibyān fī Tafsīr al-Qur'an* (Qum: Jāmi'ah Mudarrisīn, 1413 q.), vol. 5, 461.

[449] Ṭabarī, *Jāmi' al-Bayān*, vol. 12, 82-83.

The context of this tradition is definitely false, because it encourages sin. It would mean that anyone could do whatever he wanted, then apply himself to prayer as penance, not to mention the incoherence in the tradition itself and its not fitting in with the verse, which is another proof of its weakness. Furthermore, it is recorded in other narrations that most traditions containing: 'Then he recited the verse to him...' do not mean that it was revealed there and then.

The correct view in our opinion is that *Hūd* is Meccan in its entirety, in view of the singularity of its context and its innovative, scolding style, which is consistent with a Meccan chapter.

6- Joseph*(Yūsuf)*: Meccan

The Amīrī Codex says that the first three verses are exceptions, as well as:

> *Verily in Joseph and his brethren are signs for the inquiring* (12:7).

According to Jalāl al-Dīn:

> It is very weak and should not be paid any attention to.[450]

My comment is that we are surprised at the likes of Abū 'Abdillāh al-Zanjānī following what is set out in the Egyptian Codex without checking and recording it in his excellent book.[451] There can be no illusions over the weakness of the matter.

7- Abraham *(Ibrāhīm)*: Meccan

Al-Zarkashī claims:

> Except for two verses revealed about the pagans killed at Badr:
>
> *Hast thou not seen those who gave the grace of God in exchange for thanklessness and led their people down to the abode of loss, (even to) Hell? They are exposed thereto. A hapless end!* (14:28-29).[452]

The evidential basis for this is what is narrated on the authority of Sa'd, on the authority of 'Umar ibn al-Khaṭṭāb:

---

[450] Al-Suyūṭī, *al-Itqān*, vol. 1, 40.
[451] Abū 'Abdillāh al-Zanjānī, *Tārīkh al-Qur'an* (Beirut: Mu'assasat al-A'lamī, 1388 q.), 28.
[452] See Zarkashī, *al-Burhān*, vol. 1, 200.

> Those who exchanged the bounty of God with unthankfulness were the two most depraved houses of Quraysh: Banū al-Mughīrah and Banū Umayyah. As for Banū al-Mughīrah, you wiped them out at the Battle of Badr.

Alternatively, he said:

> God extirpated them at the Battle of Badr. As for Banū Umayyah, they have been allowed to enjoy themselves for a time.[453]

The same thing is narrated on the authority of Imām al-Ṣādiq, with the addition of:

> In fact, it is the whole of Quraysh.[454]

However, there is no indication therein that it was revealed at or after the Battle of Badr. The Battle of Badr was just one example of the ruin they were warned about. As for the higher interpretation, it is Hell, of which it is said 'they are exposed thereto' and is 'a hapless end.' Considering this an exception was the result of not reflecting on the allegorical interpretation (*ta'wīl*) of this verse.

8- *Al-Ḥijr*: Meccan

Jalāl al-Dīn claims:

> God's Words, *And verily We know the eager among you and verily We know the laggards* (15:24) should be considered an exception on account of what al-Tirmidhī cites, 'It was revealed in relation to the rows of [congregational] prayer.'[455]

Al-Ḥasan says:

> Except for God's Words, *We have given thee seven of the oft-repeated ...* (15:87) and, *Such as We send down for those who make divisions, those who break the Qur'an into parts* (15:90-91).[456]

My comment is that the context of verse 24 refutes its being construed as congregational prayer, as testified to by God's Words before this verse:

---

[453] Ṭabarī, *Jāmi' al-Bayān*, vol. 13, 146.
[454] *Tafsīr al-'Ayyāshī*, vol. 2, 229; Fayḍ Kāshānī, *al-Ṣāfī fī Tafsīr al-Qur'an*, vol. 1, 887-888.
[455] Al-Suyūṭī, *al-Itqān*, vol. 1, 41.
[456] See Ṭabrisī, *Majma' al-Bayān*, vol. 6, 326

> *Lo! it is We, even We, Who quicken and give death, and We are the Inheritor* (15:23).

The meaning is: 'We knew the dead who are gone and know the living who remain.'[457]

As for al-Tirmidhī's tradition, it is truncated and there is weakness in its chain of narration. Furthermore, it does not fit the verse.

Th claim that the second verse is an exception is based on Mujāhid's opinion that *The Opening* (*al-Fātiḥah*) was revealed in Medina. It was stated above that that was a slip on his part, and that the consensus supports the opposite.[458]

As for the verse about 'those who make divisions,' they claim that it was revealed in relation to the Jews and Christians, who were among those who believed in parts of the Qur'an but not others.[459] However, this is false, because the Jews did not believe in any of the Qur'an and they were not those to whom the Qur'an was revealed. It is true of their belief in the Scriptures which were revealed to them – that they would believe in some but not others.

The correct view is that the aforementioned verse was revealed in relation to the pagans who said that some of the Qur'an was sorcery, tales of the ancients, fabrication and so on. They would split up and man the gates to Mecca, turning people away from the Qur'an and telling lies about God.[460] Al-'Ayyāshī narrates on the authority of the two Imams al-Bāqir and al-Ṣādiq that it was revealed in relation to Quraysh.[461]

9- The Bee *(al-Naḥl)*: Meccan

Qatādah says:

> Except for His Words, *And those who became fugitives for the cause of God after they had been oppressed...* (16:41), and it is said that from here right up to the end of the chapter was revealed in Medina.[462]

---

457 See Ṭabarī, *Jāmi' al-Bayān*, vol. 14, 16 and vol. 14, 18.

458 See al-Suyūṭī, *al-Itqān*, vol. 1, 30.

459 Ṭabarī, *Jāmi' al-Bayān*, vol. 14, 42.

460 See Ṭabāṭabā'ī, *al-Mīzān*, vol. 12, 205.

461 *Tafsīr al-'Ayyāshī*, vol. 2, 251-252.

462 Al-Suyūṭī, *al-Itqān*, vol. 1, 41; Ṭabrisī, *Majma' al-Bayān*, vol. 6, 347 attributes it to al-Ḥasan and Qatādah.

According to 'Aṭā' ibn Yasār:

> Except for His Words, *If ye punish, then punish with the like of that wherewith ye were afflicted...*(16:126), up to the end of the chapter – three verses – which were revealed in relation to the incident at Uḥud, after Ḥamzah was killed.[463]

A tradition on the authority of Ibn 'Abbās says that the following verses were revealed in Medina:[464]

> *And purchase not a small gain at the price of God's covenant ... in proportion to the best of what they used to do* (16:95-96).

My comment is that, as far as verses 41 and 42 are concerned, there is no indication that what is meant is the second migration to Medina. In fact the apparent meaning is that it was the first migration to Ethiopia, as also narrated on the authority of Qatādah.[465]

As for the opinion that everything after verse 40 to the end of the chapter was revealed in Medina, there is no evidence for it, and the context of the verses also contradicts it.

As for verses 95 and 96, it is said that they were revealed in relation to Imru' al-Qays al-Kindī. He had seized land from 'Abdān al-Ashra' al-Haḍramawti and so the latter complained about him to the Prophet. Imru' al-Qays denied it and so 'Abdān al-Ashra' made him swear an oath, but Imru' al-Qays thought it too serious a matter to perjure himself. Thereafter, the verse was revealed.[466] The event took place in Medina.

However, the story is uncorroborated, the tone of the verse is general, and its context testifies to its fitting in perfectly with the verses aimed at fiercely scolding the stubborn pagans. A quick perusal of the verse makes us confident that it is wholly linked to verse number 91, *Fulfil the covenant of God when ye have covenanted...*, both emphasising it and strengthening the position of the believers at that time, telling them not to sell what they had covenanted to God for a paltry price, thereby

[463] Al-Suyūṭī, *al-Durr al-Manthūr*, vol. 4, 135.
[464] Ṭabrisī, *Majma' al-Bayān*, vol. 6, 347.
[465] Al-Suyūṭī, *al-Durr al-Manthūr*, vol. 4, 118.
[466] Ṭabrisī, *Majma' al-Bayān*, vol. 6, 384.

placing the life of this world on an equal footing with the great reward they had been promised.[467]

As for the verse, *If ye punish, then punish with the like of that which wherewith ye were afflicted. But if ye endure patiently, verily it is for the patient* (16:126), exegetes have three different opinions on it.

The first is that it was revealed on the day of the Battle of Uḥud, when the Prophet stood over Ḥamzah's mutilated body. It caused him distress, and he said: 'I swear by God, I will mutilate seventy [or thirty] of them in return for you!'

Thus, when the Muslims heard that, they said, 'If God gives us the upper hand over them, we will mutilate their living, never mind their dead.'

Some of them said, 'We will mutilate them in a way the Arabs have never seen,' and so Gabriel brought the verse down, the Prophet rescinded his oath, and refrained from doing what he had said.

The second opinion is that it was revealed on the Day of the Conquest. The Muslims wanted to descend upon the pagans and brutally kill them in order to make themselves feel better after what had been inflicted upon them at the Battle of Uḥud – there had been sixty-four casualties from the Helpers (*ansār*) and six from the Migrants (*muhājirūn*), including Ḥamzah ibn 'Abd al-Muṭṭalib, whom the pagans had mutilated. So the *ansār* said, 'If we have a day like this against them, we will do worse to them.' When the Day of the Conquest came and God granted the Muslims victory over the pagans, the verse was revealed in order to restrain the Muslims, so that they would not exceed the bounds of what God had revealed.

The third view is that it has a general relevance, and applies to all who are oppressed who, when God has granted them victory, then seek vengeance on the oppressor. This verse came as a compromise between just revenge and forgiveness, something which tallies with the mood of the Muslims when they were in Mecca. They say that it was abrogated by the verses commanding them to fight (*āyāt al-qitāl*):

> *And fight in the way of God against those who fight against you, but begin not hostilities. Verily God loveth not aggressors* (2:190);

and:

> *...but if they attack you then slay them* (2:191),

---

[467] See al-Suyūṭī, *al-Durr al-Manthūr*, vol. 4, 129.

which were revealed at the beginning of the Muslims' time in Medina.

Regardless of the abrogation, this last opinion is the correct one in view of the context of the verse itself and its complete compatibility with the verses before and after it.

For the Almighty said:

> *Call unto the way of thy Lord with wisdom and fair exhortation, and reason with them in the better way* (16:125);

> *If ye punish, then punish with the like of that wherewith ye were afflicted* (16:126);

and:

> *Endure thou patiently. Thy endurance is only by (the help of) God. Grieve not for them, and be not in distress because of that which they devise* (16:127).

This last verse came to give solace to the Prophet over the pagans' harassment, and to console him over his sorrow for them, not the sorrow caused by them. It is proof that the verse was revealed at the time when the pagans defied the Prophet's call and set about harassing him, and believing souls refused to put up with the wrongs they inflicted, and tried to get revenge on them no matter what hardship it entailed.[468]

10- The Night Journey *(Isrā')*: Meccan

They say that seventeen of its verses – 26, 32, 33, 57, 60, 73, 74, 75, 76, 77, 78, 79, 80, 81, 85, 88 and 107 – were revealed in Medina. This is an exaggeration, for there is no evidence regarding most of them. Some of the details are as follows:

The first of these verses is:

> *And give the kinsman his due, and the needy, and the wayfarer, and squander not (thy wealth) in wantonness* (17:26).

It is said that it was revealed in Medina after God had granted the Messenger of God victory at Khaybar, and he had given the oasis of Fadak to Fāṭimah.[469]

---

[468] See Ṭabrisī, *Majma' al-Bayān*, vol. 6, 393; al-Suyūṭī, *al-Durr al-Manthūr*, vol. 4, 135.

[469] Al-Suyūṭī, *al-Durr al-Manthūr*, vol. 4, 177; Ṭabrisī, *Majma' al-Bayān*, vol. 6, 411.

Abū Ja'far al-Ṭabarī cites Abū Daylam as saying:

Ali ibn al-Husayn asked a Syrian man, 'Have you read the Qur'an?'

He replied, 'Yes.'

He asked, 'Have you not read in *The Children of Israel*: *And give the kinsman his due...*'?

The man asked, 'Are you the kinsman to whom God, sublime is His Praise, has commanded us to give his due?'

He replied, 'Yes.'[470]

Ḥāfiẓ Ḥasakānī cites a hadith with several chains of narration that says it refers to the Prophet giving Fadak to Fāṭimah .[471]

My comment is that the apparent meaning of the verse is that it is nonetheless a general duty for every Muslim, and mentions in distinct terms the duty to maintain kinsmen and the poor – in the nature of other examples of Meccan legislation. Later the paramaters were defined after the migration to Medina.

The universal applicability (*'umūm*) of the verse includes the Prophet, for he too, like any other Muslim, is commanded to maintain relations with his kin and to support both them and the poor.

However, it may be that the verse was sent down a second time after the conquest of Khaybar. After God had provided booty for the Messenger and the believers, Gabriel brought it down, thereby reminding him of the duty to maintain relations with his kin. Thereupon he summoned Fāṭimah and gave her Fadak. There is no evidence that the verse was revealed for the first time at that point.

It is possible that the verse revealed at Khaybar on maintaining relations with kin was another one. Minhāl ibn 'Amr's hadith says, on the authority of Ali ibn al-Husayn, that it is about the following:

> *That which God giveth as spoil unto His messenger from the people of the townships, it is for God and His messenger and for the near of kin and the orphans and the needy and the wayfarer ...* (59:7).

---

[470] Ṭabarī, *Jāmi' al-Bayān*, vol. 15, 53.

[471] Ḥasakānī, *Shawāhid al-Tanzīl*, vol. 1, 338-341.

The 'people of the townships' means Banū Qurayẓah and Banū Naḍīr. The cities are Fadak, Khaybar, 'Uraynah and Yanbu', which became booty at the Muslims' disposal. The verse was revealed in relation to them at that time.[472]

If it is correct that Gabriel also brought the first of these verses, it was a reminder to the Prophet of the previous ruling, and a confirmation of the ruling at hand. This is so, providing that the narrator did not confuse one of the verses with the other.

The second verse is:

> *And come not near unto adultery. Lo! it is an abomination and an evil way* (17:32).

And the third verse is:

> *And slay not the life which God hath forbidden save with right* (17:33).

Whoever claims that these two verses are an exception does not give any explanation.[473] It may be because they mention the unlawfulness of adultery and the taking of life, and legislative matters took place in Medina.

However, what would have been missed is that the parameters and particulars of various laws were established in Medina. As for the bare bones and generalities of the religious law (*sharī'ah*), they were frequently revealed in Meccan chapters, and these two verses were revealed in Mecca in the same way.

Al-Suddī says that the verse, *And come not near unto adultery...*, was revealed at a time when there were no set punishments, for they were sent down after that in *The Light* (*Sūrah al-Nūr*), which is Medinan.[474]

Al-Ḍaḥḥāk says about the verse on slaying:

> The pagans would slay the Prophet's companions at that time, so the companions were about to do the same to them. Hence, He said, Sublime is His Remembrance, that if someone slays, his father should not be slayed in return, nor his brother, nor any of the pagans, as was the custom in the days of ignorance, which was

---

[472] Ṭabrisī, *Majma' al-Bayān*, vol. 9, 260-261; there is also an allusion to it in al-Suyūṭī, *al-Durr al-Manthūr*, vol. 6, 189.

[473] Zanjānī, *Tārīkh al-Qur'an*, 28.

[474] Al-Suyūṭī, *al-Durr al-Manthūr*, vol. 4, 179.

to kill someone's brother, or others from that person's tribe, in retaliation for one's own brother being killed. One of you should only slay the slayer himself.[475]

The fourth verse is:

> *Those unto whom they cry seek the way of approach to their Lord, which of them shall be the nearest ...* (17:57).

The verse, in the context of the verse preceding it, fits in with its having been revealed in Mecca. We cannot find any reason why the Amīrī Codex or others might have this as an exception.

The fifth verse is:

> *... and We appointed the vision which We showed thee as an ordeal for mankind, and (likewise) the accursed tree in the Qur'an* (17:60).

According to Jalāl al-Dīn, this is an exception because the verse was revealed about the Messenger's vision, in which he saw the Umayyads jumping like monkeys on his pulpit, and which saddened and troubled him so much, that he was not seen laughing again until he died.[476]

In any case, the Prophet did not have a pulpit in Mecca.

We have already stated our opinion on this, that he was shown the elevation of his blessed calling and the usurpers' hands reaching out to his divinely appointed position, and it was this that troubled him.[477]

The sixth, seventh and eighth verses are as follows:

> *And they indeed strove hard to beguile thee away from that wherewith We have inspired thee, that thou shouldst invent other than it against Us; and then would they have accepted thee as a friend. And if We had not made thee wholly firm thou mightest almost have inclined unto them a little. Then had We made thee taste a double (punishment) of living and a double (punishment) of dying, then hadst thou found no helper for thee against Us* (17:73-75).

There is no doubt that these verses are Meccan and were revealed about the pagans from Quraysh who offered the Prophet a truce with

[475] Al-Suyūṭī, *al-Durr al-Manthūr*, vol. 4, 181.

[476] Al-Suyūṭī, *al-Durr al-Manthūr*, vol. 4, 191.

[477] Stated above in relation to the chapter entitled *The Power* and in the section, 'Chapters over which there is disagreement.'

their gods. He rebuffed them and these verses were revealed to reinforce his position and to make the pagans despair once and for all of trying to coerce the Messenger of God – the propagator of pure monotheism and destroyer of polytheism – into a compromise which contradicted his call to the One God Who has no partner.[478]

We do not know any valid reason for saying these three verses are an exception, as Jalāl al-Dīn,[479] the Amīrī Codex and others have.

The ninth and tenth verses are:

> *And they indeed wished to startle thee (li yastafizzūnaka) from the land that they might drive thee forth from thence, and then they would have stayed (there) but a little after thee. (Such was Our) method in the case of those whom We sent before thee (to mankind), and thou wilt not find for Our method aught of power to change* (17:76-77).

What is given as the reason for its revelation is also the reason for making it an exception:

> The Jews came to the Prophet and said to him, 'If you are a Prophet, go to the Levant,[480] the land of the prophets, and make them believe.'
>
> He fought the Battle of Tabūk for the sole purpose of reaching the Levant, but when he reached Tabūk, God revealed these two verses to him, commanding him to return to Medina where his life, death and resurrection on the Day of Resurrection was to be.[481]

However, it is contradicted by another tradition which says that they were revealed in relation to the pagans of Mecca who plotted to expel the Messenger from Mecca in the same way. They said to him, 'The Prophets all lived in the Levant, so why do you live in this land?'

Alternatively, they tried to expel him by force, because *istifzāz* means 'shaking out by force.' The literal meaning of the verse supports the latter, because when the pagans behaved in this way, God's wont with regard to His creatures later came to bear upon them, beginning with

---

[478] See Ṭabrisī, *Majma' al-Bayān*, vol. 6, 431; al-Suyūṭī, *al-Durr al-Manthūr*, vol. 4, 194.

[479] Al-Suyūṭī, *al-Itqān*, vol. 1, 41.

[480] The Levant comprises Syria, Lebanon, Palestine and Jordan. [Trans.]

[481] Ṭabrisī, *Majma' al-Bayān*, vol. 6, 432; al-Suyūṭī, *al-Durr al-Manthūr*, vol. 4, 195.

those killed at Badr and culminating in the conquest of Mecca and the final expulsion of the pagans.[482]

The eleventh to fourteenth verses are:

> *Establish worship at the going down of the sun until the dark of night, and (the recital of) the Qur'an at dawn. Lo! (the recital of) the Qur'an at dawn is ever witnessed. And some part of the night awake for it, a largess for thee. It may be that thy Lord will raise thee to a praised estate. And say: 'My Lord, cause me to come in with a firm incoming and to go with a firm outgoing. And give me from Thy presence a sustaining power.' And say: 'Truth hath come and falsehood hath vanished away. Lo! falsehood is ever bound to vanish'* (17:78-81).

The one who says these are an exception claims that they are a conclusion to the previous two verses revealed in Medina.[483] However, this is a false claim given that the primary matter is not confirmed, let alone the secondary.

Abu Nu'aym and Bayhaqī cite on the authority of Ibn 'Abbās that God's Words:

> My Lord, cause me to come in with a firm incoming...

were revealed in Mecca shortly before the Migration.[484]

At any rate, the unbroken context of the preceding and subsequent verses itself testifies to their having been revealed in Mecca, and they do not fit the opinion that they were revealed in Medina at all.

The fifteenth verse is:

> They will question thee concerning the Spirit. Say: 'The Spirit is of the bidding of my Lord. You have only been given a little knowledge.'

A number of hadith specialists have said that the question referred to was asked by the Jews in Medina after the Migration.[485]

However, it is contradicted by a tradition which says that it was the pagans from Quraysh who asked him about the Spirit mentioned in the

---

[482] Ibid.

[483] Al-Suyūṭī, *al-Itqān*, vol. 1, 41.

[484] *Al-Suyūṭī, al-Durr al-Manthūr*, vol. 4, 198; Ṭabarī, *Jāmi' al-Bayān*, vol. 15, 100.

[485] Al-Suyūṭī, *al-Durr al-Manthūr*, vol. 4, 199; Ṭabarī, *Jāmi' al-Bayān*, vol. 15, 105.

Qur'an,[486] or that the Jews suggested that the pagans ask Muhammad the question, saying, 'If he answers you, he is not a prophet, but if he does not answer you, he is a prophet.'[487]

This is in addition to the fact that the end of the verse testifies to the fact that it was a conversation with the pagans. According to 'Aṭā' ibn Yasār the words, *You have only been given a little knowledge*, were revealed in Mecca.[488]

The sixteenth verse is:

> *Say: Verily though mankind and the jinn should assemble to produce the like of this Qur'an, they could not produce the like thereof though they were helpers one of another* (17:88).

Ṭabarī claims that this verse was revealed to the Messenger in Medina because a group of Jews had argued with him over the coherence of the Qur'an. They denied its being coherent and claimed that the Torah was more coherent.[489]

However, the reproachful tone of the verse indicates that it was revealed about the pagans from Quraysh, challenging them when they asked the Prophet for strange miracles and inane requests, rather than revelation.

It was revealed by way of an introduction to the condemnation directed at them in the following verses:

> *And they say, 'We will not put faith in thee till thou cause rivers to gush forth...'* (17:90),

up to the end of the four verses and those which follow on, up to the seventeenth verse after this, which one may refer to independently.

The last verse is the seventeenth:

> *Say: Believe therein or believe not, lo! those who were given knowledge before it, when it is read unto them, fall down prostrate on their faces, adoring...'* (17:107).

According to Jalāl al-Dīn:

---

[486] See Ṭabrisī, *Majma' al-Bayān*, vol. 6, 437; al-Suyūṭī, *al-Durr al-Manthūr*, vol. 4, 199.

[487] See Ṭabrisī, *Majma' al-Bayān*, vol. 6, 437; al-Suyūṭī, *al-Durr al-Manthūr*, vol. 4, 199.

[488] Ṭabarī, *Jāmi' al-Bayān*, vol. 15, 105-106.

[489] Ṭabarī, *Jāmi' al-Bayān*, vol. 15, 106.

> It was revealed in Medina on account of the reasons for revelation which we have cited.[490]

However, he cites nothing on the matter either in *Lubāb al-Nuqūl* or in *al-Durr al-Manthūr.*

The context of the verse testifies to its being Meccan. It was revealed as a rebuke of the pagans' defiance towards the revelation of the Qur'an and their refusal to believe it, and it alludes to the fact that their stubborn resistance was the result of the blind ignorance which enveloped their souls. As for the people of Medina and those of culture, they perceived the clear truth of the Qur'an straight away and had no doubts, and the contrast indicates just how far from knowledge and culture these pagans were – hence their scorn and disdain.

11- The Cave *(al-Kahf)*: Meccan

Some say that thirty-two verses are exceptions, claiming that they were revealed in Medina. This is excessive, because it would mean that a third of the chapter, including the first eight verses, were Medinan.

Jalāl al-Dīn claims:

> The beginning of it up to His Word[s], ... *barren dust*, verses one to eight, was revealed in Medina.[491]

There is no evidence at all for claiming they are an exception, because it is the beginning of a chapter and some of its first verses that decide whether a chapter is Meccan or Medinan. Further, the complete consensus is that *The Cave* is Meccan.[492]

It may be that the person who said they were an exception did so on account of the Almighty's Words:

> *...and to warn those who say: God hath chosen a son* (18:4).

However, just because there were Jews in Medina does not necessarily mean that it had to have been revealed in Medina. In fact it is general,

[490] Al-Suyūṭī, *al-Itqān*, vol. 1, 41; al-Suyūṭī, *al-Durr al-Manthūr*, vol. 4, 205; Ibn Jarīr cites on the authority of Mujāhid: Those given knowledge before him were some of the People of the Book who heard what God had revealed to Muhammad. However that does not mean that it was revealed in Medina as is obvious.

[491] Al-Suyūṭī, *al-Itqān*, vol. 1, 41.

[492] See al-Suyūṭī, *al-Durr al-Manthūr*, vol. 4, 208.

and is also relevant to the Christians and pagans, because a verse being revealed in relation to a Jewish story does not mean it had to have happened at the time when they were resisting Islam. There are many verses like this in Meccan chapters, because of the close link between the Jews and pagans before the Prophet's migration to Medina, as alluded to above.

> He also says that the words, *Restrain thyself along with those who cry unto their Lord at morning and evening...* (18:28), [493] are an exception.

They claim that they were revealed about 'Uyaynah ibn Ḥiṣn, who suggested to the Messenger – who was in Medina at the time – that he keep his distance from where poor believers gathered if he wanted the noblemen of the land to become Muslims.[494]

However, the correct opinion is that they were revealed about Umayyah ibn Khalaf, who suggested the same thing to him when he was in Mecca – he called on the Prophet to cast out the poor and to favour the nobles from Quraysh.[495] The tone and context of the verse also shows that.

The Amīrī Codex and al-Zanjānī's *Tārīkh al-Qur'an* claim that nineteen verses are exceptions, from *They will ask thee of Dhū al-Qarnayn...* up to ... *and who could not bear to hear* (18:83-101).

They claim that it was the Jews themselves who put this question to the Prophet. Hence the revelation of these verses as a response must have taken place in Medina.[496]

The correct view is that it was the pagans who asked this question. However, it was by Jewish instruction. The pagans had sent someone to ask the Jews about the Messenger's attributes, and they responded by providing questions to put to him. If he could answer them, he truly was a prophet.

Abū Ja'far al-Ṭabarī narrates that the Quraysh had sent al-Naḍir ibn al-Ḥarith and 'Uqbah ibn Abī Mu'ayṭ to the Jewish rabbis in Medina and told them, 'Ask them about Muhammad. Describe him to them and tell them what he has said, for they are the People of the First Book – the Torah – and they have knowledge of the prophets which we do not have.' They set off, eventually reaching Medina, and asked the Jewish rabbis

[493] See al-Suyūṭī, *al-Itqān*, vol. 1, 41; Zanjānī, *Tārīkh al-Qur'an*, 29

[494] Al-Suyūṭī, *al-Durr al-Manthūr*, vol. 4, 220.

[495] Al-Suyūṭī, *Lubāb al-Nuqūl*, vol. 1, 230; al-Suyūṭī, *al-Durr al-Manthūr*, vol. 4, 220.

[496] Al- Suyūṭī, *al-Durr al-Manthūr*, vol. 4, 340.

about the Messenger of God. They described his affair to them along with some of what he had said. They said, 'You are the people of the Torah, and we have come to you so that you can tell us about this friend of ours.' So the Jewish rabbis replied, 'Ask him about three things which we will tell you. If he tells you about them, he is a prophet sent. If he does not, he is a charlatan. Ask him what happened to the youths who went away in the First Age. Theirs is an amazing story. Ask him what the tidings were of the man who travelled around, reaching the eastern and western horizons of the earth. Ask him what the Spirit is. If he tells you about that, he is a prophet, so follow him...' The hadith is long, and at the same time curious.[497]

Al-Itqān says that four verses are exceptions:

> *Lo! those who believe and do good works, theirs are the Gardens of Paradise for welcome,*

up to the end of the chapter (18:107-110).[498]

However, he does not explain his evidence for this strange claim. It may be oversight or careless words, for nothing in the verses suffices as evidence of their being Medinan and there is no tradition interpreting them in such a way that would indicate their having been revealed in Medina.

Admittedly it is narrated in *al-Durr al-Manthūr* that Mujāhid said:

> There were among the Muslims those who fought, and wanted to see their position, and so God revealed, *and whoever hopeth for the meeting with his Lord, let him do righteous work...* (18:110).[499]

However the tone and meaning of the verse do not fit in with that. Ṭabrisī narrates on the authority of Ibn 'Abbās:

> When God's Words, *...and of knowledge ye have been vouchsafed but little* (17:85), were revealed, the Jews retorted, 'We have been given the Torah and there is much knowledge in it,' and so God revealed, *Say: Though the sea became ink for the Words of my Lord...* That is why al-Ḥasan said, 'By 'words' He means knowledge.'[500]

---

[497] Ṭabarī, *Jāmi' al-Bayān*, vol. 15, 127; vol. 16, 7; al-Suyūṭī, *al-Durr al-Manthūr*, vol. 4, 210; al-Suyūṭī, *Lubāb al-Nuqūl*, vol. 1, 228.

[498] Al-Suyūṭī, *al-Itqān*, vol. 1, 42.

[499] See al-Suyūṭī, *al-Durr al-Manthūr*, vol. 4, 255.

[500] Ṭabrisī, *Majma' al-Bayān*, vol. 6, 499.

However, this does not mean that it was necessarily revealed in Medina, as stated more than once above.

12- Mary *(Maryam):* Meccan

Jalāl al-Dīn claims that two of its verses are exceptions,[501] of which the first is the Verse of Prostration:

> *These are they unto whom God showed favour from among the prophets, of the seed of Adam and of whom We carried with Noah...they fell down, adoring and weeping.* (19:58)

What refutes this is the fact that this verse was revealed as a comment on the verses before it, from the beginning of the chapter up until this point, which talk in detail about matters pertaining to the prophets and past nations. Then praise for them all in general terms came along in this verse as a kind of summary and culmination. We either have to say that all of them, from the beginning of the chapter to this verse, are Medinan, or that they are all Meccan. There is no room for this strange exception, the evidence for which has not been explained.

The second exception he claims is:

> *There is not one of you but shall approach it. That is a fixed ordinance of thy Lord* (19:71).

This, like the previous one, is completely linked to the verses preceding and following it, which leaves no room for it alone being an exception.

13- *Ṭā Hā*: Meccan

Two verses have been said to be exceptions, the first of which is:

> *Therefore, bear with what they say, and celebrate the praises of thy Lord ere the rising of the sun and ere the going down thereof...* (20:130).

However the verse follows on from those preceding it, and its tone is exclusive to Meccan verses. There are also confirmations of its having been revealed in Mecca in traditions describing its exegesis.[502]

The second is:

---

501 Al-Suyūṭī, *al-Itqān*, vol. 1, 42.

502 Ṭabarī, *Jāmi' al-Bayān*, vol. 16, 168.

> *And strain not thine eyes toward that which We cause some wedded pairs among them to enjoy ...* (20:131).

Jalāl al-Dīn says:

> ... on account of what al-Bazzāz cites on the authority of Abū Rāfi':
>
> The Prophet had sent him to borrow food from a Jew, and he refused to do so without charging interest. The Messenger of God was sad about that and so the verse was revealed.[503]

However, this story, assuming it to be true, does not mean that the verse had to have been revealed in relation to it. Furthermore, there is no correlation at all between the story and the meaning of the verse.

14- The Prophets *(al-Anbīyā')*: Meccan

The words, *See they not how We visit to the land, reducing it of its outlying parts?* (21:44),[504] are said to be an exception, but those who say so have not provided any evidence.

However, the context is indisputably Meccan. Something similar was also said about verse 41 of *Thunder* (*al-Ra'd*). Its tone might be thought to be Meccan if it were not for the consensus of traditions on order being that it is Medinan, as stated above.

15- The Believers *(al-Mu'minūn)*: Meccan

Thirteen verses are said to be exceptions:[505]

> *Till when We grasp their luxurious ones with the punishment...*
>
> to
>
> *...they are aghast thereat* (23:64-77).

There is no evidence at all for saying so. Whoever claims so perhaps had a regard to traditions which explain chastisement as what happened to the pagans at the Battle of Badr or on the Day of the Conquest. However, he overlooks the fact that it is explanation of a promise previously made, and not a report on what currently was. See Abū Ja'far al-Ṭabarī and others.[506]

---

[503] Al-Suyūṭī, *al-Itqān*, vol. 1, 42; See Ṭabarī, *Jāmi' al-Bayān*, vol. 16, 169.

[504] See al-Suyūṭī, *al-Itqān*, vol. 1, 42.

[505] Ibid.

[506] See Ṭabarī, *Jāmi' al-Bayān*, vol. 18, 28.

16- The Criterion *(al-Furqān)*: Meccan

Three verses – 68, 69 and 70 – are said to be exceptions.

However, these verses fit in completely with verses preceding and following them, making it impossible for them to stand alone as exceptions. There is a confirmation of their having been revealed in Mecca in *Tafsīr al-Ṭabarī.*[507]

17- The Poets *(al-Shu'arā')*: Meccan

Five verses are said to be an exception:

The first verse is:

> *Is it not a token for them that the learned of the Children of Israel know it?* (26:197).

Ibn Gharas says that this is Medinan,[508] possibly on account of what tradition says by way of exegesis, that what is meant by the learned of the Children of Israel here is Asad, Usayd, Ibn Yāmīn, Tha'labah and 'Abdullāh ibn Salām.[509]

However, the object of the verse is without doubt the pagans of the Quraysh and it is a sharp rebuke to them. As for the exegesis in the tradition, it does not mean that the verse was revealed after those Jews became believers. It is just an explanation of an instance to which the verse applied, but which happened later on.

The pagans consulting the Jews about recognising the Messenger of God was referred to above.[510] They would acquaint them of his characteristics and attributes, and the verse means simply that. This is something the People of the Book knew even before the Migration. They only denied it later out of greed for the vanities of the world. The verse does not signify their belief, only their acknowledgment. Thus, the exegesis in the tradition does not serve to situate the revelation of the verse in Medina.

The next four verses are:

> *As for poets, the erring follow them* (26:224),

---

[507] Ṭabarī, *Jāmi' al-Bayān*, vol. 19, 26.

[508] Al-Suyūṭī, *al-Itqān*, vol. 1, 42.

[509] Ṭabarī, *Jāmi' al-Bayān*, vol. 19, 69; al-Suyūṭī, *al-Durr al-Manthūr*, vol. 5, 95.

[510] This was with regard to the saying God willing as per *The Cave.*

and up to the end of the chapter. The claim of this as an exception is narrated on the authority of Ibn 'Abbās.[511] The evidence of its being an exception is a narration – that it was revealed in relation to two men, one from the Helpers (*anṣār*) and the other from the Emigrants (*muhājirūn*), who ridiculed each other in satiric verse at the time of the Prophet.[512]

However it is contradicted by what has a stronger chain of narration and is reported via more sources – that it was revealed about the pagans from Quraysh whose poets ridiculed the Messenger in satiric verse, and the verse was revealed as a rebuke to their character and to criticise their hateful behaviour. Ṭabrisī gives a very detailed account of the names of these pagans.[513] Abū Ja'far al-Ṭabarī also prefers this opinion.[514]

18- The Narrations *(al-Qaṣaṣ)*: Meccan

It is said that the following four verses are an exception:

> *Those unto whom We gave the Scripture before it, they believe in it...*
>
> to
>
> *...Peace be unto you! We desire not the ignorant* (28:52-55).

It is said that they were revealed concerning a group of the People of the Book who had become Muslims, including 'Abdullāh ibn Salām, Tamīm al-Dārī, al-Jārūd al-'Abdī and Salmān al-Fārisī.[515]

Alternatively, it is said that it was revealed concerning the Negus' companions who came to Medina and participated in the Battle of Uḥud.[516]

However, if the two aforementioned interpretations are correct, it means foretelling what was to come, not reporting what was, never mind that these interpretations contradict that of it concerning a group of the People of the Book who believed in the Prophet before he was despatched, of whom there were forty men according to *Ṭabrisī's, Ṭabarī's* and others' exegeses.[517]

---

[511] Al-Suyūṭī, *al-Itqān*, vol. 1, 24 and vol. 1, 42.

[512] Al-Suyūṭī, *al-Durr al-Manthūr*, vol. 5, 99; Ṭabarī, *Jāmi' al-Bayān*, vol. 19, 78.

[513] Ṭabrisī, *Majma' al-Bayān*, vol. 7, 208.

[514] Ṭabarī, *Jāmi' al-Bayān*, vol. 19, 78.

[515] Ṭabrisī, *Majma' al-Bayān*, vol. 7, 258.

[516] Al-Suyūṭī, *al-Itqān*, vol. 1, 42.

[517] Ṭabrisī, *Majma' al-Bayān*, vol. 7, 258; Ṭabarī, *Jāmi' al-Bayān*, vol. 20, 57; al-Suyūṭī, *al-Durr al-Manthūr*, vol. 5, 133.

What we have stated is confirmed by God's Words:

> *And argue not with the People of the Book unless it be in a way that is better, save with such of them as do wrong ...* (29:46).

This verse is Meccan and came down in relation to dispute with the People of the Book.

It is also confirmed by God's Words:

> *In like manner We have revealed unto thee the Scripture, and those unto whom We gave the Scripture aforetime will believe therein...* (29:47).

This is also Meccan by consensus.

This is exactly like the verse discussed regarding foretelling what was to come.

The verse:

> *Lo! He who hath given thee the Qur'an for a law will surely bring thee home again...* (28:85),

is also said to be an exception, revealed to the Prophet when he arrived at al-Juḥfah, whilst migrating to Medina.[518] According to the second classification,[519] the verse is neither Meccan nor Medinan.

However, the generally accepted choice of classification is the first one, based on which the verse is Meccan, as stated above.

19- The Spider *(al-'Ankabūt)*: Meccan

From the beginning of it up to the eleventh verse is said to be an exception. They say that it was revealed in Medina:[520]

> The verses were revealed about Muslim people who lagged behind the Migration. Then God's Messenger's companions wrote to them and they resolved to migrate, but the Quraysh held them back, so there was fighting and violence between them.[521]

However, the verse is general, and was revealed about the believers in Mecca who fell into hardship. It was a test for them to ascertain the

518 Ṭabrisī, *Majma' al-Bayān*, vol. 7, 268.
519 *Supra* under the heading Different Ways of Telling Meccan from Medinan.
520 Al-Suyūṭī, *al-Itqān*, vol. 1, 43.
521 Al-Suyūṭī, *Lubāb al-Nuqūl*, vol. 2, 32.

truth from error. That is how Abū Ja'far al-Ṭabarī explains it.[522] There is also an tradition to that effect on the authority of Abū 'Abdillāh al-Ṣādiq,[523] not to mention the fact that if it is correct that the beginning of the chapter is Medinan, that would make the whole of the chapter Medinan according to the aforementioned classification.[524] Furthermore, no one disputes its being Meccan.

The Almighty's Words:

> *And how many a beast there is that beareth not its own provision! God provideth for it and for you. He is the Hearer, the Knower* (29:60).

According to Jalal al-Din this is an exception on account of what Ibn Abī Ḥātim narrates via a weak chain of narration on the authority of Ibn 'Umar:

> I set off with the Messenger of God until he entered one of the orchards of Medina. He started picking dates and eating them, then said:
>
> 'This is the fourth morning I have not tasted or found food.'
>
> Ibn 'Umar said, 'We remained, not moving until, *And how many a beast...*, was revealed.[525]

The tradition's chain of narration is criticised, not to mention the incoherence of its wording and the inconceivability of its import.

Moreover, it is narrated on the authority of Muqātil and al-Kalbī that the words were revealed in connection with a group of poor believers who were under pressure whilst staying in Mecca before the Migration, and had fallen into difficulty and hardship. So they were instructed to migrate to Medina, and they said. 'How can we go out to a land where we have no home, no land and no means to make a living?' Thereafter, the following verses were revealed:[526]

> *O My bondsmen who believe! Lo! My earth is spacious. Therefore serve Me only ...And how many a beast ...* (29:56-60).

---

522 Ṭabarī, *Jāmi' al-Bayān*, vol. 20, 83.

523 Ṭabrisī, *Majma' al-Bayān*, vol. 7, 272.

524 *Supra* under the heading Order of Revelation.

525 Al-Suyūṭī, *al-Itqān*, vol. 1, 43; al-Suyūṭī, *al-Durr al-Manthūr*, vol. 5, 149.

526 See Ṭabrisī, *Majma' al-Bayān*, vol. 8, 290.

The second tradition is more appropriate to the wording of the Book, and worthier of being given credence. Hence it is authentic (*ṣaḥīḥah*) and accepted (*maqbūlah*).

20- The Romans *(al-Rūm)*: Meccan

The Amīrī Codex, Abū 'Abdillāh al-Zanjānī's *Tārīkh al-Qur'an* and *Majma' al-Bayān* say that the following verse is an exception:[527]

> *So glory be to God when ye enter the night and and when ye enter the morning* (30:17).

There is no evidence for this, not to mention the verse's strong link to the verses preceding and following it.

21- *Luqmān*: Meccan

Three verses are said on the authority of Ibn 'Abbās to be exceptions:

> *And if all the trees in the earth were pens, and the sea, with seven more seas to help it...*
>
> to
>
> *...God is informed of what ye do* (31:27-29).

He explains the reason for their revelation as follows:

> The Jewish rabbis in Medina said to the Messenger of God, 'We have been given the Torah and it contains much knowledge.'
>
> So he replied, 'Next to God's knowledge, it is little.'
>
> And so the verse was revealed.[528]

However, even though the reason could hypothetically fit in with verse 27, it does not fit in with the two verses after it, and therefore this does not suffice as a reason for its revelation.

The correct view is that the three verses, like those preceding and following them, fit in with each other. They are all an exposition of the greatness of the Lord of the Worlds. There is no reason for them to be separated from the surrounding verses. Hence, there is no reason at all for saying they are an exception.

---

[527] See Zanjānī, *Tārīkh al-Qur'an*, 30; Ṭabrisī, *Majma' al-Bayān*, vol. 8, 293.

[528] Al-Suyūṭī, *al-Durr al-Manthūr*, 5:167; al-Suyūṭī, *al-Itqān*, vol. 1, 43.

If the aforementioned tradition on the authority of Ibn 'Abbās is authentic, it would have to mean that the Prophet recited them to them when they put this challenge to him, not that they were revealed there and then.

22- The Prostration *(al-Sajdah)*: Meccan

The following verse is said to be an exception:

> *Who forsake their beds to cry unto their Lord in fear and hope, spend of that We have bestowed on them* (32:16).

Jalāl al-Dīn explains that this is:

> ...on account of what al-Bazzāz and Ibn Mardawayh cite on the authority of Bilāl:
>
> We were sitting down while some of God's Messenger's companions were praying after Maghrib and 'Ishā' prayers, and so it was revealed.[529]

My comment is that the verse is general and its compatibility with the adjacent verses is plain to see, not to mention that it does not fit in at all with the purport of the tradition.

According to the Amīrī Codex and al-Zanjānī's *Tārīkh al-Qur'an*, the words:

> *No soul knoweth what is kept hid for them of joy...* (32:17),

are an exception. That may be in view of the fact that they are a culmination of the previous verse. However, the correct view, as with the previous example, is that it is general.

It is narrated on the authority of Ibn 'Abbās that the Almighty's Words:

> *Is he who is a believer like unto him who is ungodly?...*
>
> to
>
> *...a welcome (in reward) for wthat they used to do* (32:18-19),

are an exception.

This is on account of what is narrated via several well-regarded (*mu'tabarah*) routes and chains of narration – that it was revealed about

[529] Al-Suyūṭī, *al-Itqān*, vol. 1, 43; al-Suyūṭī, *al-Durr al-Manthūr*, vol. 5, 175.

an argument between Ali ibn Abī Ṭālib and al-Walīd ibn 'Uqbah ibn Abī Mu'ayṭ at the Battle of Badr. Walīd said to Ali, 'Be quiet! For you are just a boy and I am more simple-tongued than you, sharper of tooth than you and more useful to the troop.' So Ali said to him, 'Calm down! For you are ungodly and it is not as you say.'

This has been cited by Abu al-Faraj al-Iṣfahānī in *al-Aghānī*, al-Wāḥidī in *Asbāb al-Nuzūl*, Ibn Mardawayh, al-Khaṭīb al-Baghdādī and Ibn 'Asākir via routes leading back to Ibn 'Abbās. Ibn Isḥāq and Ibn Jarīr cite it on the authority of 'Aṭā' ibn Yasār. Ibn Abī Ḥātim cites it on the authority of al-Suddī and 'Abd al-Raḥmān ibn Abī Laylā. Thus the believer mentioned in the verse is Ali ibn Abī Ṭālib and the ungodly is al-Walīd.[530]

Ḥāfiẓ Ḥasakānī cites it via twelve routes which may be considered indubitable (*tawātur*).[531]

My comment is that the context of the verse is general and is linked to the rest of the adjacent verses. This becomes clear upon the slightest perusal of the chapter.

It is true that a verse may be revealed a second time on an occasion which calls for it, something which happened in several cases which we will point out. It is possible that the aforementioned dispute came to the Prophet's attention and he recited a verse appropriate to the situation. This same Walīd was called ungodly in other verses.

> *...If an ungodly man bring you tidings, verify it...* (49:6)

This was revealed specifically in connection to him, as cited by Jalāl al-Dīn via chains of narrators (*rijāl*) who are reliable (*thuqāt*).[532]

23- Sheba *(al-Saba')*: Meccan

The following verse is said to be an exception:

> *Those who have been given knowledge see that what is revealed unto thee from thy Lord is the truth and leadeth unto the path of the Mighty, the Owner of Praise* (34:6).

---

[530] See al-Suyūṭī, *al-Durr al-Manthūr*, vol. 5, 178; Ṭabarī, *Jāmi' al-Bayān*, vol. 21, 68; Ṭabrisī, *Majma' al-Bayān*, vol. 8, 332.

[531] Ḥasakānī, *Shawāhid al-Tanzīl*, vol. 1, 445-453.

[532] Al-Suyūṭī, *Lubāb al-Nuqūl*, vol. 2, 80-82.

This verse is an allusion to the fact that real people of knowledge have a sincere belief in the Book through knowledge and certainty. There is no doubt that this should be so, that reasonable, observant people and those of virtue and maturity do not hesitate to believe the Qur'an as soon as they are introduced to it. Such is the case with every clear truth. This is the interpretation favoured by 'Allāmah Ṭabrisī, who says:

> This is more appropriate on account of its general applicability (*'umūm*) ... because they reflect and ponder on it and realise through consideration and reasoning that it is not of human origin.[533]

However, Abū Ja'far al-Ṭabarī explains the verse primarily in terms of the People of the Book who became Muslims, such as 'Abdullāh ibn Salām and the like.[534] Hence, some claim that the verse is Medinan and was revealed after such people became Muslims.[535]

Nevertheless, Abū Ja'far did not rely on hadith evidence to arrive at that explanation.[536] He simply narrates on the authority of Qatādah that they were Muhammad's first and earliest companions who discovered Islam to be the plain truth, and embraced it on the basis of knowledge and certainty. There is some discrepancy between his narration and his opinion.

Seven other verses are also said to be exceptions:

> *There was indeed a sign for Sheba in their dwelling-place...*
>
> to
>
> *...and thy Lord taketh note of all things* (24:15-21).

Farwah ibn Musayk narrates that he asked the Messenger of God – or heard a man ask him – whether Sheba was a mountain or a land, a man or a woman, and the verses were revealed in response. The question was asked after returning from raids on the tribes of Sheba. The Messenger of God recalled him because he had not been commanded to go.[537]

---

[533] Ṭabrisī, *Majma' al-Bayān*, vol. 8, 378-379.

[534] Ṭabarī, *Jāmi' al-Bayān*, vol. 22, 44.

[535] Al-Suyūṭī, *al-Itqān*, vol. 1, 16.

[536] Ṭabrisī, *Majma' al-Bayān*, vol. 8, 378 states that it is what al-Ḍaḥḥāk said.

[537] Ṭabrisī, *Majma' al-Bayān*, vol. 8, 386; Ṭabarī, *Jāmi' al-Bayān*, vol. 22, 53; al-Suyūṭī, *al-Durr al-Manthūr*, vol. 5, 231.

According to Ibn al-Ḥaṣṣār:

> This means that the verses were revealed in Medina, because Farwah's migration happened after Thaqīf became Muslim, nine years AH.[538]

However, he says after that:

> It is possible that the words, *There was indeed a sign for Sheba...*, referred to what had been revealed earlier in Mecca before the Migration, not to its being revealed there and then.

My comment is that if the story is to be believed, it has to be construed as referring back, for the possibility is extremely remote of a verse being revealed in response to the question of a man whose curiosity regarding the tradition would have been satisfied by being given an answer. It would not require the detail into which the verses went. A fleeting consideration of the story of Sheba as it appears in the Qur'an suffices as proof that, like all the other stories which appear in the Qur'an, it was aimed at guiding mankind towards proper conduct, drawing their attention to errors in times gone by, so that they might learn a lesson on how to proceed in the present.

The correct view on the story of Farwah is that he asked the Prophet about the story of Saba' after he had read it in the Qur'an. He asked whether Sheba was a man or woman, a land or a mountain, and the Prophet explained to him that it was an Arab man who had such and such a number of sons.[539] This indicates that the question came after the revelation of the verse.

Finally, the tradition about Farwah is incoherent and self-contradictory, and this makes it impossible to rely on as evidence on the revelation of verses.

Ibn Abī Ḥātim cites Ali ibn Rabāḥ as saying:

> So-and-So told me that Farwah ibn Musayk al-Ghaṭafānī came to the Messenger of God and said to him, 'O, Prophet of God, Sheba were a people who had combat experience in the days of ignorance. I fear that they will apostasise from Islam. Should I fight them?'

538 Al-Suyūṭī, *al-Itqān*, vol. 1, 43.
539 Ṭabrisī, *Majma' al-Bayān*, vol. 8, 386.

> So he replied, 'I have not been given any instruction with regard to them yet.'
>
> And so the verse, *There was indeed a sign for Sheba in their dwelling-place...*, was revealed.[540]

This tradition is disorderly in terms of its chain of narration, wording and style, and what it says does not relate to the revelation of such a verse. This makes us sure that it was woven by a person who paid little attention to what he said. The same is true of other traditions on the matter.[541] If occasions such as this called for a revelation of the Qur'an, we would be better off avoiding making connections with any particular incident, for the number of them that people might find would be overwhelming.

24- The Originator (*al-Fāṭir*): Meccan

Al-Ḥasan makes an exception of two verses:

> *Surely those who read the Book of God, and establish worship, and spend of that which We have bestowed on them ...* (35:29),

and:

> *Then We gave the Scripture as inheritance unto those whom We elected...* (35:32).

The first one may be on account of the reference therein to prayer. The second one is on account of its being followed by:

> But of them are some who wrong themselves and of them are some who are luke-warm, and of them are some who outstrip (others) through good deeds...

'Ikrimah narrates on the authority of Ibn 'Abbās that those who wrong themselves are the hypocrites.[542]

However, prayer was made compulsory in Mecca, and applying 'those who wrong themselves' to the hypocrites does not mean that the verse had to have been revealed, according to the explanation of Ibn 'Abbās, in Medina, where the hypocrites were – and assuming the hadith to

---

[540] Al-Suyūṭī, *Lubāb al-Nuqūl*, vol. 2, 55.

[541] Ṭabarī, *Jāmi' al-Bayān*, al-Suyūṭī, *al-Durr al-Manthūr* and others.

[542] Ṭabrisī, *Majma' al-Bayān*, vol. 8, 399 and 409.

be correct. Furthermore, the wording is general and not restricted to a particular application.

25- *Yā Sīn*: Meccan

Two verses are said to be exceptions:

Firstly:

> *Verily, We it is Who bring the dead to life. We record that which they send before (them), and their footprints. And all things We have kept in a clear register* (36:12).

Al-Ḥākim and al-Tirmidhī cite Abū Sa'īd al-Khidrī as saying:

> Banū Salamah were on the outskirts of Medina, and they complained to the Messenger of God about the remoteness of their homes from the Mosque and praying with him, so the verse was revealed, and the Messenger of God told them, 'What you have sent before is recorded.'

Therefore they did not move house.[543]

However, this story does not account for the revelation of every part of the verse. It may be that the Prophet relied on part of it as evidence after they complained about the remoteness of their homes, because the best deeds can be the most painful ones.

And secondly:

> *And when it is said unto them: 'Spend of that wherewith God hath provided you,' those who disbelieve say unto those who believe: 'Shall we feed those whom God, if He willed, would feed?' Ye are in naught else than error manifest* (36:47).

According to Ibn 'Abbās, this was revealed in reference to the hypocrites in Medina.[544]

However, it is clearly addressed to those who became unbelievers. Also, Abū Ja'far explicitly stated that it refers to the pagans.[545] In addition, the context of the verse itself testifies to the same thing.

---

[543] Ṭabrisī, *Majma' al-Bayān*, vol. 8, 418; al-Suyūṭī, *al-Itqān*, vol. 1, 43; Ṭabarī, *Jāmi' al-Bayān*, vol. 22, 100.

[544] Al-Suyūṭī, *al-Itqān*, vol. 1, 44; Ṭabrisī, *Majma' al-Bayān*, vol. 8, 413.

[545] Ṭabarī, *Jāmi' al-Bayān*, vol. 23, 9.

The Amīrī Codex and al-Zanjāni's *Tārīkh al-Qur'an* say that verse 45 is an exception. However they may have got the number mixed up. On the assumption that it is correct, however, it is in the same context as verse 47, and what was said about that applies here as well.

26- The Troops *(al-Zumar)*: Meccan

These Words of the Almighty have been said to be an exception:

> *Say: O My bondmen who believe! Observe your duty to your Lord. For those who do good in this world there is good, and God's earth is spacious. Verily the steadfast will be paid their wages without stint* (39:10).

Al-Sakhāwī narrates on authority in *Jamāl al-Qurrā'* that it was revealed in Medina.[546]

However, the verse itself illustrates that it is Meccan and was revealed to urge the poor believers to migrate. The same is narrated on the authority of Ibn 'Abbās.[547]

The following is also said to be an exception:

> *God hath (now) revealed the fairest of statements, a Book consistent, (wherein promises of reward are) paired (with threats of punishment), whereat doth creep the flesh of those who fear their Lord...* (39:23).

Ibn al-Juzrī also narrates on the authority of one other that it was revealed in Medina.[548]

However, the resonant tone that plucks at the heartstrings testifies to the fact that it is Meccan, as does the context, so there is no reason at all for saying that it is an exception.

Similarly, three other verses are said to be exceptions:

> *Say: O My slaves who have been prodigal to their own hurt!...*
>
> to
>
> *....when ye know not...* (39:53-55).

546 Al-Suyūṭī, *al-Itqān*, vol. 1, 44.
547 Ṭabrisī, *Majma' al-Bayān*, vol. 8, 492.
548 Al-Suyūṭī, *al-Itqān*, vol. 1, 44.

It is said through a weak chain of narration on the authority of Ibn 'Abbās that they were revealed about Waḥshī, the slayer of Ḥamzah![549]

However, via an authentic chain of narration Ibn Abī Ḥātim cites Ibn 'Abbās as saying:

> This verse was revealed about the Meccan pagans.[550]

Abū Ja'far explained it the same way, on the basis of hadith evidence transmitted via many routes (*ṭuruq*).[551]

Nevertheless, Waḥshī – a monster in human form – does not deserve a verse to be revealed about him with such a tender emotional resonance and hidden allusions that are imperceptible to all but those with a mature understanding and acute faculties.

'Allāmah Ṭabrisī contends:

> It is incorrect to say that this verse was revealed about Waḥshī, because the verse was revealed in Mecca and Waḥshī became a Muslim many years after that. However, it is possible that the verse was recited to him and was the reason for his becoming a Muslim.[552]

27- The Believer or The Forgiver *(al-Mu'min* or *al-Ghāfir)*: Meccan

Three of its verses are said to be an exception.

The first is:

> *...and hymn the praise of thy Lord at fall of night and in the early hours* (40:55).

Al-Ḥasan says that this is because it refers to the sunset prayer and the dawn prayer. It is confirmed that the obligation to pray was revealed in Medina.[553]

My comment is that this is strange, because prayer was the first duty to be imposed and that happened in Mecca. The Muslims used to pray both in congregation and individually. It was stated above that prayer

549 Al-Suyūṭī, *Lubāb al-Nuqūl*, vol. 2, 63.
550 Ibid.
551 Ṭabarī, *Jāmi' al-Bayān*, vol. 24, 10.
552 Ṭabrisī, *Majma' al-Bayān*, vol. 8, 503.
553 Ṭabrisī, *Majma' al-Bayān*, vol. 8, 528.

was the first thing brought by Gabriel at the beginning of the Prophet's mission, when he taught him the ablution from minor impurity and how to pray.[554]

Furthermore, the beginning of the verse, *Then have patience. Lo! the promise of God is true. And ask forgiveness of thy sin*, is evidence that it is Meccan, not to mention its context.

The second and third verses are:

> *Verily, those who wrangle concerning the revelations of God without a warrent having come to them...*
>
> to
>
> *...but most of mankind know not* (40:56-57).

According to Jalāl al-Dīn:

> Ibn Ḥamīd and Ibn Abī Ḥātim, via an authentic chain of narration, cite Abu al-ʿĀliyah as saying:
>
> The Jews came to the Prophet and said, 'The Antichrist (*dajjāl*) is among us. He will appear at the end of time...'
>
> They began extolling his importance and so God revealed these two verses which contain:
>
> *Assuredly the creation of the heavens and the earth is greater...* (40:57).[555]

My comment is that we seek refuge in God from vain talk. How can a Qur'anic verse be revealed refuting an insignificant claim that a Jew bragged about, making a comparison between the deceit of the Antichrist and the creation of the heavens and the earth?

Abū Jaʿfar al-Ṭabarī did well[556] in not mentioning any of those vacuous hadiths with which Jalāl al-Dīn al-Suyūṭī filled his exegesis. We declare the Holy Qur'an to be completely free of them.

Next, the verse compares the creation of the heavens with the creation of mankind, making the former greater, and this is evidence of a disavowal which took place with regard to man's creation, which is something that does not fit in with such an absurd claim.

---

[554] *Supra* under 'The First to be Revealed.'

[555] Al-Suyūṭī, *al-Durr al-Manthūr*, vol. 5, 353; al-Suyūṭī, *Lubāb al-Nuqūl*, vol. 2, 65.

[556] Ṭabarī, *Jamiʿ al-Bayān*, vol. 24, 50.

It is strange that Ṭabrisī[557] should have fallen in with the likes of al-Suyūṭī with regard to this vacuousness.

28- Consultation *(al-Shūrā)*: Meccan

The following three verses are said to be exceptions:

> *Or they say: 'Hath he invented a lie concerning God?'...*
>
> to
>
> *...As for the disbelievers, theirs will be an awful doom* (42:24-26).

It is said that they were revealed about the Helpers (*anṣār*). Al-Ṭabarānī narrates this on the authority of Ibn 'Abbās via a weak chain of narration.[558]

Also, it is said that the Almighty's Words:

> *And if God were to enlarge the provision for His slaves... He is Informed, a Seer of His bondsmen* (42:27),

were revealed about the poor refugees who lived off charity (*aṣḥāb al-ṣuffah*). Al-Ḥākim cites this and declares it to be authentic.[559]

My comment is that it would be very surprising if the first of these verses were revealed about the Helpers (*anṣār*). How can the words, *'Hath he (the Prophet) invented a lie concerning God?'* conceivably be attributed to them? Next, the tradition states that the Helpers thought ill of the Messenger of God and that he was fighting exclusively in defence of the People of his Household, and so this verse was revealed!

As for the last verse, it is general. If the tradition narrated on the authority of Ali is authentic, it means that it applies to the poor refugees on account of its generality (*'umūm*), and not that it was revealed exclusively about them. Assuming that to be the case, it would be a scolding rebuke of the poor refugees who lived off charity. Far be it from the Qur'an to hurt the feelings of a group of believers on account of their poverty.

Ṭabrisī also adds:

> *Say: 'I ask of you no fee therefor, save loving kindness among kinsfolk'* (42:23).

---

557 Ṭabrisī, *Majma' al-Bayān*, vol. 8, 528.

558 Al-Suyūṭī, *Lubāb al-Nuqūl*, vol. 2, 68.

559 Al-Suyūṭī, *Lubāb al-Nuqūl*, vol. 2, 68.

Ibn 'Abbās says that when this verse was revealed, a man said, 'God has not revealed this verse!' and so God revealed:

Or say they: 'He hath invented a lie concerning God'? (42:24).

The man then repented and felt regret, and so, *And He it is Who accepteth repentance from His bondsmen... And as for disbelievers, theirs will be an awful doom* (42:25-26), was revealed.

He says on the authority of Ibn 'Abbās and Qatādah that four verses were revealed in Medina.[560] It may be with regard to the verse about love for kinsfolk being revealed regarding the Messenger's kinsfolk from his Pure Family, as we have confirmed.[561] However, that does not contradict the idea of the 'fee' for the Message being love for one's kinsfolk, and recorded as a debt owed by the believers because it was for their own good, and they would be aware of that from the beginning of their Islamic life.

Similarly, they thought:

...and whose affairs are a matter of counsel... (42:38),

was revealed after Islam was established in Medina, for the Muslims did not have an institution when they were in fear of the pagans in Mecca.

However, the verse indicates the modus operandi for a group of believers, whatever condition they are in, whether weak or strong. They should work as one wherever they settle and wherever they travel.

The Almighty's Words:

And those who, when wrong is done to them, defend themselves...

to

...there is no cause of blame against them. (42:39-41).

Ibn al-Gharas narrates on the authority of one of them that it was revealed in Medina,[562] except that the context is completely Meccan and the verses preceding and following it are definitely linked to it, making it impossible for it to be an exception. They were all revealed about the believers in Mecca in the days when they were considered weak. This cannot be doubted by anyone who refers to the verses.

[560] Ṭabrisī, *Majma' al-Bayan*, vol. 9, 20.

[561] See Ma'rifat, *al-Tamhīd*, part 8: 'Consideration of the Traditions, The Seventh Kind.'

[562] Al-Suyūṭī, *al-Itqān*, vol. 1, 44.

29- The Adornment *(al-Zukhruf)*: Meccan
The following is said to be an exception:

> *And ask those of Our messengers whom We sent before thee: Did We ever appoint gods to be worshipped beside the Beneficent?* (43:45).

According to al-Muqātil this was revealed at the Dome of the Rock at the time of the Night Journey.[563] Alternatively, it is said that it was revealed in Medina.[564] However, the verse is closely linked to the surrounding verses, and was revealed in the tone of, 'I am talking to you but I want others to listen,' so it is without a doubt Meccan, and concerns the pagans. As for its being revealed in Heaven or at the Dome of the Rock, that would not make it Medinan. It is only Meccan on account of its being revealed before the Migration, in accordance with the aforementioned classification.[565] The Amīrī Codex and those who follow it say that verse 54 is an exception, but this could be confusion over the number.

30- The Crouching *(al-Jāthiyah)*: Meccan
According to Qatādah, the following was revealed in Medina:[566]

> *Tell those who believe to forgive those who hope not for the days of God* (45:14).

The correct view is that it is one of the verses of forgiveness which were revealed in Mecca in the days when the believers were considered weak. Hence it was abrogated later, when Islam's power became strong in Medina.[567]

31- The Sand Dunes *(al-Aḥqāf)*: Meccan
The following is said to be an exception:

> *Bethink you that if it is from God and ye disbelieve therein, and a witness of the Children of Israel hath already testified to the like thereof and hath believed, and ye are too proud...* (46:10).

---

563 Ṭabrisī, *Majmaʿ al-Bayān*, vol. 9, 38; al-Suyūṭī, *al-Durr al-Manthūr*, vol. 6, 19.
564 Al-Suyūṭī, *al-Itqān*, vol. 1, 44.
565 *Supra* under 'Different Ways of Telling Meccan from Medinan.'
566 Ṭabrisī, *Majmaʿ al-Bayān*, vol. 9, 70; al-Suyūṭī, *al-Itqān*, vol. 1, 44.
567 See *Tafsīr al-Ṭabarī*, vol. 25, 87.

Ṭabarānī states that it was revealed in Medina and concerns how 'Abdullāh ibn Salām became a Muslim.[568] It is indeed odd how the exegetes seem infatuated with connecting every verse where there is an allusion to the People of the Book becoming believers with 'Abdullāh ibn Salām and his kind.

The correct view is that it is rebuke of the Quraysh for dragging their heels in believing in a religion brought at the hand of one of their own and in their native tongue, while those such as the Children of Israel and others believed in it. The only reason the Children of Israel were singled out for mention is the extra attention given them by the Arabs at the time, and the trust they had in their knowledge and culture.

Moreover, Ibn Abī Ḥātim cites Masrūq as saying:

> This verse was revealed in Mecca about the pagans.

Abū Ja'far states the same via several chains of narration.[569]

Five other verses are said to be exceptions:

> *We have commanded unto man kindness toward parents...*
>
> to
>
> *...and they will not be wronged* (46:15-19).

It is said that they were revealed about Abū Bakr – because he was kind to his parents – and his son 'Abd al-Raḥmān when he was recalcitrant towards his parents when they were trying to persuade him to become a Muslim.[570]

However, the verses are general, as evidenced by the plural form indicative of generality in both cases. Thus, they are a portrayal of anyone who is kind to his parents as compared with obstinacy towards them.[571]

In any event, deeming it to have been revealed about Abū Bakr and his son 'Abd al-Raḥmān does not mean the verses have to be Medinan, given that the relevant story – assuming it to be true – took place in Mecca.

Similarly, there is no reason for saying that God's Words:

> *Then have patience even as the stout of heart among the messengers of old had patience* (46:35),

---

[568] Al-Suyūṭī, *Lubāb al-Nuqūl*, vol. 2, 72; Ṭabarī, *Jāmi' al-Bayān*, vol. 26, 8; al-Suyūṭī, *al-Itqān*, vol. 1, 44.

[569] Ṭabarī, *Jami' al-Bayān*, 26:7; al-Suyūṭī, *al-Durr al-Manthūr*, 6:39.

[570] Al-Suyūṭī, *al-Durr al-Manthūr*, vol. 6, 41; Ṭabarī, *Jāmi' al-Bayān*, vol. 26, 13.

[571] Ṭabrisī, *Majma' al-Bayān*, vol. 9, 87.

are an exception, given their Meccan tone and their melody being directed at the pagans of Quraysh. It was revealed during the days when the Muslims were weak, and was abrogated later by the verse telling them to fight (*āyat al-qitāl*).

32- *Qāf*: Meccan

Ḥākim and others state that the following verse was revealed in Medina in response to a Jewish claim that God rested on the Sabbath after creating the heavens and the earth in six days:[572]

> *And verily We created the heavens and the earth, and all that is between them, in six days, and naught of weariness touched Us* (50:38).

Majma' al-Bayān adds:

> ...up to His Words, *and before the setting of the sun* (50:39), on the authority of al-Ḥasan.

My comment is that it is true that it was revealed in response to a false claim, but not that it was revealed in Medina. This is because the Arabs, as repeatedly stated, were in constant contact with the People of the Book, and they may have accepted teachings pertaining to the creation of the heavens and the earth from them, making them well known among the pagan Arabs. So this response – assuming it to be a response – does not prove that it was revealed in Medina. It may be that the tradition which says that it was revealed about the Jews means what we have stated – that it was revealed about teachings they had spread among the Arabs.

Testimony to the fact that the verse is Meccan, is what comes after it – one of the verses of forgiveness that were abrogated later:
...so bear with what they say...(50:39).

33- The Star *(al-Najm)*: Meccan

The following is said to be an exception:

> *He is Best Aware of you (from the time) when He created you from the earth, and when ye were hidden in the bellies of your mothers. Therefore ascribe not purity unto yourselves. He is Best Aware of him who wardeth off (evil)* (53:32).

[572] Al-Suyūṭī, *al-Durr al-Manthūr*, vol. 6, 110; al-Suyūṭī, *al-Itqān*, vol. 1, 45.

Al-Wāḥidī states that Thābit ibn al-Ḥarth al-Anṣārī said:

> The Jews would say, 'Righteous (*Ṣiddīq*),' if one of their small boys died. That came to the attention of the Messenger of God and so he said, 'They're lying. There is not a single soul created by God in his mother's womb who is not either wretched or happy.' So at that, God revealed, *He is Best Aware of you...*[573]

My comment is that if the tradition is authentic, it does not indicate that the verse was revealed in Medina. It may be that what was said by the Jews – who spread their corrupt teachings among the Arabs – reached the Messenger when he was in Mecca and thence the verse was revealed there.

However, the tradition has nothing at all to do with the import of the verse, because God's Words, *He is Best Aware of you*, are an explanation of *....wide in His forgiveness*, meaning that mankind has a propensity to succumb to base desires in accordance with human nature, which consists of tendencies and cravings, and which God knows very well. Hence, He covenanted forgiveness upon Himself as a mercy to mankind and out of compassion for man's particular position.

Nine verses are said to be exceptions, beginning with:

> *Didst thou observe him who turned away ...* (53:33-41).

It is said that they were revealed about a man who came to the Prophet when he was setting out for battle, asking him for a mount and weaponry, but none could be found. So he met up with a friend of his and said, 'Give me something.' He replied, 'I will give you this in exchange for your bearing my sins.' He agreed, and so these verses were revealed.[574]

However, the verses do not tally with the meaning of the story at all. They were simply revealed in reference to one of the leaders of Quraysh in a long story referred to by Abū Ja'far al-Ṭabarī.[575]

34- The Moon *(al-Qamar)*: Meccan

Three verses are said to be exceptions, firstly:

> *The hosts shall all be routed, and will turn and flee* (54:45).

[573] Al-Suyūṭī, *Lubāb al-Nuqūl*, vol. 2, 88-89; al-Suyūṭī, *al-Durr al-Manthūr*, vol. 6, 128.

[574] Al-Suyūṭī, *al-Durr al-Manthūr*, vol. 6, 128.

[575] Ṭabarī, *Jāmi' al-Bayān*, vol. 27, 41-42.

It is claimed that this was revealed at the Battle of Badr.[576]

The truth is that they promised the Muslims victory later on and so the Battle of Badr took place.[577]

The second and third are:

> *Surely the godfearing shall dwell amid gardens and a river in a sure abode, in the presence of a King Omnipotent* (54:54-55).

However, whoever said that these are exceptions gave no reason, nor is there any reason for their being so, given the unbroken context (*waḥdat al-siyāq*) of the verses and their being firmly in keeping with those before and after.

The Amīrī Codex says that verses 44, 45 and 46 are exceptions, but this may be because of confusion over the numeration.

35- The Inevitable *(al-Wāqi'ah)*: Meccan

The following is said to be an exception:[578]

> *A multitude of those of old and a multitude of those of later time* (56:39-40).

This may be on account of Ibn Mas'ūd's tradition about a vision the Messenger of God had. He told his companions of it, and then recited the two verses.[579] This is said to have happened in Medina.

However, his reciting it does not prove that it was revealed there and then.

Also, the following verses are said to be exceptions:

> *Nay, I swear by the places of the stars - and lo! that verily is a tremendous oath, if ye but knew - that (this) is indeed a noble Qur'an in a Book kept hidden which none toucheth but the purified, a revelation from the Lord of the Worlds. Is it this Statement that ye scorn, and make denial thereof your livelihood?* (56:75-82).

This is on account of what Muslim, Ḥākim and others narrate, that the companions were either afflicted by drought or their water ran out

---

[576] Al-Suyūṭī, *Lubāb al-Nuqūl*, vol. 2, 90.

[577] Ṭabrisī, *Majma' al-Bayān*, vol. 9, 194; see al-Suyūṭī, *al-Itqān*, vol. 1, 45 and 104; Ṭabarī, *Jāmi' al-Bayān*, vol. 27, 65.

[578] See al-Suyūṭī, *al-Itqān*, vol. 1, 45.

[579] Ṭabrisī, *Majma' al-Bayān*, vol. 9, 219.

during a journey or at the Battle of Tabūk. They then complained to the Prophet and he rose up and prayed two *rak'ahs*. He then petitioned God, Who sent a cloud which rained down on them. Thereafter some of them started whispering to each other, 'We have been given rain by the setting of such-and-such a star,' and so the verse was revealed.[580]

However, the verses do not apply to this story. They are a response to those who rejected the revelation from God, and have nothing whatsoever to do with the setting of the stars, either in their literal meaning or their import, just as the verses preceding and following them make it impossible to accept the aforementioned tradition.

36- The Kingdom *(al-Mulk)*: Meccan

It is narrated on the authority of Ibn 'Abbās that the whole chapter, apart from three verses, was revealed in relation to the people of Mecca.[581]

My comment is that this does not mean that all of it was revealed in Mecca other than three verses which were revealed elsewhere.

On the contrary, this chapter was revealed as a reprimand to the pagans of Mecca. All the verses are a threat to them except for three verses about the believers, which are as follows:

> *Surely those who fear their Lord ...* (67:12);
>
> *It is He who made the earth ... for you ...* (67:15);
>
> *Say: 'He is the All-Merciful. We believe in Him ...'* (67:29)

The correct view, as in Ibn Khudayj's hadith, is that the whole chapter was revealed in Mecca.[582]

37- The Pen *(al-Qalam)*: Meccan

Al-Sakhāwī narrates in *Jamāl al-Qurrā'* that these seventeen verses are exceptions:

> *Lo! We have tried them as We tried the owners of the garden...*
>
> to
>
> *...if they did but know* (68:17-33);

---

[580] Al-Suyūṭī, *Lubāb al-Nuqūl*, vol. 2, 92-93.

[581] Al-Suyūṭī, *al-Durr al-Manthūr*, vol. 6, 246.

[582] Ibid.

along with another three verses:

But wait thou for thy Lord's decree...

to

...and He placed him among the righteous (68:48-50).

It is claimed that these twenty verses were revealed in Medina.[583] *Majma' al-Bayān* adds verses 51 and 52.[584]

Ibn Abī Ḥātim and Ibn Jurayj state that Abū Jahl said at the Battle of Badr: 'Take them, tie them with ropes and do not kill any of them,' and so, *Lo! We have tried them...*, was revealed.[585]

However, what Abū Jahl said does not ostensibly fit in with the import of the aforementioned verses, such that it could account for their revelation.

The correct view is that they were revealed about the pagans in general, in keeping with the rest of the verses in the chapter. That is how 'Allāmah Ṭabrisī and Abū Ja'far al-Ṭabarī explain them.[586]

As for, *But wait thou for thy Lord's decree...*, they are without a doubt Meccan verses of forgiveness. We do not know the reason for the strange belief that they are an exception.

38- Enfolded *(al-Muzzammil)*: Meccan

Al-Iṣbahānī narrates that the following are exceptions:[587]

And bear with patience what they utter...

to

...and do thou respite them awhile (73:10-11).

However, the two verses are a consolation to the Prophet in the face of harassment by the pagans, and a threat to them. Thence they are Meccan verses of forgiveness, and there is no reason to think that they are Medinan.

Ibn al-Gharas narrates that God's Words:

583 Al-Suyūṭī, *al-Itqān*, vol. 1, 46.

584 Ṭabrisī, *Majma' al-Bayān*, vol. 10, 330.

585 Al-Suyūṭī, *al-Durr al-Manthūr*, vol. 6, 253.

586 Ṭabrisī, *Majma' al-Bayān*, vol. 10, 336 and Ṭabarī, *Jāmi' al-Bayān*, vol. 29, 19.

587 Al-Suyūṭī, *al-Itqān*, vol. 1, 46.

> *Lo! thy Lord knoweth how thou keepest vigil...*
>
> to
>
> *...God is Forgiving, Merciful* (73:20),

are an exception.

According to Jalāl al-Dīn:

> What Ḥākim states – that it was revealed a year after the beginning of the chapter – refutes this. That was when standing in prayer all through the night was mandatory – when Islam first came along – before the five prayers were made mandatory.[588]

'Abd ibn Ḥamīd narrates the same on the authority of 'Ikrimah:

> The Muslims carried on doing what they were doing for a whole year after, *O, thou enwrapped in thy robes, keep vigil at night...*, was revealed. It was difficult for them and their feet cracked, until the end of the chapter, *Recite, then, of the Qur'an, that which is easy for you*, abrogated it.[589]

My comment is that whoever says that the verse is Medinan relies on the belief that prayer and charity were not made obligatory in Mecca.[590] It is a strange reasoning, because prayer was the first duty to be imposed in Mecca.[591] As for charity, it does not mean compulsory almsgiving with prescribed parameters and a minimum quantity of property that incurs liability (*niṣābs*). At the time, it simply meant a discretionary but compulsory amount, as in God's Words:

> *...And who are payers of the poor-due* (23:4)

and:

> *...Who give not the poor-due, and are disbelievers in the Hereafter* (41:7).

It is true that specific rulings came about in Medina, but there was undoubtedly a compulsory foundation of alms-giving in Mecca.

---

588 Al-Suyūṭī, *al-Itqān*, vol. 1, 46.
589 Al-Suyūṭī, *al-Durr al-Manthūr*, vol. 6, 280.
590 Ṭabrisī, *Majma' al-Bayān*, vol. 10, 372.
591 See Ibn Hishām, *al-Sīrat al-Nabawiyyah*, vol. 1, 259.

The narrator might rather have relied on God's Words, *...and others fight in God's cause...*, and the fact that fighting was only made part of the law in Medina. However, that would have to be based on the presumption that what is meant by fighting is actual fighting, and not that which would be made a duty and which would take place later on. The second possibility is more likely in view of the fact that, in this verse, God mentions the reasons for which the first difficult duty would be replaced by another, easier one. A reason for fighting being made part of the law later on, was that there was no clear evidence of what was meant by actual fighting.

39- Those Sent Forth *(al-Mursalāt)*: Meccan

It is said that the following of God's Words are an exception:

> *When it is said unto them: Bow down, they bow not down* (77:48).

According to Muqātil it was revealed when the Messenger told the Banu Thaqīf to pray and they protested, 'We do not bow because that is dishonour for us.'[592] They became Muslim in Medina.

However, the complexion of the verse and its context indicates that it refers to the pagan Arabs. There is no reason for there to be a space left in the chapter for this verse, to be filled in the last years after the Migration, because that would rupture the harmony and eloquence of the chapter.

Nevertheless, in this context 'bowing' means submission to God, obeying his commandments, and not bowing in the technical sense, as a part of prayer, for example. This is Abū Ja'far al-Ṭabarī's favoured opinion,[593] in the same way as, *And perform the prayer, pay the alms and bow with those that bow* means the same thing.

See *Tafsīru Shubbar*, where it says:

> Alternatively, it means submission and obedience to the Truth.

It states with conviction regarding *Those Sent Forth*:

> *If they are told to bow*, means submitted, humbled themselves and followed.[594]

---

[592] Ṭabrisī, *Majma' al-Bayān*, vol. 10, 419 .

[593] See Ṭabarī, *Jāmi' al-Bayān*, vol. 29, 150.

[594] *Tafsīru Shubbar*, vol. 46, 545.

Therefore the verse has nothing to do with the matter of the Banu Thaqīf becoming Muslims. Instead, it talks generally about the pagans' stubborn resistance in the face of manifest Truth.

40- The Dealers in Fraud *(al-Muṭaffif īn)*: Meccan

They say that the beginning of this chapter was revealed in Medina when the Messenger of God first arrived there. The people of Medina were amongst the most unfair with regard to weights and measures, and so God revealed the first six verses, beginning with:

> *Woe unto the dealers in fraud ...* (83:1).

Thereafter, they were reformed.[595]

It was stated above that it would be extremely surprising for the Messenger to confront the Helpers (*anṣār*) with such sternly-worded verses upon his first meeting with them, when they had given him refuge in their own territory, and gone to great efforts to help him in the cause of spreading the word of Islam.

Hence, the correct view is that the whole chapter is Meccan.

There are yet more verses said to be exceptions, but we have omitted them to avoid prolixity and because they are not based on adequate evidence. Some of these are in *The Night* (*al-Layl*) and *Charity* (*al-Mā'ūn*), and are referred to by al-Suyūṭī in *al-Itqān*.

Exceptions within Medinan Chapters

It was stated above that it would be surprising if a verse remained unrecorded in a Meccan chapter until a later Medinan chapter was revealed in which it was. Others, including Ibn Ḥajar in *Sharḥ al-Bukhārī*, believe that to be a remote possibility.[596]

Nevertheless, it is said that several verses which are recorded in Medinan chapters are in fact Meccan. These will be examined in the order in which they appear in the Noble Codex (*al-Muṣḥaf al-Sharīf*) and comment on them.

---

[595] Al-Suyūṭī, *al-Itqān*, vol. 1, 47; al-Suyūṭī, *al-Durr al-Manthūr*, vol. 6, 324; Ṭabrisī, *Majma' al-Bayān*, vol. 10, 452.

[596] *Supra* under 'Verses Said to Be an Exception.'

1- The Cow *(al-Baqarah):* Medinan

Three of the verses are said to be exceptions.

The first of these is:

> *... Forgive and be indulgent (toward them) until God gives His command* (2:109).

They claim that they were revealed about the pagans in the days when the Muslims in Mecca were weak.

However, the beginning of the verse:

> *Many of the People of the Book long to...*

is testimony to its having been revealed about the People of the Book shortly after the Messenger's migration to Medina, before Islam had become strong. It was later abrogated by:

> *Fight against such of those who have been given the Scripture as believe not...until they pay the tribute readily, Being brought low* (9:29).

See Tabarsī regarding the revelation of the verse and its abrogation by a verse freeing them from obligation (*āyat barā'ah*).[597]

The second verse is the Almighty's Words:

> *The guiding of them is not thy duty...* (2:272).

This is also claimed to have been revealed regarding the pagans' stubborn resistance to accepting the Truth, as in His Words:

> *Thou guidest not whom thou lovest...* (28:56).

However, the verse was revealed in connection with the Muslims' expenditure on the disbelievers, because they had refused to do so, believing it to be forbidden because the disbelievers did not follow their religion.[598]

The third verse is:

> *And guard yourself against a day in which ye will be brought back to God ...* (2:281).

---

[597] Ṭabrisī, *Majma' al-Bayān*, vol. 1, 184-185; al-Suyūṭī, *al-Durr al-Manthūr*, vol. 1, 107.

[598] Ṭabrisī, *Majma' al-Bayān*, vol. 2, 385; al-Suyūṭī, *al-Durr al-Manthūr*, vol. 1, 357.

It is said that this was the last verse to be revealed to the Messenger of God when he was at Minā on the Farewell Pilgrimage.[599] Assuming that to be the case, it is Medinan as stated above.

2- The Women *(al-Nisā')*: Medinan

Ṭabrisī claims that the following are exceptions:

> *God commandeth you that ye restore deposits to their owners ...* (4:58),

and:

> *They ask thee for a pronouncement. Say: God hath pronounced for you concerning distant kindred...* (4:176).

However, he gives no evidence and no others agree.[600]

The reason for the first verse may be that it is said on the authority of Ibn Jurayj that it was revealed after the conquest of Mecca, and is addressed to the Prophet, instructing him to give the key of the Ka'bah back to 'Uthmān ibn Ṭalḥah, having taken it from him on the day of the conquest, intending to give it to to al-'Abbās.[601]

However, what determines whether a verse is Meccan is whether it was revealed before the Migration, as stated above. Moreover, the verse does not apply to the aforementioned story because the key was not given to the Prophet for safekeeping or as a deposit. Otherwise, far be it from the Prophet to betray a trust and have his attention drawn to it by God through the revelation of a verse. Ṭabrisī also rejects this explanation for the revelation.

As for the second verse, we neither acknowledge the reason given, nor that it is even possible. Ṭabrisī refers to explanations for its revelation which are inappropriate as evidence for saying that it is an exception.[602] The tone of the verse also cries out that it is Medinan, because it is one of the verses containing a ruling (*āyāt al-aḥkām*).

However, the declaration that it is an exception is based on the second system of classification. As for the first system, which is generally accepted,

---

599 Al-Suyūṭī, *al-Durr al-Manthūr*, vol. 1, 370.

600 Ṭabrisī, *Majma' al-Bayān*, vol. 3, 1.

601 Ṭabrisī, *Majma' al-Bayān*, vol. 3, 63.

602 Ṭabrisī, *Majma' al-Bayān*, vol. 3, 149.

whatever was revealed after the Migration is Medinan, even if it was revealed in Mecca. The verse is therefore Medinan.[603]

3- The Table *(al-Mā'idah)*: Medinan

The following Words of God are said to be an exception:

> *This day are those who disbelieve in despair of (ever harming) your religion; so fear them not, but fear Me. This day have I perfected your religion for you and completed My favour unto you, and have chosen for you as religion Islam* (5:3).

It is said that this was revealed to the Messenger of God while he was staying in 'Arafah on the Farewell Pilgrimage.[604] Abū 'Abdillāh al-Zanjānī claims the same in *Tārīkh al-Qur'an.*[605]

However, Abū 'Abdillāh al-Ṣādiq explains:

> The verse was revealed after the Messenger of God appointed Ali as the banner of the nation on the Day of Ghadīr Khumm on his way back from the Farewell Pilgrimage. So God revealed on that day:
>
> *This day have I perfected your religion for you...* [606]

So, too, is it recorded by Ibn Wāḍiḥ al-Ya'qūbī:

> It was revealed on the day he appointed Ali ibn Abī Ṭālib Commander of the Faithful at Ghadīr Khumm.

He comments:

> It is the tradition which is confirmed and clear.[607]

Hāfiẓ Ḥasakānī cites it via several routes.[608]

Furthermore, the verse being revealed at 'Arafah or at Ghadīr Khumm does not make it an exception to the Medinan chapters according to the generally accepted classification.

---

603 *Supra* under 'Different Ways of Telling Meccan from Medinan.'

604 Al-Suyūṭī, *al-Durr al-Manthūr*, vol. 2, 257.

605 Zanjānī, *Tārīkh al-Qur'an*, 27.

606 Ṭūsī, *al-Tibyān*, vol. 3, 435.

607 Ibn Wāḍiḥ, *Tārīkh al-Ya'qūbī*, vol. 2, 35.

608 Ḥasakānī, *Shawāhid al-Tanzīl*, vol. 1, 156-160.

4- The Spoils of War *(al-Anfāl)*: Medinan

The following is said to be an exception:

> *And when those who disbelieve plot against thee to wound thee fatally, or to kill thee or to drive thee forth; they devise, but God deviseth; and God is the best of devisers* (8:30).

It is said that this was revealed in relation to the story of the council hall (*dār al-nadwah*) where the Quraysh had gathered to plot against the Messenger of God, and their plot was foiled by the Messenger's Migration and Ali's sleeping on his bed.[609]

However, this does not mean that the verse had to have been revealed there and then, especially in view of the adverbial preposition of time, which indicates the past tense – *idh* (when) – at the beginning of the verse, referring to a past event.

According to the Amīrī Codex and Zanjānī's *Tārīkh*, verses 31 to 36 are exceptions in view of the fact that they were revealed about the pagans from Quraysh. However, the verse mentioned refers to a past event and there is no evidence that it was revealed there and then. Further, His Words:

> *But God would not punish them while thou wast with them, nor will He punish them while they seek forgiveness* (8:33),

also refer to the past and speak of the present, meaning that God did not punish them before because the Prophet was among them, and does not punish them now after his leaving them because of the presence of a group of believers who were unable to leave, even though they were determined to migrate. Thus God lifted the punishment from the people of Mecca out of respect for the forgiveness sought by those believers who remained among them.[610]

Moreover, Jalāl al-Dīn narrates on the authority of Qatādah:

> The verse, *And when those who disbelieve plot against thee...*, was revealed in Mecca.

However, this is refuted by what is authentically narrated on the authority of Ibn 'Abbās, that this very same verse was revealed in Medina.[611]

---

[609] Ṭabrisī, *Majma' al-Bayān*, vol. 4, 537.
[610] Ṭabrisī, *Majma' al-Bayān*, vol. 4, 539.
[611] Al-Suyūṭī, *al-Itqān*, vol. 1, 39.

It is stated in *Asbāb al-Tanzīl* on the authority of Ibn 'Abbās that the verse was revealed after the Prophet's arrival in Medina.[612]

Ibn al-'Arabī and others say that the following of God's Words are an exception:[613]

> *O Prophet! God is sufficient for thee and those who follow thee of the believers* (8:64).

This is on account of what is stated by Abū Muhammad via Ṭāriq on the authority of 'Umar ibn al-Khaṭṭāb:

> I was the fortieth to become Muslim and so, *O Prophet, God is sufficient for thee and those who follow thee of the believers*, was revealed.

The same is narrated on the authority of Ibn 'Abbās.[614]

However, it is contradicted by what is narrated on the authority of al-Kalbī. He says that this verse was revealed in the desert at the Battle of Badr.[615] According to al-Wāqidī, it was revealed in Medina about Banī Qurayẓah and Banī al-Naḍīr.[616]

Moreover, the context of the verse testifies to its being Medinan. It was revealed when fighting was first made lawful both with the pagans and with the People of the Book. The verse is preceded by the Almighty's Words:

> *Those of them with whom thou hast made a pact, then at every opportunity they break their pact ...* (8:56);
>
> *If thou comest upon them in the war, deal with them...* (8:57);
>
> *And let not those who disbelieve suppose that they can outstrip (God's purpose). Lo! they cannot escape.* (8:59);
>
> *Make ready for them all thou canst of (armed) force and of horses tethered...* (8:60);
>
> *And if they incline to peace, incline thou also to it...* (8:61);
>
> *And if they would deceive thee, then lo! God is sufficient for thee. He it is that supporteth thee with His help...* (8:62).

---

612 Al-Suyūṭī, *Lubāb al-Nuqūl*, vol. 1, 170.
613 Al-Suyūṭī, *al-Itqān*, vol. 1, 39.
614 Al-Suyūṭī, *al-Durr al-Manthūr*, vol. 3, 200.
615 Ṭabrisī, *Majma' al-Bayān*, vol. 4, 557.
616 Ṭūsī, *al-Tibyān*, vol. 5, 152.

Then comes:

> *O Prophet! God is sufficient for thee and those who follow thee of the believers* (8:64);

followed by:

> *O Prophet! Exhort the believers to fight...* (8:65).

Looking at the verse within its context, each part of which fits in with the others, makes us confident that it is a part of a coherent whole that was revealed together.

Furthermore, it makes no sense, since they were still a weak force, as if forty men becoming Muslim was enough. This confirms that the verse was revealed in Medina, because the Muslims' power was increasing by the day.

This is how Abū Ja'far al-Ṭabarī explains it:

> He says to them, Sublime is His Praise, 'Resist your enemy, for God will suffice you, and do not let the size of their numbers and the paucity of yours frighten you. For God will support you with His Help.'

He refers to traditions in support of this explanation and does not address any of the traditions which claim that it was revealed in relation to 'Umar ibn al-Khaṭṭāb's becoming a Muslim.[617]

5- The Repentance *(al-Barā'ah)*: Medinan

Four verses have been said to be an exception.

The first and second are:

> *It is not for the Prophet, and those who believe, to pray for the forgiveness of idolaters, even though they may be near of kins...*
>
> to
>
> *...Abraham was soft of heart, long-suffering* (9:113-114).

It is claimed that they were revealed about Abū Ṭālib when death came upon him. The Prophet went to see him and Abū Jahl and 'Abdullāh ibn Abī Umayyah were with him. The Prophet said, 'Say: 'There is no god but God,' Uncle, and I will rely on it as evidence in God's presence.' So the two

[617] Ṭabarī, *Jāmi' al-Bayān*, vol. 10, 26.

Qurayshi men said, 'Do you have a distaste for 'Abd al-Muṭṭalib's religion?' Every time the Prophet put the testimony of faith to him they repeated what they had said. Abū Ṭālib's last words were that he followed 'Abd al-Muṭṭalib's religion and refused to say that there is no god but God, so the Prophet said, 'I will seek forgiveness for you provided I am not told otherwise.' Thereafter, the verse was revealed, as also was:

> *Thou guidest not whom thou lovest, but God guideth whom He will...* (28:56).[618]

It is also said that it was revealed about the parents of the Prophet; he wanted to seek forgiveness for his father, and similarly, sought his Lord's permission to visit his mother's grave, and was granted it. It occurred to him to seek forgiveness for her, and so the verse was revealed telling him not to. The Messenger of God was never seen crying more than he did that day.[619]

My comment is may God destroy ignorant fanaticism. It is an Umayyad leaning set on detracting from the Hashimites' dignity and on distorting the image of the Prophet's relatives, making out that his parents were pagans and that Abū Ṭālib died an unbeliever, when in fact he was the first protector and only defender in his time of the Messenger of God. The Almighty said:

> *...and those who are akin are nearer one to another in the ordinance of God* (8:75).

There is no doubt that Abū Ṭālib was the first to give him refuge, help him and defend him with his life and property. The verse above is a general testimony which undoubtedly includes him.[620]

What he said in his ode (*qaṣīdah*) in which he defended the Messenger of God suffices as evidence of his sincere belief:

> *They know that none of us calls our son a liar and that he does not occupy himself with telling falsehoods;*

---

[618] See al-Suyūṭī, *al-Durr al-Manthūr*, vol. 3, 282; *Ṣaḥīḥ al-Bukhārī*, vol. 2, 119; 6:87.

[619] Ṭabarī, *Jāmi' al-Bayān*, vol. 11, 319.

[620] Al-Sayyid 'Abdallāh Shubbar, *Ḥaqq al-Yaqīn fī Ma'rifat Usūl al-Dīn* (Beirut: Mu'assasat al-A'lamī, 1997), vol. 1, 100.

He became the most laudable among us in origin short of which the vehemence of the insolent falls;

I took care of him by myself, protected him with shelter and chests;

The Lord of the servants supported him with His help and manifested a religion, the truth of which is not falsehood.[621]

As for us, the Imāmiyyah, the fundamentals of Shi'a beliefs dictate the necessity of the purity of the Prophet and the Imams' ancestors, both male and female, unpolluted in the slightest by the stain of polytheism. They continued throughout the generations, as the seventh salutation (*ziyārah*) of Imām Abū 'Abdillāh says:

> I testify that you were light in the noble loins and pure wombs. The days of ignorance did not sully you with impurity or clothe you in darkness.

A hadith from Ibn 'Abbās on the authority of the Prophet says:

> God kept moving me from the noble loins to the pure wombs, cleansed and refined.[622]

An interpretation of the Almighty's Words says the same:

> *...and your movement among those who fall prostrate (in prayer)* (26:219);

that is to say, your seed moved from believer to believer. Mujāhid explains:

> ...from Prophet to Prophet until you were brought out as a Prophet.[623]

According to 'Allāmah Ṭabrisī :

> It is said on the authority of Ibn 'Abbās, narrated by 'Aṭā' and 'Ikrimah, that it means your turning over in the loins of the monotheists, from Prophet to Prophet until you were brought out as a Prophet. It is what is narrated on the authority of Imam Muhammad ibn Ali al-Bāqir and Abū 'Abdillāh Imām Ja'far ibn Muhammad al-Ṣādiq:

---

621 Ibn Hishām, *al-Sīrat al-Nabawiyyah*, vol. 1, 299.
622 Al-Suyūṭī, *al-Durr al-Manthūr*, vol. 3, 294.
623 Al-Suyūṭī, *al-Durr al-Manthūr*, vol. 5, 98.

> ...in the loins of Prophets, Prophet after Prophet until He took him out of his father's loin, via marriage, not fornication, from the time of Adam.[624]

The correct view on the reason for the revelation of this verse is what Abu Ali al-Ṭabrisī says:

> The Muslims came to the Prophet asking him to seek forgiveness for their dead who had passed on as unbelievers or hypocrites. They said, 'Will you not seek forgiveness for our forefathers who died in the days of ignorance?' and so the verse was revealed.[625]

What proves the authenticity of this narration is that the verse is worded: 'It is not for the Prophet and those who believe...' If the first narration were authentic, there would be no conceivable reason to include other believers with him in this severe rebuke.

Finally, this verse – verse 80 – and verse 84 were revealed in the same way. The reason for their revelation is one thing: that the believers hoped that the Prophet would invoke mercy upon their kinsfolk who had died as unbelievers, begging the Prophet to help them. The following verses were revealed to scupper this hope, if they knew that their kinsfolk had remained polytheists until they died:

> *Lo! God forgiveth not that a partner should be ascribed unto Him. He forgiveth (all) save that to whom He will...* (4:48),

and:

> *Lo! God pardoneth not that partners should be ascribed unto him. He pardoneth all save that to whom He will* (4:116).

For more clarification, see the exegesis of the two verses.[626]

The third and fourth verses are the following:

> *There hath come unto you a messenger, (one) of yourselves, unto whom aught that ye are overburdened is grievous, full of concern for you, for the believers full of pity, merciful. Now, if they turn away say: God sufficeth*

---

[624] Ṭabrisī, *Majma' al-Bayān*, vol. 7, 207.

[625] Ṭabrisī, *Majma' al-Bayān*, vol. 5, 76.

[626] Ṭabarī, *Jāmi' al-Bayān*, vol. 10, 137 and 141; Ṭabrisī, *Majma' al-Bayān*, vol. 5, 54 and 56; al-Suyūṭī, *al-Durr al-Manthūr*, vol. 3, 264 and 266.

> *me. There is no god save Him. In Him have I put my trust, and He is Lord of the Mighty Throne* (9:128-129).

They are the last two verses of the chapter.

According to Ibn al-Gharas they are Meccan. Jalāl al-Dīn says that this is strange given that it is said that they were the last thing to be revealed.[627]

My comment is that the claim that the two verses were revealed in Mecca is not corroborated, and the one who claimed that they were gives no evidence for it. The placing of the verse in a Medinan chapter – especially the last Medinan chapter – is in itself proof that it was revealed in Medina, given that the first principle of situating verses is to place them where they naturally belong, in line with revelation, and in addition to what is said regarding the reason for its revelation. When the Messenger of God first came to Medina, Juhaynah came to ask him for a promise of security, and so the two verses were revealed.[628] Similarly, it is narrated that they were the last Qur'anic verses to be revealed in Medina.[629]

6- The Thunder *(al-Ra'd)*: Medinan

Abū Sheikh reports from Qatādah:

> *The Thunder* is Medinan except for the Almighty's Words:
>
> > *...As for those who disbelieve, disaster ceaseth not to strike them because of what they do, or it dwelleth near their home, until the threat of God come to pass...* (13:31).[630]

According to Ṭabrisī :

> *Had it been possible for a Qur'an to cause the mountains to move...* (13:31)
>
> to the end of the verse and what follows it are an exception.[631]

However, the verse is a rebuke of the pagans' fluctuating position and intimidation of them, just as it announces the glad tidings of the Muslims' imminent victory. Therefore, since it is nothing but a conclusion to the previous verses, it is more likely to have been revealed about the

---

[627] Al-Suyūṭī, *al-Itqān*, vol. 1, 39; al-Suyūṭī, *al-Durr al-Manthūr*, vol. 3, 296.

[628] Al-Suyūṭī, *al-Durr al-Manthūr*, vol. 3, 297.

[629] Al-Suyūṭī, *al-Durr al-Manthūr*, vol. 3, 297; Ṭabrisī, *Majma' al-Bayān*, vol. 5, 86.

[630] See al-Suyūṭī, *al-Itqān*, vol. 1, 40.

[631] Ṭabrisī, *Majma' al-Bayān*, vol. 5, 273.

treaty of Ḥudaybiyyah.[632] It is said on the authority of 'Ikrimah that it was revealed in Medina concerning the Prophet's raiding parties. The 'striking' is the raiding party which would subjugate them, and the 'threat' is the conquest.[633]

7- The Pilgrimage *(al-Hajj)*: Medinan

According to Jalāl al-Dīn, three verses, beginning with the following, were revealed in Medina:[634]

> *These twain (the believers and the disbelievers) are two opponents...* (22:19).

My comment is that, on that basis, one would have to go all the way to verse 22, or even verse 24 – six verses – in view of the tight link between them, which indicates that they cannot be separated.

In addition, there is no evidence for saying that these verses constitute an exception. Hence it is a strange claim, especially when considered in conjunction with a solid tradition which says that they were revealed in connection with three believers, Ḥamzah ibn 'Abd al-Muṭṭalib, 'Ubaydah ibn al-Ḥārith and Ali ibn Abī Ṭālib, and three of the unbelievers, 'Utbah and Shaybah, sons of Rabī'ah, and Walīd ibn 'Utbah, who went out to meet each other in combat. Ali said: 'I will be the first to fall on his knees before God in the dispute on the Day of Resurrection,'[635] and so the verse was revealed either during or after the Battle of Badr.[636]

Four other verses are also said to be an exception:

> *Never sent We a messenger or a prophet before thee but when he recited (the message) Satan proposed (opposition)...*
>
> to:
>
> *...the doom of a disastrous day* (22:52-55).

---

[632] See Ṭabrisī, *Majma' al-Bayān*, vol. 6, 292.

[633] Ṭabarī, *Jāmi' al-Bayān*, vol. 13, 105.

[634] Al-Suyūṭī, *al-Itqān*, vol. 1, 24.

[635] *Ṣaḥīḥ al-Bukhārī*, vol. 6, 123 and 124; *Ṣaḥīḥ Muslim*, vol. 8, 246.

[636] Al-Suyūṭī, *al-Durr al-Manthūr*, vol. 4, 348-349; Ṭabarī, *Jāmi' al-Bayān*, vol. 17, 99.

Ibn Mundhir states on the authority of Qatādah that they are Meccan.[637] They say that they were revealed in Mecca in relation to the cranes story.[638]

We have shown the cranes hadith to be a fabrication concocted by the atheists to damage the reputation of Muhammad and the Qur'an.[639]

The verses allude to the innovations which beset the prophets' codes of religious law (*sharā'i' al-anbiyā'*) at the hands of forgers. However, God preserves His religion at the hands of His scholars in every age, who foil the innovations of mischief-makers, as the hadith says.[640] These alternative narrations are a temptation for those with sickness in their hearts.

According to the Amīrī Codex and Zanjānī's *Tārīkh*, the verses were revealed between Mecca and Medina. However, there is no known rational or orally transmitted basis for this qualification.

8- *Muhammad*: Medinan

The following is said to be an exception:

> *And how many a township stronger than thy township which hath cast thee out, have We destroyed, and they had no helper!* (47:13).

Al-Sakhāwī reports in *Jamāl al-Qurrā'*:

> It is said that when the Prophet set off on his migration towards Medina, he stopped and looked towards Mecca and wept, and so it was revealed as a consolation for his noble heart.[641]

However, the context of the verse fits in snugly with the verses preceding and following it, leaving no scope to claim that they can be separated. Either they are all Meccan or all Medinan.

Given that the chapter is a stern rebuke of the pagans, and a general incitement for the believers as a prelude to making fighting lawful, it is Medinan, and revealed in a sharp tone that enumerates the misdeeds committed by the Quraysh, threatening them with terrible failure and

---

[637] Al-Suyūṭī, *al-Durr al-Manthūr*, vol. 4, 342. See also Zarkashī, *al-Burhān*, vol. 1, 202.

[638] Ṭabrisī, *Majma' al-Bayān*, vol. 7, 90; Ṭabarī, *Jāmi' al-Bayān*, vol. 17, 131; al-Suyūṭī, *al-Durr al-Manthūr*, vol. 4, 366.

[639] *Supra* under 'The Myth of the Cranes.'

[640] Sheikh Abbās Qummi, *Safīnat al-Biḥār wa Madīnat al-Ḥikam wa al-Āthār* (Tehran: Dār al-Uswah, 1414q.), vol. 1, 204 under article a-w-l.

[641] Al-Suyūṭī, *al-Itqān*, vol. 1, 55-56; al-Suyūṭī, *al-Durr al-Manthūr*, vol. 6, 48.

a quick death in return for their stubborn resistance to the Truth. The aforementioned verse fits this pattern, without departing from the other verses in its context.

9- The Chambers *(al-Ḥujurāt)*: Medinan

It is said that Ibn 'Abbās claimed that the following is an exception:[642]

O mankind! Lo! We have created you male and female... (49:13).

It may be on account of its being addressed to 'mankind,' which some believe to be one of the proofs that a passage was addressed to Meccans. We stated above that this proves nothing, as is clear from the occurrence in *The Cow* of:

O mankind! Worship your Lord... (2:21).

10- The Merciful *(al-Rahmān)*: Medinan

The following is said to be an exception,[643] but the reason for this strange claim is unknown:

All that are in the heavens and in the earth entreat Him... (55:29).

11- The Dispute *(al-Mujādalah)*: Medinan

The following is said to be an exception,[644] but the reason for this is also unknown:

There is no secret conference of three but He is their fourth... (58:7).

12- The Prohibition *(al-Tahrīm)*: Medinan

According to Qatādah, the first ten verses are Medinan and the rest is Meccan.[645] This is refuted by the fact that the last two verses are a conclusion to the similitude struck by God by way of advice to the Messenger's wives who had been insolent to him. If they are separated from the rest of the verses of the chapter, there would be nothing innovative about them.

---

642 See Ṭabrisī, *Majma' al-Bayān*, vol. 9, 128.

643 Al-Suyūṭī, *al-Itqān*, vol. 1, 45.

644 Al-Suyūṭī, *al-Itqān*, vol. 1, 46.

645 Al-Suyūṭī, *al-Itqān*, vol. 1, 46.

13- The Man *(al-Insān)*: Medinan

The following verse up to the end of the chapter is said to be an exception:

> *So submit patiently to thy Lord's command...* (76:24).

It is claimed that these verses were revealed about Abū Jahl.[646]

However, the verse follows on from the previous verses, so to separate it from them is out of the question. Nevertheless, the instruction to be patient in the face of stubborn opposition and the aberrations of ignorant people is a particularity of the prophets at all stages of their lives of striving for good. Hence, it is said that the verse is general, and applies to any disobedient person, sinner or unbeliever.[647]

There are other Medinan chapters which are said to contain strange exceptions, but which we have not included, since the discussion is already protracted, and what we have already said is enough to prove that there is no basis at all for claiming that they are exceptions. This applies to both Meccan and Medinan chapters. Such claims are either based on guesswork or weak traditions, and there is no reason to rely on them.

This concludes the discussion, and praise be to God, the First and the Last.

---

[646] Al-Suyūṭī, *al-Durr al-Manthūr*, vol. 6, 302; *Ṭabrisī, Majma' al-Bayān*, vol. 10, 402 and 413.

[647] Ṭabrisī, *Majma' al-Bayān*, vol. 10, 413.

CHAPTER IV

THE REASONS FOR REVELATION

ASBĀB AL-NUZŪL

Knowing the Reasons for Revelation

The Qur'an was revealed serially, in periods separated from each other and on various occasions which called for the revelation of a verse or verses to deal with the context. These occasions have been termed 'reasons for revelation' (*asbāb al-nuzūl*) or 'background to revelation' (*sha'n al-nuzūl*) – there is a difference between the two – and it is an important and noble science pertaining to the very essence of the meaning of revelation, and directs the exegete in search of guidance and the jurist who seeks to deduce rulings on the straight path.

In order to carry out this study comprehensively, we must look at a number of issues. What is the value of this knowledge and its contribution in the fields of jurisprudence and exegesis? How can one be guided to an understanding of the reasons for a revelation? Is there a difference between the expressions 'reason for' and 'background' to a revelation, or between reasons for revelation and allegorical interpretation (*ta'wīl*); and similarly, the exoteric (*ẓāhir*) and esoteric (*baṭn*) meaning of a verse according to the terminology of the original generation (*salaf*)? What does it mean when it is said that a verse was revealed about such and such a thing? Is it necessary for the original narrator of the reason for revelation to have been present at the scene? Is what matters most the general meaning of the wording or the specifics of the situation in which it was revealed? What does it mean that the Qur'an was addressed to one person but that others should pay attention? Or that it courses like the sun and moon? How can one be guided to the main pointers in the Qur'an and by what means do we find them? There are wide-ranging and extensive discussions of this type.

The Value of This Knowledge

Knowing the background to the revelation plays an important role in understanding the meaning of the Qur'an, and solves problems of exegesis in both the fields of fundamentals (*uṣūl*) and secondary issues (*furū'*). It lifts the veil on many aspects of verses that were revealed to address problems contemporary to that time. However, at the same time, these verses also have a general message for the problems of a nation throughout its duration. It may be that pausing over the original reason is one of the best ways to clear up ambiguity in a verse, for there would most certainly be an allusion to that within it.

According to al-Wāḥidī:

> It is not possible to know the exegesis of a verse without pausing over the story behind it and explaining the reason for its revelation.

Al-Suyūṭī contends that the benefits of knowing the reasons for revelation are the arrival at an accurate meaning and the removal of ambiguity.[648] He considers this unavoidable, given that the verse is linked to the incident which provoked its revelation.

Al-Qushayrī explains:

> Clarifying the reasons for the revelations is a robust way of understanding the meanings in the Mighty Book.[649]

There are examples of that in the Revelation itself:

> *Ṣafā and Marwa are among the indications of God. It is therefore no sin for him who is on pilgrimage to the House (of God) or visiteth it to go around them ...* (2:158).

The expression 'it is...no sin for him' has confused some exegetes, because it removes blame without meaning that there is any obligation. Therefore, the verse means that it is permissible, not compulsory, to pass back and forth (*al-sa'y*) between Ṣafā and Marwa, even though the consensus considers it compulsory.

However, if we know the reason why it was revealed, there is no confusion. That is because the rites of the *ḥajj* and *'umrah* were well known since the age of ignorance, except that the Arabs had polluted these rites with innovations they had made, including the placing of an idol in the form of a man called Isāf on Ṣafā, and an idol in the form of a woman called Nā'ilah on Marwa, claiming that they had fornicated in the Ka'bah and God had transfigured them into two stones, which they

---

[648] Al-Suyūṭī, *al-Itqān*, vol. 1, 82.

[649] Zarkashī, *al-Burhān*, vol. 1, 22.

placed on the two mountains so that a lesson could be learned from them. Then, after much time had passed, the Arabs began worshipping them out of ignorance, and would rub them to seek a blessing as they passed back and forth between them.

Then, when Islam came along and the idols were smashed, the Muslims refrained from this passing back and forth, believing that obtaining blessings from the two idols was an innovation from the days of ignorance. However, the verse was revealed in order to remove this misconception from the minds of the Muslims.[650]

According to Imām al-Ṣādiq:

> The Muslims believed that Ṣafā and Marwa were among the innovations of the people of ignorance, and so God revealed this verse.[651]

It is also narrated on his authority that it was when making up for the missed *'umrah* (*'umrat al-qaḍā'*). That was because the Messenger of God had imposed a condition upon the Quraysh to remove their idols, and one of the companions had seen that they had been put back. They came to the Messenger and asked him about it. He was told that So-and-So had not passed back and forth between them, because the idols had been replaced. Thereafter, God revealed this verse.[652]

God has said:

> *There shall be no sin (imputed) unto those who believe and do good works for what they may have eaten (in the past). So be mindful of your duty (to God), and believe, and do good works; and again: be mindful of your duty, and believe; and once again: be mindful of your duty and do right. God loveth the good.* (5:93).

It might be claimed that there is no harm in drinking wine if a man's faith is strong and his deeds are good, because drinking moderately does no harm. This is what 'Amr ibn Mu'dī Karb is said to have claimed.[653] Alternatively, it is said that it was a claim made by Qudāmah ibn Maẓ'ūn,[654]

---

650 See Al-Wāḥidī, *Asbāb al-Nuzūl*, 25.

651 Ṭabrisī, *Majma' al-Bayān*, vol. 1, 240.

652 *Tafsīr al-'Ayyāshī*, vol. 1, 70.

653 Al-Suyūṭī, *al-Itqān*, vol. 1, 83.

654 Al-Dhahabī, *al-Tafsīr wa al-Mufassirūn*, vol. 1, 60.

except that this verse was revealed in connection with those who had done so in the past but had repented, become a believer, and done good deeds. They had then been guided, and God forgave what was in the past.

The Almighty said:

> *It is not righteousness that ye go to houses from the backs thereof, but the righteous man is he who wardeth off (evil). So go to houses by the gates thereof, and observe your duty to God, that ye may prosper* (2:189).

The beginning of the verse states:

They ask thee of new moons. Say, 'They are fixed seasons for mankind and for the pilgrimage.'

The reason for the link between the two is obscure, as is the reference to entering houses.

However, if we refer to the reason for the revelation concerning the entering of houses, which is that the puritans (*al-ḥums*)[655] or six Arab tribes who, when they were in the state of pilgrim sanctity, would refrain from entering tents and houses any other way than from the back, and would accordingly make a hole to pass through, then the confusion is cleared up on both counts.

Again, the Almighty said:

> *The postponement (al-nasī') (of a sacred month) is only an excess of disbelief whereby those who disbelieve are misled; they allow it one year and forbid it (another) year, that they may make up the number of the months which God hath hallowed, so that they allow that which God hath forbidden. The evil of their deeds is made fairseeming unto them* (9:37).

The Arabs used to believe in the sanctity of four months as a throwback to Abraham's religion. However, it was difficult for them to go for thee whole months without raiding, or if a war were in progress when the crescent moon heralding one of the holy months appeared, thus making it difficult for them to abandon fighting. Therefore they would postpone the month to another time, allowing them to continue raiding and plundering.

---

[655] *Al-Ḥums* with a *ḍammah* followed by a *sukūn* is the plural of *aḥmas* and *ḥamsā'*, meaning 'rigorous in his religion and school of thought.' It was said of the six well-known tribes: Quraysh, Khuzā'ah, Kinānah, Thaqīf, Jashm and Banī 'Āmir ibn Ṣa'ṣa'ah. See Ṭabrisī, *Majma' al-Bayān*, vol. 2, 284.

Similarly, they would postpone the pilgrimage so that it coincided with springtime every year. Before the Farewell Pilgrimage, the pilgrimage fell in Dhū al-Qa'dah. When the Prophet went on his pilgrimage the following month, he said in his sermon:

> Lo! Time has rotated the same as the first day on which the Lord created the heavens and the earth. Surely the number of months with God is twelve months, in God's ordinance, since the day when He created the heavens and the earth, of these four being sacred, three consecutive ones – Dhū al-Qa'dah, Dhū al-Ḥijjah and Muḥarram – and Rajab which is between between Jumādā and Sha'bān...

By this he meant that the holy months had been returned to their rightful places, the pilgrimage had been returned to Dhū al-Ḥijjah, and that postponement was wrong.[656]

Ascertaining the Reasons for Revelation

There are accepted ways of ascertaining the correct reasons for revelation that specialists normally use, such as ensuring that the attribution is authentic, or that the narration is widespread (*mustafīḍ*) or indubitable (*mutawātir*). With these one can be sure that the incident truly occurred. However, there is another way which may be more precise and reliable, and more in keeping with the principles of the study of history, that is, the oral tradition that provides the background of the revelation, since this can completely clear up any apparent ambiguity in a verse and solve the problem of its exegesis, provided it is not incompatible with the fundamentals of religion or counterintuitive to sound reason. This alone suffices as testimony to the authenticity of a hadith, no matter what its chain of narration may be.

It is worth bearing in mind in this section that the majority of hadiths on the background to revelation are characterised by weak or broken chains of transmission and unknown narrators, not to mention fabrications, interpolations and forgery. This is how the imams describe them:

According to Imām Badr al-Dīn al-Zarkashī:

[656] Ṭabrisī, *Majma' al-Bayān*, vol. 5, 29.

> One must be wary of ones with weak chains of narration and fabricated ones, because there are many.

Al-Maymūnī says:

> I heard Imām Aḥmad ibn Ḥanbal say, 'There are three types of hadith which do not have any basis,' or 'There is no basis to three types of hadith: the battles (*maghāzī*), apocalyptic (*malāḥim*) and exegesis (*tafsīr*),' meaning that there is no basis which can be relied upon. The careful researchers among his companions say, 'It means that the majority do not have authentic, unbroken chains of narration. Otherwise, much of it would be authentic.'[657]

Jalāl al-Dīn al-Suyūṭī complains:

> Very little of it is authentic. In fact it is extremely rare for there to be an evidential basis of an unbroken chain of narration.

Al-Suyūṭī, at the end of his book, refers to approximately three hundred hadiths with unbroken chains (*marfū'*) ranging from weak to 'thin' to problematic. The rest are narrated omitting the narrator in between the successor and the Prophet (*mursal*), and which are of no evidential value at all.[658]

What the early Muslims (*salaf*) can be accused of is their sloppiness with regard to the recording of events. Hence, what we know today about the matter is extremely little, and is of little help to the exegete.

Al-Wāḥidī himself inclined towards collecting anomalies amongst the reasons for revelation, therefore he could not have been wary of weak and unknown narrators and of that which is of no evidential value. For example, we see that he often narrates on the authority of Ibn 'Abbās via al-Kalbī, on the authority of Abū Ṣāliḥ.

According to Jalāl al-Dīn al-Suyūṭī:

> The weakest line of exegesis is via al-Kalbī on the authority of Abū Ṣāliḥ, on the authority of Ibn 'Abbās. If the narration of Muhammad ibn Marwān al-Suddī al-Ṣaghīr is appended to that

[657] Zarkashī, *al-Burhān*, vol. 2, 156.

[658] Al-Suyūṭī, *al-Itqān*, vol. 4, 181, 214-257.

> it is a chain of falsehood. Al-Tha'labī and al-Wāḥidī often quote from the latter chain.[659]
>
> He says regarding God's Words, *When they meet those who believe they say: 'We believe,'...* (2:14), that al-Wāhidī and al-Tha'labī state via al-Suddī on the authority of al-Kalbī, on the authority of Abū Ṣāliḥ, on the authority of Ibn 'Abbās, 'This verse was revealed about 'Abdullāh ibn Ubayy and his companions...'
>
> He then says, 'This chain is very weak, for al-Suddī al-Ṣaghīr is a liar, as is al-Kalbī, and Abū Ṣāliḥ is weak.'[660]
>
> With regard to The Almighty's Words, *God is not ashamed to strike a similitude...* (2:26), he says what al-Wāḥidī states via 'Abd al-Ghanī ibn Sa'īd al-Thaqafī – who is very weak.[661]

There are misprints in the printed edition of *Asbāb al-Nuzūl*. There is reference to a tradition on the authority of 'Abd al-'Azīz ibn Sa'īd,[662] but there is no reference to him in the catalogues of narrators (*kutub al-tarājim*).

The following was revealed as a response to the Jews over their recrimination of the Muslims for changing the direction in which they prayed (*qiblah*), as stated above:

> *Unto God belong the East and the West, and whithersoever ye turn, there is the Face of God...* (2:115).

According to al-Suyūṭī:

> The chains of narration of the traditions which say this are strong. The import is also meaningful, so it can be relied upon.[663]

He says:

> There are other, weak traditions on the verse...including what al-Wāhidī and others narrate on the authority of Ash'ath al-Sammān.[664]

---

[659] Al-Suyūṭī, *al-Itqān*, vol. 4, 209.
[660] Al-Suyūṭī, *Lubāb al-Nuqūl*, vol. 1, 9.
[661] Al-Suyūṭī, *Lubāb al-Nuqūl*, vol. 1, 11, ft.
[662] Al-Waḥidī, *Asbāb al-Nuzūl*, 13.
[663] Al-Suyūṭī, *Lubāb al-Nuqūl*, vol. 1, 24.
[664] Al-Wāhidī, *Asbāb al-Nuzūl*, 20.

He explains:

> Ash'ath is reckoned as weak regarding hadith.[665]

Al-Dhahabī's comment is:

> Ash'ath ibn Sa'īd Abu al-Rabī' al-Sammān is weak. Al-Dāraquṭnī and others disregard him.[666]

We see reliance on narrations that omit the narrator between the successor and the Prophet, and narrations with unknown narrators by Jalāl al-Dīn al-Suyūṭī himself, who criticises al-Wāḥidī, embroiling him in unlikely things contrary to reason and religion in some of his explanations of the causes of revelation in his book *Lubāb al-Nuqūl*.

For example, he narrates via Bayhaqī on the authority of Abū Hurayrah that the Prophet stood over Ḥamzah, who had been martyred and mutilated at Uḥud, and said, 'I will mutilate seventy of them in return for you,' as the background for the following:[667]

> *If ye punish, then punish with the like of that wherewith ye were afflicted. But if ye endure patiently, verily it is better for the patient. Endure thou patiently. Thine endurance is only (by the help of) God. Grieve not for them, and be not in distress because of that which they devise. Surely God is with those who keep their duty unto Him and those who are doers of good* (16:126-128).

He says:

> Al-Tirmidhī states on the authority of Ubayy ibn Ka'b:
>
> Sixty-four of the Helpers (*anṣār*) and six of the Emigrants (*muhājirūn*) were struck down at Uḥud, including Ḥamzah who had been mutilated. The Helpers said, 'If we get a day like this against them, we will do worse to them.' When the day of the Conquest came, God revealed these verses.

This is in spite of knowing that *The Bee* (*al-Naḥl*) is Meccan. All its verses were revealed in Mecca before the Migration, as stated above.

---

665 Al-Suyūṭī, *Lubāb al-Nuqūl*, vol. 1, 25.
666 Al-Dhahabī, *al-Mughnī*, vol. 1, 91.
667 Al-Suyūṭī, *Lubāb al-Nuqūl*, vol. 1, 213.

Nevertheless, al-Suyūṭī himself noticed the aforementioned weakness. Hence, he resorted to supposing that the verse was revealed three times – before the Migration, after it at Uḥud, and then again in Mecca on the day of the Conquest.[668]

What makes matters worse is the presence of strange things like this in major hadith collections like *Bukhārī*, *Muslim* and others, which according to Sunni understanding are the most authentic books of hadith. However, in spite of this claim, they are full of such myths which are unbecoming to the sacredness of Islam.

We spoke above about the myth of the cranes and the story of Ibn Nawfil – deemed to be authentic by the people, but which violate the sanctity of the Qur'an and the holiness of the station of prophethood. Here is another example from al-Suyūṭī:

> Ṭabarānī, Ibn Abī Shaybah in his *Musnad*, al-Wāḥidī and others state via a chain of narration including someone who is unknown, on the authority of Ḥafṣ ibn Maysarah al-Qarashī, on the authority of his mother, on the authority of her mother Khawlah who was God's Messenger's servant, that a puppy entered the Prophet's house, went under his bed and died. Three days went by without the Prophet's receiving any revelation so he said, 'Khawlah, what has happened in God's Messenger's house? Does not Gabriel come to me?' So I said to myself, 'What if I clean the house?' So I got down to clean under the bed and got the puppy out. The Prophet came along, trembling with shame – whenever revelation came down to him he would be overcome with trembling – and God revealed, *By the morning hours... up to ...so that thou wilt be content* (93:1-5).[669]

Ibn Ḥajar says in *Sharḥ al-Bukhārī*:

> The story about Gabriel's delay because of there being a puppy under his bed without his noticing is well known. However, its being a reason for revelation would be strange. In fact it is odd and refuted.[670]

---

[668] Al-Suyūṭī, *al-Itqān*, vol. 1, 96; al-Suyūṭī, *Lubāb al-Nuqūl*, vol. 1, 214.

[669] See al-Suyūṭī, *al-Itqān*, vol. 1, 92; al-Suyūṭī, *Lubāb al-Nuqūl*, vol. 2, 135-136.

[670] Ibn Ḥajar, *Fatḥ al-Bārī*, vol. 8, 545.

My comment is that the alleged story is Medinan, but no one disputes that the chapter is Meccan. However a liar's memory betrays him.

The two Sheikhs (Bukhārī and Muslim) state on the authority of al-Musayyab:

> When death came to Abū Ṭālib, the Prophet came to see him. Abū Jahl and 'Abdullāh ibn Abī Umayyah were with him. The Prophet said, 'Uncle, say, 'There is no God but God,' and I will rely on it as evidence in God's presence.' So Abū Jahl and 'Abdullāh said, 'Abū Ṭālib, do you have a distaste for 'Abd al-Muṭṭalib's religion?' Then the Prophet said, 'I will seek forgiveness for you provided I am not told not to.' Thereafter was revealed:[671]

> *It is not for the Prophet and those who believe to pray for the forgiveness of idolaters, even though they may be near of kin after it hath become clear that they are people of hell-fire* (9:113).

What refutes this claim, or rather this fabricated lie, is the fact that Abū Ṭālib died three years before the Migration and was the Messenger's strong support. As for the verse of *The Repentence* (*al-Tawbah*), it was revealed in the ninth year after the Migration, i.e., twelve years after Abū Ṭālib's death. This is not to mention the abundant proofs of Abū Ṭālib having become a Muslim which we have cited.

Al-Suyūṭī resorted to the verse's having been revealed twice.[672]

The traditions on the reasons for revelation which appear in the major books of hadith giving chains of narration, plus those with broken chains, those which omit the narrator between the successor and the Prophet, and those with narrators who are unknown, all demonstrate the pedigree of the narrations we have on this subject. Now that one is aware of their value, one can appreciate what Imām Aḥmad said:

> There is no reliable basis to three types of hadith: the battles (*maghāzī*), apocalyptic (*malāḥim*) and exegesis (*tafsīr*).

Take another example from al-Suyūṭī, who gives five explanations for the following:

> *...whithersoever ye turn, there is the Face of God* (2:115).

---

[671] See *Ṣaḥīḥ al-Bukhārī*, vol. 6, 87 and vol. 2, 119.

[672] Al-Suyūṭī, *al-Itqān*, vol. 1, 95.

1) It is about the change of the direction in which one should pray (*qiblah*) and the Jews' doubt regarding that, according to Ibn Jarīr, Ibn Abī Ḥātim via Ali ibn Abī Ṭalḥah on the authority of Ibn 'Abbās.

2) One should pray in whichever direction one's mount faces. Al-Ḥākim and others state that on the authority of Ibn 'Umar.

3) It was on a journey on a dark night. Every man prayed in whichever direction he was facing, not knowing the direction of the *qiblah*. Al-Tirimidhī states this from 'Āmir ibn Rabī'ah's hadith, and similarly, al-Dāraquṭnī does so from Jābir's hadith.

4) When *Call upon Me and I will answer you* (40:60) was revealed, they asked, 'Where to?' and so it was revealed. Ibn Jarīr states that on the authority of Mujāhid.

5) Qatādah says that the Prophet said, 'Your brother has died, so perform the funeral prayer for him. They protested, saying, 'He did not used to pray towards the qiblah,' and so it was revealed.

Al-Suyūṭi's comment is:

> These are five different reasons, the weakest of which is the last one on account of its enigmatic nature, followed by the one before it on account of its omission of the narrator between the successor and the Prophet, followed by the third one on account of the weakness of its narrators. The second is authentic; however, it says, 'It was revealed about such and such a thing,' and does not explicitly state the reason. The first one is authentic and explicitly states the reason, so it is the one which can be relied upon.[673]

Reasons for Revelation (*Sabab al-Nuzūl*) versus Background to Revelation (*Sha'n al-Nuzūl*)

What is the difference between the 'reason for revelation' and the 'background to revelation'?

A cause or reason for a Qur'anic revelation to appear would be if there had been a present problem which did not have a clear-cut solution.

This is more specific than the background to revelation, because the background is more general. According to the scholastic terminology, the background refers to any matter for which a verse or chapter of the

[673] Al-Suyūṭī, *al-Itqān*, vol. 1, 93.

Qur'an was revealed in order to clarify or explain. A majority of the stories of people of ages past, including the lives of prophets and saintly people, have been distorted. Hence the Qur'an was revealed to deal with such things and to clarify the truth of the matter by explaining what really happened. In this way, doubts and confusion are dispelled, and the holy name of the noble friends of God is restored.

Thus the difference between cause and background according to the terminology is that the former refers to an existing problem presented by some event, whereas the latter refers to any matter in need of clarification, either present or past. This, then, is the terminology, over which there is no dispute.

When they say 'it was revealed about such and such,' it could mean either of the two: a present cause or something which happened in the past. Sometimes, the clarification of a religious duty is intended. Al-Zarkashī explains:

> It is known to have been the custom of the companions and successors for one of them to have meant, if he said that this verse is about (*fī*) such and such a thing, that the verse contains this ruling and not that this was the reason for its revelation.[674]

However, al-Suyūṭī believes that the term 'reason' for revelation exclusively refers to the first kind, and that a clarification of something in the past cannot be a reason for the revelation of a Qur'anic chapter or verse. Hence, he challenges what al-Wāḥidī says in *Asbāb al-Nuzūl*:

> *The Elephant* was revealed in relation to the story of Abrahah's companions who came along to destroy the Ka'bah.[675]

His response is:

> What is clear with regard to the reason for revelation is that the verse was not revealed during the days when it happened so as to justify what al-Wāḥidī said about *The Elephant* – that the reason for it was the story of the Ethiopians' coming – because that was by no means one of the reasons for its revelation. On the contrary, it falls under the heading of relating past events, like the stories

---

674 Zarkashī, *al-Burhān*, vol. 1, 31-32.

675 Al-Wāhidī, *Asbāb al-Nuzūl*, 259.

> of the people of Noah, and of 'Ād and Thamūd, the building of the House and so on.[676]

This is in spite of the fact that al-Wāḥidī did not explicitly state that it was the reason. On the contrary, he only stated that it was revealed about (*fī*) the people with the elephant. Thus, there is no reason for al-Suyūṭī's constraining himself and others, given that what are termed reasons for revelation are the events which were the reasons for the revelation of the Qur'an, irrespective of whether they were current events, a disagreement over a secondary legal (*shar'iyyah far'iyyah*) or doctrinal matter, a historical account with a lesson to learn, or any other disagreement which Almighty God wanted to clarify.

Exoteric (*tanzīl*) and Esoteric Meaning (*ta'wīl*)

Al-Fuḍayl ibn Yasār asked Imām Abū Ja'far al-Bāqir about the well-known hadith: There is not a single verse in the Qur'an which does not have an exoteric and esoteric meaning.

> He said: 'Its exoteric meaning (*ẓāhiruhu*) is the reason for its revelation (*tanzīluhu*) and its esoteric meaning (*bāṭinuhu*) is its allegorical interpretation (*ta'wīluhu*). Part of it is what is past and part of it is what has not yet been, coursing the way the sun and moon course...[677]

He also said:

> The exoteric meaning of the Qur'an refers to those about whom it was revealed and its esoteric meaning refers to those who do as they do...[678]

That is because the verse has an aspect linked to an event which occurred, which caused it to be revealed, and another aspect which has a universal context. Therefore, its particularity addresses a given problem, whereas it also has a timeless and universal application.

Imām Abū Ja'far said:

---

676 Al-Suyūṭī, *Lubāb al-Nuqūl*, vol. 1, 5.

677 Muhammad ibn al-Hasan al-Ṣaffār, *Baṣā'ir al-Darajāt* (Qum: Maktabat Aytollah Mar'ashī, 1404 q.), 196

678 *Tafsīr al-'Ayyāshī*, vol. 1, 11.

> If a verse is revealed solely about a people and those people die, the verse would die and nothing would be left of the Qur'an. However, the beginning of Qur'an proceeds in accordance with the end of it for as long as the Heavens and Earth remain. There is good or ill derived therein for every people that recite it.[679]

Hence, the wisdom in the revelation of a verse or chapter is not just a temporary cure for a particular problem, such that its benefit ends with a change in circumstances. On the contrary, every verse and chapter of the Qur'an was revealed to remedy problems throughout all time. This is what the following alludes to:

> The Qur'an was revealed by way of: 'I'm talking to you, but I want the neighbour to listen.'[680]

This universality is the greater revelation hidden behind the particular, shedding light from behind an exoteric veil.

Part of the uniqueness of the Qur'an is its having two sides to its meanings – the particular and the universal. Hence it has a meaning which is *tanzīl* (for a particular situation) and one which is *ta'wīl* (a universal application). The former is the exoteric meaning and the latter is the esoteric meaning.

However, understanding the hidden meanings of the verses and knowledge of the esoteric meaning of the Qur'an is exclusive to those firmly rooted in knowledge (*al-rāsikhūna fī al-'ilm*), who have been firm on the path and to whom their Lord has given *copious water to drink* (72:16).

Hence, Imām Abū Ja'far said after reciting this verse, 'We know it,'[681] i.e., its interpretation (*al-ta'wīl*). Another tradition states, 'The Imāms know it.'[682]

The Almighty says:

> *Unto God belong the East and the West, and whithersoever ye turn, there is the Face of God. Lo! God is All-Embracing, All-Knowing* (2:115).

This verse is an example of the verses which have two sides – that for which they were revealed (*tanzīl*) and their true interpretation (*ta'wīl*),

---

679 *Tafsīr al-'Ayyāshī*, vol. 1, 10.
680 *Tafsīr al-'Ayyāshī*, vol. 1, 10.
681 Al-Ṣaffār, *Baṣā'ir al-Darajāt*, 196.
682 Ibid.

the exoteric and esoteric meanings. Only those with insight into religion, the Infallible Imams, know the universally applicable hidden secret.

On the face of it, this verse appears to contradict those verses instructing the believers to face towards the Sacred House in prayer (2:144, 149, 150). However, taking into consideration the reason for its revelation – that it was to refute a misconception held by the Jews, and to dispel their doubt over the change of direction in which one prays (*qiblah*) – it becomes clear that there is no contradiction, and any ambiguity is cleared up. That is because the direction in which one faces in prayer and other acts of worship is purely subjective, and ultimately depends on God and the interests He sees as dictated by circumstances and situations. God's Face is not limited to the Holy Mosque of Jerusalem or the Blessed Ka'bah.

Thus, any initial problem presented by the verse is solved and its ambiguity is cleared up. It is not simply a licence to face in any direction.

However, the Imāms also deduced something else from the hidden meaning of the verse – since allegorical interpretation is an ongoing process – that it is permissible to perform supererogatory prayers in whatever direction one's mount is facing, and that if the direction of the *qiblah* is not known, one can pray in any direction. We have found traditions explicitly stating this on the authority of the Imāms of the People of the Household.[683]

Sayyid Ṭabaṭabā'ī says that if one peruses the words of the Imāms on the general and particular and the unqualified and qualified within the Qur'an, one will often find a deduction of one ruling from the general meaning of the verse followed by another ruling deduced from its particular meaning. Commendability (*istiḥbāb*) may be understood from the general meaning of a verse and obligation from its particular meaning. Similarly, unlawfulness or reprehensibility (*karāhiyya*) may be understood from different interpretations of a verse.

He explains:

> Through this criterion one may discover principles which are the keys to many things locked away in the verses. One will only find them in their words, no one else's.

He continues:

---

683 See al-Ḥurr al-'Āmilī, *Wasā'il al-Shī'ah* vol. 3, 225 and 239 and *Tafsīr al-'Ayyāshī*, vol. 1, 56-57.

> Thus one can deduce two fundamental rules from the gist of what is said regarding Qur'anic knowledge:
>
> Firstly, that every element within a single verse means something and sheds light on one of the laws of the *sharīʿah*. Then along with the element which follows it, it produces another rule and along with the third one, a third rule and so on.
>
> For example, in God's Words:
>
> *Say: 'God,' and leave them to their idle chatter* (6:91)
>
> 'Say: 'God,'' produces a complete meaning. Along with 'and leave them' it means something else which is also complete. And similarly, along with 'to their idle chatter' there is a complete statement which means something complete.
>
> The same can be applied to any of the Qur'an's verses.
>
> Secondly, if two stories or two meanings share a sentence or the like, they both refer to the same concept.

And:

> These are two secrets beneath which there are many secrets, and God is the Guide.[684]

It is narrated on the authority of Saʿīd ibn Jubayr that God's Words:

> *And the places of worship (al-masājid) are only for God, so pray not unto anyone along with God* (72:18),

are said to concern the *jinn* who sought the Messenger's permission to attend his mosque, but for whom it was difficult because they were spread throughout the earth. Therefore it was revealed that any place on earth can be a place for the worship of God. The only provision is that the worship has to be of Him alone.[685]

This is if *al-masājid* is understood to mean places of worship (*al-maʿābid*). It may be interpreted as meaning the verbal noun – that all acts of worship are for God alone. It is not permissible to worship anyone else apart from Him. This is narrated on the authority of al-Ḥasan.

---

[684] Ṭabāṭabāʾī, *al-Mīzān*, vol. 1, 262.
[685] Al-Suyūṭī, *Lubāb al-Nuqūl*, vol. 2, 121.

A number of exegetes, such as Sa'īd ibn Jubayr, al-Zajjāj and al-Farrā', say that there are seven parts of the body with which one prostrates. They belong to God because He created them, and He it is who blessed mankind with them. One should not use them to worship anyone else apart from Almighty God.[686]

Imām Abū Ja'far Muhammad ibn Ali al-Jawād adopted this explanation when al-Mu'taṣim al-'Abbāsī asked him about this verse. He told him:

> It means the seven parts of the body on which one prostrates.[687]

This hadith appears in the story of a thief who was brought to al-Mu'taṣim's royal court. The jurists present disagreed with each other over the 'cut-off point' for the hand. The Imām believed that it should be cut off at the finger joints. When al-Mu'taṣim asked him why, he answered that the palm of the hand is one of the seven parts of the body on which one prostrates (*mawāḍi' al-sujūd al-saba'ah*), and that the parts on which one prostrates (*al-masājid*) belong to God and should therefore not be cut off.[688]

Thus, in this unique way he deduced a legal ruling from the words of the Qur'an which was a decisive, permanent solution to the jurists' problem.

This is part of the hidden and esoteric meaning of the Qur'an – known to the Imāms of every time – which 'flows' with every age in accordance with the need of that time. According to Imām al-Ṣādiq:

> The Qur'an has an esoteric meaning (*ta'wīl*). Some of it concerns what has already been, and some of it concerns what is yet to come. If the *ta'wīl* occurs in the time of one of the Imāms, the Imām of that time knows it.[689]

Imām Abū Ja'far al-Bāqir explains:

> No one but the Executors can claim that he has the whole of the Qur'an – both its literal meaning and its hidden meaning.[690]

---

[686] This is how the Imāms from the People of the Household explained it according to hadith-based exegesis (*al-tafsīr bi al-ma'thūr*). See also Ṭabrisī, *Majma' al-Bayān*, vol. 10, 372 and Baḥrānī, *Tafsīr al-Burhān*, vol. 4, 394-395.

[687] Ṭabrisī, *Majma' al-Bayān*, vol. 10, 372.

[688] Al-Ḥurr al-'Āmilī, *Wasā'il al-Shī'ah*, vol. 18, 490.

[689] Al-Ṣaffār, *Baṣā'ir al-Darajāt*, 195.

[690] Kulaynī, *al-Kāfī*, vol. 1, 228.

Al-Ṣādiq said:

> I swear by God that I know the Book of God from beginning to end as though it is in my hand. It contains information on Heaven and information on the Earth, information on what was and is. It contains an exposition of everything, as the Almighty says.[691]

Does the Person Narrating the Cause of Revelation Have to Have Been Present?

Al-Wāḥidī states:

> It is only permitted to speak of the causes of revelation on the basis of hearing from those who witnessed the revelation, who knew the reasons for it, and seeking knowledge of them.[692]

This condition is only to ensure that what is narrated is first-hand witness evidence and not personal judgment or guesswork. We then know that the narrator is truthful, reliable and alert in what he says, avoiding conjecture and uncertainty. Such a person may be trusted, even if he was not present at the scene. Hence we can rely on the best of the companions, even if they do not explicitly state that they were there, and similarly, the reports of their successors and the imams after them.

For the same reason, we can rely on what our Infallible Imams say concerning the exegesis of the Qur'an, the reasons for its revelation and its esoteric meaning (*ta'wīl*), because they are the most knowledgeable in the sciences of the Qur'an and both its literal and hidden meaning. It is important to know that narrations attributed to them are authentic and indubitable.

The general meaning is what matters, rather than specific use

This is a general *uṣūlī*[693] rule with regards to all laws of the *shariah*. Whatever issues from the Source of Revelation to explain God's Laws and

---

[691] Kulaynī, *al-Kāfī*, vol. 1, 229. This refers to 16:89: *'And We reveal the Scripture unto thee as an exposition of all things...'*

[692] Al-Wāḥidī, *Asbāb al-Nuzūl*, 4.

[693] Usul al-Fiqh is a study of legal presumptions, e.g., the presumption that what is said is what is meant, what is not said is not intended, that things are as they were

the servant's duties to Him is not specific to one situation and exclusive of others. The law did not come along simply to deal with current events, but for all time, and this is why jurists overlook specifics in order to glean a universally applicable law (*iṭlāq al-ḥukm*), on the basis of the wording (*lafẓī*) and a full explanation (*maqāmī*)[694] of the terminology.

This applies to all the laws of the *shariah*, both from the Sunnah and the Scripture, even though it is more definite with regard to the Scripture. One is already familiar with the traditions which explicitly refer to this universality in the verses of the Qur'an. Thus the jurists look at all the laws and duties that appear in the verses of the Qur'an as universal legislation, without attaching undue significance to the specifics of where they appear.

Of course, there are some messages addressed to particular groups of the time as specific propositions (sing. *qaḍiyyah khārijiyyah*).[695] This means that the specifics do not literally apply to everyone, whereas the principle involved may apply universally if it can be determined with certainty. There are many examples of this in the Qur'an.

The Almighty said:

(*istiṣḥāb*), and that with regard to a given matter one has no obligation either way until proven otherwise (*aṣālat al-barā'ah*). (Trans.)

[694] A reference to the general applicability to be inferred from *maqām al-bayān*. *Maqām al-bayān* is the status of a speaker who intends to explain his intention fully. For example, a woman must switch to a *ḥajjah mufradah* followed by an *'umrah mufradah* if she begins menstruating before entering the state of pilgrim sanctity (*iḥrām*), or can choose to do so if she starts menstruating after entering *iḥrām*. In either case, she is not required to perform *ḥajj al-tamattu'* the following year. This is because in the traditions which say that she should perform a *ḥajjah mufradah* say nothing about the need to perform *ḥajj al-tamattu'* the following year. Had that been incumbent upon her, the Imām would have drawn attention to it. For in his speech, we presume that the Imām is in the position of intending to explain fully what he means (*maqām al-bayān*) with regard to what it is she is required to do. Therefore, by saying nothing about *ḥajj al-tamattu'*, the meaning is that she is not required to perform one the following year, and this is based on the assumption that the speaker is in the position of intending to explain fully what he means and not qualifying his statement (*itlāq maqāmī*). (Trans.)

[695] A term used in logic meaning that the subject in the proposition is already present, as when it is said for example, 'Treat with deference whoever is in the school,' the meaning applies to whoever is currently in the school at that time, and does not apply to all times or all schools.

> *As for those who heard the call of God and His messenger after the harm befell them (in the fight): for such of them as do right and ward off (evil), there is great reward. Those unto whom men said: 'Lo! the people have gathered against you, therefore fear them.' (The threat of danger) but increased them in faith and they cried: 'God is sufficient for us! Most Excellent is He in Whom we trust!'* (3:172-173).

The verses were revealed about the believers after they dispersed from the Battle of Uḥud. They were badly wounded and Abū Sufyān tried to make a comeback and regretted leaving the fighting. News of this reached the Muslims, and the one who spread the news was Nu'aym ibn Mas'ūd al-Ashja'ī according to the hadith on the authority of the two Imāms al-Bāqir and al-Ṣādiq.[696] It is said that the riders Abū Sufyān slipped in were to spread lies among the believers. It is also said that they were the hypocrites in Medina.

However the sincere believers remained firm in belief and resolved to confront the enemy with all their efforts, and the Messenger of God commissioned them to terrify the pagans. At the forefront of those commissioned was the Commander of the Faithful.

This is indicated in the words, *those unto whom men said*, which is an allusion to known people or a known individual. What is meant here by 'men' is those who had been gathered together for them, i.e., Abū Sufyān's cohorts.

The whole incident teaches us to remain firm in belief and not fear an enemy, and that we should not doubt the truth for God helps us and cares for us, excellent Master and Helper that He is.

As for the Almighty's Words:

> As for the unbelievers, alike it is to them whether thou has warned them or has not warned them, they do not believe. God has set a seal on their hearts and on their hearing, and on their eyes is a covering, and there awaits them a mighty chastisement...

This indicates only those who were unbelievers at the time, who stubbornly resisted and were unyielding, even after the truth was clear with shining proof, and not necessarily unbelievers thereafter. This was

[696] Ṭabrisī, *Majma' al-Bayān*, vol. 2, 541.

an instruction to the Prophet to desist, so that his soul would not be distressed over them.

According to 'Allāmah Ṭabaṭabā'ī:

> It would not be surprising if what is meant is the chiefs of Quraysh and the elders of Mecca who stubbornly resisted and were unyielding with regard to the matter of religion, and spared no effort in that, because it is not possible to carry on saying this about all unbelievers. Otherwise, the door of guidance would be closed. It is more likely that the unbelievers (*alladhīna kafarū*) here and elsewhere refers to the unbelievers of Mecca at the outset of the Mission unless there is a contextual indicator to the contrary. Likewise, what is meant in the Qur'an by 'those who believe,' if there is nothing in the context to indicate that all believers are meant, is the vanguard, the first of the believers, exclusively addressed as such out of deference to them.[697]

Similarly, he says by way of exegesis of *The Unbelievers*

> Those are people previously referred to, not every unbeliever. What proves it is the instruction to the Prophet to tell them of his disavowal of their religion and their refusal to accept his religion.[698]

Thus the problem presented by many verses in which this and similar expressions appear is solved.

Nevertheless, this rule also applies to those who are like them, in terms of stubborn resistance to the truth, once it has become clear.

---

[697] Ṭabāṭabā'ī, *al-Mīzān*, vol. 1, 50.

[698] Ṭabāṭabā'ī, *al-Mīzān*, vol. 20, 526.

CHAPTER V

INIMITABILITY (*I'JĀZ*) OF THE QUR'AN

I'jāz is derived from the root word *'ajaza*, which means 'to render incapable.' This can be interpreted two ways, one of which is when a particular ability is forcibly taken from someone and he is rendered incapable. For example, if a person has wealth and position and these are taken from him by force, he is 'made incapable.' The other is when one does something and others are incapable of doing the same thing, without them being actively prevented from doing so. For instance, someone may advance to a state of excellence that others cannot achieve, and they may give up out of disappointment. If it is said: 'So-and-so rendered his adversary incapable,' then he has advanced beyond the shortcomings of others who are no match for him. The poet says:

> *To the grief and sorrow of those who envy him and the anger and anxiety of his enemies;*
>
> *It is enough for the seer to open his eyes and for the listener to lend his ears.*

In other words, his virtue is so pervasive that anyone who opens his eyes and lends his ears cannot but see or hear anything else, and thus those who envy him have to give up.

The *i'jāz*, or inimitability, of the Qur'an is of this second type. Therefore, in rhetoric, eloquence, consistency, clarity of expression, gnosis, legal rulings and other features, it is far beyond any human ability. For this reason, the Qur'an is known as 'the eternal miracle.'

Background of the Discourse

The inimitability of the Qur'an has been discussed by scholars from the very beginning. According to Ibn al-Nadīm,[699] one of the first to deal with this topic in writing was the great theologian Muhammad ibn Zayd al-Wāsiṭī (d. 307/919), who wrote the theological works *al-Imāmah* and *I'jāz al-Qur'ān fī Naẓmih wa Ta'līfih* ('The Inimitability of the Harmony and Authority of the Qur'an'). Some have mentioned Abū 'Ubaydah Mu'ammar ibn al-Muthannā (d. 209/824), who wrote a two-volume tract on the same topic, and a book by Abū 'Ubayd Qāsim ibn Salām (d. 224/839). However, none of these writings are extant today.

The oldest available book on this subject is a treatise entitled *Bayān I'jāz al-Qur'ān*, written by Abū Sulaymān Ḥamad ibn Muhammad ibn Ibrāhīm

---

[699] See Ibn al-Nadīm, *al-Fihrist*, 63, 259.

Khaṭṭābī Bostī[700] (d. 388/998). This work has recently been published in a collection entitled *Thalāth Rasā'il fī I'jāz al-Qur'ān*.[701] The author has dealt with the material in an interesting fashion, and covers the rhetoric of the Qur'an and the harmonious and perspicacious choice of words.

Another treatise in this collection was written by Abū al-Ḥasan 'Alī ibn 'Īsā al-Rummānī (d. 386/996), who was one of the great theologians and scholars in the Muslim world. His writings on Qur'anic sciences are invaluable, and are much referenced by Shaykh al-Ṭā'ifah Abū Ja'far al-Ṭūsī in his important exegesis *al-Tibyān*. Another treatise is *al-Shāfiyah* by Shaykh 'Abd al-Qāhir al-Jurjānī (d. 471/1078), who was the founder of the science of rhetoric (*balāghah*) as a specific discipline. This great personality in the field of knowledge and literature has left for posterity two other books on this subject, namely, *Asrār al-Balāghah* and *Dalā'il al-I'jāz*. His treatise *al-Shāfiyah* is a summary of the discussions in these two books, and serves as an introduction to a discussion on inimitability.

Abū Bakr al-Bāqillānī (d. 403/1012), Imām Fakhr al-Dīn Rāzī (d. 606/1209) and Kamāl al-Dīn Zamalkānī (d. 651/1253) each wrote an extensive book in this field. Imām Yaḥyā ibn Ḥamzah ibn 'Alī al-'Alawī al-Zaydī (d. 749/1348) wrote *al-Ṭarāz fī Asrār al-Balāghah wa Ḥaqā'iq al-I'jāz* in three volumes, in volume 3 of which he compares the rules and secrets of eloquence and literary techniques within the Qur'anic verses. In addition, Jalāl al-Dīn al-Suyūṭī (d. 910/1504) wrote three volumes under the title *Mu'tarak al-Aqrān fī I'jāz al-Qur'ān*.

Recognising the Divine Miracle

The miracle of the Qur'an is such that the people of the time recognised its sublimity. This is so for all time, because it is necessary to make clear that the function of the prophets is totally beyond human ability, since they are inspired by the Will of a supernatural Being. If one were to say hypothetically that they functioned in conventional terms, and that this remained concealed from others, it would mean that the prophets skilfully deceived the people with their claims of prophethood.

---

[700] Bost is a district near Kabul where he lived.

[701] See the introductions to *Thalāth Rasā'il fī I'jāz al-Qur'ān*, (Cairo: Dār al-Ma'ārif, 1976), and Ma'rifat, *al-Tamhīd*, vol. 1, 8.

Yet the prophets performed deeds far beyond human capabilites. Perhaps the most outstanding characteristic of the Arabs of the time was their language and speech. The miracle of Islam is the Qur'an, which was presented in the most eloquent and expressive form of the Arabic language, so full of meaning that the Arabs could easily recognise that it could never have been composed by a human being. In terms of harmony, content or any other characteristic, the zenith of the Arabic language is the Qur'an.

Walīd ibn Mughīrah al-Makhzūmī, who was a powerful speaker and a high-ranking chief of the Arabs, said this of the Qur'an: 'By God! What the son of Abī Kabshah[702] recites is neither poetry, nor magic, nor the vainglory of the unwise, and indeed it is nothing but the word of God.'

Also, upon passing the Prophet and hearing him recite some verses of *Sūrah al-Mu'minūn* in prayer, he said:

By God! Recently I have heard speech from Muhammad which is neither like that of a man nor like that of a *jinn*. By God! His speech has a special melody and elegance. It is like a tall abundant tree whose branches are full of fruits, whose trunk is firm with roots well entrenched. Indeed it is superior [to other speech] and none can surpass it.[703]

Ṭufayl ibn 'Amr al-Dūsī, who was known as a leading poet, thinker and noble man of Quraysh, went to the Ka'bah. Some people surrounded him in order to prevent him from approaching the Prophet and listening to him, but they failed. After listening to the words of the Prophet, he hurriedly returned to his tribesmen and told them what he had experienced, and all of them subsequently embraced Islam and he himself became one of its most outstanding propagators. He narrates thus:

I found Muhammad in the mosque and listened to his speech. He welcomed me. I followed him and told myself: 'Woe to you as you listened

---

[702] This is what the polytheists would call the Holy Prophet, thereby associating him with Abū Kabshah who belonged to the tribe of Khuzā'ah and opposed the Quraysh in matters of religion. It is said that he was a maternal forefather of the Prophet, who was for this reason associated with him.

[703] See *Tafsīr al-Ṭabarī*, vol. 29, 98; *Sīrah Ibn Hishām*, vol. 1, 288; Suhaylī, *al-Rawḍ al-Anaf*, vol. 2, 21; Ibn al-Athir, *Usd al-Ghābah*, vol. 2, 90; Ibn 'Abd al-Barr, *al-Istī'āb*, vol. 1, 412; Ibn Ḥajar, *al-Iṣābah*, vol. 1, 410; Qāḍī 'Ayāḍ, *al-Shifā'*, 220; Ghazālī, *Iḥyā' 'Ulūm al-Dīn*, vol. 1, 281; Sayyid Hibat al-Dīn Shahristānī, *al-Mu'jizah al-Khālidah*, 21; Naysābūrī, *al-Mustadrak 'alā al-Ṣaḥīḥayn*, vol. 2, 507; al-Suyūṭī, *al-Durr al-Manthūr*, vol. 6, 283.

to him! Accept if he tells the truth, and if not, disregard it.' I followed him up to his house and told him: 'Present to me whatever you have.' He presented Islam to me and recited to me some verses of the Qur'an. By God! I had not heard such eloquent and elegant speech before, nor more valuable content. As such, I embraced Islam and verbally testified to the truth from my heart and soul.[704]

Naḍr ibn Ḥārith ibn Kaldah was one of the chiefs of Quraysh and had a brilliant mind, but he was an open enemy of the Prophet. Hence, the testimony of someone like him regarding the greatness of the Qur'an and its influence in the advancement of the mission is worth considering. Concerning how they should deal with the Prophet, he said to the chiefs of Quraysh:

By God! Something has happened to you for which you have not yet thought of a solution. Amongst you is Muhammad, a handsome youth, acceptable to all; he is the most truthful in speech and the most trustworthy. It was so until his beard turned white and he brought what he brought. Then you said: 'He is a sorcerer.' No, by God! He is no sorcerer. You said: 'He is a magician.' No, by God! His words are not those of a magician. You said: 'He is a poet.' No, by God! His speech is not poetry. You said: 'He is mad.' No, by God! His behaviour does not indicate that he is mad. So, you yourselves must know and realise that something great has happened which must not be taken lightly.[705]

Aspects of the Qur'an's Inimitability

Scholars have studied extensively the significance of the inimitability (*i'jāz*) of the Qur'an and have put forward different ideas on the subject, amongst which there are some divergent opinions. Early scholars had a particular understanding, while contemporary scholars have a different one and have added certain points to the views of their predecessors. The different views could be summed up as follows:

1) Arab litterateurs and rhetoricians regard the Qur'an as inimitable due to its high degree of eloquence and rhetoric. The clarity of diction and

[704] *Sīrah Ibn Hishām*, vol. 2, 21-25; Ibn al-Athīr, *Usd al-Ghābah*, vol. 3, 54.

[705] *Sīrah Ibn Hishām*, vol. 1, 320-321; al-Suyūṭī, *al-Durr al-Manthūr*, vol. 3, 180. For more information on the testimonies of Arab rhetoricians and prominent personalities on the Qur'an, see Ma'rifat, *al-Tamhīd*, vol. 4.

fluency of expression observed in the choice and ordering of words have created a cohesive composition in every verse and chapter. All of these features point to the power and force of the Divine Speech. Moreover, the choice of words is so distinctive that substituting them with other words could never be possible. This is a secret discovered by men of knowledge and literature, who have said it would be impossible to change any word in the Qur'an, because no other could be found that conveyed the same meaning and harmony, or that was in such unison with those preceding and following it. This shows that the words have been chosen with a precision beyond human ability. Such comprehensive precision demonstrates that no matter how advanced and prepared a person is in the knowledge of the particularities of words, he would never possess such overarching wisdom. It has been said in this respect: 'If one word of it were taken from its place, and then all the Arabic language searched for a similar word to replace it, nothing would be found.'[706]

2) The modes of expression, composition and arrangement in the Qur'an are totally unprecedented and inimitable. Although the arrangement and composition were different, they were not outside the framework of Arabic styles of expression. The forms of verbal expression that were common amongst the Arabs were poetry, prose and rhyming prose, each of which has its own merits and drawbacks. The value of poetry is its elegance, which makes it attractive and reaches the depths of the heart, but the constraints of rhyme and a specific measure somehow deprive the speaker of freedom. On the other hand, the merit of prose lies in the freedom given to the speaker. He freely chooses any words and expressions that suit his intended meaning, but it lacks the grandeur and attractiveness of poetry. It is true that sometimes rhyming prose is seemingly elegant and may be considered a kind of oral art, but the difficulty in composing it sometimes entails the use of unsuitable words that diminish it.

The Qur'an combines these three types of speech, with the merits of each, but without their drawbacks. This is one of the wonders of the Qur'anic style. It has the splendour of poetry, the freedom of prose, and the

[706] The quotation is from Abū Sulaymān Ḥamad ibn Muḥammad Bostī, Ibn 'Aṭīyyah Ghanāṭī, the author of *Tafsīr al-Muḥarrar al-Wajīz* and Shaykh 'Abd al-Qāhir Jurjānī, and other authorities in learning and literature whose details are given in Ma'rifat, *al-Tamhīd*, vols. 4-5.

beauty of rhyming prose. These astonishing features have been obvious to Arab rhetoricians and verbalists from the very beginning. Many great scholars and men of letters, including Shaykh 'Abd al-Qāhir Jurjānī, Sakkākī and Rāghib Iṣfahānī, regarded this as the most outstanding feature of the Qur'an's inimitability.

Successive scholars have added that the language is composed in such a melodious way that it soothes the soul. The harmony of the letters of every word in relation to the letters of the adjacent words is so accurate that it bespeaks of ever-increasing melodies of serenity. All the appeal of poetry is manifested in this rhymed prose.

Both short and long phrases in the Qur'an are composed in such a way that they are in unison with voice tones and melodies, and unless the reciter is familiar with the range of voice tones, he cannot recite the Qur'an in the way its phrases are formed. This is a truth which the Holy Prophet stated from the very beginning and has been emphasised by the Imāms of guidance, and which is widely acknowledged today.[707]

3) The Qur'an contains transcendent knowledge and wise teachings which were beyond human ability to acquire at the time. The astonishing wisdom of the Qur'an about the secrets of creation and the wonders of existence; its exposition of the Attributes of Beauty and Majesty; the philosophy regarding the Divine spark hidden in the human constitution; man's origin and ultimate destiny: these are all amongst the uncertainties of the time that were clarified by the Qur'an.

A brief perusal of the unestablished notions of the time and the contradictory statements of today's secular scholars, compared with the wisdom of the Qur'an, demomstrates very well the superiority of the teachings of the Qur'an and is evidence of its inimitability.[708]

4) The style of reasoning in the Qur'an is unique, and this can be considered to be one of the forms of literary inimitability in the combination of two styles, namely, the demonstrative and persuasive. In essence, these two styles are at odds, for demonstrative reasoning is based upon definitive premises (*a priori* data and axioms), where the emphasis is on the elite who need definite proof; but the persuasive style relies on conjectural premises (widely accepted facts and common sense) and

---

[707] See Ma'rifat, *al-Tamhīd*, vol. 5.

[708] See Ibid. vol. 6.

its goal is to convince the common people. The Qur'an has reconciled these two apparently conflicting styles and addresses both groups. With a single message, it has been able to win the acceptance of both the elite and the generality. The arguments of the Qur'an – notwithstanding their simplicity of expression – have much depth and profundity. The common people who are not well-versed in the secrets of rational arguments are convinced by persuasive arguments. The elite, however, benefit from the precision of expression and the secrets contained therein.

In this regard, Ibn Rushd al-Andalusī has cited a clear example in his valuable book *al-Kashf 'An Manāhij al-Adillah*:[709]

> In order to know the Essence of God, the Qur'an has given the metaphor of light:
>
> *God is the Light of the heavens and the earth (24:35).*

This simple metaphor for knowing the Essence of God, and His Station in the world of being is sufficient for the common people and can convince them. Yet, at the same time, it is so accurate and descriptive that it can be regarded as the most eloquent and accurate way of likening an intangible to a tangible. It is a metaphor which reflects all aspects of the Essence of God.

God is the Necessary Being (*wājib al-wujūd*) and all existence depends on Him. His Essence is utterly hidden whilst at the same time His Being is perceptible within existence to all.

Nothing in the tangible world can be found with these characteristics other than the example of light. Its radiance encompasses all creatures and manifests all things; the appearance of everything depends on light. Yet, the appearance of light is self-generated. The substance or reality of light itself is unknown, but its luminosity and the effects of its existence are known and apparent to all. If a sage wanted to express a metaphor for the Essence of God, no better could be found than this Qur'anic symbol.

5) Unique scientific indicators, in the sense that occasionally we encounter in the Qur'an some passing indications that reflect the Author's knowledge of the secrets hidden in nature:

> *Say: The (Qur'an) was sent down by Him Who knows the Mystery (that is) in the heavens and the earth* (25:6).

[709] Ibn Rushd, *al-Kashf 'an Manāhij al-Adillah*, 92-93.

In the expressions of the Qur'an, some of the secrets of nature are sometimes indicated by God, although the essential intention or main goal is not to state them; they are never emphasised or elaborated upon, since the main intent is to give spiritual precepts and guidance. Only erudite scholars can detect these secrets and passing indications, which constitute a proof of the Qur'an's uniqueness.

Of course, it should be pointed out that scientific achievements must not be imputed to the Qur'an, because they are impermanent, while the content of the Qur'an is unalterable truth compared to which there is nothing.

However, according to some, established scientific facts can be used to understand some of the scientific indications in the Qur'an, although not with definitive certainty. The reason for this is that if this apparently fixed scientific theory changes, it would not undermine the status of the Qur'an. According to this view, whenever a verse of the Qur'an apparently contradicts a scientific hypothesis or proven scientific theory, the words of the Qur'an prevail, and we should regard the supposed scientific theory or hypothesis as erroneous.

In my opinion, the scholars who have accepted such a theory are mistaken. I have cited elsewhere many instances where definitive technical research has unveiled some of the scientific hints in the Qur'an.[710]

6) Unique firmness of expression. The text of the Qur'an is homogeneous and free of inconsistencies and contradictions. Although the Qur'an was revealed gradually over a relatively long period in different places, and in some instances has repeated certain ideas and statements, never has there been any inconsistency. If it were human speech, certain inconsistencies would be expected over the course of a long period in differing circumstances when reiterating particular topics. The words of the Qur'an give this as one of the proofs of its inimitability:[711]

> *Do they not consider the Qur'an (with care)? Had it been from other than God, they would surely have found therein much discrepancy* (4:82).

7) The concept of *ṣarfah*, whereby certain scholars are not convinced by the explanations given for the inimitability of the Quran and impossibility

---

[710] See Maʿrifat, *al-Tamhīd*, vol. 6, 'On the Scientific Inimitability.'

[711] Ibid. vol. 7, 'On Removing Scepticism.'

of challenging it in those areas. They have put forward a very different view regarding inimitability. Great personalities like Abū Isḥāq al-Naẓẓām (d. 231/845) and his student, Jāḥiẓ (d. 255/869), Sayyid Murtaḍā (d. 436/1044) and Ibn Sinān al-Khafājī (d. 466/1073) are of the opinion that the secret behind the inimitability of the Qur'an lies in the concept of *ṣarfah*, in the sense that God Himself is the deterrent of those who want to challenge the Qur'an. According to this view, although it is possible for individuals to challenge the Qur'an, they are prevented from doing so by the overpowering Will of God.

> *Those who behave arrogantly on the earth in defiance of right – them will I turn away from My signs* (7:146).

According to those who subscribe to the notion of *ṣarfah*, *turn away from My signs* here means preventing them from harming the Qur'an by challenging it or disproving it.

However, this verse has many different interpretations; many have considered 'turn away' to mean the refutation of objections made by the arrogant who wanted to corrupt the Signs of God, meaning that God presents His proofs so clearly that any avenue for doubt or distortion is closed.[712]

Critics state that *ṣarfah* deprives the Qur'an of merit, and attributes the inimitability of the Qur'an to an external cause which overrides any alternative by forceful prevention. However, this claim conflicts with the apparent – and at times even explicit –ntrinsic.

The notion of *ṣarfah* can be interpreted in three ways, as stated by Amīr Yaḥyā ibn Ḥamzah al-'Alawī al-Zaydī (d. 749/1392):[713]

(i) that God would deprive individuals of their intention to challenge the Qur'an. That is, the motive or drive which prompts them to challange the Qur'an would die down at the time of acting upon it, and they would experience a state of disinterest and indifference.

(ii) that God would deprive them of the relevant faculties of knowledge or skills necessary for challenging the Qur'an, since these facilities are not in man's control. This is exactly the meaning of *ṣarf* in the

[712] See Ṭabrisī, *Majma' al-Bayān*, vol. 4, 477-478.

[713] Amīr Yaḥyā al-'Alawī, *al-Ṭirāz* (Beirut: Dār al-Kutub al-'Ilmiyyah, n.d.), vol. 3, 391-392.

abovementioned verse. Also the following verse states that mankind does not have at its disposal the knowledge contained in the Quran:

Nay, they charge with falsehood that whose knowledge they cannot compass... (10:39).

If this is the case, by what means are they to challenge it? Also, another verse states that the turning aside of the hearts is the outcome of their own incompetence to discern the truth:

God hath turned their hearts (from the light); for they are a people who understand not (9:127).

(iii) that they are forcibly dissuaded. Although they have the necessary means at the time of executing their plan, they would experience a state of lethargy, and would thereby be unable to vilify the Qur'an.

The difference between this and the first interpretation is that in the first one, their motive, enthusiasm and ambition would be suppressed, while here the motive remains but they would lose the courage to take action. It is like someone who is hindered by force despite his efforts and strong motive.

It seems that the first and the third interpretations and the first part of the second view are contrary to historical knowledge and incompatible with the propositions of the Arabs of that time, for if it were really so, then the Arabs should have been bewildered by the change in their inner state, rather than being astonished by the pleasant and attractive melody of the Qur'an. This is especially true in view of the fact that some like Abū Jahl and others in the tribe of Quraysh would plug the ears of their tribemen when entering the Sacred Mosque (*al-masjid al-ḥarām*), or prevent them from getting close enough to hear the recitation of the Qur'an. This in itself is testimony to the appeal of the Qur'an and its spiritual attraction, its inimitability and the impossibility of challenging it.

Admittedly, the concluding part of the second interpretation seems reasonable to some extent, and it is implied in the opinions of Sayyid and other great personalities. However, in reality, all good is embedded in the essence of the Qur'an, and mankind is incapable of challenging it.[714]

---

[714] See Ma'rifat, *al-Tamhīd*, vol. 4, 135-190.

The Challenge of the Qur'an (*taḥaddī*)

Taḥaddī literally means to challenge. Technically it is the challenge the Qur'an has repeatedly posed to those who deny it, which is in effect that if you do not believe that this Qur'an is the word of God and you suppose that it is a human invention, then this is easy to test. Persuade your litterateurs and orators to join forces and compose an oration as eloquent, consistent and full of wisdom as the Qur'an. You could never do so, because you know very well that the Qur'an is totally unlike human speech.

The Stages of Challenge

The Qur'an has put forth several challenges:

1) to produce something similar:

> *Or do they say: 'He fabricated it (the message)'? Nay, they have no faith! Let them then produce a recital like unto it – if (it be) they speak the truth* (52:33-34).

2) to produce just ten chapters (*sūrahs*), no matter how short:

> *Or they may say: 'He forged it.' Say: 'Bring ye then ten sūrahs forged, like unto it, and call (to your aid) whomsoever ye can, other than God! – if ye speak the truth!'* (11:13).

3) then to produce just one *sūrah* like the Qur'an:

> *Or do they say: 'He forged it'? Say: 'Bring then a sūrah like unto it...* (10:38).

4) then again a most decisive statement regarding the unbelievers' inability:

> *And if ye are in doubt as to what We have revealed from time to time to Our servant, then produce a sūrah like thereunto; and call your witnesses or helpers (if they are any) besides God, should you be truthful.*
>
> *But if ye cannot – and of a surety ye cannot – then fear the Fire whose fuel is men and stones – which is prepared for those who reject faith* (2:23-24).

5) and the Qur'an declares its inimitability and a challenge for all times to come:

> *Say: 'If the whole of mankind and jinns were to gather together to produce the like of this Qur'an they could not produce the like thereof, even if they backed up each other with help and support'* (17:88).

It is interesting that in the verses that lay down a challenge – especially the last two verses – there is a striking remark which clarifies more than anything else the secret of uniqueness. In verse 24 of *Sūrah al-Baqarah*, the expression *and of a surety ye cannot* informs us regarding the future in absolute terms, in that it is impossible to challenge the Qur'an for all time to come. In verse 88 of *Sūrah al-Isrā'*, all the *jinns* as well as mankind are incapable of challenging the Qur'an. This is an account of the unseen which could not come from anyone else but 'the Knower of the seen and the unseen.'

To draw a parallel, an athlete who wants to challenge others will try as much as he can to assess the strength of his opponents against his own in order to tell whether or not he is superior. But no one would dare consider himself superior to all future challengers, because he has no knowledge of them. Yet, the Qur'an has the confidence to do so, by declaring that mankind is impotent to challenge the Qur'an for all time to come. This boldness is the greatest proof of the inimitability of the Qur'an.

Challenge on the Superiority of Language

People do not have the same abilities when it comes to the art of oration and powers of expression, which differ from person to person according to their zeal, taste, thought patterns and insight. Also, the styles of writing and speaking of each person differ from one another. So how can one compare them if people cannot compete with one another in this respect?

In reply, it must be stated that the essence of the Qur'an's challenge to others is not that they might produce speech similar or identical to that of God, in such a way that the syle of expression is completely identical, for such a similarity is impossible except by imitation.[715] The challenge is rather to bring forth speech which is like the Qur'an in terms of sublime spirituality in the most eloquent rhetoric. Based on

[715] This kind of imitation is that which was done by Musaylamah the Liar and others, whereby they merely embarrassed themselves. See Ma'rifat, *al-Tamhīd*, vol. 4, 228, 257.

specific criteria, rhetoricians have determined levels of superiority and inferiority in terms of every word.

We do not deny that every person's speech is a product of an inner constitution and particular disposition, and it is never possible for anyone to be identical to another in their way of thinking. But the point here concerns correspondences in the degree of excellence of literature, which would determine the superiority of one form of literature over another. Such a comparison is based upon the powers of expression, lucidity and subtleties of speech.

After enumerating the criteria for the evaluation of literature, al-Sakkākī writes in *Miftāḥ al-'Ulūm*:

> The elevation or demotion of the status of literature depends on the observance of the above points and subtleties. The more these points are observed, the more elevated the literature becomes, and the less they are observed, the more its status diminishes. Rhetoric progressively excels until it reaches the level of inimitability which is the highest degree in the art of rhetoric or somewhere close to it.[716]

It can be inferred from this statement that the stage of inimitability has different degrees, but the stage of the Qur'an is at a level beyond human reach.[717]

In sum, the superiority or similarity of two forms of speech depends on points of rhetoric and other subtleties. The rhetorical criteria mentioned in the science of rhetoric give more importance to the meaning and content than to the words and expressions. As Shaykh 'Abd al-Qāhir Jurjānī states:

If an expert of literature who is acquainted with the values of speech appreciates a poem or commends prose, he would say the following words: 'It is pleasant and fine; it is beautiful and graceful; it is lucid and pleasing; it is interesting and charming.' So, be it known that this description does not bespeak the melody of its words. Neither does it depend on the order of the words. Rather, it has something to do with a

---

[716] Sakkākī, Yūsuf ibn Abī Bakr, *Miftāḥ al-'Ulūm* (Cairo: Maṭba'ah Muṣṭafā al-Bābī al-Ḥalabī, 1356 q.), 80, 84, 196.

[717] See Sa'd al-Dīn Mas'ūd ibn 'Umar Taftāzānī, *al-Muṭawwal* (Islāmbūl, 1330 s.), 31.

dimension which affects the human heart, and it is a superiority which illuminates reason.[718]

Inna al-kalāma la fī al-fu'ādi wa innamā

Ju'ila al-kalāmu 'alā al-fu'ādi dalīlā

That is to say, all speech is an indication of the truth that dwells within the heart.

The Dimensions of Inimitability

Nowadays three essential aspects of the uniqueness of the Qur'an are discussed: the rhetorical, the scientific and the legislative.[719]

Rhetorical inimitability deals mostly with the terminology, the use of apposite expressions, and oratorical features and subtleties in which meaning and content play a pivotal role.

Scientific inimitability deals with the passing suggestions of some of the secrets of nature which are sometimes spontaneously found amongst the phraseology of the Qur'an, which scholars have discovered with the passage of time and advancing scientific knowledge.

The legislative inimitability pertains to the original approach that the Qur'an adopted in terms of wisdom and edicts, which at the time was inaccessible to mankind, and even since then is impossible to achieve without the guidance of religion. The Qur'an contains a comprehensive ontology as well as a multi-dimensional system of legislation.

1. Rhetorical Inimitability

The rhetorical inimitability of the Qur'an can be divided into five areas: (i) the choice of words, (ii) the mode and style of expression, (iii) the harmonious melody, (iv) thematic unity and consistency, and (v) beauty and subtlety.

i) The Choice of Words

The choice of words in the Qur'an is perfectly measured. If any word were replaced with another, the new word would be lacking in certain

[718] 'Abd al-Qāhir Jurjānī, *Asrār al-Balāghah* (Beirut: Dār al-Ma'rifah, n.d.), 3.

[719] In this summary we discuss the first two dimensions only.

respects. This is because the words in the Qur'an have a symmetry whereby the sounds of the letters of adjacent words are concordant, thus making the recitation of the Qur'an easy and smooth. Secondly, there is a spiritual congruence of words, which forms cohesive combinations of meanings. Moreover, the choice of words according to the conditions of eloquence set by the science of rhetoric is observed completely. These three aspects closely take into account the special features of every word. In sum, each word is specifically placed in such a way that it cannot be substituted.

In this regard, Ibn 'Aṭiyyah says:

> 'The Book of God is such that if a word were taken out and all the Arabic language were searched to replace it with something better, nothing could be found.'

Abū Sulaymān Bostī says:

> Known that the basic foundation of rhetoric of the Qur'an which combines together the above qualities is that all kinds of terms – in which the above particularities are present – is correctly used in its place, which is exclusive and suitable, such that if another term is used in its place, either the meaning would totally change and lead to a distortion of the intended meaning, or it would lose its smooth flow and resplendence and fall from the ideal level of rhetoric.[720]

Shaykh 'Abd al-Qāhir Jurjānī states:

> Litterateurs and rhetoricians were completely enamoured by the choice of words in the Qur'an, for they have not found any word which is unsuitable in a given place or located in a strange place, or another word more suitable, more deserving or more appropriate. Instead, they have found such cohesion and accurate arrangement that the wise have been astounded, and everybody has been rendered incapable of imitating it.

Such praise from great rhetoricians and men of letters for the unique choice of words in the Qur'an is plentiful. Of course, this accuracy in the choice of words depends on two conditions which are by nature impossible for mankind to fulfil: a comprehensive knowledge of the specific

[720] Ma'rifat, *Thalāth Rasā'il fī I'jāz al-Qur'ān*, 29.

aspects of each word, to the extent that the particularities throughout the language are known and can be used appropriately; and a thorough comprehension of each word so that no vacillation or confusion occurs. It seems impossible for common individuals to fulfil these conditions .

The most illustrious example in this regard is the verse on retaliation (*qiṣāṣ*):

> *Wa lakum fī al-qiṣāṣi ḥayātun yā ulī al-albāb la'allakum tattaqūn.* (2:179)
>
> *And there is for you in legal retribution (saving of) life, O ye (people) of understanding, that ye may restrain yourselves* (2:179).

In order to easily memorise their civil and penal laws, the Arabs were accustomed to stipulating them in concise, elegant statements, and they sought the assistance of their outstanding orators to codify their laws in the most concise and articulate way. They eventually agreed to coin the expression *al-qatl anfā li al-qatl*, that is, killing is the best deterrent for killing, but their choice overlooked certain points. First of all, nothing negates itself, and it is a big mistake to regard killing as such as the antidote for killing. It can only be regarded as a deterrent if it is done as retribution.

Secondly, in the opposition of 'retribution' (*qiṣāṣ*) and 'life' (*ḥayāt*) in the verse, the special pun of *ṭibāq* is used, which is a combination of opposites. Retribution, which is a type of killing, is the opposite of life, yet in the verse it is regarded as the source of life.

Thirdly, in the same expression, the comparative form is used without mentioning the noun with which the comparison is made. From a literary point of view this is deficient, for it is a source of ambiguity; in other words, it is not clear what killing is more of a deterrent for.[721] Nevertheless, such a deficiency does not exist in the verse. The guarantee of life hinges solely on retribution (*qiṣāṣ*).

Fourthly, the verse is affirmative while the stated expression is negative. From a literary point of view, an affirmative expression is superior to a negative one, especially in the codification of legal matters.

And finally, by the use of the word *qiṣāṣ*, the concept of legal justice is invoked, and suggests that the law emanates from a source of justice. This

[721] If the ellipsis is *min kulli shay'* (from all things), it is totally incorrect, and if it is *min ba'ḍ al-ashyā'* (from certain things), it is ambiguous, and should not be so in legal texts.

is while using the word *qatl* at the beginning, previously unmentioned, lacks this property. Moreover, the word *qatl* is somewhat aversive, whereas *qiṣāṣ* affirms a sense of justice, peace of mind and retribution.[722]

ii) The Mode and Style of Expression

There is no similarity or parallelism between the style of expression in the Qur'an with any other conventional style of Arabic.

The wonder of the Qur'an is that it has a style which is acceptable to Arabic speakers even though it is different from their conventional styles of speaking. What is more remarkable is that it possesses all the merits of conventional linguistic styles, but with no trace at all of any of their drawbacks.

It was stated above that each of the three conventional styles of poetry, prose and rhyming prose, has its own merits and drawbacks. The Qur'anic style has the charm and elegance of poetry, the liberty of prose, and the beauty and fineness of rhyming prose, without the restrictions of rhyme, rhythm or any difficulty in composition. This was why the Arab orators were astounded by it.

iii) The Harmonious Melody

One of the most striking dimensions of the rhetorical uniqueness of the Qur'an – which recently has been given more attention by scholars – is its melody, which is so elegant that from the very beginning the Arabs had to confess that the language of the Qur'an was beyond human capability, and could only be words from God.

In this respect Sayyid Quṭb thus says:

> Such melody is produced as a result of a special orderliness and symphony of letters in a word, as well as the concordance of words in a space. For this reason, the Qur'an has the peculiarities of prose as well as the salient features of poetry. This superior rhetoric in the Qur'an has rendered it needless of the restrictions of rhyme, and it has a complete liberty of expression. At the same time, among the features of poetry, it possesses its own inner music and intervals which create a kind of rhythm.

---

[722] See Ma'rifat, *al-Tamhīd*, vol. 5, 90-130.

At the time of reciting the Qur'an, its inner tune can be completely felt. This tune is more manifest in short *sūrahs* with their short intervals, and in descriptions and depictions as a whole, and less manifest in long *sūrahs*, but the system of its tune is alway intact. For example, we read thus in verses 1-22 of *Sūrah al-Najm*:

Wa [a]l-najmi idhā hawā

Mā ḍalla ṣāḥibikum wa mā ghawā

Wa mā yanṭiqu 'an al-hawā

In huwa illā waḥyun yūḥā

'Allamahū shadīd al-quwā

Dhū mirratin fastawā

Wa huwa bi [a]l-ufuqi [a]l-a'alā

Thumma danā fatadallā

Fa kāna qāba qawsayni aw adnā

Fa awḥā ilā 'abdihī mā awḥā

These intervals have an approximately equal rhythm – but not according to the Arab system of prosody – and rhyme is observed in it as well, and out of the concordance of the letters of words and the symphony of words within the sentences, a musical rhythm is produced. Because of inner feeling and musical perception, this peculiarity makes one rhythm differ from another, even though they might have the same intervals and metres.

As we have said, such a melody in the verses and intervals is obvious throughout the Qur'an. The reason for our claim is that if we change a word which is used in a particular form to another of its other forms which has the same meaning, or if we omit or change the word order, there would be a disruption of this tuneful order.

An example of the first kind is the story of Prophet Ibrāhīm (Abraham) in *Sūrah al-Shu'arā'* (26: 75-82), where, in order to maintain rhyme with such words as *ta'budūn*, *al-aqdamūn*, *al-dīn* and the like, *yā' al-mutakallim* in the words *yahdīn*, *yasqīn*, *yashfīn* and *yuḥyīn* is omitted.

Another example can be found in these verses (*Sūrah al-Fajr* 89:1-5):

Wa [a]l-fajr

Wa layālin 'ashr

Wa [a]l-shaf'i wa [a]l-watr

Wa [a]l-layli idhā yasr

Hal fī dhālika qasamun li dhī ḥijr

Here the original *yā'* of the word *yasr* is omitted for concordance with *fajr*, *'ashr*, *al-watr* and *ḥijr*.

Another example is in *Sūrah al-Kahf* 18:64:

Qāla dhālika mā kunnā nabgh *fartaddā 'alā āthārihimā qaṣaṣā*

Here, if we prolong the letter *yā'* of *nabghi* according to general rule, the rhythm would be somehow disrupted.

Hence, as stated earlier, there is a kind of inner music in the words of the Qur'an that can be felt but is beyond description. This music is hidden in the warp and woof of the words as well as in the composition of the sentences, and it can only be discerned with that inward sense which is a sublime faculty.[723]

As Rāfi'ī writes:

> The Arabs were contesting with one another in writing prose and reciting poetry, thereby taking pride in themselves. Yet their style of speech was always based on a single manual. They were free in logic and expression, knowing the art of oration. Of course, the Arabs' eloquence, on the one hand, was innate, and on the other, was inspired by nature. When the Qur'an was revealed, however, they observed that the Qur'an was put forth in a different scheme. The words were the same as those they used to know, but it flowed successively without any interruption, and the composition, symphony and harmony were exquisite. The Arabs were astonished by its splendour, realising the fundamental weakness and insignificance of their mental framework. The eloquent Arabs also heard a kind of speech which was previously unknown to them. They could discern a resplendent melody in

[723] Sayyid Ibrāhīm Husayn al-Quṭb, *al-Taṣwīr al-Fannī fī al-Qur'an* (Beirut: Dār al-Kitāb al-'Arabī, 1980), 80-83.

> the letters, words and sentences of this new kind of speech. All these words were so compatibly grouped together that they are as if a single unit. The Arabs readily sensed this melody in the words, which left them weak and helpless.

All those who can discern the musical secret and psychological philosophy of the Qur'an believe that no kind of art can rival the natural harmony and melody of the Qur'anic text, nor can any fault be found in it. This being said, it should be noted that the Qur'anic melody is much superior to music, to the extent that it cannot be called music.

In the musical tones, variation of the voice, flow, resonance, subtlety, vigour and the different accompanying movements, in addition to the modulation and vibration known as the 'rhetoric of sound' in musical language, bring about a spiritual stirring. If we take this dimension of the Qur'an into account in recitation, we find out that no language could be more eloquent than that of the Qur'an, and it is this very dimension which arouses feelings in people, whether Arabic speakers or not. Taking this into consideration, the exhortation to recite the Qur'an in a loud voice becomes clear.

The intervals with which the Qur'anic verses end are complete silhouettes of the musical sentences. Each of these intervals is itself compatible with the sounds, and has a unicity with the type of voice in which it is expressed. In addition, most of these intervals end with one of the two letters *nūn* and *mīm*, both of which are common in music, or with letters with a stretching sound (*madd*).[724]

Some experts have said that most of the intervals in the Holy Qur'an end with *madd* and *līn* letters and the addition of the letter *nūn*, and the reason for this is to create a kind of melody. Sībawayh has also said:

> Whenever the Arabs wished to give a melody to what they said, they would add the letters *alif*, *yā'* or *nūn*, thereby prolonging the words, and if this were not their intention, they would refrain from adding those letters. This method is also used in the Qur'an, but in a richer way. However, if a word cannot end with one of these letters – for example, if it should end with a *sākin* letter – then, of course, this letter becomes in line with the tone of

[724] Ma'rifat, *Thalāth Rasā'il fī I'jāz al-Qur'ān*, 188-216.

> the sentence and the grouping of its words, and maintaining consistency with the tune of the statement, it is placed in the most appropriate way. Such letters mostly occur in short sentences and from *qalqalah* (shaking, echoing)[725] letters or similar ones, which in music are believed to contain melody. The effect in people's hearts is but natural. In a recitation of the Holy Qur'an, the unmatchable tunefulness of the voice addresses all – both those who can understand the language and those who cannot.

It is said that this unmatchable dimension of the Qur'an is traceable to the multi-layered feelings in the heart of the reciter or listener. In other words, the letters are placed alongside each other in an unprecedented manner, such that by listening to them unaided by any template of music, rhyme, rhythm or poetic metre, the resplendent cadence of the words can be heard.

The Inward Melody of the Qur'an

Melody in literature might refer to such manifest artistic achievements as rhyme, metre, the division of rhymed speech into equal hemistiches, and other conventional rhythms and measures which can all be regarded as abstract verbal frameworks. However, the 'inward' melody is a result of the beauty of expression that emanates from the substance of literature. The difference between these two types is immense, for in the second type, words and meaning are elegantly interwoven in a way that produces a melody that caresses the spirit and arouses the inner self.

Professor Muṣṭafā Muhammad writes: 'This secret is one of the most profound secrets of the rhetorical structure of the Qur'an. The Qur'an is not poetry, prose or rhyming prose, but rather a sort of speech architecture which discloses inward music.'

One should be aware of the great difference between straightforward harmony and an inner harmony. For example, let us recite a couplet from the poems of 'Umar ibn Abī Rabī'ah whose poems are known for being accompanied by music and melody:

Qāla lī ṣāḥibī li ya'lama mā bī

---

[725] Whenever one of the letters *qāf*, *ṭā'*, *bā'*, *jīm* or *dāl* carries a *sukūn*, the letter is 'shaken' or echoed (*qalqalah*). [Trans.]

atuḥibbu al-qatūla ukhta al-rubābī

When people listen to this couplet, they are aroused by its music, but the music is of an outward nature. Two equal hemistiches with a homologous rhyme – an elongated *yā'* – in either of the two hemistiches has helped make the couplet melodious. But the music comes from outside and not from within. In other words, rhyme, rhythm and cadence create a musical harmony. But when we recite the following verse:

Wa [a]l-ḍuḥā

Wa [a]l-layli idhā sajā

By the glorious morning light, and by the night when it is still... (93:1-2),

we are faced with a hemistich with no conventional rhyme or rhythm, and yet it is full of melody, and each of the letters produces a pleasant sound, an inner melody. How and from what does this melody originate? Inward melody is one of the architectural secrets of the Qur'an, and no other literary structure has ever compared. The following verses have an intrinsic musical structure whose melody emanates from within in an astonishing manner:

Al-raḥmānu 'ala al-'arsh istawā,

The All-Merciful is firmly established on the throne (20:5);

Qāla rabbi innī wahana al-'aẓmu minnī washta'ala al-ra'su shaybā wa lam akun bi du'āika rabbi shaqiyyā,

He said: 'O my Lord! indeed my bones have become feeble, and the hair of my head doth glisten with grey, but never am I unblest, O my Lord, in my prayer to Thee!' (19:4);

Inna [a]l-sā'ata ātiyatun akādu ukhfīhā litujzā kullu nafsin bimā tas'ā...,

'...Verily the Hour is coming – My design is to keep it hidden – for every soul to receive its reward by the measure of its endeavour...' (20:15);

Innahū man ya'ti rabbahū mujriman fa inna lahū jahannama lā yamūtu fīhā wa lā yaḥyā,

Verily he who comes to his Lord as a sinner (at Judgement) – for him is hell; therein shall he will neither die nor live (20:74).

When the Qur'an gives the account of the Prophet Moses, it adopts a wonderful symphonic approach, thus:

> *Wa laqad awḥaynā ilā Mūsā an asri bi 'ibādi faḍrib lahum ṭarīqan fi al-baḥri yabasā lā takhāfu darakan wa lā takhshā,*
>
> *We sent an inspiration to Moses: 'Travel by night with My servants, and strike a dry path for them through the sea, without fear of being overtaken (by Pharaoh) and without (any other) fear (20:77-79).*

The words are an effortless concordance. Such words as *yabasan* or *lā takhāfu darakan* – which means *lā takhāfu idrākan* – are an embodiment of sympathetic accord. It is as if the words melt in the hands of their Creator, acquire a harmony, and a unique melody manifests in them.

There is no similarity whatsoever between this melody and either the poetry of the Age of Ignorance (*al-jāhiliyyah*) or contemporary poetry and prose, and notwithstanding those enemies who wished to undermine the status of the Qur'an, not a single example of anything similar has been recorded in history. Amidst all this clamour, the Qur'anic text has preserved its distinctive features as an indescribable phenomenon. The only convincing explanation for this is that the Qur'an emanates from something beyond the reach of man.

Reciting the Qur'an Melodiously

And recite the Qur'an with a measured tone (73:4).

> As we become generally familiar with the wonderful inner melody of poetical sound and tone in the Qur'an, we realise why reciting the Qur'an in melodious tone has been recommended. The reciter is enjoined to observe all the subtle points of recitation, including voice range, pitch, resonance and the like. There are some traditions in this regard:

The Messenger of God said:

> Everything has an ornament, and the ornament of the Qur'an is a beautiful voice;
>
> Amongst the most beautiful things are beautiful hair and a pleasant voice;

> Recite the Qur'an in [clear] Arabic tones, but avoid the [vulgar] tone of those who are corrupt;[726]
>
> A beautiful voice is an ornament for the Qur'an;
>
> Make the Qur'an pleasant with your voice, for a pleasant voice increases the beauty of the Qur'an;
>
> Embellish the Qur'an with melodious tones.

On the interpretation of *And recite the Qur'an in a measured tone* (73:4) Imām al-Ṣādiq has said: 'This means that you should recite it with reflection and make your voice pleasant.'[727]

Imām al-Bāqir has said: 'Recite the Qur'an tunefully, for God, the Almighty, likes the Qur'an to be recited with a beautiful voice.'[728]

The Messenger of God said: 'The Qur'an has been revealed in a melancholic tone. So, recite it with weeping [out of ecstasy], and if you cannot weep, have a weeping tone and recite it with a pleasant tune, for whoever does not recite it with a pleasant tune is not of us,' and 'He is not of us who does not recite the Qur'an with a pleasant tunefulness.'[729]

Imām al-Ṣādiq said: 'The Qur'an has been revealed with melancholy. So, recite it in a melancholic tone.'[730]

Of course, there are plenty of sayings of the Holy Prophet narrated by his companions, as well as proof to substantiate those sayings.

iv) Thematic Unity and Consistency

Another salient feature of the Qur'an is the consistency of the concepts and meanings throughout the verses, even though they may not have been revealed together, but a little at a time over longer or shorter periods. The dispersion of the revelations due to various circumstances would seem to dictate that there would not be a relationship or consistency in the verses, and that this would be clear. Particularly in recent times, close examination of content of each *sūrah* by scholars has meant that, on the whole, they have come to the conclusion that all the verses in each *sūrah*

---

[726] Kulaynī, *al-Kāfī*, vol. 2, 614-616.

[727] Majlisī, *Bihār al-Anwār*, vol. 89, 'Kitāb al-Qur'ān,' 190-195.

[728] Kulaynī, *al-Kāfī*, vol. 2, 616.

[729] Majlisī, *Biḥār al-Anwār*, vol. 89, 191.

[730] Kulaynī, *al-Kāfī*, vol. 2, 614.

are summed up by a particular purpose expressed in the whole *sūrah.* This is nowadays called the 'thematic unity' of the *sūrah.* It is the same thematic unity which constitutes the unity of style of that *sūrah*, and an aspect of inimitability originates from this point.

The scholars cite certain proofs to substantiate this claim, amongst which is the different number of verses in the *sūrahs*. This cannot be accidental, because it would indicate a lack of reason, calculation and wisdom, and it is impossible for any uncalculated action to have come from a Wise Agent. Most *sūrahs* of the Qur'an, especially the short ones, were revealed in a complete form. The longer *sūrahs* of the Qur'an would also begin with *Bismillāhi al-raḥmāni al-raḥīm* (In the Name of God, the All-Beneficent, the All-Merciful), and every subsequent verse would be recorded by instruction of the Holy Prophet until another *Bismillāhi al-raḥmāni al-raḥīm* indicating the conclusion of one *sūrah* and the beginning of the next. Hence, the number and arrangement of the verses of every *sūrah* is intentional, through revelation and the instruction of the Prophet.

Now, this question is raised: what is the reason for this difference in the number of verses of the *sūrahs*? The correct answer has been stated. That is, every *sūrah* pursues a certain goal, and having done that a *sūrah* would end, and this accounts for different numbers of verses in the *sūrahs*. It was never accidental or without a reasonable cause, and this is something which constitutes the thematic unity or unity of style in every *sūrah*; that is, there is a conceptual relationship and close harmony amongst the verses of every *sūrah.*

Contemporary exegetes have realised this fact and worked hard to discover the specific aim of each *sūrah* with a certain amount of success. Amongst them is Sayyid Quṭb who, in the introduction to an exegesis of each *sūrah*, briefly explains its intention according to his understanding. One of his students, 'Abd Allāh Maḥmūd Shaḥātah, in his book *Ahdāf Kull Sūrah wa Maqāṣiduhā*, has also attempted this with some success.

Professor Muhammad 'Abd Allāh al-Darrāz also says in this regard: 'Although the Qur'an has been revealed according to the demands of particular circumstances at various times, it has preserved a logical and literary unity, and this is the greatest testimony to the inimitability of the Qur'an.'[731]

---

[731] Muhammad 'Abd Allāh al-Darrāz, *al-Madkhal ilā al-Qur'an al-Karīm* (Cairo, 1957), Preface.

Professor Muhammad Muhammad al-Madanī, Dean of the Faculty of Theology at al-Azhar University, also emphasises this point, believing that an accurate understanding of the objectives of each *sūrah* is the best way to understand the meaning as a whole. He says: 'Unless you look at the general picture of the *sūrah* with an open mind, you will never be able to discern the details drawn out throughout the *sūrah*.'[732]

In sum, contemporary scholars acknowledge that every *sūrah* is cohesive throughout, and this plays a role in the integration and connectivity of the verses, and the primary duty of the exegete, before embarking on the exegesis of a verse, is to understand the all-encompassing unity prevailing in the *sūrah* in order to detect its objectives. Moreover, rhetoricians have regarded the 'good opening' (*ḥusni maṭla'*) and 'good ending' (*ḥusni khitām*) of each *sūrah* as one of the axiomatic merits of the Qur'an. As such, every *sūrah* begins with an elegant opening and ends with a subtle conclusion. It is said that the essence of rhetoric dictates that the speaker commence his speech with the utmost agility by preparing the listener and indicating the main point of the speech. This way of beginning a speech is called the 'the excellence in opening' – the skill to draw the attention of the listener. Ibn Ma'ṣūd, the famous accomplished litterateur, says: 'The beginnings of all the *sūrahs* of the Holy Qur'an observed this fundamental principle of rhetoric in the best and most effective manner.'[733] Ibn Athīr also mentions the beginning of the *sūrahs* of the Qur'an as the best example.[734]

Regarding the 'good ending' (*ḥusn khitām*), Ibn Abī al-Iṣba' says:

> The speaker must end his speech with the utmost elegance, because the effect of the final phrases remains in the mind of the listener. So he must try to end his speech with the most expressive and appropriate turn of phrase.

He then goes on to elaborately examine each of the *sūrahs* and clarifies the style of each of the endings from the perspective of oration.[735]

The rhetoricians have a consensus of opinion that the endings of the *sūrahs*, like their openings, are expressed with the utmost subtlety and

---

[732] Muhammad Muhammad Madanī, *al-Mujtama' al-Islāmī* (Cairo: Dār al-Iḥyā', 1935), 5-7.

[733] Ibn Ma'ṣūm, *Anwār al-Rabī' fī Anwā' al-Badī'* (Najaf: Maṭba'at al-Nu'mān, 1389 q.), vol. 1, 34.

[734] 'Izz al-Dīn ibn al-Athīr, *al-Mathal al-Sā'ir,* (Cairo: Maṭba'at al-Thā'ir, 1379 q.), vol. 3, 98.

[735] Ibn Abī al-Iṣba', *Badī' al-Qur'ān,* (Cairo: Nahḍat Miṣr, 1377 q.), 343, 346-353.

elegance. Ibn Ma'ṣūm says: 'The closing parts of the surahs, like their beginnings, all accord with the strictest rules of rhetoric.' Thereafter, he mentions the ending of some *sūrahs* and presents their merits, and concludes: 'And if you ponder on the closing sentences of all the other surahs, you will find them at the peak of eloquence and ultimate beauty.'[736]

In his book *Mu'tarak al-Aqrān*, Jalāl al-Dīn al-Suyūṭi has dealt extensively with this topic.[737]

2. Scientific Inimitability

The scientific inimitability of the Qur'an refers to points which are indicated by certain verses without being the main purport, for the Qur'an is not a book of science but a guidance for mankind. As such, if we sometimes encounter a scientific clue in the Qur'an, it is because the source of the text is divine Wisdom, the fountainhead of infinite knowledge.

> *Say: 'It was sent down by Him Who knows the mystery (that is) in the heavens and the earth'* (25:6).

It is to be expected that the statements of any learned person – even when talking about something outside his expertise – will sometimes contain expressions that reflect his area of expertise. For example, if a jurist (*faqīh*) speaks on a common subject, those who are familiar with jurisprudence might detect from his expressions that the speaker is a jurist, even though he may not deliberately intend it. This is how it is with scientific indications in the Qur'an, which are but sprinklings within the main purpose of the text. Before presenting some examples of these clues, there are three points worth considering:

1) There are some who suppose that within the Qur'an are comprised all the fundamentals of natural sciences, mathematics, astronomy, and even industrial sciences, technology and the like. They have attempted to illustrate this false notion with passages from the Qur'an such as the following:

> *...and We have sent down to thee a Book explaining all things* (16:89);

---

[736] Ibn Ma'ṣūm, *Anwār al-Rabī'*, vol. 6, 325.

[737] Jalāl al-Dīn 'Abd al-Raḥmān al-Suyūṭī, *Mu'tarak al-Aqrān* (Beirut: Dār al-Fikr al-'Arabī, n.d.), vol. 1, 75-79; al-Suyūṭī, *al-Itqān*, vol. 3, 316-319. See Ma'rifat, *al-Tamhīd*, vol. 5, 290-304.

Nothing have We neglected in the Book (6:38);

...nor anything fresh or withered but is (inscribed) in a record clear (6:59).

It is thus stated in a tradition narrated by 'Abd Allāh ibn Mas'ūd: 'Whosoever desires knowledge of the people of the past and of the people of the future should reflect on the Qur'an.'[738] Had such notions not issued from certain prominent figures[739] or been attributed to them, we would not have contested them, because the weakness of their bases is obvious.

The first question that should be asked is how and where can these sciences, crafts, and ever-increasing discoveries be inferred from the Qur'an? Why were our predecessors not aware of them, and why do our contemporaries not pay attention to them? Moreover, the verses cited are unrelated to the claim. The verse in *Sūrah al-Naḥl* concerns the all-encompassing provision of the religious law, and aims to exhaust the arguments of the unbelievers regarding the Day of Resurrection, when every prophet will be called as a witness to the actions of his community, as the Holy Prophet is the witness to his community. Hence, everything is laid down complete in the Book and the law (*sharī'ah*) sent to him:

...and We shall bring thee as a witness against these (thy people); and We have sent down to thee a Book explaining all things... (16:89).

That is to say: 'We have not left any shortcoming in the guidance, mercy and good news sent to the Muslims.' By examining the background to this revelation, it becomes very clear that 'explaining all things' refers to the comprehensive nature of the religious law.

In principle, the scope of the meaning of each word should be determined by the status of the speaker. For example, Muhammad ibn Zakariyyā, who wrote *Man Lā Yaḥḍuruh al-Ṭabīb*, declared as an expert physician that whatever is needed is provided in that book. What he meant by 'whatever is needed' is within the framework of medicine. In the same way, Shaykh Ṣadūq wrote *Man Lā Yaḥḍuruh al-Faqīh* in a bid to present whatever was needed within the domain of jurisprudence. In the same

---

738 Ghazālī, *Iḥyā' al-'Ulūm*, vol. 1, section 4, 'Ādāb Tilāwat al-Qur'ān,' 296.

739 Among them are Abū al-Faḍl Marsamī (d. 655/1257) and Abū Bakr Ibn al-'Arabī al-Ma'āfarī (d. 544/1149), and implications in the statements of Abū Ḥāmid al-Ghazālī, Zarkashī and al-Suyūṭī also seem to agree. Of course, these statements are subject to other interpretations, as we have stated in the introduction to volume 6 of *al-Tamhīd*.

manner, since God is the Legislator, He uses such expressions in relation to the books and codes of law (*sharāʾiʿ*) solely to imply the universality of the legislation.

The same applies to the words *Nothing have We neglected in the Book* (6:38), if 'the Book' in this case refers to the Qur'an. However, the apparent meaning is something else, and refers to the Book of Creation and the eternal Knowledge of God. The whole verse is as follows:

> *There is no animal (that lives) on the earth, nor a being that flies on its wings, but (forms part of) communities like you. Nothing have We omitted from the Book, and they (all) shall be gathered to their Lord in the end* (6:38).

The following verse makes it even clearer that all creatures and their actions and thoughts are recorded and actually present in the Knowledge of God:

> *With Him are the keys of the unseen, the treasures that none knoweth but He. He knoweth whatever there is on the earth and in the sea. Not a leaf doth fall but with His knowledge; there is not a grain in the darkness (or depths) of the earth, nor anything fresh or withered, but it is in a record clear* (6:59).

However, the tradition of Ibn Masʿūd relates only to the field of religious science with which he was acquainted, and 'the first (*awwalīn*) and the last (*ākhirīn*)' means the earlier and succeeding prophets and their respective doctrines as presented in the Qur'an.

2) A second point is that it is extremely difficult to draw conclusions about science from the Qur'an, because scientific claims change with the passage of time. In many cases a scientific theory assumes the status of fact for a while before being displaced. Therefore, if we equate Qur'anic concepts with unreliable theories, we will undermine the unchangeable and truth-based meanings of the Qur'an with unstable interpretations. Therefore it seems inappropriate to draw conclusions about scientific achievements from the Qur'an.

If ever a scientist manages by scientific means of which he is certain to explain some of the ambiguities in the clues supplied by the Qur'an, it might be acceptable provided that he uses the provision 'perhaps,' and concedes that perhaps this is what the verse means. In this way, even if there is some change of theory, it would not arbitrarily affect the Qur'an, and we would know that the scientist's interpretation was wrong. A firm connection between a definitive religious vision and changeable scientific views cannot be established.

3) The third point concerns whether the challenge of the Qur'an or *taḥaddī* as a manifestation of the Qur'an's inimitability also covers this scientific dimension of the Qur'an, in the sense that it also challenges any rival with these scientific clues. Or, is it the case that the discovery of previously unknown scientific facts hinted at by the Qur'an is part of the clarification of its inimitability? In other words, after scientists have explained with the tools at their disposal what were previously ambiguous clues, do we then realize that the clues in the Qur'an could only have originated from God's Knowledge as Lord of the Universe? This is one more reason why the question of the scientific inimitability of the Qur'an is raised.

Some believe that these scientific clues are a proof of inimitability, although there is no *taḥaddī* in this regard. This is because the challenges in those particular verses are addressed to people unacquiainted with the sciences in question. On this basis, from a scientific perspective, the Qur'an is the same as other books with a heavenly origin which did not challenge their audience, although scientific clues in them may well be a proof of inimitability (*i'jāz*).[740]

Examples of Scientific Clues

1. Contraction (*Ratq*) and Expansion (*Fatq*) of the Universe

Do not the unbelievers see that the heavens and the earth were a joined entity (ratq) and We clove them asunder (fatq)? (21:30).

Ratq means to be interwoven, while *fatq* indicates an unravelling. It is stated in this verse that the heavens and the earth were at first interwoven and then unravelled. Most exegetes were of the opinion that the interweaving and unravelling refer to the opening of the sky and the pouring down of rain:

> *So We opened the gates of heaven, with water pouring forth* (54:11).

It is also suggested that it means the opening up of the earth and the growing of plants:

---

[740] See Aḥmad Abū Ḥijr, *al-Tafsīr al-'Ilmī li al-Qur'ān fī al-Mīzān* (Beirut: Dār al-Fikr, 1970), 131.

And We split the earth in fragments, and produce therein grain (80:26-27).

'Allāmah Ṭabrisī says in this regard: 'This interpretation has been narrated from two Imāms (Imām Abū Ja'far al-Bāqir and Abū 'Abdillāh al-Ṣādiq).'[741] In *Rawḍat al-Kāfī* there is a tradition with a weak chain of transmission from Imām al-Bāqir, while in *Tafsīr al-Qummī* there is a tradition from Imām al-Ṣadiq which has no continuous chain of transmission.

Another interpretation tells us that initially the heavens and the earth were once interwoven and then split and expanded to how they are today. For instance, we read in *Sūrah Fuṣṣilat*:

> *Then He turned to the heaven while it was smoke and said to it and to the earth: 'Come ye together, willingly or unwillingly' They said: 'We do come willingly.' And He completed them as seven firmaments* (41:11-12).

This verse bespeaks a scientific fact which modern science has more or less realised, and that is that the origin of the universe was gaseous in form. In this case, the Arabic word *dukhān* (smoke) is the most opportune for describing the original matter that constituted the universe.

As recorded in *Nahj al-Balāghah*, the Commander of the Faithful has time and again pointed this out. In the first sermon of *Nahj al-Balāghah* concerning the creation of the universe, we read:

> Then the Almighty created the openings of the atmosphere, the expanse of the firmament and the strata of winds.[742]

And in Sermon 211:

> Then He made it from layers, and separated them into seven skies after they had joined together.[743]

Therefore, in his commentary on *Rawḍat al-Kāfī*, 'Allāmah Majlisī comments on the two traditions; he mentions: 'These two traditions are inconsistent with what has been transmitted from the Commander of the Faithful.'[744]

---

741 Ṭabrisī, *Majma' al-Bayān*, vol. 7, 45.

742 Al-Raḍī, *Nahj al-Balāghah*, Sermon 1.

743 Ibid. Sermon 211.

744 'Allāmah Muhammad Bāqir Majlisī, *Mir'āt al-'Uqūl* (Tehran: Dār al-Kutub al-Islāmiyyah, 1394 q.), vol. 25, 232. As such, the abovementioned two traditions cannot be cited on account of weakness in the chain of transmission. Only the statement of the Commander

The Role of Mountains in the Stability of the Earth

In nine places in the Qur'an mountains are referred to as *rawāsī* (13:3; 27:61; 15:19; 50:7; 16:15; 31:10; 21:31; 41:10; 77:27):

> *And We have set on the earth mountains standing firm, lest it should shake them* (21:31).

Mountains are described as *rawāsī* because they are the 'firm ones' based on strong foundations. The term *rawāsī* is derived from *rasā al-safīnah*, which means 'the ship anchored.' Because of the anchor, the ship remains stable in the middle of the raging sea, and as such, the mountains are like anchors that prevent the earth from shaking with its tectonic movements.

Mountains are also referred to as *awtād*, meaning 'pegs,' for they keep the earth from falling apart:

> *Have We not made the earth as a wide expanse, and the mountains as pegs?* (78:6-7).

In this regard, the Commander of the Faithful said the following:

> He also created high hills, rocks of stones and lofty mountains. He put them in their positions and made them remain stationary. Their peaks rose into the air while their roots remained in the water. In this way He raised the mountains above the plains and fixed their foundations in the vast expanse wherever they stood. He made their peaks high and made their bodies lofty. He made them like pillars for the earth and fixed them in it like pegs. Consequently, the earth became stationary; otherwise it might bend with its inhabitants or sink inwards with its burden, or shift from its positions. Therefore, glorified is He who preserved it after the flowing of its waters.[745]

This means that, notwithstanding its movements, the earth is prevented from shaking and falling apart. From this it can be inferred that the earth has various movements, yet despite these movements, it remains stable and firm; that the earth's surface is firm and solid so that its inhabitants

---

of the Faithful which has an authentic chain of transmission can be an interpretation of the verse. See Ma'rifat, *al-Tamhīd*, vol. 6, 129-139.

[745] Al-Raḍī, *Nahj al-Balāghah*, Sermon 211, 328.

and the forms upon it do not sink into it; and that in its rotation and other movements, the earth is constant and firm, and does not swerve from the axis determined for it. These points have been confirmed by scientific research. In view of the vital role the mountains have in making life possible on earth, they are scattered on the surface of the earth like chains around it.

Now we can better grasp the subtle elements in what Imām 'Alī says in the first sermon of *Nahj al-Balāghah*, in which instead of *jibāl* (mountains) the word *ṣukhūr* (rocks) is used. In an interpretation of the verse:

> *And We have set on the earth mountains standing firm, lest it should shake with them* (21:31).

The Imām connects the mountain's being *ṣakhrah* to the stability and firmness of the earth.

The mountain ranges, with their curves and contours, therefore play a vital role in maintaining the stability of the earth's surface, notwithstanding the fiery activity beneath the surface.

Difficulty in Breathing with the Increase in Height

> *Those whom He willeth to leave astraying - He maketh their breast close and constricted, as if they had to climb up to the skies* (6:125).

This verse deals with the difficulties faced by the misguided ones, and likens them to those who ascend to the higher layers of the atmosphere where they would experience difficulty in breathing and narrowness of the breast.

Earlier exegetes had different views regarding the nature of the metaphor in this verse. Some of them were of the opinion that it refers to anyone who tries in vain to fly in the air like the birds. Since this is not possible for him, he becomes intensely frustrated and breathing becomes difficult. Others have said that it refers to young trees that desire to grow in a thick jungle: the thick foliage of the mature trees closes their path, and the young trees hardly have any space to grow. But none of this clearly conveys the meaning of the verse.

Today, however, because of the discovery of the correlation of air pressure with blood pressure inside the body causing external and internal pressure, the nature of simile becomes clearer than the earlier explanations, whose mistake lies in the interpretion of *yaṣṣa'adu fī [a]l-samā'* – with an emphatic (*tashdīd*) *ṣād* and *'ayn*, and the preposition *fī* (in) – as an endeavour to ascend to the sky. If this were actually so, then the preposition *ilā* (to/toward) should have been used instead of *fī*. Moreover, lexically the word *yaṣṣa'adu* does not convey the meaning of *ṣu'ūd* or ascending. Instead, this word – in the *tafa'ul* verb form (*taṣa'ud*) – is used to indicate the constriction of breathing due to intense difficulties. *Taṣa'ada nafsuhu* means difficulty in breathing, a narrowing of the breast and the feeling of anxiety and pain. The words *ṣa'ūd* and *ṣa'ada*, on the other hand, mean passing through difficult terrain, and are used to describe any extremely difficult task. It is thus stated in *Sūrah al-Jinn*:

> *But if any turns away from the remembrance of his Lord, He will cause him to undergo a growing* (ṣa'adā) *penalty* (72:17).

Also, in *Sūrah al-Muddaththir*:

> *Soon I will visit him with a mount of calamities* (ṣa'ūdā) (74:17).

As such, the meaning of *ka annamā yaṣṣa'adu fī [a]l-samā'* is that he is like someone who experiences hardship and extreme difficulty in breathing at elevated heights. In reality, anyone who forgets God in his life is like one who climbs such heights, experiencing pain, distress and difficulty in breathing. Hence, it can be easily inferred from this expression that someone located in an elevated place with no means of protection will experience these problems.

Water as the Origin of Life

> *We made from water every living thing* (21:30).

The Holy Prophet has said: 'Everything is created from water.'[746] According to the verse above and this saying of the Prophet, all creatures have derived their existence from water. Shaykh Ṣadūq narrates on the authority of Jābir ibn Yazīd al-Ju'fī – who is regarded as one of the prominent figures amongst the Successors (*tābi'ūn*)[747] – that Imām Baqir was asked questions regarding the origin the universe, and the Imām replied: 'The

[746] Majlisī, *Biḥār al-Anwār*, vol. 54, 208; al-Suyūṭī, *al-Durr al-Manthūr*, vol. 4, 317.

[747] *Tābi'ūn* (Successors) refers to the second generation of Muslims who came after the Companions, who had met the Companions but had not seen the Prophet.

first thing He created from amongst His creation is something through which everything originates, and that is water.'[748]

In *Rawḍat al-Kāfī*, Shaykh Kulaynī has recorded a tradition from Imām al-Bāqir which was a reply to a man from the Levant:

> He created first the thing through which all things emanate, and that thing from which all things are created is water. As a result, God traces the origin of everything to water, but traces no origin to water.[749]

Also, Muhammad ibn Muslim, a man with a prominent reputation, has narrated from Imām al-Ṣādiq:

> *Everything was water and His Throne was upon the water;*[750]
>
> *He it is Who created the heavens and the earth in six days – and His Throne was upon the water...* (11:7).

This verse shows that prior to the emergence of the universe – including the heavens and the earth – there was water, because in the expression *and His Throne was upon the water* the word *'arsh* alludes to the Throne of measure and management (*tadbīr*), by which is meant God's Knowledge to do whatever was good and necessary for the creation at a time when nothing existed other than water. As such, the verse alludes to the fact that in the beginning was God and there was nobody with Him, that God made water prior to the creation of the universe, and that all other creatures were created from water. And in several places the Holy Qur'an identifies the source of life – whether as the origin or the essential substrate – as water:

> *...and We made every living thing of water* (21:30);
>
> *God has created every living thing from water* (24:45).

And regarding mankind:

> *It is He who has created man from water* (25:54).

---

748 Ṣadūq, *al-Tawḥīd*, 67.

749 Kulaynī, *al-Kāfī*, vol. 8, 94.

750 Ibid. 95.

Here, water may mean the same water which is the source of all beings, as stated in the other verses, or it may mean semen, as in the following:

> *He is created from a fluid emitted* (86:6);
>
> *Did We not create you from a base fluid?* (77:20).

Most exegetes, however, have maintained that the *mā'* in the verse refers to the same initial substance from which all phenomena emanated: 'The first thing created by God was water.'[751] This is because the seed of the first living being only comes from water, the same primary seed which changed into simple creatures as well as those with complex parts composed of billions of cells.

However, the origin of life in the seas is one of the most complex issues yet to be resolved by empirical science. The theory of evolution – in whatever form it has been presented – has examined the stage after the emergence of the living cell, but what was prior to that remains unknown. What is known so far is that life came into being by the divine Will which has power over all existence, and there is no option other than accepting this, for both infinite regress and self-creation are impossible, as empirical science today admits.[752]

The Atmosphere as Protection for the Earth

> *We made the sky as a canopy well guarded; yet they turn away from its portent* (21:31).

The planet earth is surrounded by an atmospheric covering estimated at about anything up to 1000 kilometres thick, and as consisting of approximately 78% nitrogen, 21% oxygen, 0.93% argon, 0.04% carbon monoxide, and small amounts of water vapour and other gases. This atmospheric covering is like an impenetrable shield surrounding the earth, protecting it from meteoroids that approach the earth in abundance from all directions[753] and are seen as a terrible threat.

The fact that the earth's inhabitants are protected from the manifold rocks that fall from the sky as well as the menace of radiation is in itself

751 Rāzī, *al-Tafsīr al-Kabīr*, vol. 24, 16.

752 See Ma'rifat, *al-Tamhīd*, vol. 6, 31-61.

753 Every day innumerable rocks fall from the sky to the earth.

a manifestation of the divine Mercy, for otherwise life on earth would be impossible. Moreover, the ozone layer around the earth is also vitally important, since it protects the earth from the harmful rays of the sun. Without it life on earth would be unsustainable, therefore it must be declared that:

> *Glorified is He Who hath subdued these for us, and we were unable to have control over it* (43:13).

INDEX